I0132143

Anonymus

# History of the sect of Mahárájas in western India

Anonymus

**History of the sect of Mahárájas in western India**

ISBN/EAN: 9783742858382

Manufactured in Europe, USA, Canada, Australia, Japa

Cover: Foto ©Thomas Meinert / pixelio.de

Manufactured and distributed by brebook publishing software
(www.brebook.com)

Anonymus

# History of the sect of Mahárájas in western India

# HISTORY

OF THE

# SECT OF MAHÁRÁJAS,

## OR VALLABHÁCHÁRYAS,

IN

# WESTERN INDIA

"HAVE NO FELLOWSHIP WITH THE UNFRUITFUL WORKS OF DARKNESS, BUT RATHER
REPROVE (OR EXPOSE) THEM."—EPHESIANS V. 2.

LONDON:

TRÜBNER & CO., 60, PATERNOSTER ROW.

1865.

STEPHEN AUSTIN,

PRINTER, HERTFORD.

# PREFACE.

It is still a general complaint that comparatively little is known of the religious, moral, and social state of the Hindus. This ignorance of their actual condition results not so much from a want of research and observation, as from the limits imposed on inquiries respecting the people of India, conducted by distinguished scholars on the one hand, and by popular writers on the other. Their creed and customs are supposed by many to be not only of an immeasurable antiquity, but of a well-nigh unchangeable fixedness. The Orientalist, attracted by the singular philological and mythological curiosities which are discovered in the Vedas, the oldest of Sanskrit works, breathes so much their ancient spirit, and sympathizes so much with the pretensions ages ago urged in their behalf, that he believes they must, to the present day, have no small share of their ancient authority and respect. The popular observer looks merely to

the surface of Hindu society, forgetful that the
lousy and secresy of caste conceal to a great c:
the mainspring and action of Hindu life. Even :
ligent natives themselves look little beyond their
immediate sphere, having no care or interest in
affairs of their neighbours. Hinduism is consequ
imagined to be•very much an abiding and univ
system of faith and manners, without reference t
great changes which it has undergone in the cou
time, and the great diversity of the forms whi
has assumed over the wide extent of this great
diversified country. The fact is that, within a cc
range, Hinduism has been ever on the move.
Vedik songs recognized, if not very clearly, the
tence of the great Creator and Governor of
Universe. They contained many fresh and bea
allusions to the phenomena of nature, and :
striking personifications of the forces and age
intermediately regulating these phenomena.
lively spirit of these primitive songs had well
entirely disappeared at the time of the compositi
the Bráhmanas (or Brahmanical Directories),
reverential worship was to a great extent laid asid
the art of the magician and conjurer, dealing with
gods through *mantras*, charms, and complicated

monial manipulations. The Philosophical Schools,
originating in the revolt of the inquiring mind of the
country from the puerilities and inanities thus mani-
fested, formed a new era, in which atheistic and
pantheistic speculation became predominant. These
Schools prepared the way for the Buddhist Revolution,
which gave social and religious liberty to all its adherents, in opposition to the Caste system, which had
begun to be fostered by the Brahmans shortly after
the entrance of the Áryas into India; and which
almost completely altered the national creed. The
revival of Brahmanism by the craft of its partisans,
and the persecution resorted to by its kingly adherents, after a thousand years' depression, was not
effected in its pristine form. Its strength lay in its
religious orders; and its great champions, such as
Śankaráchárya, and his associates and successors,
assumed an importance never before conceded to mere
individuals of the priesthood. They became the ora-
cles and pontiffs of the country; but they did not
long maintain an undivided sway among its various
tribes. The people of India had their favourite gods
in the extensive pantheon of Brahmanism, and, particularly, in its now established triads. The aggrega-
tion of legends connected with individual gods, gave

scope to the popular choice; and the spirit of sectarianism became rampant among them. The devotees
of the different gods were the leaders in this movement, and everywhere they had a large following.
One sect was for the supremacy of Vishnu; another
for that of the deified king Krishna, set forth as an
avatára of Vishnû; a third for that of Śiva; and a
fourth for that of his consort (the *Devi*, or goddess,
emphatically so called), or of the female energies in
general.

In all these changes—for an elucidation of which
in their main features the reader is referred to Professor H. H. Wilson's valuable Sketch of the Religious
Sects of the Hindus—the moral restraints of Hinduism, such as they were in its earlier days, have nearly
perished. Krishna's conversion into the god of love
and lust, and the worship of the *Śaktis*, or female
energies, have introduced a moral plague into India,
the ravages of which are both appalling and astounding. The readers of this History of the Maháráj or
Vallabháchárya Sect, and of the various documents
included in its Appendix, will find this assertion but
too amply vindicated. It is put forth simply in the
interests of truth and purity. Its author does not
apologize for its revelations, which have all been

tested by the keen and impartial investigations of a Court presided over by British judges; but he expresses the hope that they will not be lost, either upon the European or Indian public. The lessons which they teach are so obvious, that is not necessary to draw them in this place.

# CONTENTS.

## CHAPTER I.

### INTRODUCTION.

## CHAPTER II.

### RELIGIOUS SECTS OF THE HINDUS.

## CHAPTER V.

### RELIGIOUS DOCTRINES OF THE SECT.

## CHAPTER VI.

### WORSHIP AND PSALMODY.

## CHAPER VII.

### EFFECTS OF THE DOCTRINES AND WORSHIP OF THE VALLABHÁCI

## CHAPTER VIII.

### PROFLIGACY OF THE MAHÁRÁJAS.

## CHAPTER IX.

### OPPRESSIVE EXACTIONS OF THE MAHÁRÁJAS.

## CHAPTER X.

### THE MAHÁRÁJAS IN DIFFICULTIES.

# CHAPTER XI.

## THE MAHÁRÁJ LIBEL CASE.

# APPENDIX.

## SPECIMENS OF THE EVIDENCE IN THE MAHÁRÁJ LIBEL CASE.

# HISTORY

OF THE

# SECT OF MAHÁRÁJAS,

## OR VALLABHÁCHÁRYAS,

### IN WESTERN INDIA.

## CHAPTER I.

### INTRODUCTORY REMARKS.

WE propose to give in the following chapters a history of a corrupt, degraded, and licentious sect in Western India, usually denominated the sect of Mahárájas, but also known as the sect of the Vallabháchárya, Rudra Sampradáya, or Pushti Márga. To show how widely the tenets and practices of this sect vary from the doctrines which form a fundamental basis of the Hindu religion, it will be desirable to present a succinct view of this religion in its primitive condition.

The primitive elements of the Hindu Religion are found in the Veda. Professor Max Müller observes—" The key-note of all religion, natural as well as revealed, is present in the hymns of the Veda. . . . There is the belief in God, the perception of the difference between good and evil, the conviction that God hates sin, and loves the righteous."* Mr. H.

* Müller's Ancient Sanskrit Literature, p. 538.

1

T. Colebrooke remarks—"The real doctrine of the whole Indian scripture is the unity of the deity, in whom the universe is comprehended."*

The collective title of the Holy Books comprising the entire body of the primitive religion of the Hindus, both doctrinal and ceremonial is— *Vedas.* They consist of several divisions, each branching off into further sub-divisions, comments, and explanations, as follows :—

### The Four Vedas.

| 1. | RIG-VEDA. | 3. | SÁMA-VEDA. |
| 2. | YAJUR-VEDA. | 4. | ATHARVA-VEDA. |

### Six Vedángas.

| 1. | SÍKSHÁ. | 4. | NIRUKTA. |
| 2. | CHHANDA. | 5. | JYOTISHA. |
| 3. | VYÁKARANA. | 6. | KALPA. |

### Four Vedopángas.

| 1. | MIMÁNSÁ. | 3. | DHARMA-SÁSTRA. |
| 2. | NYÁYA. | 4. | PURÁNAS. |

### Four Upavedas.

| 1. | AYURVA. | 3. | GANDHARVA. |
| 2. | DHANARVA. | 4. | ARTHA-SÁSTRA. |

All of these have other sub-divisions, either explanatory, commentatorial, or in the shape of illustrative indexes. Having given the general view to assist in following out the description of the several divisions, we will now proceed.

The primary books, whence all the rest emanate, are the *Vedas,* which are said "to have been revealed by Bramhá, and to have been preserved by tradition until they were arranged in the present order by a sage who thence obtained the surname of *Vyása* or *Vedavyása,* that is, the compiler of the *Vedas.*"† The word *Veda* means knowledge, and its root signifies light or fire. These *Vedas* are written in Sanskrit, the ancient sacred language of the Bráhmans, with

* Colebrooke on the Hindu Religion, p. 68.        † Ibid, p. 1.

the Devanagari character; and are supposed to have originally
consisted of three, namely, the *Rig-veda*, the *Yajur-veda*, and
the *Sáma-veda*. To these, the *Atharva-veda*, which is not
considered of equal sanctity, and is of less authority than the
others, was subsequently added.

Each of these *Vedas* consists of two distinct parts: the
*Sanhitá*, or collection of *Mantras*, and *Bráhmana*. The
Sanhitá is "the aggregate assemblage, in a single collection,"
of the prayers and hymns; the Bráhmana is "a collection of
rules for the application of the mantras, directions for the
performance of particular rites, citations of the hymns," illus-
trations, and legendary narrations.*

The RIG-VEDA takes precedence of the rest; for, as Mr.
Muir says, "the Taittiríyas, or followers of the *Black
Yajur-veda*, record that whatever sacrifical act is performed
by means of the *Sáma-* and *Yajur-veda* is comparatively
slender; whatever is done by means of the *Rig-veda* is
strong:"† and the Kaushítaki Bráhmana, which does not
mention the *Atharva-veda*, calls the *Yajur-* and *Sáma-veda*
"the attendants of *Rig-veda*." ‡ The first of the four *Vedopángas* also, the *Mimánsá*, makes mention only of the
three first *Vedas;* and what still further establishes the
priority of the *Rig-veda* is that some of the hymns of the
*Yajur-veda* and all those of the *Sáma-veda* are derived from
those of the *Rig-veda.* •

It is probable that originally there was but one text of the
four *Vedas*. Tradition says that "*Vyása* having compiled
and arranged the scriptures, theogonies, and mythological
poems, taught the several *Vedas* to as many disciples. These
disciples instructed their respective pupils, who, becoming
teachers in their turn, communicated the knowledge to their
own disciples, until at length, in the progress of successive

---

* Wilson's Rig-veda Sanhitá, i., Introduction, p. ix. and x.
† Muir's Orig. Sansk. Texts, i. p. 86. ‡ Müller's Anc. Sansk. Lit., p. 457.

instructions, so great variations crept into the text, the manner of reading and reciting it, and into the sacred precepts for its use and application, that the hundred different schools of scriptural knowledge arose

The *Charaṇavyuha*, which treats of these schools, m several by name, and states that five, sixty-eight, a the and nine, were the respective numbers of the *Charc* the *Rig-*, *Yajur-*, *Sáma-*, and *Atharva-vedas*. Had original *Sákhás* been extant in modern times they perhaps, have accounted for some of the superstitions days, said to be founded on, but not countenanced present text of the *Rig-veda Sanhitá*.

"All the verses of the *Yajur-veda* and all the verses *Sáma-veda* are used in one sacrificial act or another, l is not the case with the verses of the *Rig-veda*. Many latter, indeed, are likewise indispensable for sacrifici poses, as we are taught by the ritual books connect this *Veda:* yet a large number remain, which stand aloof from any ceremony. This class bears purely a p or mystical character; and it may be fairly inferred th the strong tendency of later ages to impress an sacrificial stamp on each of these Vedas, broke down the natural and poetical power that had evidently call these songs, as it could not incorporate them amon liturgic hymns."[†] One of these we will give as an of the class: it is from the tenth mandala, and is teresting, as shewing the Hindu original and mystical of the origin of things. It runs thus:—

"Then there was no entity nor nonentity; no world nor aught above it; nothing anywhere in the happiness of involving or involved; nor water deep and dangerous. D not; nor then was immortality, nor distinction of day o But THAT breathed without afflation, single with (*Swadhá*)

---

[*] Colebrooke on the Hindu Religion, p. 4.
[†] Goldstücker's Paper on Veda—Cyclopædia, p. 577.

is within him. Other than him, nothing existed (which) since (has been). Darkness there was; (for) this universe was enveloped with darkness, and was undistinguishable (like fluids mixed in) waters; but that mass, which was covered by the husk, was (at length) produced by the power of contemplation. First, desire was formed in his mind, and that became the original productive seed; which the wise, recognising it by the intellect in their hearts, distinguish, in nonentity, as the bond of entity. Did the luminous ray of these (creative acts) expand in the middle? or above? or below? That productive seed at once became providence (or sentient souls) and matter (or the elements): she who is sustained within himself was inferior; and he, who heeds, was superior. Who knows exactly, and who shall in this world declare, whence and why the creation took place? The gods are subsequent to the production of this world; then who can know whence it proceeded? or whence this varied world arose? or whether it upholds itself or not? He who in the highest heaven is the ruler of this universe, does indeed know; but not another can possess this knowledge."

This high-toned mysticism of the early Hindu religion became, as we shall see, degraded to a debasing and anthropomorphic superstition which converted this spirituality to a gross personification. "There is further evidence to show that the collection of the Rig-veda cannot have borne originally a ritual stamp. When songs are intended only for liturgic purposes they are sure to be arranged in conformity with the ritual acts to which they apply; when, on the contrary, they flow from the poetical or pious longings of the soul, they may, in the course of time, be used at, and adapted for, religious rites; but they will never submit to that systematic arrangement which is inseparable from the class of liturgic songs. Now, such a systematic arrangement characterises the collection of the Yajur-veda and Sáma-veda hymns : it is foreign to the Rig-veda Sanhitá."*

To give a notion of the elaborate subdivision of the Vedas we may cite that of the *Sanhitá* of the Rig-veda, which itself now exists only in the text of the Sákhala school. This

* Goldstücker's Paper on Veda—Cyclopædia, p. 578.

Sanhitá is divided, or arranged, on two methods. "Acco
to the first it is divided into eight *ashtákas*, or eighths
of which is again subdivided into *adhyáyas*, or lectures
*adhyáya* consisting of a number of *vargas*, or sections,
*varga* of a number of *rich*, or verses, usually five. Acco
to the second method, the Sanhitá is divided into ten
*dalas*, or circles, subdivided into eighty-five *annaváka*
lessons, which consist of one thousand and seventeen (or
eleven additional hymns, of one thousand and twenty-e
súktas, or hymns; these again, containing ten thousan
hundred and eighty and a half *rich*, or verses. The first
of these *mandalas* begin with hymns addressed to *Agni*,
are followed by hymns addressed to *Indra*. After the
come generally hymns addressed to the *Viswa Devas*,
gods collectively, and then those which are devoted to
divinities. The ninth mandala is wholly addressed t
*Soma-plant*," so distinguished in the sacrificial rites;
the tenth *mandala* has chiefly served for the collection of
*Atharva-veda* hymns."[*]

The YAJUR-VEDA consists of two different Vedas,
have separately branched out into various Sákhás. Th
termed *Black* and *White Yajur-veda*, or *Taittiríya* and
*saneyi*. The Taittiríya, or Black Yajur-vedu, is more ce
in regard to mantras than the White Yajur-vedu.
Sanhitá, or collection of prayers, is arranged in seven l
containing from five to eight lectures, or chapters.
chapter, or lecture, is subdivided into sections (annuv
which are equally distributed in the third and sixth l
but unequally in the rest. The whole number exceed
hundred and fifty."[†]

"The Vájasaneyi, or White Yajur-vedu, is the short
the Vedas; so far as respects the first and principal

---

[*] Goldstücker's Paper on Veda—Cyclopædia, pp. 578-9
[†] Colebrooke on the Hindu Religion, p. 43.

which comprehends the mantras. The Sanhitá, or collection of prayers and invocations belonging to this Veda, is comprised in forty lectures (adhyáya), unequally subdivided into numerous short sections (kándiká), each of which, in general, constitutes a prayer or mantra. It is also divided, like the Rig-veda, into annavákas, or chapters. The number of annavákas, as they are stated at the close of the index to this Veda, appears to be two hundred and eighty-six: the number of sections, or verses, nearly two thousand." *

The Yajur-veda "has largely drawn on the Rig-veda hymns. But the first difference we observe is that its contents are not entirely taken from the principal Veda, and the second is marked by the circumstances that it often combines with verses, passages in prose, which are called Yajus (*lit.* 'that by which the sacrifice is effected,') and have given to Yajur-veda its name. Besides, the ceremonial for which this Veda was made up is much more diversified and elaborate than that of the Sáma-veda ; and the mystical and philosophical allusions, which now and then appear in the Rig-veda, probably in its latest portions, assume a more prominent place in the Yajur-veda. In one word, it is the sacrificial Veda, as its name indicates. Hence we understand why it was looked upon in that period of Hindu civilization which was engrossed by superstitions and rites, as the principal Veda, superior, in fact,. to the Rig-veda, where there is no system of rites." †

SÁMA-VEDA.—"A peculiar degree of holiness seems to be attached, according to Indian notions, to the Sáma-veda ; if reliance may be placed on the inference suggested by the etymology of its name, which indicates the efficacy of this part of the *Vedas* in removing sin. The prayers belonging to it are composed in metre and intended to be chanted, and

---

* Colebrooke on the Hindu Religion, p. 31.
† Goldstücker's Paper on Veda—Cyclopædia, p. 584.

their supposed efficacy is apparently ascribed to this mode of uttering them."* "The Sanhitá (of the Sáma-veda) consists of two parts, the Archika and Staubhika. The Archika, as adapted to the special use of the priests, exists in two forms, called Gúṇas, or Song-books, the Veyagáṇa and Araṇya-gáṇa. The Staubhika exists in the same manner as Uha-gúṇa and Uhyagáṇa."† As regards the Bráhmaṇas of the *Sáma-veda*, Sayana enumerates eight : of these the first two are the most important, and treat of the sacrifices which are performed with the juice of the *Soma-plant.* The third is remarkable on account of the incantatory ceremonies it describes."‡

THE ATHARVA-VEDA.—" The Sanhitá, or collection of prayers and invocations belonging to this *Veda*, is composed of twenty books (kandas), subdivided into sections, hymns, and verses."§ "The Atharva-veda," says Madhusúdana, " is not used for the sacrifice ; it only teaches how to appease, to bless, to curse," etc. Its songs, as Professor Müller observes, " formed probably an additional part of the sacrifice from a very early time. They were chiefly intended to counteract the influence of any untoward event that might happen during the sacrifice. They also contained imprecations and blessings, and various formulas, such as popular superstition would be sure to sanction at all times and in all countries."‖

There are in the Vedic age, as Professor Max Müller remarks, " four distinct periods which can be established with sufficient evidence. They may be called the *Chhandas period,* *Mantra period,* *Bráhmaṇa period,* and *Sútra period,* according to the general form of the literary productions which give to each of them its peculiar historical character."¶ According to this, the Bráhmaṇas which form the sacrificial and

---

* Colebrooke on the Hindu Religion, p. 47.    † Müller's Anc. Sansk. Lit., note to p. 473.         ‡ Goldstücker's Paper on Veda—Cyclopædia, p. 590.
§ Colebrooke on the Hindu Religion, p. 53.
‖ Müller's Anc. Sansk. Lit., p. 447.              ¶ Ibid, p. 70.

ceremonial portions of the Vedas were written in the third period of the Vedic age. With regard to the Sanhitás-collection of hymns and prayers, those of the Rig-veda only belong to the first period. The Sanhitás of other Vedas " were more likely the production of the Bráhmaṇa period." *

The hymn we have extracted in a former passage from the tenth mandala of the Rig-veda points to the fact that the Vaidik creed established but one God, or principle of creation, and that the many gods which occur in the Vaidik hymns are but poetical allegories of the One Great Soul. "The deities invoked," as observed by Mr. H. T. Colebrooke, " appear on a cursory inspection of the Veda to be as various as the authors of the prayers addressed to them ; but, according to the most ancient annotations on the Indian scripture, those numerous names of persons and things are all resolvable into different titles of three deities, and, ultimately, of one God. The *Nighánti,* or glossary of the Vedas, concludes with three lists of names of deities,—the first comprising such as are deemed synonymous with fire ; the second, with air ; and the third, with the sun. In the last part of the *Nirukta,* which entirely relates to deities, it is twice asserted that there are but three gods : ' *Tisra iva devatáh.*' The further inference, that these intend but one deity, is supported by many passages in the *Veda ;* and is very clearly and concisely stated in the beginning of the index to the *Rig-veda,* on the authority of the *Nirukta* and of the *Veda* itself." †

The chief deities addressed in many of the hymns of the Rig-veda are *Agni* and *Indra ;* and there are besides *Súrya, Vishṇu,* and *Varuṇa,* and *Mitra* of inferior distinction. *Agni* is the God of Fire as it exists on earth, in the fire of lightning and in the fire of the sun. Deities subordinate to him are the *Marutas,* or winds. *Indra* is the God of the Firmament. It is he who fixed the stars in their position, and raised the

* Müller's Anc. Sansk. Lit., p. 457.   † Colebrooke on the Hindu Religion, p. 12.

sun aloft; but he is peculiarly the conqueror of *Vritra* (the enveloper), the demon who hides the sun; and he pierces the clouds which threaten to withhold their waters from the earth with his thunderbolt, and the waters are let down. *Vishṇu* is identified with the sun in its three stages of rising, culmination, and setting; and *Varuṇa* is the all-embracing heaven, the orderer and ruler of the universe, who established the eternal laws which govern the movements of the world, and which neither immortal nor mortal may break : he regulates the seasons; appoints sun, moon, stars, and their courses; and gives to each creature that which is peculiarly characteristic. From his station in heaven he sees and hears everything; nothing can remain hidden from him : he grants wealth, averts evil, and protects cattle. *Mitra* is the divinity that presides over the day, and is "a dispenser of water." *

"We must not," says Professor Max Müller, "compare the Aryan and the Semitic races. Whereas, the Semitic nations relapsed from time to time into polytheism, the Aryans of India seem to have relapsed into monotheism. . . . There is a monotheism that precedes the polytheism of the Veda; and, even in the invocations of their innumerable gods, the remembrance of a God, one and infinite, breaks through the mist of an idolatrous phraseology, like the blue sky that is hidden by passing clouds." †

"Thus we read, 'I know not what this is that I am like; turned inward I walk, chained in my mind. When the firstborn of time comes near me, then I obtain the portion of this speech.'

"In the 30th verse of the same hymn we read : 'Breathing lies the quick-moving life, heaving, yet firm, in the midst of its abodes. The living one walks through the powers of the dead : the immortal is the brother of the mortal.' Sometimes when these oracular sayings have been pronounced, the poet

---

* Wilson's Rig-veda, i., p. xxxiv.    † Müller's Anc. Sansk. Lit., p. 558-9.

claims his due. 'One who had eyes,' he says, 'saw it; the blind will not understand it. A poet, who is a boy, he has perceived it; he who understands it will be the father of his father.'

"In the same hymn one verse occurs which boldly declares the existence of but one Divine Being though invoked under different names (R. V. i. 164, 46).

"'They call (him) Indra, Mitra, Varuṇa, Agni; then he is the well-winged heavenly Garutmat; that which is One the wise call it many ways; they call it Agni, Yama, Mátarisvan.' *

"I add only one more hymn, in which the idea of one God is expressed with such power and decision, that it will make us hesitate before we deny to the Aryan nations an instinctive monotheism (R. V. x. 121).

"'In the beginning there arose the Source of golden light. He was the only born Lord of all that is. He stablished the earth, and this sky;—Who is the God to whom we shall offer our sacrifice?

"'He who gives life, He who gives strength; whose blessing all the bright gods desire; whose shadow is immortality; whose shadow is death;—Who is the God to whom we shall offer our sacrifice?

"'He who through His power is the only king of the breathing and awakening world; He who governs all, man and beast;—Who is the God to whom we shall offer our sacrifice?

"'He whose power these snowy mountains, whose power the sea proclaims, with the distant river; He whose these regions are, as it were, his two arms;—Who is the God to whom we shall offer our sacrifice?

"'He through whom the sky is bright, and the earth firm; He through whom the heaven was stablished—nay, the highest heaven; He who measured out the light in the air;—Who is the God to whom we shall offer our sacrifice?

"'He to whom heaven and earth, standing firm by His will, look up, trembling inwardly; He over whom the rising sun shines forth;—Who is the God to whom we shall offer our sacrifice?

"'Wherever the mighty water-clouds went, where they placed

* Müller's Anc. Sansk. Lit., p. 567.

the seed and lit the fire, thence arose He who is the only life of the bright gods;—Who is the God to whom we shall offer our sacrifice?

"'He who by His might looked even over the water-clouds, the clouds which gave strength and lit the sacrifice; He *who is God above all gods;*—Who is the God to whom we shall offer our sacrifice?

"'May He not destroy us, He the creator of the earth; or He, the righteous, who created the heaven; He who also created the bright and mighty waters.—Who is the God to whom we shall offer our sacrifice?'"*

We have shown the tendency of this Vaidik creed, that we may shortly display its application to the existing worship; and we now proceed to the further elucidation of the several divisions of the Śástras. In speaking of the Vedas, we should not feel justified in leaving unnoticed that class of works known by the name " *Upanishads,*" which are so intimately connected with them, and which were held by later generations in the same awe as the Vedas. They contain the theological or theosophical writings which have sprung from the *Bráhmana.* The word *Upanishad* signifies the science which destroys erroneous ideas or ignorance, or the entering into that which is hidden. The knowledge which the Upanishads intend to convey is chiefly that of the production and nature of the world, of the properties of a Supreme Divinity, and of the human soul, which they conceive to be part of it. They contain the highest authority on which the various systems of philosophy in India rest. "The old Upanishads did not pretend to give more than 'guesses at truth,' and when, in course of time, they became invested with an inspired character, they allowed great latitude to those who professed to believe in them as revelation. Yet this was not sufficient for the rank growth of philosophical doctrines during the latter ages of Indian history; and when none of the ancient Upanishads could be found to suit the

* Müller's Anc. Sansk. Lit., p. 568–70.

purpose, the founders of new sects had no scruple and no difficulty in composing new Upanishads of their own."*

The *Vedángas* are called the Limbs of the Vedas, and display the mode in which scientific research sprung from the sacred texts. The first Vedánga is *Śikshá*, which treats of the science of orthoepy, or proper pronunciation; the second, called *Chhandas*, treats of prosody; the third, named *Vyákarana*, treats of grammar. Upon this the celebrated *Pánini* wrote a treatise which is considered as equal to the best grammatical works of any nation or age: it is in eight chapters, consisting of thirty-two sections and three thousand nine hundred and ninety-six rules. So great was the renown of this wonderful labour (of which we have an admirable edition edited by Dr. Goldstücker), that it was supposed to have been inspired by the god *Śiva* himself, and it is still to the present day the standard of Sanskrit speech. The fourth Vedánga is *Nirukta*, which treats of etymology; the fifth is *Jyotisha*, which treats of astronomy; and the sixth Vedánga is the *Kalpa*, or ceremonial, and constitutes the code of the Brahmanic rites. Two other classes of Śástras complete the code of these Kalpa works, and are the *Grihya* and the *Sámayáchárika* Sútras; the former describes the domestic ceremonies as distinct from the great sacrificial acts, and consists of the marriage ceremonies, those performed on conception, at various periods before birth, at birth, on naming the child, of carrying him out to see the sun, of feeding him, of cutting his hair, and "of investing him as a student and handing him to a *guru*, under whose care he is to study the sacred writings. . . . It is only after he has served his apprenticeship and grown up to manhood that he is allowed to marry, to light the sacrificial fire for himself, to choose his priests, and to perform year after year the solemn sacrifices prescribed by *Śruti* and *Smriti*. The latter

* Müller's Anc. Sansk. Lit., p. 317.

are described in later books of the *Grihya-sútras*, ɛ
last book contains a full account of the funeral cerɛ
and of the sacrifices offered to the spirits of the depa
The Sámayáchárika Sutras regulate the relations o:
day life, and in them we have to look for the origi
the metrical law books, such as *Manu, Yájnavalkya,* ɛ
rest.†

The next class are the *Vedopángas*, which are divid
four, viz. : first, the *Mimánsá*, which explains portions
Veda, both doctrinal and ceremonial; the second
which contains a refutation of atheism, by way of reaɛ
the third, *Dharma Sástra*, containing the ordinat
*Manu*, a complete code of morality, and a poetical acc
God, spirits, and the origin of the world and man ; ɛ
fourth class are the *Puránas*, which consist of eight
which are appended as many *Upapuránas*, or comp
and explanations. Taken collectively they are of n
and philosophical contexture, cosmogonical, theogonic
chronological; and contain extensive legendary nar
We will briefly enumerate them, with their contents :-

1. *Vishnu Puránu*, the history of Vishnu and his i:
tions, in 23000 *Slokas.* 2. *Náradya Puránu*, the hi:
Nárad, as god of music, in 25000 *Slokas.* 3. *Bh*
*Puránu*, the history of Krishna or Vishnu, in twelve
11000 *Slokas.* 4. *Garuda Puráns*, in 19000 *Slok*
*Padma Puránu*, the history of Lakshmi, the Con
Vishnu, in 55000 *Slokas.* 6. *Varáha Puránu*, the
of the third incarnation of Vishnu, in 24000 *Slol*
*Matsya Puránu*, the history of the first incarnation of
in 14000 *Slokas.* 8. *Linga Puránu*, the history of ɪ
11000 *Slokas.* 9. *Siva Puránu*, in 24000 *Sloka.*
*Skanda Puránu*, the history of Skanda, the son of ɪ
81000 *Slokas.* 11. *Agneya Puránu*, the abstract of al'

---

ledge, in 15500 *Slokas.* 12. *Kurma Puráṇa,* in 17000 *Slokas.* 13. *Brahmáṇda Puráṇa,* the history of Rámachandra, in 12000 *Slokas.* 14. *Brahma Vaivartta Puráṇa,* which is especially dedicated to Krishṇa as Govinda, and is principally occupied by him and his mistress Rádhá : it is also full on the subject of Prakriti, or personified nature, in 18000 *Slokas.* 15. *Márkandeya Puráṇa,* the history of Durgá, which contains the famous *Chandi Pátha,* in 9000 *Slokas.* 16. *Bhavishya Puráṇa,* in 14500 *Slokas.* 17. *Vámana Puráṇa,* in 10000 *Slokas.* 18. *Brahma Puráṇa,* in 10000 *Slokás.*

The four *Upavedas* comprise—1. *Ayurva,* which treats of surgery and physic. 2. *Dhanarva,* which treats of the art of war. 3. *Gandharva,* which treats of music and dancing. And 4. *Artha-Sástra,* which treats of political economy.

Together with these canonical books may be classed the two ancient and excellent Epics—namely, the *Rámáyaṇa,* the work of *Válmika,* containing the history of Ráma, king of Ayodhyá, the seventh *avatár* of Vishṇu ; and the *Mahábhárata,* containing the war between *Pándavas* and *Kauravas,* the descendants of the ancient Indian king *Bhárata,* in eighteen books and more than 100,000 *Slokas,* the celebrated episode of which, the *Bhagavad Gítá,* is well known.

# CHAPTER II.

## RELIGIOUS SECTS OF THE HINDUS.

In the last chapter we took a brief and rapid review
sacred writings of the Hindus. It was to be expected
many conflicting opinions would originate in such a m
doctrine, commentary, and interpretation, the heterogo
subjects introduced, and the errors and misconceptions
polated by transcribers in the lapse of centuries.
opinions led progressively to divergent views, strained
times to excess by the subtle artifices of a crafty pries
prompted by the instigations of a paramount self-int
and sometimes by the enthusiam of the devotee, who
scientiously conceiving that he had, in his medita
detected the true path, was anxious that his contempo
and posterity should not be lost in intricate by-ways, a
promulgated his peculiar views, which ensured advocate
followers. Thus, in the thousand and one modes by
new opinions are disseminated and adherents found
Hindu religion, like the other religions of the world
generated sects and sectaries, and the number of thos
are dissentient in their tenets and their ceremonies is a
tudinous.

"The worship of the populace, being addressed to dif
divinities, the followers of the several gods naturally sep:
into different associations, and the adorers of *Brahmá, V*
and *Śiva*, or other phantoms of their faith, become di
and insulated bodies in the general aggregate. The co
of opinion on subjects on which human reason has nev

agreed, led to similar differences in the philosophical class, and resolved itself into the several *Darśanas,* or schools of philosophy." *

"To the internal incongruities of the system, which did not affect its integral existence,. others were, in time, superadded that threatened to dissolve or destroy the whole. Of this nature was the exclusive adoration of the old deities, or of new forms of them; and even,. it may be presumed,. the introduction of new divinities. In all these respects,. the *Puránas* and *Tantras* were especially instrumental; and they not only taught their followers to assert the unapproachable superiority of the gods they worshipped, but inspired them with feelings of animosity towards. those who presumed to dispute that supremacy. In this conflict the worship of *Brahmá* has disappeared, as well as, indeed, that of the whole pantheon, except *Vishṇu, Śiva,* and *Śakti,* or their modifications. With respect to the two former, in fact,. the representatives have borne away the palm from the prototypes, and *Krishṇa, Ráma,* or the *Linga,.* are almost the only forms under which *Vishṇu* and *Śiva* are now adored in most parts of India.

"The varieties of opinion kept pace with those of practice; and six heretical schools of philosophy disputed the pre-eminence with their orthodox brethren. We have little or no knowledge of these systems, and even their names are not satisfactorily stated: they seem, however, to be the *Saugata,* or *Bauddha; Árhata,* or *Jaina;* and *Várhaspatya,* or atheistical, with their several subdivisions.

"Had the difference of doctrine taught in the heretical schools been confined to tenets of a merely speculative nature, they would, probably, have encountered little opposition, and excited little enmity among the Brahmanical class, of which latitude of opinion is a very common characteristic. *Vrihaspati,* the founder of the atheistical school, however,

* H. H. Wilson's Works, vol. i. p. 2.

2

attacks both the *Vedas* and the *Brahmans,* and asserts that
the whole of the Hindu system is a contrivance of the
priesthood, to secure a means of livelihood for themselves;
whilst the *Bauddhas* and *Jainas,* equally disregarding the
*Vedas* and the *Brahmans,* the practice and opinions of the
Hindus, invented a set of gods for themselves, and deposed
the ancient pantheon. These aggressions provoked resentment: the writings of these sects are alluded to with every
epithet of anger and contempt, and they are all anathematised
as heretical and* atheistical. More active measures than
anathemas, it may be presumed, were had recourse to. The
followers of *Vrihaspati,* having no worship at all, easily
eluded the storm; but the *Bauddhas* of Hindustan were
annihilated by its fury, and the *Jainas* apparently evaded it
with difficulty, although they have undoubtedly survived its
terrors, and may now defy its force.

"The varieties thus arising from innovations in practice
and belief, have differed, it may be concluded, at different eras
of the Hindu worship. To trace the character of those which
have latterly disappeared, or to investigate the remote history
of some which still remain and are apparently of ancient
date, are tasks for which we are far from being yet prepared:
the enquiry is in itself so vast, and so little progress has been
made in the studies necessary to its elucidation, that it must
remain in the obscurity in which it has hitherto been
enveloped."*

The adorers of these divinities, as *Vishnu, Śiva,* and *Śakti,*
about nine centuries ago spread into a multitude of sects, a
mere catalogue of the names of which, without the discrimination of their creeds, would be an almost profitless labour;
for it would want the muscular flesh to give the skeleton
form. The learned Brahman *Śankara,* did, indeed, about this

* H. H. Wilson's Works, vol. i. p. 3 to 6.

period endeavour, by great exertions, to suppress these different sects, and to re-introduce the sole recognition and worship of Brahmá, Para Brahmá, the Supreme and sole ruler of the universe; but he saw no reason to distrust the faith of those who worshipped the personifications of Brahmá, Vishṇu, and Śiva, they not being competent to the abstraction and elevation of mind requisite for the comprehension of the one Great First Cause and animating principle. For he observed : "In the present impure age, the bud of wisdom being blighted by iniquity, men are inadequate to the apprehension of pure unity; they will be apt therefore again to follow the dictates of their own fancies, and it is necessary for the preservation of the world, and the maintenance of civil and religious distinctions, to acknowledge those modifications of the Divine Spirit which are the works of the Supreme."

His success was not of permanent duration; for, in the course of time, other teachings were introduced, and ultimately and gradually resolved themselves into the present condition of the Hindu religion. The worshippers of this faith consist now of the *Vaishṇavas, Śaivas* and *Śáktas;* or the adorers of *Vishṇu, Śiva,* and *Śakti.*

Amongst these must not be enumerated the few learned Brahmans who may be found, and who consider themselves as the sole orthodox adorers, admitting the Vedas, the Law Books, the Puráṇas, and the Tantras as the only ritual they recognise; although they even select some particular deity as their Ishta Devatá, or chosen god. A very remarkable feature of sectarianism in the present day is that the distinction of caste almost merges in the identity of schism. The following list * enumerates, if not all, at least the chief of the sects into which the Hindu religion is now divided :

* H. H. Wilson's Works, vol. i. p. 31.

attacks both the *Vedas* and the *Brahmans*, and assert
the whole of the Hindu system is a contrivance ‹
priesthood, to secure a means of livelihood for thems
whilst the *Bauddhas* and *Jainas*, equally disregardin
*Vedas* and the *Brahmans*, the practice and opinions
Hindus, invented a set of gods for themselves, and do
the ancient pantheon.   These aggressions provoked i
ment : the writings of these sects are alluded to with
epithet of anger and contempt, and they are all anathem
as heretical and* atheistical.   More active measures
anathemas, it may be presumed, were had recourse to.
followers of *Vrihaspati*, having no worship at all,
eluded the storm ; but the *Bauddhas* of Hindustan
annihilated by its fury, and the *Jainas* apparently eva
with difficulty, although they have undoubtedly surviv
terrors, and may now defy its force.

"The varieties thus arising from innovations in p]
and belief, have differed, it may be concluded, at differei
of the Hindu worship.   To trace the character of those
have latterly disappeared, or to investigate the remote h
of some which still remain and are apparently of a
date, are tasks for which we are far from being yet pre]
the enquiry is in itself so vast, and so little progress ha
made in the studies necessary to its elucidation, that it
remain in the obscurity in which it has hitherto
enveloped."*

The adorers of these divinities, as *Vishṇu*, *Śiva*, and
about nine centuries ago spread into a multitude of s
mere catalogue of the names of which, without the dis
nation of their creeds, would be an almost profitless k
for it would want the muscular flesh to give the sk
form.   The learned Brahman *Śankara*, did, indeed, abo

* H. H. Wilson's Works, vol. i. p. 3 to 6.

The *Vaishṇavas* comprise the—

1. "Rámánujas, or Śri Sampradáyís, or Śri Vaishṇavas.
2. Rámánandís, or Rámávats.
3. Kabír Panthís.
4. Khákis.
5. Malúk Dásís.
6. Dádú Panthís.
7. Ráya Dásís.
8. Senáís.
9. Vallabháchárís, or Rudra Sampradáyís.
10. Mírá Báís.
11. Madhwáchárís, or Brahmá Sampradáyís.
12. Nímávats, or Sanakádi Sampradáyís.
13. Vaishṇavas of Bengal.
14. Rádhá Vallabhís.
15. Sákhí Bhávas.
16. Charaṇ Dásís.
17. Hariśchandís.
18. Sadhná Panthís.
19. Mádhavís.
20. Sannyásís, Vairágís, and Nágás.

The *Śaivas* comprise the—

1. Daṇdís and Dasnámís.
2. Jogís.
3. Jangams.
4. Paramahansas.
5. Urddhabáhús, Akás Mukhís, and Nákhís.
6. Gúdharas.
7. Rúkharas, Súkharas, and Ukharas.
8. Kará Lingís.
9. Sannyásis, etc.

The *Sáktas* comprise the—
1. Dakshinís.
2. Vámís.
3. Kánchalyás.
4. Karáris.

There is a further miscellaneous class which cannot be arranged with the above, whose tenets again differ, and some of which, even amongst themselves, admit of further sub-division, as they deviate in their belief from their own branch.

These *Miscellaneous Sects* are the—
1. Gánapatyás.
2. Saurapatas, Súrya-Upashakas.
3. Núnak Sháhís, of which there are seven classes, viz.
    *a.* Udásís.
    *b.* Ganjbakhshís.
    *c.* Rámráyís.
    *d.* Suthrú Sháhís.
    *e.* Govind Sinhís.
    *f.* Nirmalas.
    *g.* Nágús.
4. Jainas, of two principal orders :
    *a.* Digambaras.
    *b.* Śwetámbaras.
5. Bábá Lálís.
6. Prán Náthís.
7. Sádhs.
8. Śatnámís.
9. Śiva Núráyúnís.
10. Śúnyavádís.

This long enumeration might be still further lengthened did we introduce the many sub-sects and affiliated commu-

nities which adopt modifications of the doctrine ar
monial of the sects from which they have seceded;
may be well considered that the multitude of these
make the Hindu religion a maze of confusion, the
minable intricacies of which cannot be threaded for w
clue.

We shall now briefly notice a few of the sects give
preceding list, in order to shew the leading features
doctrines.      -

## VAISHNAVAS.

The *Vaishnavas* are usually distinguished into fo·
cipal *Sampradáyas*, or sects, viz.: Rámánuja, Vishṇu
Mádhaváchárya, and Nimbárka; of these, the most
and respectable is the first, called also the *Śrí Samp*
founded by the Vaishṇava reformer *Rámánuja*, ab
middle of the twelfth century.

### RÁMÁNUJAS.

" The worship of the followers of *Rámánuja* is add
*Vishṇu* and to *Lakshmí*, and their respective inca
either singly or conjointly; and the *Śrí Vaishṇavas*, v
general name the sect is known, consist of correspond
divisions, as *Náráyaṇa* or *Lakshmí*, or *Lakshmí Nárá*
*Ráma* or *Sítá*, or *Sítá Ráma* or *Krishṇa*, or *Ruk*
any other modifications of *Vishṇu*, or his consort, is
ferential object of the veneration of the votary." *

" The most striking peculiarities in the practice
sect are the individual preparation and scrupulous p
their meals: they must not eat in cotton garme
having bathed, must put on woollen or silk: the
allow their select pupils to assist them, but, in ge
the *Rámánujas* cook for themselves; and should t
during this process, or whilst they are eating, atti

* H. H. Wilson's Works, vol. i. p. 38.

the looks of a stranger, the operation is instantly stopped, and the viands buried in the ground. A similar delicacy, in this respect, prevails amongst some other classes of Hindus, especially the *Rájaput* families; but it is not carried to so preposterous an extent.

"The chief ceremony of initiation in all Hindu sects is the communication, by the teacher to the disciple, of the *Mantra*, which generally consists of the name of some deity, or a short address to him: it is communicated in a whisper, and never lightly made known by the adept to profane ears. The *Mantra* of the *Rámánuja* sect is said to be the six syllable *Mantra*, or *Om Rámáya namah;* or Om, salutation to *Ráma*.

"Another distinction amongst sects, but merely of a civil character, is the term or terms with which the religious members salute each other when they meet, or in which they are addressed by the lay members. This amongst the *Rámánujas* is the phrase *Dáso'smi*, or *Dáso'ham*, I am (your) slave; accompanied with the Praṇám, or slight inclination of the head, and the application of the joined hands to the forehead. To the *Áchárya*s, or supreme teachers of this sect, the rest perform the *Ashtánga Daṇdawat*, or prostration of the body, with the application of eight parts—the forehead, breast, hands, knees, and insteps of the feet, to the ground."*

"The chief religious tenet of the Rámánujas is the assertion that *Vishṇu* is *Bráhmá;* that he was before all worlds, and was the cause and the creator of all. Although they maintain that *Vishṇu* and the *Universe* are one, yet, in opposition to the *Vedánta* doctrines, they deny that the deity is void of form or quality, and regard him as endowed with all good qualities, and with a two-fold form: the supreme spirit, *Paramátmá*, or cause, and the gross one, the effect, the universe or matter. The doctrine is hence called the *Visishthádwaita*, or doctrine of unity with attributes. In

* H. H. Wilson's Works, vol. i. p. 39 and 40.

these assertions they are followed by most of the *Va:*
sects." *  The *Rámánujas* are decidedly hostile to th
sect, and are not on very friendly terms with the :
votaries of *Krishṇa,* although they recognise that deit
incarnation of *Vishṇu.*

### RÁMÁNANDÍS.

" The followers of Rámánand are much better knov
those of Rámánuja in Upper Hindustan : they are
considered as a branch of the *Rámánuja* sect, and
their devotions peculiarly to *Rámachandra,* and the
manifestations connected with *Vishṇu* in that incarna
*Sítá, Lakshmaṇa,* and *Hanumán.*" †

" The especial object of the worship of *Rámánanɑ*
lowers is *Vishṇu,* as Rámachandra : they, of course, re
all the other incarnations of *Vishṇu,* but they maint
superiority of *Ráma,* in the present or *Kali Yug :*
they are known collectively as *Rámávats,* although tl
variety prevails amongst them as amongst the *Rámáɪ*
to the exclusive or collective worship of the male and
members of this incarnation, or of *Ráma* and *Sítá* si
jointly, or *Sítá Ráma.*  Individuals of them also pa;
cular veneration to some of the other forms of *Vishn*
they hold in like estimation, as the *Rámánujas* anɩ
*Vaishṇava* sect, the *Sálagrám* stone and *Tulasí* plant.
forms of worship correspond with˚ those of the
generally ; but some of the mendicant members of t
who are very numerous, and are usually known as *℩*
or *Viraktas,* consider all forms of adoration supɩ
beyond the incessant invocation of the name of *Kris.*
*Ráma.*" ‡

### KABÍR PANTHÍS.

" Amongst the twelve disciples of *Rámánand,* t:
celebrated of all, and one who seems to have ɪ

directly or indirectly a greater effect on the state of popular belief than any other, was *Kabír*. With an unprecedented boldness he assailed the whole system of idolatrous worship, and ridiculed the learning of the *Pandits* and doctrines of the *Sástras*, in a style peculiarly well suited to the genius of his countrymen to whom he addressed himself; whilst he also directed his compositions to the Musalmán, as well as to the Hindu faith, and with equal severity attacked the *Mullá* and *Korán*. The effect of his lessons, as confined to his own immediate followers, will be shown to have been considerable, but their indirect effect has been still greater; several of the popular sects being little more than ramifications from his stock, whilst Núnak Sháh, the only Hindu reformer who has established a national faith, appears to have been chiefly indebted for his religious notions to his predecessor *Kabír*."[*]

"The moral code of the *Kabír Panthís* is short, but, if observed faithfully, is of a rather favourable tendency. Life is the gift of God, and must not therefore be violated by his creatures. *Humanity* is consequently a cardinal virtue, and the shedding of blood, whether of man or animal, a heinous crime. *Truth* is the other great principle of their code, as all the ills of the world, and ignorance of God, are attributable to original falsehood. *Retirement* from the world is desirable, because the passions and desires, the hopes and fears, which the social state engenders, are all hostile to tranquillity and purity of spirit, and prevent that undisturbed meditation on man and God which is necessary to their comprehension."[†]

## DÁDU PANTHÍS.

"This class is one of the indirect ramifications of the *Rámánandi* stock, and is always included amongst the *Vaishnava* schisms: its founder is said to have been a pupil of one

---

[*] H. H. Wilson's Works, vol. i. p. 68-9.      [†] Ibid, p. 94.

of the *Kabir Panthi* teachers and to be the fifth in
from *Rámánand*, according to the following geneology

1. *Kabir.*                    4. *Vimál.*
2. *Kamál.*                   5. *Buddhan.*
3. *Jamál.*                   6. *Dádú.*

The worship is addressed to *Ráma*, but it is restricted
*Japa*, or repetition of his name, and the *Ráma* intende
deity, as negatively described in the *Vedánta* the
temples and images are prohibited."*

## MADHWACHARIS.

"The institution of this sect is posterior to that of
Vaishṇavas, or Rámánujas."† "The essential dogma
sect, like that of the *Vaishṇavas* in general, is the ide
tion of *Vishṇu* with the Supreme Spirit as the pre-
cause of the universe, from whose substance the wo
made. This primeval *Vishṇu* they also affirm to be e
with real attributes, most excellent, although indefina
independent. As there is one independent, howeve
is also one dependent, and this doctrine is the charai
dogma of the sect, distinguishing its professors fr
followers of *Rámánuja*, as well as *Śankara*, or the
maintain the qualified or absolute unity of the deit
creed of the *Mádhaws* is *Dwaita*, or duality. It
however, that they discriminate between the princ
good and evil, or even the difference between spi
matter, which is the duality known to other sects
Hindus. Their distinction is of a more subtle charac
separates the *Jivátmá* from the *Paramátmá*, or the p
of life from the Supreme Being. Life, they say, is
eternal, dependent upon the Supreme, and indissolul
nected with, but not the same with him. An im
consequence of this doctrine is the denial of *Moksh*

* II. H. Wilson's Works, vol. i. p. 103.          † Ibid, p. 1

more generally received sense, or that of absorption into the universal spirit, and loss of independent existence after death."*

## NIMBÁRKA, OR NIMÁVATS.

"This division of the Vaishṇava faith is one of the four primary ones, and appears to be of considerable antiquity: it is one also of some popularity and extent, although it seems to possess but few characteristic peculiarities beyond the name of the founder, and the sectarial mark. *Nimbáditya* is said to have been a *Vaishṇava* ascetic, originally named *Bháskar Áchárya*, and to have been, in fact, an incarnation of the *sun*, for the suppression of the heretical doctrines then prevalent."†

"The *Nimávats* are distinguished by a circular black mark in the centre of the ordinary double streak of white earth, or *Gopíchandan*: they use the necklace and rosary of the stem of the *Tulasí*: the objects of their worship are *Krishṇa* and *Rádhá* conjointly: their chief authority is the *Bhágavat*, and there is said to be a *Bháshya* on the *Vedas* by *Nimbárka*: the sect, however, is not possessed of any books peculiar to the members, which want they attribute to the destruction of their works at *Mathurá*, in the time of Aurengzeb."‡

## SAIVAS.

The worship of *Śiva* "appears to be the most prevalent and popular of all the modes of adoration, to judge by the number of shrines dedicated to the only form under which Śiva is reverenced, that of the *Linga*."§  "*Sambhu* is declared by Manu to be the presiding deity of the Brahmanical order, and the greater number of them, particularly those who practice the rites of the *Vedas*, or who profess the study of the *Sástras*, receive *Śiva* as their tutelary deity, wear his insignia, and worship the *Linga*, either in temples, in their

---

* H. H. Wilson's Works, vol. i. p. 143-45.  † Ibid, p. 151.
‡ Ibid, p. 150.  § Ibid, p. 188.

houses, or on the side of a sacred stream, providing
latter case, extempore emblems kneaded out of the
clay of the river's bed." *

"There are no teachers of ancient repute except
*áchárya*, and his doctrines are too philosophical and
tive to have made him popular." †

### DANDÍS.

"The *Dandí* is distinguished by carrying a small *l*
wand, with several processes or projections from it
piece of cloth dyed with red ochre, in which the Brah
cord is supposed to be enshrined, attached to it: h
his hair and beard, wears only a cloth round his lo
subsists upon food obtained ready-dressed from the h
the Brahmans once a day only, which he deposits
small clay pot that he carries always with him. Th
has no particular time or mode of worship, but sp
time in meditation, or in practices corresponding wi
of the *Yoga*, and in the study of the *Vedánta* works, es
according to the comments of *Śankaráchárya*." ‡

### YOGÍS, OR JOGÍS.

"The term *Jogí*, or *Yogí*, is properly applicable
followers of the *Yoga* or *Pátanjala* school of phi
which, amongst other tenets, maintained the practi
of acquiring, even in life, entire command over elei
matter by means of certain ascetic practices." §

"According to standard authorities, the perfect fu
of the rites which the *Yogí* has to accomplish rec
protracted existence and repeated births, and it is dec
be unattainable in the present, or *Kali*, age. The at
therefore prohibited, and the *Yoga* is proscribed in
times. This inhibition is, however, disregarded, ε

individuals who are the subjects of our enquiry, endeavour to attain the superhuman powers which the performance of the *Yoga* is supposed to confer. They especially practise the various gesticulations and postures of which it consists, and labour assiduously to suppress their breath and fix their thoughts until the effect does somewhat realise expectation, and the brain, in a state of over-wrought excitement, bodies forth a host of crude and wild conceptions, and 'gives to airy nothings a local habitation and a name.'" "Some who have commenced their career in this line have carried the practice to several hours' duration, at which time they have described themselves as becoming perfectly exhausted, with strange objects passing before them, and sparks of fire flashing in their eyes."[*]

### JANGAMS.

"One of the forms in which the *Linga* worship appears is that of the *Lingáyats*, *Lingavants*, or *Jangamas*, the essential characteristic of which is wearing the emblem on some part of the dress or person. The type is of a small size, made of copper or silver, and is commonly worn suspended in a case round the neck, or sometimes tied in the turban. In common with the *Śaivas* generally, the *Jangamas* smear their foreheads with *vibhúti* or ashes, and wear necklaces, and carry rosaries, made of the *Rudráksha* seed. The clerical members of the sect usually stain their garments with red ochre."[†]

### PARAMAHANSAS.

"The *Paramahansa* is the ascetic who is solely occupied with the investigation of *Brahmá*, or spirit, and who is equally indifferent to pleasure or pain, insensible of heat or cold, and incapable of satiety or want. Agreeably to this definition, individuals are sometimes met with who pretend to have

---

[*] H. H. Wilson's Works, vol. i. p. 207-8.      [†] Ibid, p. 224-25.

attained such a degree of perfection; in proof of which they
go naked in all weathers, never speak, and never indicate any
natural want: what is brought to them as alms or food, by
any person, is received by the attendants, whom their supposed sanctity, or a confederation of interest, attaches to
them; and by these attendants they are fed and served on
all occasions, as if they were as helpless as infants."*

## ŚÁKTAS.

"The worshippers of the *Śakti*, the power or energy of the
divine nature in action, are exceedingly numerous amongst
all classes of Hindus. This active energy is, agreeably to the
spirit of the mythological system, personified, and the form
with which it is invested, considered as the especial object of
veneration, depends upon the bias entertained by the individuals towards the adoration of *Vishṇu* or *Śiva*. In the former
case the personified *Śakti* is termed *Lakshmí* or *Máhá Lakshmí*,
and in the latter, *Párvatí*, *Bhaváni*, or *Durgá*. Even *Saras-
vatí* enjoys some portion of homage, much more than her
lord, *Brahmá;* whilst a vast variety of inferior beings of
malevolent character and formidable aspect receive the
worship of the multitude."† "The worship of the female
principle, as distinct from the divinity, appears to have
originated in the literal interpretation of the metaphorical
language of the *Vedas*, in which the *will or purpose to create*
the universe is represented as originating from the creator,
and co-existent with him as his bride, and part of himself."‡

"Another set of notions of some antiquity which contributed to form the character of the *Śakti*, whether general
or particular, were derived from the *Sánkhya* philosophy.
In this system, nature, *Prakriti*, or *Múla Prakriti*, is defined
to be of eternal existence and independent origin, distinct
from the supreme spirit, productive though no production,

* H. H. Wilson's Works, vol. i. p. 231-32.    † Ibid, p. 240-41.    ‡ Ibid, p. 241.

and the plastic origin of all things, including even the gods. Hence *Prakriti* has come to be regarded as the mother of gods and men, whilst, as one with matter, the source of error, it is again identified with *Máyá*, or delusion ; and as co-existent with the supreme as his *Śakti*, his personified energy, or his bride." * "These mythological fancies have been principally disseminated by the *Puránas*, in all which *Prakriti*, or *Máyá*, bears a prominent part. The aggregate of the whole is given in the *Brahma Vaivartta Purána*." †

### DAKSHINIS.

"When the worship of any goddess is performed in a public manner, and agreeably to the *Vaidik* or *Puránic* ritual, it does not comprehend the impure practices which are attributed to a different division of the adorers of *Śakti*, and which are particularly prescribed to the followers of this system. In this form it is termed the *Dakshina*, or right-hand form of worship. The only observance that can be supposed to form an exception to the general character of this mode is the *Bali*, an offering of blood, in which rite a number of helpless animals, usually kids, are annually de-capitated. In some cases life is offered without shedding blood, when the more barbarous practice is adopted of pum-melling with the fists the poor animal to death : at other times blood only is offered without injury to life." ‡

### VÁMÍS.

"The *Vámís* mean the left-hand worshippers, or those who adopt a ritual contrary to that which is usual, and to what indeed they dare publicly avow." "The worship of the *Vámá-cháris* is derived from a portion of the *Tantras*." "The object of the worship is, by the reverence of *Deví* or *Śakti*, who is one with *Śiva*, to obtain supernatural powers in this

* H. H. Wilson's Works, vol. i. p. 243.    † Ibid, p. 244.    ‡ Ibid, p. 250-1.

life, and to be identified after death with *Śiva* and *Śakti*.
According to the immediate object of the worshipper is the
particular form of worship ; but all the forms require the use
of some or all of the five *Makáras, Mánsa, Matsya, Madya,
Maithuna,* and *Mudrá,* flesh, fish, wine, women, and certain
mystical gesticulations." *   "In this, and many of the observances practised, solitude is enjoined ; but all the principal
ceremonies comprehend the worship of *Śakti,* and require for
that purpose the presence of a female as the living representative and the type of the goddess. This worship is mostly celebrated in a mixed society, the men of which represent *Bhairavas*
or *Víras,* and the women *Bhairavís* and *Náyikás.* The *Śakti*
is personated by a naked female, to whom meat and wine are
offered, and then distributed amongst the assistants, the
recitation of various *Mantras* and texts, and the performance
of the *Mudrá,* or gesticulations with the fingers, accompanying
the different stages of the ceremony ; and it is terminated
with the most scandalous orgies amongst the votaries.   The
ceremony is entitled the *Śrí Chakra,* or *Púrnábhisheka,* the
Ring, or Full Initiation."†   "The occurrence of these impurities is certainly countenanced by the texts, which the
sects regard as authorities, and by a very general belief of
their occurrence.   The members of the sect are enjoined
secrecy, which, indeed, it might be supposed they would
observe on their own account ; and consequently, will not
acknowledge their participation in such scenes."‡

### KÁNCHALYÁS.

"The worship is that of *Śakti,* and the practices are similar
to those of the *Kaulas* or *Vámácháris.*   It is said to be distinguished by one peculiar rite, the object of which is to
confound all the ties of female alliance, and to enforce not

---

* H. H. Wilson's Works, vol. i. p. 254-56.          † Ibid, p. 257-8.
‡ Ibid, p. 259-60.

only a community of women amongst the votaries, but disregard even to natural restraints.   On occasions of worship, the female votaries are said to deposit their upper vests in a box in charge of the *Guru*.   At the close of the usual rites, the male worshippers take each a vest from the box, and the female to whom the garment appertains, be she ever so nearly of kin to him, is the partner for the time of his licentious pleasures."*

* H. H. Wilson's Works, p. 263.

# CHAPTER III.

## ORIGIN OF THE SECT OF MAHÁRAJAS.

THE Vaishṇavas, or worshippers of Vishṇu, are, as we have seen, sub-divided into a multiplicity of sects, some of which are absolute ascetics, and others of a bold and inquiring spirit; but the opulent, the luxurious, and the indolent, in the large mass of society, and especially females, attach themselves to the worship of Krishṇa, adored under this name, and his mistress Rúdhá, either conjointly or singly, by the names of Vishṇu and Lakshmi. But there is a still more popular form of the worship of the divinity than this, although its legends are much interwoven with those of the others. This is the worship of the Bála Gopála, or Bála Krishṇa, the infant Krishṇa, a worship widely diffused throughout all ranks of Indian society, and which was first promulgated by the founder of the sect under the name of Rudra Sampradáya. The name of the instituter of this sect was Vallabhá-

Bála Krishṇa.

chárya, whose history we shall proceed to relate, remarking merely that the heresy itself is possibly better known from the title of its teachers, as the religion of the Gokulastha Gosáins.

In tracing it, however, to its spring-head and source, we shall find that the first teacher of the philosophical tenets upon which the present doctrines of the sect are founded was Vishṇu Svámi, who was a commentator on the texts of the Vedas. He was followed in his teaching by Dnána Deva, who was succeeded by Keśáváchárya, and he by Hirálál, who had six sons, the most distinguished of whom was Śrídhar, who, after a time, was succeeded by Bilava Mangala, who strengthened the sect. Bilava Mangala was succeeded, but how soon is not known, by Vallabháchárya, who was the second son of Lakshman Bhatt, a Tailingá Brahman. This Lakshman Bhatt was descended from a Brahman named Náráyaṇ Bhatt, dwelling in a village called Kánkrava, and was the fourth in direct descent from him. He lived somewhere about the commencement of the sixteenth century, but the particulars of the exact period are not preserved. He promulgated the idea, which the people in their monstrous credulity and ignorance put entire faith in, that he had been promised by Krishṇa that he should have three sons, and that his second son should succeed him as the incarnation of himself, the god. His wife's name was Elmágár, and the first son of the marriage was Ráma Krishṇa.

After the birth of this child, Lakshman Bhatt, taking his family with him, went on a pilgrimage by the route of Alláhabád to Benares, where, after dwelling some time, a violent dispute took place between the Mussulmáns and the Sannyásis, which resulted in a bloody conflict. Lakshman Bhatt, apprehensive for the safety of his family, fled away with them. In the course of their flight through the country they eventually arrived at a wild spot called Champáranya. The terror of the flight, combined with the wild savageness of the country through which they were fleeing, had the effect upon the intimidated Elmágár of accelerating labour, she being at the time pregnant with her second child; and in

the wilderness of this entangled forest she gave birth to an
eight-months' child, on Sunday, the 11th of Vaisákh Vddya,
Samvat 1535 (A.D. 1479).

In a work called Nijvártá, it is stated that when Vallabha
was born in Champáranya, a palace of gold sprung up on the
spot, and the gods from the heavens showered down flowers,
the houries danced around, and the Gandharvas (heavenly
songsters) sang: divine music filled the air, and gods descended in vimán (celestial cars) to see the prodigy. Whether, embarrassed by the encumbrance of this offspring, or
prompted by confidence in the promise of Krishna that this
infant should be his incarnation, and so trusting to his pro-
vidential intervention to protect it, they forthwith abandoned
it, placing it gently upon leaves in the shade of a wide-
branched tree. Still pursuing their flight, they at length
arrived at a place called Chowdá-nagar, where, after residing
some time, intelligence at length reached them that quiet
was completely restored at Benares, upon which they set out,
to return to that place, and taking purposely the route by
which they had come, they speedily reached the spot where
they had deserted their helpless infant.

Here they found their faith in the promise of Krishna
verified, for they beheld the little creature alive and well,
and playing in the midst of a flame of sacrificial fire, in a pit
sunk on the spot. This miracle exalted their hopes, and,
after some short repose and refreshment they resumed their
journey, taking it with them to Benares which they eventually
reached. The name they gave the child was Vadtrabha, but
who was afterwards called Vallabha, and acquired celebrity
as the founder of a widely prevailing sect in Western India,
but whose divergent corruptions which derogate from the
doctrines on which he founded his teaching, he had not the
prophetical inspiration to foresee. In the course of time,
prompted by their zeal and love, his followers erected a

temple upon the spot of his birth, which is still in existence. His younger brother's name was Keśava.

When Vallabha had reached the age of six or seven years he was placed for instruction under the tuition of Náráyan Bhatt; and the legend of his life, written in Brijabháshá, asserts that the rapidity of his apprehension was so great and miraculous, that in the short space of four months he succeeded in learning the whole of the four Vedas, the six Śástras (schools of philosophy), and the eighteen Puránas— an accomplishment which a mature scholar cannot hope thoroughly to acquire by the prolonged labour of a whole life. But, of course, the supernatural attended him throughout, and the incarnation of Krishna would receive by intuition, and momentarily, what would be hopeless to the laborious application of the uncanonized throughout any time. Vallabha on attaining his eleventh year lost his father. The following year he took leave of his mother, and bidding farewell to Gokul, the village of his residence, on the left bank of the Jamuná, a short distance from Mathurá, he started on his pilgrimage through India.

On arriving at a certain town in the South of India, he became acquainted with the son of a rich and important man of the place, whose name was Dámodardás, and who by the force of his arguments, or the plausibility of his reasoning, was made a proselyte to his doctrines. For it is to be understood that Vallabha had already framed his tenets and scheme of tuition, and, with a view to their promulgation, had undertaken his pilgrimage. They then both proceeded together onward and arrived at the city of Vijayanagar, where the maternal parents of Vallabha resided. Krishna Deva was the king of this place, to whose court he was introduced. Here he was invited to a religious disputation with the Śaivists, the followers of Śiva, at the court of this king, who was so pleased with Vallabha for the ability he

displayed, that he bestowed upon him rich presents of gold
and silver. A portion of these he devoted to the manufacture
of a handsome golden waist-ornament with which to decorate
the image of the deity in a temple of that city, and another
portion he appropriated to the discharge of debts incurred
by his father and left unpaid at his death. The fourth only.
of the presents did he reserve to himself to meet the possibility of his needs.

It was his success in this disputation with the Smártá
Bráhmans which caused him to be elected by the Vaishṇavas
as their chief, with the title of Áchárya, and thence dates
the rise of his great influence. "He travelled to Ujayin,
and took up his abode under a *pípal* tree, on the banks of
the Siprá, which is said still to exist and is designated as his
baithak, or station. Besides this we find traces of him in
other places. There is a baithak of his amongst the gháts of
Muttrá ; and about two miles from the fort of Chanár is a
place called his well, *Áchárj Kúán*, comprising a temple and
*math*, in the court-yard of which is the well in question. The
saint is said to have resided here sometime."* He then proceeded onwards to Alláhabád, and thence to Benares, where he
remained to complete his studies, preparatory to inculcating the
doctrines he had been always meditating. His pilgrimage still
continued, and he went to Badri-kedár and thence to Haridwár.

He travelled for nine years throughout different parts of
India, considered by the Hindus as exclusively comprising
the world, twice circling this world, and in his peregrination
passing over a space of twelve thousand miles. On his return to Brindávan, as a reward for his fatigues and for his
faith, he was honoured by a visit from the god Krishṇa in
person, who then enjoined him to introduce the worship of
Bála Gopála or Bála Krishṇa, the infant Krishṇa, and found
his faith, which became widely diffused throughout Western

* H. H. Wilson's Works, vol. i. p. 120.

India, under the sectarian name of Rudra Sampradáya. Owing, however, to the fearful corruptions which subsequently, and by degrees, crept in, through the perverted sensuality of his descendants, this worship is now declining, and it is hoped, for the sake of degraded humanity, approaching extinction, unless healthy reforms be introduced to restore it to comparative purity.

Vallabháchárya ultimately settled at Benares, and it was whilst dwelling there, either at first, or subsequently, or during his previous travels, that he is said to have composed the works which bear his name, and in the composition of which he is reported to have had the assistance of certain learned Bráhmans, paid by him as his amanuenses. Some of these are, however, reputed to be suppositious. The works thus written are chiefly the following, which, although styled works, consist in some cases of but a few pages, or even merely a few lines. They are—

| | |
|---|---|
| व्यास सूच भाष्य | Vyás Sútra Bháshya. |
| जैमिनी सूच भाष्य | Jaiminí Sútra Bháshya. |
| तत्त्व दीप निबंध | Tattva Dípa Nibandi. |
| भागवत टीका सुबोधिनी | Bhágavata Tíká Subodhiní. |
| सिद्धांत मुक्तावली | Siddhánta Muktávalí. |
| पुष्टि प्रवाह मर्यादा | Pushti Praváha Maryádá. |
| सिद्धांत रहस्य | Siddhánta Rahasya. |
| अंतः करण प्रबोध | Antah-karana Prabhodha. |
| नव रत्न | Nava Ratna. |
| विवेक धैर्याश्रय | Viveka Dhairásraya. |
| कृष्णाश्रय | Krishnasraya. |
| भक्ति वर्धनी | Bhakti Vardhaní. |
| जलभेद् | Jalabheda. |
| सन्यास निर्णय | Sannyás Nirnaya. |
| निरोध लक्षण | Nirodha lakshan. |
| सेवाफल | Seváphala. |
| पुरुषोत्तम सहस्रनाम | Purushottam Sahasranáma. |

The fourth of these works, the Bhágavata Tíká Subodhiní, is the commentary of Vallabháchárya upon the Bhágavata, the chief source of the doctrines of the sect, and to which we shall have occasion subsequently to refer. But the most popular writings current in the sect, and which is also, attributed to Vallabha, are the Vishṇu padas, stanzas written in Brijabháshya in praise of Vishṇu. It was at Benares, after the composition of several of these works, that Vallabha married a Bráhman girl of the name of Máh Lakshmi, shortly after which he went to Vraja, where he established an image of Śrí Náthji, in Samvat 1576, corresponding to A.D. 1520, on a sacred hill called Govardhan Parvata,* which had been removed by the Muhammadans.

It was at one of the former visits of Vallabháchárya to Benares that he is stated to have posted on the walls of the temple the challenge to a disputation, such as frequently took place in the universities of Europe during the middle ages, immediately after the invention of printing, and in which the learned men of the day or place participated. This invitation was responded to especially by the followers of Śankaráchárya, the great Hindu philosopher, whose comment on the Vedas is held in such high esteem; and the books of the Mahárájas narrate that they were all defeated. It is evident that Vallabháchárya derived considerable repute from this occurrence; and it is most likely that a man of such disputatious renown, and so prominent and esteemed for his sanctity and knowledge, would have frequently to enter into these discussions upon his arrival at any celebrated city, or seminary.

In Samvat 1567 (A.D. 1511) Vallabháchárya's first son was born, and was named Gopinátha. His second son, named Vithalnáthji, was born in Samvat 1572 (A.D. 1516), in the

---

* This hill is fabled to have been rendered sacred by the circumstance that on one occasion, while Krishṇa was playing there with his companions, it began to rain, and that he, to protect those who were with him from the shower, lifted the hill up on one of his little fingers as an umbrella over them.

village of Parṇát, and it was to this son only that the incarnation of the parent descended. Vallabhácháyra himself educated both his sons, thus fitting them for their progress through life, after which he withdrew from his family to Benares, where he became Sannyási, which implies absolute asceticism, or total abstinence from all intercourse with the world and all participation in its doings. He dwelt at the place only forty-two days, when he died, as it is said, on a hill called Hanumán Gháta, in the vicinity; but his followers asserted that he had been translated to Lílá, which means amorous sport. Another report gives a different account of the miracle in which he disappeared. It states that he "finally settled at Jethan Bér, at Benares, near which a *math* still subsists; but at length having accomplished his mission, he entered the Ganges at Hanumán Gháta, and, when stooping into the water, passed out of sight: a brilliant flame arose from the spot, and in the presence of a host of spectators he ascended to heaven, and was lost in the firmament."

From the time Vallabhácháyra began to inculcate his new creed, which he called Pushti Márga, or the eat-and-drink doctrine, up to the day of his death, he had made eighty-four devoted proselytes. The record of the lives of these disciples is contained in a large volume entitled the Stories of Chorási Vaishṇavas, and written in Brijabháshá. At the period of his quitting the earth Vallabhácháyra was fifty-two years and thirty-seven days old. On his death it is said a dispute ensued between his sons relative to the succession to his gadi, which literally means "his seat," but implies his position as a teacher. This dispute, it appears, was decided by the intervention of the late king of Delhi in favour of the eldest son, Gopinátha, who dying, together with his son, Vithalnath became the sole representative of Vallabhácháyra.

Vithalnath is represented as an able successor of his father, having made two hundred and fifty-two devoted proselytes to the new creed, whose history is also narrated in a thick book. He likewise made long journeys, visiting Mathurá and Gokul, towns in the province of Agra which possessed a traditional celebrity, being renowned as the birthplace of Krishṇa. He resorted also to Dwárká, a place situated in Gujarát, sacred in the annals of Hindu superstition. The original Dwárká is said to have been swallowed up by the ocean, and the spot where it is supposed to have stood lies about thirty miles south of Porabandar. From Dwárká he progressed to Cutch, and thence proceeding to the centre of India, he conveyed his doctrines to Málwa and Mewár, making proselytes everywhere. He thence turned southward and visited Pandarpura, in the province of Bijapúr. This was another sacred locality, where he propagated his doctrines very extensively, his conversions taking a wide range. He made proselytes among the Baniás, or bankers; the Bháttiás, the Kanbis, or cultivators; the Sutáras or carpenters; and the Lowárs, or blacksmiths : a few Brahmans became also his followers, as well as some Musalmáns. It is a circumstance of a remarkable character that these sectaries, who belonged to different castes, were permitted to eat and drink on the same table, which is a complete violation of the system of caste. These privileges have, however, long been rescinded.

Vithalnáthji, who is also known by the name of Gusáinji, went in Samvat 1621 (A.D. 1565) to Gokul, the birthplace of Krishṇa, with the full determination of passing the rest of his days there. After residing at this place for some time he was induced to alter his intention, prompted by a cause which does not appear, and he accordingly removed to Mathurá. Vithalnáthji evidently had very strong locomotive propensities, for he is said to have visited Gujarát six times during his life, and he even now seems to have been considerably unsettled, or he had accomplished the sectarian object which induced him to visit Mathurá; for we find him, in Samvat 1629 (A.D. 1573), eight years afterwards, again at Gokul. It was in consequence of his ultimate permanent residence in this sacred city that he acquired the name of Gokul Gusáinji, which is perpetuated in all his male descendants.

He appears to have written several works of repute, and especially commentaries upon older treaties. In one of these works, Vidvanmandan, he has severely criticised and abundantly abused the sect and works of Śankaráchárya.

At the ripe age of seventy years and twenty-nine days, in Samvat 1649 (A.D. 1583), Vithalnáthji quitted the earth on the sacred hill of Govardhan Parvata, where the image was set up by his father. He was twice married, the name of his first wife being Rukmiṇí, and that of the second Padmávatí. By these wives he had seven sons and four daughters. The name of the first son, born in Samvat 1597, was Girdharji; that of the second, born in Samvat 1599, Govinda Ráy; the third was Bálkrishnaji, born in Samvat 1606; the fourth, Gokulnáthji, born in Samvat 1608; the fifth, Ragunáthji, born in Samvat 1611; the sixth, Jadunáthji, born in Samvat 1613; and the seventh, Ghanashyamji, born in Samvat 1618. His daughters' names were Śobhá, Jamuná, Kamalá, and Devaká.

All these seven sons, upon the death of Vithalnáthji, established each his own *gadi*, or seat, assuming to be the incarnation of Krishṇa, and they dispersed throughout India to diffuse their doctrines and make proselytes.

It was the fourth son, Gokulnáthji, who became the most celebrated of all the descendants of Vithalnáthji. He is distinguished for having written a commentary on the Siddhánta Rahasya, and others. It is the vitality which he infused into the tenets of his particular community that has given it its persistency; for even to the present day the followers of his

descendants keep themselves separate from all the communities of his brothers, considering their own Gosáins as
the only legitimate teachers of the faith. The followers of
the other sons of Vithalnáthji have an equal degree of
veneration for all the communities of the descendants of
Vithalnáthji, whilst restricting their exclusive preference to
their own particular division.

It was about the period of this dispersion of the sons of
Vithalnáthji, that it is presumed they first acquired the title
of Maháráj, which effectually conveys in its significance the
full force of their wide sway and influence. They have many
distinctive titles; they are called, for instance, Maháráj
Gusáinji, Gusáinji Maháráj, Vallabha Kula, Agni Kula,
Agni Svarupa, Áchárya, Guru, Máh Prabhu, etc.; but the
name for which they have the greatest respect appears to be
that of Gausvámi, which signifies Lord of Cows, applicable
also to Krishṇa.

The heads of this division of the sect are usually called
Gokul Gosáins, or Gokulastha Gosáins. The worshippers of
this sect are also widely diffused throughout Bombay, Cutch,
Kattywár, and central India, and especially the province of
Málwá. In all these places they are numerous and opulent,
comprising the most wealthy merchants and bankers, and
consisting chiefly of bháttiás, baniás, and lowanas. They
have many establishments throughout India, especially at
Mathurá and Brindávan, which latter place contains some
hundreds, amongst whom are three persons of great opulence.
In Benares the sect has two temples of great repute and
wealth. The city of Jagannáth, in the east, as one of the
great centres of Hindu worship, is particularly venerated by
them; and the city of Dwárká, in the extreme west, at the
extremity of the peninsula of Gujarát, which completes the
zone of India, has equal respect paid to it.

There are at present about sixty or seventy Mahárájas

dispersed throughout India. In Bombay there are eight or ten, fifteen or sixteen at Gokul, and one or two at each of the following places, namely, Surat, Ahmedabád, Nagar, Cutch, Porabandar, Amreli, Jodapur, Bundi, Koti, etc. Of these sixty or seventy Mahárájas, there are only two or three who have any knowledge of Sanskrit : the rest are grossly ignorant and indulge merely in sensuality and luxury. They, however, fear no desertion, owing to the infatuation of their followers, and never take the trouble to preach, but give as an equivalent public exhibitions in their temples to divert attention. "Vallabháchárya taught that privation formed no part of sanctity, and that it was the duty of the teacher and his disciples to worship their deity not in nudity and hunger, but in costly apparel and choice food; not in solitude and mortification, but in the pleasures of society and the enjoyment of the world. . . . . In accordance with these precepts the gosáins, or teachers, are always clothed in the best raiment, and fed with the daintiest viands, by their followers, over whom they have unlimited influence. . . . . These gosáins are often largely engaged in maintaining connection amongst commercial establishments in remote parts of the country : they are constantly travelling over India under pretence of pilgrimage to the sacred shrines of the sect; and on these occasions they notoriously reconcile the profits of trade with the benefits óf devotion. As religious travellers, however, this union of objects renders them more respectable than the vagrants of any other sect." Priestly craft is ever alert to obtain by fair means, or foul, the wealth needful to the sustentation of its power and self-indulgence. This is a vice not limited in its operations to India, or to the chiefs of the sects of the Hindu religion : it pervades all human society, with greater or lesser energy. The scheme is supported by very plausible and just reasoning, for it is but right that those whose function is exercised for the behoof of society at

large, and who are precluded from obtaining the means of
livelihood from those sources common to the majority, should
be supported by that majority for whom their labours are
performed ; and it is only when urged to excess, for culpable
purposes, that this becomes reprehensible. The Mahárájas,
consequently, as teachers of a doctrine and priests of a
religion, when duly restricting themselves within their province, are thoroughly entitled to the means of living at the
hands of those whom they teach. It is merely perversion
and excess that can be complained of. The source of the
permanent revenue of these priests is a fixed *lágá*, or tax,
upon every article of consumption which is sold. This tax,
although but trifling in each individual case, amounts to a
considerable sum upon the innumerable commercial transactions that take place, and is always multiplied in each case
where articles pass from hand to hand for a consideration.
There seems to exist an unlimited power on the part of the
several Mahárájas to impose this tax and to add *lágá* upon
*lágá*. When, therefore, we consider the swarming population, the great consumption and consequently the thriving
business which is carried on, and the fact that the fixed
revenue is often greatly augmented by the presents and
votive offerings which are made by their followers from
affection, or fear—the wealth, indolence, and luxury of the
Mahárájas follow as a matter of course, and the corruption of
society ensues as the result of their dissolute and effeminate
teaching.

It is not necessary that we should further particularise the
branches of the genealogical tree springing from the root of
Vallabháchárya : it suffices that, like the deadly upas, they
overshadow society with their malignant influences, in Western
India especially ; and it is with a view to counteract this
blighting tendency that the present work has been undertaken,
in the hope that the exposure of their acts and doctrines may

eventually bring their converts to reflect upon the depravity
of their practices and the utter incompatibility of such vicious
doings with a pure faith. The original teachers may have
been well disposed men, but their descendants have widely
diverged from their courses. The infatuation of the Vaishnavas is so great, that all the descendants of the Mahárájas
are held from infancy in extreme veneration, and are nurtured in ignorance, indolence, and self-indulgence: they are
empowered by their votaries to gratify through life every
vicious propensity; and, when, exhausted by vice, they pass
away in premature old age, they are held by their votaries
to be translated to the regions of perfect and ecstatic bliss;
for, as remarked by Mr. H. H. Wilson, it is a peculiarly
remarkable feature in this sect that the veneration paid
to their gosáins is paid solely to their descent, without
any reference to their individual sanctity or learning: and,
although totally destitute of every pretension to even personal respectability, they nevertheless enjoy the unlimited
homage of their followers.

# CHAPTER IV.

## CHIEF AUTHORITY OF THE SECT.

In treating generally of the sacred writings of the Hindus, we have briefly noticed the eighteen Puránas, which are evidently the productions of the later or nonvedic period. The Bhágavata Puráṇa is the chief authority of the sect of Mahárájas, or Vallabhácháryа. It consists of twelve books, in the tenth of which the history of Krishṇa,* as the eighth incarnation of Vishṇu, is given in ninety chapters. This tenth book has been translated from the Sanskrit into Brija-bháshá, under the name of "Prem Ságar, or the Ocean of Love;" and it was this that Vallabháchárya selected, on which to found doctrines he designed to teach. To this work we must look as the source whence the Mahárájas deduced originally the ideas which they have gradually expanded into the desecrating libertinism which they practise.

We shall commence by quoting those portions of the "Prem Ságar" which we conceive have most directly led, by the force of example and possibly by infatuation, to the practices at present followed in the temples of the Mahárájas. Vyása (believed to be the metamorphosed Vishṇu) is the reputed author of this work, and it is therefore held as a revelation from the deity himself, is considered of the highest authority,

---

* The worship of deified heroes is no part of the Vedic system; nor are the incarnations of the deities suggested in any other portion of the text which I have yet seen. According to the notions which I entertain of the real history of the Hindu religion, the worship of *Ráma* and *Krishna* by the Vaishṇavas, and of *Mahádeva* and *Bhaváni* by S'aivas and S'áktas, has been generally introduced since the persecution of the Bauddhas and Jains. The institutions of the Vedas are anterior to Bauddha, whose theology seems to have been borrowed from the system of Kapila.—*Colebrooke on the Hindu Religion, p.* 67, 68.

and is received with profound respect. Doubtless its true character is symbolical or allegorical, whereas the Mahárájas, by interpreting it literally, have thus converted its abtruse significations into a code of vicious immorality,—not merely sanctioning, but inculcating the most hideous sensuality.

. The following are extracts from the " Prem Ságar," describing the amorous sports of Krishṇa with Gopis, or female cowherdesses (known as the *lílá* of Krishṇa), from Mr. E. B. Eastwick's English version of the work :

"As soon as the Autumnal Season departed, Winter came on (November and December), and excessive cold and frost commenced. At that time the young women of Braj began to say, one to the other, 'Listen, companions! from bathing in the month Aghan (the 8th Hindú month) the sins of every successive birth are removed, and the wish of the heart is attained. Thus we have heard it said by aged people.' Having heard this, it entered into the minds of all to bathe in Aghan, in order that they might surely obtain the divine Krishn as a bridegroom.

"With these reflections all the youthful women of Braj rose at early morn, and having put on their clothes and ornaments, came to the Yamuná to bathe. Having made their ablutions, and offered an oblation of eight ingredients to the Sun, they came forth from the water, made an earthen image of Gaur (a name of the goddess Parvatí), offered to it sandal wood, unbroken grains of rice, flowers and fruits; and setting before it incense, lamps, and consecrated food, performed their worship, and with joined hands and bent heads, having propitiated Gaur, said, "O goddess! repeatedly we ask this boon of you, that the divine Krishn may be our husband.' In this manner the cowherdesses continually bathed, and fasting the whole day, at evening, having eaten curds and rice, slept on the earth, in order that the fruit of their religious abstinence might quickly be obtained.

"One day all the young women of Braj went together to an unfrequented place, furnished with steps to descend to the river, and on arriving there took off their clothes, and, having laid them on the bank, entered naked into the stream, and began singing the praises of Hari, and to sport in the water. At that time the divine Krishn, also seated in the shade of an Indian fig-tree, was tending the herds. It chanced that, having heard the sound of their songs,

4

he also silently approached, and began from his concealed position, to look on. At last, as he gazed, a thought entered into his mind, whereupon, having stolen all the clothes, he ascended into a Kadam tree, and having tied them in a bundle, placed them before him. Meanwhile, when the cowherdesses looked, the clothes were not on the bank; then, being confounded, they began to stretch forth their necks and look in all directions, and to say one to the other, 'Just now not even a sparrow has come here; sister, who has carried off our clothes?' Meanwhile, one cowherdess observed that, 'with a diadem on his head, a staff in his hand, an ornamental mark on his forehead made with saffron, wearing a necklace of wild flowers, clothed in yellow silk, having the clothes tied up in a bundle, and maintaining profound silence, the divine Krishn, mounted on a Kadam tree, is seated concealed.' She, on beholding him, cried out, 'Companions! see him, the stealer of our hearts, the stealer of our clothes, holding the bundle, is seated, enjoying himself in the Kadam tree.' Having heard these words, all the other young females of Braj beholding Krishn, were abashed, and, plunging into the water, with joined hands and bent heads, said, in a supplicating, coaxing manner,

"'Friend of the poor!—grief-dispeller!—dear one! please, Mohan! give us back our clothes.'

Hearing this, Kanhái said, 'Thus will I not give them, I swear by Nand; One by one come forth, then receive ye back your clothes.'

"The girls of Braj angrily replied, 'A goodly lesson this which you have learned, to bid us come forth naked! now, if we go and tell our fathers and our brothers, then they will come and seize you, raising the cry of "Thief!" and if we tell Jasodá and Nand, they will teach you a pretty lesson. We have some modesty; you have done away with all respect.'

"As soon as he heard these words, Krishn, enraged, said, 'Now you shall get back your clothes when you send and fetch them; and if not, not.' Hearing this, the cowherdesses said, alarmed, 'Kind to the poor! thou who carest for us, thou truly art the protector of our husbands. Whom shall we bring? For your sake it is that, fasting, we bathe in the month of Magashir.' Krishn said, 'If you are bathing in the month Aghan for me, giving me your affection, then lay aside your bashfulness and evasion, and come and take your clothes.' When the divine Krishn Chand spake thus, then all the cowherdesses, having consulted with one another, began to say, 'Come on, companions! what Mohan says, that alone is to be attended to; since he knows all the secrets of our minds and bodies, what place for bashfulness with him?' Thus having determined amongst themselves, and obeying the words of Krishn, hiding with their hands their breasts and the parts which modesty conceals, the young women all issued from the water, and, having bent their heads, stood before him on the bank. Then Krishn, laughing, said, 'Now let each join her hands and advance, then I will give the clothes.' The cowherdesses said,

> "'Why does Nand's darling act deceitfully to us, simple maidens of Braj?
> He has tricked us; our consciousness and sense are gone, such pranks have you played, O Hari!
> Taking courage, we have done what we are ashamed to do; now, O lord of Braj! perform your part.'

"When the cowherdesses, having spoken these words, joined their hands, then the divine Krishn Chand gave them their clothes, and approaching them, said, 'Do not take this matter ill; this is a lesson which I have taught you, for in the water is the habitation of the god Varun. Whoever, therefore, bathes in the water naked, all his moral and religious qualities pass away. Seeing the affection of your mind I was pleased, and have revealed this secret to you. Now go to your houses, and, returning in the month of Kátik (the second Hindú month), dance with me the circular dance.'"

. . . . . . . . . . . . . . . . . .

"One woman of Mathurá, whose husband would not suffer her to go, fixed her thoughts on Krishn, and, quitting her body, went, and, before them all, was united with him, as water goes and unites itself with water; and, after her, all the others, proceeding on, arrived there, where the divine Krishn Chand, together with the cowherds, was standing, under the shade of a tree, leaning with his hand on the shoulder of a comrade, with a triple bend in his body, and holding in his hand a lotus-flower. Soon as they arrived, they placed before him the plates, and making their obeisance, and gazing in the face of Hari, began to say to one another, 'Sister! this is he, the son of Nand, whose name we have heard from time to time, and on whom we have fixed our thoughts. Now, beholding his moon-like countenance, gratify your eyes, and enjoy the fruition of life.' Thus having spoken, and having joined their hands, with humble supplication they began to say to the divine Krishn, 'Compassionate Lord! without thy favour, where is a sight of thee accorded to any one? Happy is our fate this day, that we have obtained a sight of you, and become free from the sins of each successive birth.

"' The foolish, sordid, and proud Bráhman, whose mind is soiled by riches, pride, and avarice,
Regards the Deity as man : blind with this world's illusions, how should he recognize the truth?
For whose sake you perform invocation, penance, and sacrifice ; on him wherefore not bestow food?

Sire! that riches, those relations, and that shame, is worthy of praise, which is useful to you, and that alone is penance, invocation, and knowledge, into which thy name enters.' Having heard these words, the divine Krishn Chand, having inquired after their welfare, began to say, -

"' Make no reverential salutation to me! I am but the blue boy of the chieftain Nand.

Do they who cause the wives of Bráhmans to pay homage to them, obtain high estimation in the world? You, deeming us hungry, showed kindness to us, and, coming into the forest, took thought for us. Now what hospitality can we show you here?

'Brindában, our home, is far away; how can we show you courtesy?

Had we been there, we would have brought some flowers and fruits and offered them. You, for our sake, undergoing trouble, have come into the jungle, and here we are quite unable to perform the duties of hospitality, and our chagrin on this account will always continue.' Thus courteously having spoken, again he said, 'It is long since you came; now depart to your homes, because the Bráhmans, your husbands, will be expecting your return, since, when wives are absent, the oblation is not attended with happy results.' Having heard these words from Krishn, the Bráhman women, having joined their hands, said, ' Sire! we have attached ourselves to your celestial feet, and have abandoned all regard for our family, and, hence, how can we return to the house of those whose words we have disobeyed, in hastening hither? It is better, therefore, that we should remain under your protection, and, Lord! one woman of our company, having formed the desire of meeting you, was coming, when her husband stopped her; upon which that woman, being afflicted, surrendered her spirit.' Soon as he heard, the divine Krishn Chand smiled, and showed her, who, having abandoned her body, had come to him. 'Attend!' he said, 'He who shows affection to Hari, shall never suffer death ;—this woman came and joined me before you all.' "

Thus far having recited, the saintly Shukadev said, "Sire! soon as they beheld her, all were, for the moment, astonished. Afterwards their understanding returned, and then they began to sing the praises of Hari. Meanwhile the divine Krishn Chand, having eaten food, said to them, 'Now depart to your own abodes; your husbands will not rebuke you.'

. . . . . . . . . . . . . . . . . . . .

. "When the divine Krishn carried off their clothes, he then gave this promise to the cowherdesses, that in the month Kátik, he would dance with them the circular dance. From that time the cowherdesses, cherishing the hope of this dance, remained solicitous in mind, and continually, when they rose up, used to propitiate especially the month Kátik. It happened that as they persevered in their propitiations, the pleasure-giving Autumnal Season arrived.

"From the time when the month Kátik commenced, an end was put to fierce heat, cold, and rain,
The lakes were full of pellucid water, and the expanding lotus was freshly blooming.
The night-flowering lotus and the Bartavelle, like lover and mistress, gazed, rejoicing, on the moon at night.
The ruddy goose with the lotus droop, who ever regard the sun as their friend.

"One day the divine Krishn Chand, issued from the house on the night of the full moon in the month Kátik, and beheld the stars sprinkled in the clear sky, and the moonbeams spread in the ten quarters. A cool and gentle breeze, fraught with odours, continued blowing, and on one side the appearance of the thick forest imparted exceeding beauty to the scene. On seeing such a scene, it occurred to the mind of Krishn, that he had promised to the cowherdesses, that in the Autumnal Season he would dance with them the circular dance, and that the promise must be fulfilled. Having thus reflected, the divine Krishn entered the woods, and played on the flute. Having heard the sound of the Bambú, all the young women of Braj, who were inflamed with desire, through separation (from Krishn) were greatly agitated. At last, abandoning all regard for their relations, dashing from them the modesty belonging to the well-born, and forsaking their household duties, in great confusion, with their ornaments put on at random, they arose and hastened. One cowherdess, who, when she arose from beside her husband, to go, was stopped on the road by her husband, led back to the house, and not permitted to depart, fixed her thoughts on Hari, and, quitting her body, went and joined him before all the rest.

Beholding the affection of her mind, the divine Krishn Chand immediately conferred on her beatitude."

Thus far having heard, king Paríkshit inquired of the saintly Shukadev as follows, "Gracious Lord! the cowherdesses not knowing the divine Krishn to be God, did not regard him as such; they only looked upon him as a sensual object. How had that woman salvation conferred on her? This explain to me and tell, that the doubt of my mind may depart." The saintly Muni Shukadev said, "Incarnation of Justice! they who even ignorantly sing the praises of the greatness of the divine Krishn Chand, they too undoubtedly obtain the reward of faith and final beatitude. Just as if any one, without knowing what it was, should drink nectar, he also becoming immortal would live (for ever); and, if he drank it with knowledge of its properties, it would affect him in the same way. This all know, that the quality of a thing and its fruit cannot but result; and just such is the powerful efficacy of worship paid to Hari; whoever worships him, with whatever disposition of mind, obtains beatitude. It is said,

"'Invocation, the rosary, the denominational and sectarial marks,* all of them are useless.

"'The vain-minded man plays his antics (lit. dances) to no purpose; the true only please Rám.'

"And, attend! I will now relate to you the different persons, and their different feelings towards the divine Krishn, who obtained beatitude from him. Nand and Jasodá looked on him as their son, the cowherdesses as their lover; Kans worshipped him through fear; the cowherds, regarding him as their friend, repeated his name; the Pándavs as their darling; Sisupál respected him as an enemy; the family of Yadu held him to be one of their own members; and Jogis, Jatis, and Munis, knowing him to be the Supreme Being, fixed their meditations upon him: but in the end all, without exception, obtained beatification. If, therefore, one cowherdess, by fixing her thoughts on the Deity, passed the ocean of existence, what marvel is it?"

Having heard this, Paríkshit said to the saintly Muni Shukadev, "Gracious Lord! the doubt of my mind has departed; now be gracious enough to continue the history." The saintly Shukadev said, "Sire, when all the cowherdesses, each in her own different company, ran and joined the Light of the World, the Ocean of

* Of a lotus, trident, etc., made on the body or forehead of worshippers of Vishnu and other gods.

Beauty, the divine Krishn Chand, as, during the four rainy months, the rivers run violently and mingle with the ocean, then the scene was such that Bihárí Lál has no power to express the beauty of that adornment, for Hari, decked out with ornaments, and dressed as a juggler, appeared so heart-delighting, beautiful, and charming, that the young women of Braj, beholding him, remained amazed. Then Mohan, after inquiring after their welfare, assumed a peevish tone, and said, ' Tell me how, at this time of night—the hour of goblins and ghosts—you have passed this dread road, and come into the vast forest, with your clothes and ornaments cast on at random, in a state of extreme agitation, and having abandoned the regard due to your family? It behoves not women to act so boldly. It is said, that "should a woman have a husband, who is a coward, vicious, stupid, deceitful, ugly, leprous, blind of one eye or of both, lame of hand or foot, poor, or aught else, even then she ought to serve him, and from this alone her welfare and estimation in the world arise." It is the duty of a well-born and chaste lady not to leave her husband, even for a moment, and that wife who, quitting her own spouse, goes to another man, finds, in successive births, hell as her habitation.' Thus having spoken, he added, ' Hearken! you have come, have seen the dense forest, the clear moonlight, and the beauty of Yamuná's bank ; now return home, and, with earnest-ness of purpose, wait on your husbands. By this your welfare will be in every way consulted.' Soon as they heard these words from the mouth of the divine Krishn, all the cowherdesses were for a time indeed, bereft of sense, and buried in a boundless ocean of thought ;—afterwards,

"With downcast looks they drew deep sighs, and stood scratching the ground with the nails of their feet ;
From their eyes a stream of tears descended, like a broken necklace of pearls !

"At length, being deeply agitated by grief, they began with sobs to say, 'Ah, Krishn! you are a great deceiver ! At first, indeed, by playing on the flute, you stole away our judgment, thoughts, mind, and all that we possessed ; and now, turning pitiless, and practising deceit, you desire, by your cruel words, to deprive us of life.' Thus having spoken, they added,

"'Folk, kinsmen, house, and husband, we have left; neglected, too, the re-proach of people, to which we are exposed.
We are defenceless, there are none to aid us; give us protection, Lord of Braj !

And those people who attend on thy celestial footsteps, they care not for wealth, corporeal things, character, or greatness; of them, indeed, you are the husband, from birth to birth, O Deity! O soul's Beauty!

"'Where shall we go and make our abode?' our spirits are bound up in affection for you.'

"On hearing these words, the divine Krishn Chand smiled,-and called all the cowherdesses to him, and said, 'If you are imbued with this affection, then dance the circular dance with me.' Having heard these words, the cowherdesses laid aside their grief, and gladly assembled on all sides, and, continually gazing on the face of Hari, began to reap the enjoyment of their eyes.

"The dark-blue Krishn, with body of the hue of clouds, stood in the midst; and such was the beauty of the fair ones, as they sported, That they resembled golden creepers, growing from beneath a blue mountain.

"Then the divine Krishn gave this command to his Illusive Power, 'We will engage in the circular dance, wherefore do thou prepare a fair place, and remain standing here, and whoever shall ask for anything, whatever it may be, do thou bring and give it.' Sire! the Illusive Power, on hearing this, went to the bank of the Yamuná, and prepared a large circular terrace of pure gold, and having studded it with pearls and diamonds, fixed on all sides plaintain trees with young shoots, for pillars, fastened on them gay festoons of various kinds of flowers, and, returning to the divine Krishn Chand, told him. On hearing it, Krishn was pleased, and, taking with him all the young women of Braj, went to the bank of the Yamuná. Having arrived there, they saw that the brilliance of the circular terrace erected for the circular dance, was four times more beautiful than that of the moon's orb, and on all sides of it the sand was spread out like the moonbeams. A cool, sweet, fragrant breeze, continued blowing, and on one side the verdure of the dense forest derived increased loveliness from the night.

"On beholding this scene, all the cowherdesses were much delighted. Near that spot was a lake named Mán Sarowar, to the banks of which they went and put on clean robes and ornaments, such as their minds desired, and having adorned themselves from head to foot, returned, playing in harmony on fine instruments, such as the lute and timbrel. Then, intoxicated with love, they laid aside all care and diffidence, and, in company with the divine Krishn, began to play on instruments, to sing and dance. At that time the divine Govind, in the midst of the circle of the cowherdesses, appeared as beautiful as the moon in a circlet of stars."

Thus far having related, the saintly Shukadev said, " Hearken, Sire! when the cowherdesses, having abandoned, in the dance, judgment and discernment, mentally regarded Hari as their natural husband, and thought him utterly under their influence; then the divine Krishn Chand reflected in his heart as follows:

" ' These now imagine me subjected to them; they mentally regard me as a
   . natural husband;
   Their judgment is gone; modesty has left their persons; they twine themselves around me, and with fond affection embrace me, as their beloved
   one.
   They have forgotten knowledge and reflection; I will go and leave them,
   since their pride has increased.'

" ' Let us see what they will do in the forest without me, and what will be their condition?' Thus having reflected, the divine Krishn Chand, taking with him the divine Rádhiká, disappeared from sight."

. . . . . . . . . . . . . . . . . .

The saintly Muni Shukadev said, " Sire! upon the sudden dis-appearance of the divine Krishn Chand, it became dark before the eyes of the cowherdesses, and being much afflicted, they were as distressed as a snake that has lost its crest-gem. Hereupon one of them began to say,

" ' Tell me sister! where is Mohan departed, having left us?
   But lately he clasped my neck with his arm, and embraced me.

Just now, in truth, closely united with us, he was dancing and re-joicing. In these short moments where has he departed? Did no one among you see him as he left us?' Having heard these words, all the cowherdesses, deeply dejected at separation from their be-loved one, said, drawing deep sighs,

" ' Whither shall we go, what shall we do? To whom shall we call aloud and
   tell (our loss)?
   Do not you know at all where he is? How shall we rejoin Murári?'

" Thus having spoken, being intoxicated with the love of Hari, all the cowherdesses began, as they searched, and sang the praises of Krishn, to exclaim, lamenting, thus:

" ' Why have you left us, Lord of Braj? We have bestowed all we possess
   upon you.'

" When they found him not, then all, as they went on, said amongst themselves, ' Sister! here, indeed, we see no one; of whom shall we ask the road which Hari has taken!' Thus having heard, one of the cowherdesses said, 'Hearken, Sister! an idea has occurred to me, that all the beasts and birds and trees which are in this forest, are Rishis and Munis, which have descended on earth to behold the sports of Krishn: ask ye them! These standing here are spectators. They will point.out to you the direction which Hari has taken.' On hearing these words, all the cowherdesses, distressed at their separation (from Krishn), began to question each individual thing, both inanimate and animate :

> "'O fig-trees of various kinds! you have obtained your lofty stature by your meritorious acts!
> You, most of. all, have been beneficent to others, in that you have taken on Earth the form of trees.
> You have endured the pain inflicted by heat, cold, and rain, and for the sake of others you have remained standing.
> O bark! blossoms! roots! fruit! and branches! with which (ye trees) advantage others!
> Nand's darling has bereft us all of mind and property; say, kind beings! has he passed this way?
> O Kadam! mango! and Kachnár! have you seen Murári going in any direction?
> O Asoka, Champaca, and oleander! have you seen Balbír passing by?
> O blooming Tulsí, very dear to Hari! Thou whom he never separates from his person,
> Has Hari to-day come and met you? Who will tell us? who will point out the way?
> Dear jasmine, Juhí, Málti! did the youthful Kanhái come in this direction?'
> To the Antelopes the women of Braj called aloud, 'Have you seen the forester (Krishn) passing here?'"

Thus far having recited, the saintly Shukadev said, "Sire! in this manner all the cowherdesses, continually inquiring of beasts, birds, and creeping shrubs, and filled with (thoughts of) Krishn, began, in childish sport, to imitate the slaughter of Pútaná, and all the other exploits of the divine Krishn, and, at the same time, to search on. At last, as they continually searched, after proceeding some distance, they saw the footsteps of the celestial feet of the divine Krishn Chand, together with the lotus, barley, banner, and iron goad (imprinted) on the sand, continue glittering. Soon as they saw this, the women of Braj, having made a reverential obeisance to the dust, which gods, men, and Munis search for, placed it on their heads, and, resuming a confident hope of meeting Hari, proceeded on. Then they beheld that near the traces of those celestial feet the footstep of a female also was ever imprinted. Beholding this, surprised, they went forward, and saw that in one place there had fallen, upon a bed of soft leaves, a fair and jewelled mirror. Of it they began to ask, but when, filled with the pangs of separation, it also was silent, then they began to inquire of one another, 'Tell, me, Sister! why did he take this with him?' Then one, who knew well the feelings of lover and beloved one, made answer, 'Friend! when the lover sate down to wreathe the long back hair of his mistress, and his lovely form was hid from sight, at that time the fair one took the mirror in her hand, and showed it to him she loved, and then the image of his divine face appeared before her.' Having heard these words, the cowherdesses felt no resentment, but began to say, 'Well must she have worshipped Shiva and Párvatí, and great must have been the penance she performed, that alone she is privileged to sport securely with the soul's Lord.'

"Sire! all the cowherdesses indeed in this direction were wandering about in search (of Krishn) bewildered with the emotions caused by separation from him, prattling and talking, and in the other direction the divine Rádhiká, enjoying excessive delight in the society of Hari, supposed her lover was entirely under her influence, deemed herself the principal person of all, and admitting pride into her mind, said, 'Dear one! I am now unable to proceed further, take me on your shoulders and so go on with me.' Immediately on hearing these words the divine Krishn Chand, the destroyer of pride and searcher of hearts, sat down smiling and said, 'Come! be pleased to mount upon my shoulders.' When having stretched forth her hand she was about to mount, then the divine Khrishn vanished from sight and she (Rádhiká) remained standing with extended arm as (at first) she put forth her hand, just as having parted from the cloud the lightning would remain separate, or as the moonbeams at variance with the moon (might appear) when left behind by it. And the dazzling brightness cast from her white body shadowed upon the earth was beautiful, like a lovely woman standing on a golden ground. From her eyes a stream of water continued flowing, and she was unable even to drive away the black bees which, attracted by the sweet perfume, came perpetually and settled on her mouth. Thus uttering deep sobs, she remained alone in the forest, weeping through the pangs of separation in such a manner that, hearing the sound of her lamentation, all beasts and birds, trees and creeping things, were weeping, and she continued exclaiming thus—

'Alas, Lord! chief of benefactors! Whither, O capricious Bihári, hast thou gone? I am thy suppliant at thy feet, thy slave! Ocean of mercy! recall me to thy thoughts.

"Meanwhile all the cowherdesses also searching on, arrived beside her, and continually embracing her, all of them, as they in turn came up, received such gratification as he does who, having lost great riches, finds moderate treasure, or half of that he lost.

"At length, all the cowherdesses perceiving her deep distress, took her with them, and penetrated into the great forest, and as far as they could see the moonlight, so far the cowherdesses sought for the divine Krishn in the forest. When in the darkness of the dense forest they could not find their way, then they all returned thence, and, taking courage, and assuring themselves of rejoining Krishn, came and sat down on that same bank of the Yamuná, where the divine Krishn Chand had conferred much delight upon them."

The saintly Shukadev said, "Sire! all the cowherdesses seated on the banks of the Yamuná, intoxicated with love, began to sing the exploits and virtues of Hari, saying, 'Beloved one! since you came to Braj, ever since that time, having come here, you have diffused new joys. Lakshmi, placing her confidence on your celestial feet, has come and fixed here her perpetual abode. We cowherdesses are your handmaids, shew compassion and quickly direct your thoughts to us. Since we beheld your dark, comely, and piquant figure, we have become your slaves without purchase. The arrows of your eyes have smitten our hearts, and therefore, dear one! wherefore should not they be accounted your own? Our lives are departing; now, then, compassionate us. Lay cruelty aside, and quickly return to our sight. If it was really your purpose to slay us, then wherefore did you save us from the venomous serpent, fire and water, and why suffered you not us then to die? You are not merely the son of Jasodá; Brahmá, Rudr, Indr, and the other gods, by their humble supplications, have brought you for the protection of the world.

"O souls' Lord! at one thing we greatly marvel, that. if you will slay those who are your own, whom will you defend? Beloved one! you are the searcher of hearts, why do you not remove our distress, and fulfil the hope of our minds? What, is it against weak women that you will display your valour? O dearest! when we recall your gentle smiling glances, full of love, and the arch of your eyebrow, and your coquettish eyes, the bend of your neck, and your gay discourse, then what pangs are there which we do not suffer! And when you were going into the forest to pasture the cows, at that time from fixing our thoughts on your celestial feet, the gravel and thorns of the forest came thence and were rankling in our hearts. Departing at dawn, you were returning at eve, yet still those four watches appeared to us four ages. When seated before you we were gazing on your handsome form, then we used to think in our minds that 'Brahmá is an utter dolt to have made the eyelid, as it were, to impede our steadfast gaze.'"

Thus far having recited, the saintly Shukadev said, "Sire! during this same night, all the cowherdesses, afflicted with the pangs of separation, sang on in many various ways the virtues and exploits of the divine Krishn Chand till they were exhausted, but still Bihárí came not. Then truly being very dejected, yet still cherishing a hope of union (by death) they abandoned all confidence of surviving him, and through extreme impatience, became insensible, and falling down, so wept and exclaimed that, on hearing them, animate and inanimate things also were oppressed with heavy affliction."

The saintly Shukadev said, "Sire! when the divine Krishn Chand, searcher of hearts, perceived that the cowherdesses could not survive without him,

Then amongst them appeared Nand's son, just as
A juggler eludes the sight, lies hid, and again displays himself.
When they saw Hari returned, all started up to consciousness,
As when life is infused into a corpse, the senseless members revive.
Deprived of seeing him, the minds of all had become agitated,
As though a mind-agitating snake had bitten all and departed.
Their lover, knowing their grief to be unfeigned, came arriving,
He watered the creepers with nectar, and revived them all.
As the Lotus dejected at night, so were the fair ones of Braj ;
Having seen the beauty of the sun's orb, their large eyes expanded."

Thus far having recited, the saintly Shukadev said, "Sire! on beholding the divine Krishn Chand, the root of joy, all the cowherdesses having suddenly emerged from the ocean of painful separation, approached him, and were as delighted as one who, drowning in an unfathomable sea, réjoices on finding a ford. And being collected on all sides they stood. Then the divine Krishn, taking them with him, came where he had first indulged in the circular dance, and other delights. On arriving a cowherdess took off her mantle and spread it for Krishn to sit down on. When he sat on it, some of the cowherdesses, incensed, said, 'Great sir! you are very deceitful, and know how to take away the minds and wealth of others, but you never acknowledge the favours of any one.' Thus having spoken, they began to say among themselves, 'Good qualities he forsakes, and takes the bad, deceit continues pleasing to his mind. See, sister! and reflect, how shall we deal with him effectually ?' Having heard this, one among them said, 'Companion! do you stand aside, since from our own words we derive no advantage. Lo! I will make Krishn himself avow it.' Thus having spoken, she asked the divine Krishn with a smile, 'Sire! One person confers favours (or is grateful) without having received any; a second reciprocates a benefit; a third, in return for benefits, gives back the reverse; a fourth does not so much as even admit into his mind the sense of having received a favour at all; of these four, which is the good, and which is the bad man—this do you explain to us and tell.' The divine Krishn Chand said, 'Attend, all of you and listen! I will point out to you the good and the bad. The best, then, is he who confers kind offices without receiving them, as the father loves his son; and to do good for good done is not meritorious, as in the case of the cow which yields milk for the food given her. As for the man who looks on a benefit as an injury, know him to be an enemy who does that. The worst of all is the ungrateful man, who obliterates all sense of obligation.'

"When, on hearing these words, the cowherdesses, looking in one another's faces, began to laugh, then, indeed, the divine Krishn being confused, said, 'Attend! I am not to be reckoned among these four, as you suppose, and are, therefore, laughing; but my way is this, that whoever desires anything of me, whatever it may be, I fulfil the desire of his mind. Perhaps you will say, if this be your custom, then why did you thus forsake us in the forest? The reason of that is this, I put your affection to the proof; do not take this matter ill, but consider what I say to be true.' Thus having spoken, he added,

"Now I have made trial of you; you persevered in remembrance, and thought of me.

You have increased your affection for me, like a poor man who has obtained wealth.

Thus you came for my sake, and cast away regard for popular report, and respect for the Vedas.

As the Bairági (an ascetic) abandons his dwelling, and with entire purpose of mind, fixes his affection on Hari.

How can I give you exaltation? (though I recompense you) the obligation I owe you will not receive its equivalent.

Though we should live a hundred years of Brahmá, yet the debt I owe you will not be discharged."

The saintly Muni Shukadev said, "King, when the divine Krishn Chand had thus fondly spoken, then, indeed, all the cowherdesses, laying aside their anger, were pleased; and, having risen, enjoyed various delights in the society of Hari; and, filled with emotions of joy, began to indulge in sports. At this time,

Krishn used the Jogí's illusive power,—the particles of his body became many different bodies.

To all he gave pleasure to the full of their desire, sporting with perfect affection.

As many cowherdesses as there were, just so many bodies did the divine Krishn Chand assume, and, taking all with him to that same terrace of the circular dance, he again commenced dancing and delight.

Rás Mandala, or Circular Dance.

The cowherdesses joined hands two and two, between each two was Hari, their companion;

Each thought him beside her—so thought all; none perceived his other forms;

Each put her fingers into the fingers of another, and danced gaily, circling round, taking Hari with them;

Here, intermediate, (danced) a cowherdess, there, intermediate, the son of Nand, like dense clouds on all sides, and between them the flashing lightning,—

Krishn, of the dark blue hue, and the fair girls of Braj—like a necklace of gold beads and sapphires.

Sire! in this manner the cowherdesses and Krishn, standing up, began to blend the tunes of various kinds of instruments, and running over in prelude the notes of very difficult airs, to play and sing, and, selecting tunes in a high key, pleasing and full of contrast, and others raised half a tone higher, or a whole tone, or two tones, and others which they extemporised while they sang them, represented, by the dance, the emotions they were intended to convey. And their joy was so exuberant that they retained no longer their consciousness, corporeal or mental. In one place, the breasts of some of them were uncovered; in another, their diadems fell off. Here, necklaces of pearls, snapping asunder, were falling down; there, wreaths of forest flowers. The drops of perspiration on their foreheads glittered like strings of pearls; and the ringlets on the fair faces of the cowherdesses were, in their dishevelled state, like young snakes, which, through desire of nectar, had flown up and fastened themselves on the Moon. At one time, a cowherdess, blending her voice with the sound of Krishn's flute, was singing in a treble key; at another, one of them sang, unaccompanied. And when a cowherdess, having stopped the sound of the flute, was bringing from her throat its entire note with exact agreement, then Hari remained fascinated with delight, just as a child, beholding its image in a glass, stands riveted.

"In this manner, singing, and dancing, and displaying various kinds of emotions, and blandishments, and coquetry, they were giving and imparting delight; and mutually pleased, and laughing gaily, they were embracing, and making a propitiatory offering of their clothes and ornaments. At that time, Brahmá, Rudr, Indr, and all the other deities and celestial musicians, seated on their cars, together with their wives, beholding the bliss of the circular dance, were, through joy, raining down flowers, and their wives, beholding those pleasures, and filled with desire, were saying in their hearts, 'Had we been born in Braj, we also should have enjoyed the circular dance, and other delights, with Hari.' Such was the concert of musical modes (the Rágs of which there are six), and airs (the Ráginís of which are thirty), that, hearing them, even the winds and waters ceased to move, and the moon, with the circle of stars, being fascinated, was pouring down nectar with its rays. Meanwhile, the night advanced, and six months passed away, and no one was aware of it, and from that time the name of that night has been—the night of Brahmá."

Thus far having related, the saintly Shukadev said, "Earth's

Lord! sporting on in dances and diversions, a fancy entered into the mind of the divine Krishn Chand; whereupon, taking the cowherdesses with him, he went to the bank of the Yamuná, and, having plunged into the water, and sported there, he dispelled his fatigue, and came forth, and thus, having accomplished the wishes of all, he said, 'Now, four *gharis* (about one hour and a half) of the night remain; do you all depart to your own homes.' Having heard these words, the cowherdesses, being dejected, said, 'Lord! how can we go home, quitting your celestial lotus-feet? Our greedy hearts listen no whit to this direction.' The divine Krishn said, 'Listen! as Jogís fix their thoughts on me, so too do you abstract and fix your minds: wherever ye may be there will I remain with you.' On hearing this, all were pleased, and taking leave, departed to their own houses; and none of the inmates knew of this secret, that the women had been away."

. . . . . . . . . . . . . . .

### Krishna speaks to his father.

'Listen, father! Kans has sent for us; our uncle Akrúr has brought these tidings. Take milk, sheep, and goats; it is the sacrifice of the bow; there offer them. Let all accompany you: the king has said it; the case admits not of delay.

When the divine Krishn Chand, with such explanations and advice, had addressed Nand, then that chieftain, at that very time, having summoned criers, caused a proclamation to be made throughout the city to this effect, 'To-morrow, at early dawn, all will together proceed to Mathurá: the king has summoned us.' On hearing this intelligence, all the inhabitants of Braj, as soon as it dawned, came, bringing presents; and Nand also, taking with him milk, curds, butter, sheep, goats, and buffaloes, having caused the cattle in his carts to be yoked, went with them. Krishn and Baladev also, taking with them the cowherd youths, their companions, mounted on their cars,—

In front were Nand and Upanand; in rear of all, Haldhar and Govind."

The saintly Shukadev said, "Lord of the earth! all of a sudden, having heard of the departure of the divine Krishn Chand, all the cowherdesses of Braj, much agitated and distressed, left their homes, and arose and hastened in confusion, and lamenting and talking incoherently, stumbling and falling, came where the divine Krishn Chand was seated in his car. On coming up, they stood around the car, and, joining their hands, began to say with humility, 'Why, O Lord of Braj! do you forsake us? we have given all we possessed to

you. The affection of the good never suffers decrease: it ever remains, like the writing in the lines of the hand; but the regard of
the fool is not lasting, but resembles a wall of sand. What such
crime have we committed against you that you are departing and
turning your back upon us?' Having thus addressed the divine
Krishn Chand, the cowherdesses, having turned their eyes towards
Akrúr, added,—

> 'This Akrúr* is very cruel; he is altogether ignorant of our pain.
> That being—to be deprived of whose company for a single moment renders
> us desolate—him he takes away along with him.
> He is deceitful, cruel, and stern of heart. Who vainly gave him the name
> of Akrúr?
> O Akrúr! cruel, and void of understanding. Wherefore do you injure weak,
> dependent woman?'

Using such harsh words, and abandoning all consideration and reserve, they laid hold of the car of Hari, and began to say among
themselves, 'The women of Mathurá are very wanton, artful,
beautiful, and accomplished; Bihárí, having formed an attachment
for them, and being overcome by their good qualities and taste, will
take up his abode entirely there. Then how will he remember us?
Great is their good fortune, indeed, that they will remain with their
beloved one. What such fault has occurred in our invocation and
penance from which the divine Krishn Chand forsakes us?' Thus
having spoken among themselves, they again addressed Hari, 'Your
name truly is the Lord of Cowherdesses; wherefore do you not take
us along with you?

> How will each moment pass without you? If you are absent for an instant
> our bosoms burst with sorrow.
> After shewing us affection, why separate from us? relentless, pitiless, you feel
> no attachment.'
> Thus the fair ones uttered their supplications there, and were thoughtful
> plunged in a sea of grief:
> They remained stedfastly gazing in the direction of Hari,—like a fascinated
> antelope, or the Chakor looking at the moon;
> The tears fell dropping from their eyes; and their curls, falling loose, were
> spread over their faces.

The saintly Muni Shukadev said, "King! at that time this indeed
was the state of the cowherdesses, which I have described to you;
and the lady Jasodá—with the tenderness of a mother—embraced
her son, and, weeping, was saying, with intense affection, 'Son!

---

* There is an *equivoque* here. A-krúr signifies "not cruel," though it is here
a proper name.

take with you, as you go, provisions sufficient for the number of days (which will elapse) till you return thence. And when you have arrived there, place your affections on none; but quickly return, and present yourself to the sight of her who gave you birth.' Hearing these words, the divine Krishn, having dismounted from his car, and having comforted and admonished all, took leave of his mother, and, having made his obeisance, and received her blessing, again mounted his car and departed. At this time, in the one direction, Jasodá, with the cowherdesses, in great emotion and sobbing, were calling out 'Krishn! Krishn!' and, in the other direction, the divine Krishn, standing up in his car, and calling out, was saying, as he departed, 'Do you go home, and have no anxiety; I will return in four or five days at most.'"

. . . . . . . . . . . . . . . . . . . .

"Sire! these cowherdesses, distracted by separation from the divine Krishn, and singing his praises alone, in their several companies, with their thoughts fixed on their beloved one, began on their way to sing of the exploits of the Supreme Being.

One said, 'Kanhái met me;' another, 'He has run off and hidden himself.
From behind he seized my arm; there stands he, Hari, in the shade of the Indian fig.'
One says, 'I saw him milking;' another, 'I beheld him at early dawn.'
One avers that, 'He is pasturing the cattle; listen! given ear, he plays the flute
By this road, sister, we will not go; the youth Kanhái will demand alms of us;
He will break our water-pots, and untie the knots (of the cords on which we carry them), and, having surveyed us a little (*i.e.* with a mere glance), will steal away our senses;
He is concealed somewhere, and will come running; then how shall we be able to escape?'
Thus speaking, the women of Braj departed, their frames being greatly agitated through separation from Krishn."

The saintly Muni Shukadev said, "Lord of the Earth! when Udho had finished repeating his whispered invocations, then, having issued from the river, having put on his clothes and ornaments, and taken his seat in his car, when he took his way from the bank of the Kalindí towards the house of Nand, then the cowherdesses, who had gone forth to fill water, beheld his car on the road, coming from a distance. On beholding it, they began to say among themselves, 'Whose is this car which is coming towards us? Let us take a survey of this, then let us advance.' Hearing this, one cowherdess among them said, 'Sister! it may be, perhaps, that the deceitful Akrúr may have come, who led the divine Krishn Chand

to Mathurá, and caused him to dwell there, and brought about the
death of Kans.' Having heard this, another of them said, 'For
what has this betrayer of confidence come? on one occasion, indeed,
he has carried off the root of our life; now will he take our life
itself?' Sire! having spoken many such things among themselves,

> The women of Braj remained standing there; they set down their water-pots,
> having lifted them from their heads.

Meanwhile, when the chariot drew near, then the cowherdesses,
having seen U'dho from a small distance, began to say among themselves, 'Sister! this truly is some one of a dark-blue colour, with
lotus eyes, and a diadem on his head, wearing a garland of wild
flowers, dressed in yellow silk, and with a silken scarf of the same
colour, who, seated in the car of the divine Krishn Chand, comes
looking towards us.' Then one cowherdess from among them said,
'Sister! this person has, since yesterday, come to the house of Nand,
and his name is U'dho, and the divine Krishn Chand has, through
him, sent some message.'

"On hearing these words, the cowherdesses, seeing that it was a
solitary place, abandoned reserve and modesty, and ran up and
approached U'dho, and, knowing him to be a friend of Hari, made
obeisance to him, and, having inquired after his welfare, joined their
hands, and stood surrounding the chariot on all sides. Having seen
their affection, U'dho also descended from his car. Then all the
cowherdesses, having caused him to sit down under the shade of a
tree, themselves also took their seats, surrounding him on all sides,
and, with much tenderness, began to address him:

> 'Well have you done, U'dho, in coming; you have brought us tidings of
>      Mádho (Krishn);
> You have always remained near Krishn; give us the message which he
>      delivered to you.
> You were sent only for the sake of his mother and father; he takes thought
>      for no one else;
> We have given all we possessed into his hands; our souls are entangled in
>      his feet.
> He pursues only his own objects; he has now afflicted all, without exception,
>      in departing.

And as the bird deserts the tree which is destitute of fruit, just so
Hari has abandoned us; we have bestowed on him our all; but still
he has not become ours.' Sire! when the cowherdesses, inspired
with love, had in this manner spoken many such words, then U'dho,
having beheld the firmness of their affection, when he was about to

rise with the intention of making his obeisance to them, then, immediately, a cowherdess, having seen a black bee sitting upon a flower, under pretence of addressing it, said to U'dho,—

"'O honeymaker! thou has drunk the juice of the lotus-feet of Mádhav; hence hast thou the name of Madhukar (the honeymaker), and thou art the friend of a deceitful one; for this very reason he has made thee his messenger, and sent thee; touch not thou our feet, for we know that all of a dark-blue hue are deceitful; such as thou art, just such is Krishn; wherefore, do not thou salute us. Just as thou wanderest about, drinking the juice of various flowers, and belonging to none, just so Krishn also makes love, yet is constant to none.' The cowherdess was thus speaking, when another black bee came, seeing which, a cowherdess, named Lalitá, said,—

'O bee! do you remain apart from us, and go and tell this in the city of Madhu,

Where the divine Krishn Chand and his humpbacked consort dwell at ease; for why should we speak of one birth? this very custom is yours through successive births. King Bali gave you all he possessed; him you sent to Pátál, and a virtuous wife like Síta, you, innocent as she was, expelled from your house. When you brought this condition on even her, then what great loss have we suffered?' Thus having spoken, all the cowherdesses together joined their hands, and began to say to U'dho, 'Illustrious U'dho! we, deprived of the divine Krishn, are widowed; do you take us with you.'"

The saintly Shukadev said, "Sire! on these words proceeding from the mouth of the cowherdesses, U'dho said, 'The message which the divine Krishn Chand sent, that I will explain to you and tell—do you listen with attention. It is written, "Do you abandon the hope of sexual delight and practise devotion, I will never separate from you;" and Krishn says, "Night and day you fix your thoughts on me, and for this same reason I hold none so dear as yourselves."'

"Thus having spoken U'dho added, 'He who is the First Male, the Imperishable One, Hari, on him you have always fixed your affection, and whom all extol as the Invisible, the Unseen, the Impenetrable, him you regard as your husband; and as earth, wind, water, fire, and air dwell in the body, so the Supreme Being dwells in you, but by the quality of illusion appears separate. Continue to fix your recollection and your thoughts on him; he always remains accessible to his votaries, and from contiguity, perception and meditation are destroyed; on this account, Hari has gone to a distance and fixed his habitation, and the divine Krishn Chand

explained this also to me and said, that, playing on the flute he
called you to the woods, and when he saw your love and the pain
you felt at separation evinced, then he danced together with you
the circular dance.

When you forgot his divinity, the chief of Yadu vanished from sight.

" ' Again, when recovering your perception, you mentally fixed
your thoughts upon Hari, then forthwith, knowing the devotion of
your hearts, the Supreme Being came and appeared to you.' Sire!
soon as these words issued from the mouth of Udho,

Then said the cowherdesses, incensed, 'We have heard your words, now
remain apart from us;
You have told us of knowledge, devotion, wisdom; you tell us to abandon
meditation, and point out to us the sky,—
On whose sports our mind is fixed; him you call Nárayan.
He who, from his childhood, bestowed pleasure upon us, how has he become
Invisible—the Unseen?
He who is possessed of all good qualities, and gifted with all beauties of
form, how can he be quality-less and form-less;
Since in his dear body our souls are wrapped up, who will give ear to your
words?"
One of the company arose, and, after reflection, said, 'Conciliate Udho.
Say nothing to him, sisters! but hear his words, and continue gazing on his
countenance.'
One said, ' It is not his fault; he came sent by Kubjá.
Now, as Kubjá has instructed him, that very strain he sings.
Krishn would never speak thus, as, since his arrival in Braj, he has spoken.
By hearing such words, sister! thorns pierce us—we cannot endure to hear.
He tells us to abandon sexual delight and practise devotion; how can Múdho
(Krishn) have spoken thus?
Inaudible repetition of the Divine name, penance, abstinence, vows, and
religious observances; all these are the (befitting) practices of widows.
May the youth Kanháí live on through successive ages; he who bestows
happiness on our heads.
While one's husband survives, who makes use of the ashes of cowdung? tell
us where this custom is observed!
For us vows, devotion, fasting are in this, to regard with unceasing affection
the feet of the son of Nand.
Who will impute blame to you, Udho? Kubjá has led us all this dance.

Thus far having related, the saintly Muni Shukadev said, " Sire!
when Udho heard from the mouths of the cowherdesses words such
as these, imbued with affection, he then mentally regretted that he
had spoken to them of penance, and with a feeling of shame he
preserved silence and remained with bent-down head. Then a cow-

herdess said, ' Say, is Balbhadr well ? and does he, too, thinking on the affection of his childhood, ever recall us to his mind or not ?'

"Having heard this, another cowherdess from among them said, in answer, 'Companions! you, indeed, are but rustic cowherds' wives, and the women of Mathurá, are fair to see; captivated by them, Hari indulges in delight; why should he now take thought of us? Since he went and dwelt there, O companions! from that time he has become the spouse of others. Had we known this at first, how would we have suffered him to depart? Now, we gain nothing by our regrets, whence it is better to abandon all grief, and remain with hopes fixed on the stipulated time. For just as during eight months the earth, the forests, and the mountains, in expectation of the rainy clouds, endure the heat of the sun, and when the rain comes it cools them, so Hari also will come and visit us.'

" One said, ' Hari has effected his purpose, has slain his foes, and assumed the government,
Wherefore should he come to Brindában ? Why should he abandon empire to feed cows ?
Abandon, O companions ! hope of the promised return ! anxiety is gone, for it has become despair.'
One woman said, disquieted, 'Wherefore should we abandon hope of (seeing) Krishn ?

" ' In the forest, hill, and on the bank of the Yamuná, wheresoever the divine Krishn and Balarám had sported, beholding these same places, recollection truly returns of our souls' Lord Hari.' Thus having spoken, she added,

" ' This Braj has become a sea of grief, his name is a boat in the midst of a stream ;
Those who are sinking in the water of the pangs of separation ; when will Krishn bring them across ?
How has the recollection that he was the Lord of Cowherdesses departed ?
Does he not feel some sense of shame on account of his name ?'

"Having heard these words, Udho, having reflected in his inmost heart, began to say, 'All praise to these cowherdesses, and to their firmness ! that they have abandoned all they possessed, and remained immersed in contemplation of the divine Krishn Chand.' Sire! Udho, indeed, having beheld their affection, was just then applauding them in his heart of hearts, when, at that moment, all the cowherdesses arose and stood up, and conducted Udho, with much ceremony to his house. Having perceived their affection, he also, having arrived there, and having taken his food and reposed him-

narrated stories and Puránas; good and holy men sang the praises
of Hari during the eight watches; charioteers, yoking continually
chariots and cars, brought them to the royal gate; demigods, heroes,
champions, and warriors of the race of Yadu, mounted on cars,
chariots, elephants, and horses, came to salute the king; skilful
persons amused him by dancing, singing, and playing; panegyrists
and bards, chanting eulogiums, received elephants, horses, clothes,
weapons, grain, money, and ornaments of gold, studded with
jewels."

Having related thus much of the history, the saintly Shukadev
said to the king, "Sire! in that direction indeed, in the royal city
of king Ugrasen, in this manner, various kinds of amusement were
going on, and in this direction the divine Krishn Chand, the Root
of Joy, with his sixteen thousand one hundred and eight youthful
wives ever indulged in sports. At times, the youthful ladies, overpowered by their love, dressed themselves in the guise of their Lord;
at times, the enamoured Hari adorned his wives. And the sports
and pastimes which they mutually practised exceed description; I
cannot describe them, that could only be done by a spectator."

Having said this much, Shukadev said, "Sire! one night the
divine Krishn Chand was diverting himself with all his youthful
wives., and beholding the various actions of the Supreme Being,
celestial choristers and musicians, playing on lutes, timbrels, pipes,
and kettle-drums, were singing the excellences (of the Deity), and
there was a harmonious concert, when, as they sported, a thought
entered the mind of the Supreme Being, whereupon, taking all with
him, he went to the bank of a lake, and, entering the water, began
to sport therein. Then, as they played in the water, all the women,
being filled with blissful love for the divine Krishn Chand, lost their
corporeal and mental consciousness, and seeing the male and female
*Anas Casarca* seated on opposite sides of the lake, and calling to each
other, they said,

'O ruddy goose! why dost thou call out mournfully? why sleepest thou not
at night from separation from thy lover?

Deeply agitated, thou callest ever for thy husband; to us thou ever dis-
coursest of thy spouse.

We, indeed, are become the slave-girls of Krishn;' thus having spoken,
they went on.

"Again they began to address the ocean, saying, 'O Sea! thou
who drawest deep sighs, and wakest night and day, art thou then
separated from any one, or grievest thou for the fourteen gems thou

hast lost?' Having spoken thus again, beholding the moon, they said, 'O Moon! why remainest thou with wasted body and sad mind; what, hast thou consumption, that thy frame daily wanes and increases; or whilst thou beholdest the divine Krishn Chand, art thou fascinated in body and mind as we are?'

Having related thus much of the history, the saintly Shukadev said to the king, "Sire! in this same manner, all the youthful women addressed many words to the wind, the clouds, the cuckoo, the mountains, rivers, and swans, which you can imagine. Afterwards, all the women sported wtth the divine Krishn Chand, and ever continued in his service, and in singing the praises of the Supreme Being, and derived enjoyment such as their minds desired; while Krishn discharged his duties, as a householder, as became him. Sire! to the sixteen thousand one hundred and eight queens of the divine Krishn Chand, whom I have before mentioned, to each of them was born ten sons and one daughter, and their offspring was numberless; I cannot describe it. But I know thus much, that there were thirty millions, eighty-eight thousand, and one hundred schools, for teaching the offspring of the divine Krishn, and as many teachers. Moreover, among all the sons and grandsons of the divine Krishn Chand, not one was deficient in beauty, strength, prowess, wealth, or piety; every one was superior to the other; I am unable to describe them."

Having said thus much, the Rishi said, "Sire! I have sung of the sports of Braj and of Dwáriká, which give pleasure to all. Whoever recites them with affection shall, without doubt, obtain supreme beatitude. Whatever advantage results from performing penance, sacrifice, alms, and religious vows, or bathing at places of pilgrimage, the same results from hearing the history of Hari."

# CHAPTER V.

## RELIGIOUS DOCTRINES OF THE SECT.

VALLÁBHÁCHARYA, his son Vithalnáthji, and all his descendants, are known as the incarnations of the god Krishna.
The object of their incarnation has been stated in Nijvártá.
According to this authority, the residence of Krishna is
denominated Gouloka, a place far above the three worlds,
and having, at five hundred millions of yojans below it, the
separate regions of Vishnu and Śiva. The region of Krishna
Gouloka is indestructible, whilst all the rest is subject to
annihilation. In the centre of it abides Krishna, of the colour
of a dark cloud, in the bloom of youth, clad in yellow raiment,
splendidly adorned with celestial gems, and holding a flute.
He is in the full and eternal enjoyment of his wife Rádhá
and three hundred millions of gopis or female companions,
each gopi having a separate palace of her own, with three
millions of female attendants. Two of these gopis, named
Priyá and Chandrávati, once quarrelled about Krishna. Priyá
sent for Krishna to spend a night with her; and as Krishna
was, according to engagement, going to her palace, he unfortunately met Chandrávati, who, knowing his intention,
contrived to seduce him to her own palace, telling Krishna
that she saw Varshabhánu, Priyá's father, going along the
road. Krishna, fearing the anger of Priyá's father, went
with Chandrávati. When this came to the knowledge of
Priyá, the two gopis quarrelled, and cursed each other, their
imprecations being to the effect that they should fall from

heaven to the earth with all their retinue and everything belonging to them. Upon this Krishna, out of affection to both of them, promised that he would descend as a man to work out their salvation, and restore them to their original abode in the highest of heavens. Priyá, who was the first to fall from heaven, appeared on the earth as a new born babe at a spot called Champáraṇya. The fall of Chandrávati followed, and she made herself known as a child at Charaṇádiri. Krishṇa followed them both, aṇd appeared first incarnate in the person of Vallabháchárya, at Champáraṇya, and at the moment of his birth effected salvation for Priyá. In his second incarnation, in the person of Vithalnáthji, Vallabháchárya's son, at Charaṇádiri, he effected salvation for the second gopi, and thus restored them both to their former state of bliss in the highest of heavens. Each of the gopis had, previous to their descent to the earth, three millions of attendants in the heavens, some of whom accompanied their mistresses at the time of their fall; while, of those who remained behind, multitudes are daily descending, one after the other, in the persons of the followers of the sect, to secure whose recovery to the heavenly abode the successive generations of Vallabháchárya are born as incarnations of the god Krishṇa. They redeem their followers by sending them to Gouloka, where the disciple, if a male, is changed into a female, who obtains the everlasting happiness of living in sexual intercourse with Krishṇa in the heavens.

We now come to the doctrines promulgated by Vallabháchárya, and which constitute his claim to be the founder of the sect. He condensed his teachings into the compact form of the Pushti Márga, or the way of enjoyment, a sort of creed for the convenience of those of his votaries who had neither leisure, education, nor inclination to study his doctrines in detail, and who were satisfied to adopt the faith in which they had been brought up.

According to Dwárkesh, there are ten principles of the Pushti Márga, or the sect of Vallabháchárya. They are known as DAS MARAMS, meaning ten principles or ten sects, and are as follows :—

(1.) To secure the firm support of Vallabháchárya.
(2.) To exercise chiefly the worship of Krishna.
(3.) To forsake the sense of public or Vaidik opinion, and be supplicant to Gopisha (Krishna).
(4.) To sing praises with feelings of humility.
(5.) To believe that I am a gopi * of Vraj.
(6.) To swell the heart with the name of Krishna.
(7.) To forsake not his commands for a moment.
(8.) To put faith in his words and doings.
(9.) To adopt the society of the good, knowing them divine.
(10.) To see not the faults, but speak the truth.

Whether the Siddhánta Rahasya be intended as a commentary upon this Pushti Márga or not, it is evidently an amplification of some of the tenets of the sect; Vallabháchárya gives it as a direct revelation with which he was inspired. The text and the translation of it are as follows :—

श्रावणस्यामले पचे एकादश्यां महानिशि । साचाङ्गभगवता प्रोक्तं
तद्वरप्र उच्यते ॥ १ ॥ ब्रह्मसंबंधकरणात्सर्वेषां देहजीवयोः । सर्वदो-
षनिवृत्तिर्हि दोषाः पंचविधाः स्मृताः ॥ २ ॥ सहजा देशकालोत्या
लोकवेदनिरूपिताः । संयोगजाः स्पर्शजाश्च न मन्तव्याः कदाचन ॥ ३ ॥
अन्यथा सर्वदोषाणां न निवृत्तिः कथंचन । असमर्पितवस्तूनां तस्मा-
द्वर्जनमाचरेत् ॥ ४ ॥ निवेदिभिः समर्प्यैव सर्वं कुर्यादिति स्थितिः । न
मतं देवदेवस्य स्वामिभुक्तिसमर्पणम् ॥ ५ ॥ तस्मादादौ सर्वकार्ये सर्ववस्तु-
समर्पणम् । दत्तापहारवचनं तथा च सकलं हरिः ॥ ६ ॥ न ग्राह्यमिति
वाक्यं हि भिन्नमार्गेपरं मतम् । सेवकानां यथा लोके व्यवहारः प्रसिध्य-
ति ॥ ७ ॥ तथा कार्यं समर्प्यैव सर्वेषां ब्रह्मता ततः । गङ्गाम्बे सर्वदोषाणां

---

* Female companion of Rádha, one of Krishna's wives.

गुणदोषादिवर्णनम् ॥ ८ ॥ गङ्गाखिन निरूप्यं खान्तवद्चापि चैव हि ॥ ९ ॥

"At midnight on *Ekádashi*, in the month of Shráwan-shud, God visibly uttered the (following) words which are here repeated word for word:

"By entering into relation with BRAHMA, all persons' sins of body and mind are washed away. These sins are said to be of five kinds, viz., those which are congenital; those which owe their origin to time and place; those described in profane works and in the Vedas; those which are results of intimate association, and such as are produced by contact. These sins are not, and are never believed in, (after the above relation has been established). Otherwise (that is when such a relation has not been contracted) expiation of sins never takes place. That which has not been in the first instance dedicated should not be accepted. Offerers, after making their offerings, should do with them what they like; such is the rule. That offering which has (in the first instance) been enjoyed by its owner is not acceptable by the God of gods. Therefore in the first instance, in all doings, all things should be dedicated. That that which is given should not be taken, because the whole comes to belong to Hari, is the doctrine of other sects. (With us) the relation which subsists in the world between (a master and his) servants holds good; and everything should be done accordingly; that is, after dedicating, it should be enjoyed: hence it is that the Brahmatva, or the quality of BRAHMA, is obtained. As when all merits and demerits obtain the quality of Gangá,* all of them promiscuously have the quality of Gangá; so now such is the case here. Thus is concluded, in Siddhánta Rahasya, composed by Vallabháchárya."

Here we have the doctrine of the origin of sin, and its mode of expiation or absolution; and here is the first insinuation of the paramount importance of the Gosáinji, or Guru, as the direct mediator.

In the next extract we give will be found the punishments awarded by the doctrines of this sect to those who neglect due respect to their spiritual teachers, which is enforced as a paramount duty, the neglect of which involves fearful consequences.

* The sacred river (Ganges).

6

The extracts given are translations of some of the articles of a work in Brijabháshá, written by Hariráyaji, the work itself being entitled "The sixty-seven sins and atonements, and their consequences."

32. Whoever holds (his) spiritual guide, and S'ri Thákurji (or god) to be different and distinct, shall be born a Sicháná.*

34. Whoever disobeys the orders of (his) spiritual guide, shall go to Asipátra† and other dreadful hells, and lose all his religious merits.

37. Whoever divulges the secrets of (his) spiritual guide, or of Sri Thákurji, shall for three births be born a dog.

39. Whoever, before his spiritual guide, or S'ri Thákurji, sits in the posture called Padmásan, shall be born a serpent.

54. Whoever displays (his) learning before his spiritual guide, shall for three births be dumb. For three births he shall be a dog (or) an ass.

55. Whoever displays activity before his spiritual guide shall be born a jarakha.

56. Whoever, without paying his respects to his spiritual guide, performs worship, (his worship) shall become entirely fruitless.

59. Whoever shows the soles of his feet to his spiritual guide, or to S'ri Thákurji, shall be born a serpent for ten years.

The next extract we shall give is a sort of commentary upon the Pushti Márga, enforcing its tenets, with the penalties attached to the neglect of them. It is written by the celebrated Śri Gokulnáthji, the fourth son of Vithalnáthji, whose followers are so exclusive as to avoid all intercourse with other sectaries. The work is written in Brijabháshá, and is entitled "Vachnámrat (Precept as sweet as nectar) of the Pushti Márga."

"He who, getting angry in his heart, maligns (his) Guru, and utters harsh terms towards his Guru, becomes dumb, and after that he becomes a serpent. He is then born a creature of the region of the vegetable kingdom, and after that he is born a creature of the region of the dead (or ghost). As he (Vaishnava) remembers S'ri Bhagván (god), in the same way he remembers and repeats in his

---

* A kind of bird.                    † The name of a dreadful hell.

mind the name of his Guru. One having become a Vaishṇava should not see faults of (or in) others. He should not hear them with his ears. Even if he should see them with his eyes and hear them with his ears, still he should not consider anything of them in (his) mind. He understands or (says to himself) as follows :—I, who having fallen into this avidya (ignorance) in the form of máyá (delusion) see nothing but the faults; (but) there is not a particle of fault therein. . . . . . He does not consider himself happy by the acquisition of anything. By hearing the Sástras of the duties of *Grahasta* doctrines from any one, he does not allow himself to be absorbed into the Lowkik and Vaidik. The moral precepts of the Sástras connected with the Pushti Márga should be freely heard and related. All other Sástras cause one to swerve from the Pushti Márga. This should be firmly believed in one's own mind."

Herein the Guru is assimilated to Śri Bhagván, and severe punishment threatened for evil acts towards the teacher.

The next extract is a laudation of Śri Gosáinji or Vithalnáthji, the son of Vallabháchárya. It is fulsome in its comparison, and is extracted from a manuscript in Brijabháshá, entitled Astákshar Tiká. Its evident object is distinctly to enhance the supremacy of the Mahárájas, by the commendation of their ancestors, whose qualities it is here insinuated they inherit. It runs thus :—

"Behold! how is Śri Gosáinji.* He is totally without desires; he is without wants; he is with desires fulfilled; he desires all virtues; he is possessed of all virtues; he is the very personification of the most excellent being (God); he is all incarnations; he is as beautiful as a million of Kándevas;* he is possessed of the six virtues; he is the head of all those who appreciate sensual or intellectual pleasure, or poetry; he is desirous of fulfilling the wishes of his devotees. Such is Śri Gosáinji. Why should he want anything? He is himself the creator of the endless crores of worlds wherein his glory has diffused all over. He is the inspirer (or propeller) of the souls of all animated beings. He is praised by Brahma, Śiva, Indra, and other gods. Such is Śri Gosáinji."

We next take a passage from a commentary, in Brijabháshá, on a work called the "Chaturślocki Bhágvat," the

* Vithalnáthji, son of Vallabháchárya.　　　† Kandeva is god of love.

object of which is to exhibit the paramount importance of the Guru.

"Therefore in Kali Yuga there is no means of salvation similar to worship. Therefore when a man seeks protection of Sri Acháryaji* alone, all his wishes are fulfilled. We should regard our Guru as God, nay, even greater than God; for if God gets angry, the Guru-deva is able to save (one from the effects of God's anger); whereas if Guru is displeased nobody is able to save (one from the effects of the Guru's displeasure)."

The next extract also makes the Guru superior to Hari (god) himself, in his power of salvation, and ordains offerings and promulgates the idea of the Mahárájas being the manifest incarnation of the deity. It is from a work in Brijabháshá, entitled "Guru Seva, or Guru Worship."

"When Hari (god) is displeased (with any one) the Guru saves him (from the effects of Hari's displeasure). But when Guru is displeased with any one no one can save him (from the effects of the Guru's displeasure). Therefore a Vaishṇava should serve the Guru with his body and money, and please the Guru.

"But the principal Gurus are Sri Acháryaji and Sri Gosáinji and the whole family called the Vallabha family. They are all Gurus as is mentioned in the Sarvottamji.

"Therefore God and the Guru are necessarily to be worshipped. If a man worships God he goes to Vyápi Vaikuntha.† But, by the worship of God, he goes to Vyápi Vaikuntha only when he worships the Guru. The worship of the Guru is to be performed in the same way as the worship of God.

"Offerings are to be made to the Guru. There is no particular quantity of offerings (ordained). You are to make such an offering as you feel inclined to make. But you are to reflect thus: 'In this world there are many kinds of creatures: of them all we are most fortunate that we have sought the protection of the illustrious Vallabhácháryaji, Sri Gosáinji, and their descendants, who are manifestly (incarnations of) God the excellent Being himself.'"

Here we have the manifestation of the Mahárájas in their extreme cupidity. In order that the offerings to them should be as unlimited as possible, it is not prescribed what they are

---

* Vallabháchárya.    † The highest of heavens, Gouloka.

to be. It is also ordained that they should be worshipped, and the promised reward for this is the highest heaven, whereas the mere worship of God entitles only to an inferior paradise.

We come now to a most important series of extracts, which fully develope the entire doctrine of adulterine intercourse. These are evidently inculcated to satisfy the lewd propensities of a libidinous priesthood, who, under the shield of religion, avert the avenging hand of outraged manhood, which suffers the chastity of its females to be openly violated, and the sacred purity of home defiled. They may well ask, "are these my children?" when the first form of adjuration that their religion demands is the Samarpan, the consecration of *tan, man,* and *dhan,* viz., "of body, organs of sense, life, heart, and other faculties, and wife, house, family, property, and self," to Krishna, or his representative, the Maháráj. The term *tan* implies the body in all its relations; *man* is the mind, with all its faculties and qualities; and *dhan,* as explained by the Mahárájas, signifies that the sectaries should place at their disposal sons, wives, daughters, and everything else before applying them to their own use.

The first passage we shall cite is from a commentary by Gokulnáthji (in Sanskrit, called "Virchita Bhakti Siddhánta Vivruti") upon his grandfather's work called "Siddhánta Rahasya."

तस्मादादौ स्वोपभोगात्पूर्वमेव सर्वेवस्तुपदेन भार्यापूत्रादीनामपि समर्पणं कर्तव्यं विवाहानन्तरं स्वोपभोगे सर्वकार्ये सर्वकार्यनिमित्तं तत्कार्यौपभोगिवस्तुसमर्पणं कार्यं समर्पणं कृत्वा पश्चात्तानि तानि कार्याणि कर्तव्यानीत्यर्थः॥

"Therefore in the beginning, even before ourselves enjoying, wives, sons, etc., should be made over; because of the expression, "Sarvavastu" (*i.e.* all things). After marriage, even before ourselves using her, [her (the wife's) offering should be made with the view that she may become useful to ourselves. So likewise, even after the birth of a son, sons, etc., should also be made over]. On all occasions, and on account of all occasions, the thing to be used on that occasion should be made over. After making the things over, the different acts should be done."

This commentary thus enjoins on the sectaries total abnegation of self in behoof of the Maháráj. The next extract designates the Maháráj by the character which he is so ambitious to sustain among his deluded and outraged votaries. In Vithalesha-ratnavivarana :

"The Áchárya is called ' Shrishá,' which is rendered by the commentator to mean the 'Priya,' or husband of many women. He is also described as ' the ocean of the Rás lilá,' and as one whose sole aim is the Rás lilá, which means amorous sports with many women."

A confirmation of this is found in a manuscript copy, in Brijabháshá, of Pushti Praváha Maryádá Tiká, by Hararáiji.

"It is stated in Pushti Márga that God abides in the houses of the Vaishnavas by the adulterine love which (I) now describe : as when we bring another's son to our house, and (or) when we keep another's husband in our house by any mode whatsoever, he is won over by excessive affection. If we serve by our body, mind, wealth, or by any other mode, then another's son or husband will remain with us. In the same way does God ever abide in our house in union."

We may ask how should God abide in these houses but by his conceptions in the progeny of the Vaishnava, through the medium of the Maháráj.

It would seem that the fatuity of the sect of the Vaishnavas has attained its culmination ; for in the next extract, which is rather long, and of modern date, being published in Oct. 1860, by the Vaishnava Dharma Prasáraka Mandali (Society for the diffusion of the Vaishnava Religion), in a book printed in Gujarati, called "Swadharma Vardhak and Sanshaya Chhedak," that is to say, "Promoter of our religion and destroyer of doubt," the apology or explanation of " adulterine love" was attempted. It was clearly understood by these sectaries that society was aroused, and that it was necessary to do something to allay the ferment. The extract commences at page 27 of No. 2, vol. i., and runs thus:—

"In the above chapter it is stated that God himself has become, by parts, all the forms : consequently this whole universe is his spirit ; consequently he is at play with his own spirit. With God, therefore, (the relation of) my-own-and-another's does not exist. All is his own. Consequently the sin of adultery does not affect Him. The sin of enjoying other people's things affects this world. With God nothing whatever is alien. God has therefore ordained the sin of adultery for this world. Now the ignorant say this : ' Should a daughter or a son propose to (her or his) father to become his wife, what sin and immorality are contained therein. How sinful, therefore, are those who entertain towards God the adulterine love.' Thus have they argued. Now the intelligent should consider this matter as follows: The gopis made the adulterine love with Sri Krishna, (is it to be maintained that) therefore they committed sin? Further, Mahádevaji and Rámachandraji married women of this world, namely, Párvatiji and Sitáji; and Sri Krishna married sixteen thousand princesses; (now) it would follow from the argument of these fools that they too acted improperly. If, as between God and this world, there has existed only the relation of father and children (as maintained by them), then Sri Krishna would not have married these maidens. But in God all relations abide. Both man and woman have sprung from God. Wherefore, with God, the two species of man and woman do not exist. Both these are the spirit of God. Consequently he is at play with his own spirit. In that no sin is incurred either by God or by (this) world. If any sin be committed (by such conduct) Sri Krishna would not have married the daughters of the kings. Thus (you) see how much contrary to the Sástras have they represented the subject, and confounded the ignorant.

"If there be any sin committed in entertaining the adulterine love towards God, then the most excellent Being would never have granted to the Vedas their request to entertain the adulterine love. The story is related by Brahmaji to Bhrigu Rishi in Brahád Váman Purán, which we now recount for the information of the people.

"Having heard the long offered prayers of the Vedas, the Lord spoke in a heavenly voice: 'Oh! you Traditions, I am pleased with

qualified like the gopís, nor could our souls have immediate connection with God.  We will illustrate this by an anecdote.  A certain woman was one evening going to her paramour.  At the same time a Fakír was sitting in her way praying to God.  But as it was dark she did not observe the Fakír, and accidentally struck him with her foot in passing, of which she was unconscious.  Just then the Fakír did not say anything; but when that woman returned, the Fakír addressed her thus: ' Oh hussy, you struck me with your foot and passed on; but then, my attention being fixed on God, I did not speak.'  Thereupon the woman replied thus: ' Had your attention been so fixed on God, you would not have been conscious of my having struck you with my foot.  See, owing to my contemptible love in my paramour, I did not observe you, and was not even conscious of having struck you with my foot.  Oh man, had your love really been in God, and your attention fixed upon him, how could you have known of my foot having struck you?'  No sooner had the Fakír heard this than he seized his own ear, and prostrated himself at her feet and said: ' Oh mother, what you have now observed is true.  From this day I have adopted you as my spiritual guide.'  In this anecdote also a lesson is drawn from love.  As Dattatraya Rishi derived instruction from twenty-four things, so should we draw the moral from the adulterine love."

We shall now see how the position of their sectaries is strengthened by a further citation from the works of Gokulnáthji, in a tract written by him in the Brijabháshá, entitled " Rasabhávana " (Love Faith).  It is as follows :—

"Thus came Krishna to be called a great charioteer (a warrior).  Similarly in this Pushti system (*i.e.* doctrines taught by Vallabháchárya), the most excellent Lord himself having conquered millions of Sváminijis in the Vrij devotees' forest of sexual enjoyment, came to be called a great charioteer.  Therefore he began to dance with Srí Sváminiji (the chief mistress) when he could not cope in dancing with Sváminiji, and was defeated in other sexual commerce.

"Thereafter the female companions (of Srí Sváminiji) having collected all her hair, and twisted it with a string, and tied it into a knot, wherefore the same should be regarded thus :—The string in the form of Srí Sváminiji, and the hair in the form of Krishna, having coupled together after enjoying in a contrary manner.

"There are maidens in the house of Jasodáji (mother of Krishṇa; they regard Krishṇa (who is now a child) as their husband. The maidens, therefore, prepare a swinging bed instead of a cradle, whereon they lay Krishṇa, and enjoy with him.

"The Lord plays with the followers of Pushti Márga (*i.e.* followers of Vallabháchárya). Such play is fearful to the opponents, whereas such play is poetic happiness (ecstacy) to devotees or initiated.

"The elephant's ivory toys are (symbolic) of the internal desires of Sri Sváminiji (the chief mistress). So when she goes into the forest Sri Sváminiji, by means of those toys, she enkindles (in him) the desire to amuse or enjoy like elephants.

"Sri Chandrávaliji, and Sri Yamunáji, and the virgins, and all the married women of Vrij, join together in an humble speech to Sri Sváminiji thus: 'Let us become your servants. We are not like you. We are your servants. How can we reach God in your presence? Still we are yours.' Having heard this humble speech, Sri Sváminiji addressed them us: 'Though sagacious and possessed of the sixty-four good qualities, yet she is guileless; though the foremost among the accomplished, yet she is guileless.' Wherefore Sri Sváminiji, seeing the humility of all the females, was pleased, and spoke thus: 'Your name is Vrij Ratna (*i.e.* the jewel of Vrij), for you are the jewel in Vrij; for there is no other love as the love of husband which you cherish towards God. Therefore you are the most excellent among the excellent. Therefore your love for him is greater than mine. Firstly, you keep yourselves always holy; you have no connection with any gopi. Even sons, husbands, etc., in this world are for show in the world's intercourse, but they have no connection with you. And, secondly, you are harmless. You are useful in your sexual commerce. You have no harm or jealousy in you. Thirdly, you are penetrated with the passion of love. Your passion is for the different modes of sexual commerce. You are very dear in my heart. In your coupled form, you act as our servants, and with affection wait on us. Therefore Sri Sváminiji. being pleased, tells God thus: 'Because they are dear to you, they are exceedingly dear to me. They should be therefore allotted separate groves, so that you might carry on sexual commerce separately with them.'

"Then Sri Sváminiji produces from her person millions of female companions. They were named Lalitá, Visákhá, and so forth. Those that were exceedingly skilful and beautiful in sexual com-

merce are called Lalitá; those that are very expert in the inverted
and other postures or positions (at sexual commerce) are called
Visákhás."

Here we have an exaltation of the Prem Ságar itself. Its
most voluptuous verses are less lascivious than this; and
"Love Faith" here mantles with its wings "the Ocean of
Love," hovering over the deep abyss.

A remarkable instance of how strongly these doctrines impress the imagination of young females is related by the same
Gokulnáthji, in his account of the two hundred and fifty-two
devotees of his father, Vithalnáthji, the Srí Gosáinji Maháraji.
It is written in Brijabháshá. The following is the story :—

"Now there was Ganga Kshatriáni, a female devotee of Srí
Gosáinji, who was living in that Máhában. This is an account of
her. The mother of that Gangábái was very beautiful, and she was
also very good looking, and she was in the bloom of her age. On
one occasion Gosáinji went to the Máhában and put up at the house
of a Vaishnava, and that Kshatriáni was then residing close to the
house of that Vaishnava. That Kshatriáni paid her homage to Srí
Gosáinji, whon she witnessed a very great beauty equal to a crore
of Kandrapas.* Feelings of lust were then excited in that Kshatriáni,
and she then became very much enamoured; so that she did not
feel easy without seeing Srí Gosáinji once daily. So she daily got
up and came to Srí Gokul, and having seen Srí Gosáinji, she used
then to go to her house ; and she constantly said in her mind, 'Were
I to meet him in a solitary or private place, the wishes of my heart
would be fulfilled.' But she could not find an opportunity. Then
one day that Kshatriáni thought in her mind, ' When Srí Gosáinji
goes to the privy I will go there.' So one day that Kshatriáni remained concealed in the privy, and afterwards Srí Gosáinji went to
the privy, when that Kshatriáni said, "Maháráj, pray fulfil the wishes
which I have in my heart.' But Srí Gosáinji refused, saying, 'I do
not know anything about that matter.' That Kshatriáni then became
very obstinate, when Srí Gosáinji, getting angry, said, "Do not be
obstinate, and the wishes of your heart will now be fulfilled without
your leaving your house. These are my prophetic words, and therefore you may go home.' That Kshatriáni, having heard these words

* Kandrapa is a god of love.

of Sri Gosáinji, went away. Afterwards one day, when that Kshatriáni was asleep, she dreamed a dream in her sleep that she had connection with Sri Gosáinji, and from that very day that Kshatriáni was in the family way. Afterwards, when the time of pregnancy was completed, she was delivered of a daughter. She was extremely beautiful, and was a fountain of good qualities. She was then named Gangábai. Then that girl grew up; after which she was caused to tell her name to Sri Gosáinji.'

The next extract will show what care the Mahárájas take to free from blame the immoral practices which their doctrines inculcate. It is a story of adultery between two low persons, expiated in blood, but rewarded by a re-birth in a very high social position.

"A narrative related first of all by Sri Áchárysji with his own mouth to the Vaishnavas on a certain occasion, and afterwards related by Sri Gopináthji to the Vaishnavas. There was a Bhil and a Bhilan, being two persons, husband and wife. They used to go to a jungle and to bring firewood daily, and they used to maintain themselves by selling the wood. There was another Bhil, who was also in the habit of going to the same jungle to fetch wood, and an intimacy then rose between the wife of the one Bhil and the other Bhil. At first the two persons, husband and wife used to go together for wood. She then fell in love with the other man. Afterwards that woman commenced going for wood to another jungle with the other or (stranger) man, with whom she had contracted an intimacy. So the woman went with him to a jungle, and there was a temple of God in a certain spot in that jungle. The two persons having gone there used to sweep and clean the temple, and then rest themselves there. They did so for several days, when, being overpowered with love, they took to singing. They then both got up from that place and went to their respective houses. Afterwards some one came and told the husband of the woman that his wife lived, or was in love, with such and such a man, and that those two persons were in the habit of going to such and such a place in such and such a jungle. Afterwards, one day, the husband of the woman followed his wife to the jungle. The two persons went first, and having gone there they swept and cleared the spot all around the place of God that was there, and then sat there in happiness. The husband of the woman then witnessed, while standing there, all the acts of the two persons, and when the two persons had completed their worldly (or carnal) pleasures, the husband of the woman killed them both on the spot. The angels of Dharmarája then came for the two persons, and immediately after them came the angels of Vishṇu; when the angels of Vishṇu said to the angels of Yam, 'Why have you come here? Sri Thákurji (God) has conferred on them the best place (in the heaven), and these two persons will moreover obtain better and a more desirable place than this (in the heaven).' The angels of Vishṇu then took the two persons with them, and having gone there they made them stand before Sri Thákurji (God). When Sri Thákurji told the two persons to ask for anything they liked; they then, having folded their hands together (in a suppliant manner), made the following representation :—'Maháráj, we have committed a very mean act; what is the cause of your showing so great a regard towards us?' When the angels of Vishṇu told them as follows :—'It is true you two persons have committed a mean act, but you cleaned the temple of (God) and Sri Thákurji (God) has favorably accepted the service performed by you; and therefore you both have now obtained the best place (in the heaven). Having therefore become pleased with you, I tell you two persons that you may ask (for anything you like).' The two persons then said, 'Maháráj, if you are pleased with us, and wish to confer a favour, then we pray that we may be born in the mortal world, and that we, having become husband and wife, may serve you. Pray favour us with a compliance with this (request).' When Sri Thákurji (God) said, 'Go, your wishes will be fulfilled.' Then the two persons became incarnate in this world. The man was born a son of a Rájá, and the woman was born a daughter of a Rájá."

We are heartily glad we are approaching the termination of this odious subject, for the next extract will close the series. We have considered it necessary to make these quotations in order fully to elucidate the reprehensible tendencies of the doctrines of these sectaries in reference to "adulterine love." Perhaps, without such positive and certain proofs obtained from the Mahárájas themselves, our readers might have suspected us of misrepresenting or exaggerating the foul practices of these priests. Here, however, the public has the "plain unvarnished tale" of their hideous immorality.

The following extract suggests some remarks upon the strange infatuation of a people who might evidently be made pure and good if the delusion which corrupts them could be removed. The writer evidently had a heart to feel the virtue of the Banian, although not to loathe the perverting doctrines of his sect. The translation is from a book in Brija-bháshá, containing the account of the eighty-four Vaishnavas.

"A narrative of Krishnadás Brahmin, a devotee of Sri Áchárуaji, the great lord. Krishnadás was living in a village: he was a worshipper of Bhagvant (God). There were five or ten Vaishnavas who, on one occasion, were going to Ádel for the purpose of paying their homage to Sri Áchárуaji, the great lord. They came to the house of Krishnadás. At that time Krishnadás was not at home: he had gone out on some business, and the wife of Krishnadás was at home. When the Vaishnavas came to the village, Sri Krishnadás had gone out to some other village. After that she went inside the house and began to consider as to what she should do now. She then recollected that Banian Daimaro always said to her that she should meet him, and that he would give her what she might ask for. So she said to herself, 'I will fetch provisions and other articles from his shop to-day, and will tell him, I will meet you to-day; give me the provisions and other articles that I require.' Having made this determination, she set out, went to his shop, and having given a promise to him, the woman brought all the provisions and other articles, and having come home, prepared the dinner, and presented an offering of it to Sri Thákurji (God); and having removed the offering at the due time, she caused the Vaishnavas to feast on the blessed food, of which the Vaishnavas partook in good style. After that Krishnadás came home in the evening, met all the Vaishnavas, and after saluting them, he entered his house and asked his wife what the news was, and whether she had given food to the Vaishnavas. She replied that she had given them food. Then Krishnadás inquired whence she had got the provisions and other articles, when the woman related to him all that had taken place: Krishnadás was thereupon much pleased with his wife. Afterwards the husband and wife both jointly partook of the blessed food, and Krishnadás then went to the Vaishnavas and passed the whole night in talking of the praise of God. When it was morning, Krishnadás having dispatched all the Vaishnavas, they walked away, and Krishṇadás went with them for a short distance to see them off. Afterwards he came home, presented the food offering to Śri Thákurji (God), and then, having removed it, as usual he covered it up and placed it aside. When Krishnádas returned home in the evening, both the husband and the wife jointly partook of the blessed food. Krishṇadás then said to his wife, 'You gave a promise yesterday to the Banian, and the Banian must be expecting you, and therefore the promise given to him must be fulfilled.' The wife thereupon, having rubbed her body with an ointment, and bathed herself, and having ornaments, as are usual among the women, she set out. It was the rainy season, and it had rained that day, and there was mud on the road, in consequence whereof Krishṇadás said, 'If you place yourself on my shoulder I will convey you there and return, otherwise your feet will be soiled with mud, as there is a great deal of mud on the road; and if your feet should get soiled, the Banian would treat you with disrespect.' Krishṇadás thereupon placed his wife on his shoulder, and put her down near the shop of the Banian, when the woman called out to the Banian and asked him to open the door. The Banian then opened the door and took the woman inside, and then brought her some water to wash her feet with, when the woman said to the Banian, ' My feet are not soiled with mud.' The Banian then said, ' There is a great deal of mud on the road, and how is it that your feet are free from it?' Then the woman said to the Banian, ' You had better proceed with your business;' when the Banian said, ' You must tell me the circumstance.' The woman then said to the Banian, ' My husband placed me on his shoulder, brought me here, and went away.' On hearing the account, the Banian was struck with wonder, and he questioned her on the whole subject, and asked the cause of it, and requested her to tell him all, when the woman related to him all that had occurred. On hearing it the Banian thought of himself with contempt, and said, ' Happy is your life whose mind is so pure;' and having put his hands together in a suppliant manner, he saluted her, and said, ' Pardon me my offence: regard me with kindness; you are my sister.' "

We have thus terminated our account of the Mahárâj doctrines. We think it cannot be read without exciting indignation against the priesthood who promulgate these immoralities; and perhaps not without provoking pity and contempt for those who submit to their domination. We hope that the full exhibition of these enormities made in the extracts already given, and in the next following chapters, will help towards the eradication of a vile and debasing superstition. If this work should at all contribute to that good end, we shall have reaped a rich reward.

We shall conclude this chapter with a list of the various books, written in Brijabháshá language, which are considered as authorities by the sect. The first thirty-nine are translations from the Sanskrit, with commentaries, and the rest are original, in Brijabháshá language :

| | | | |
|---|---|---|---|
| 1. Sarvottam. | 25. Sarn-áshtaka. |
| 2. Vallabh-áshtaka. | 26. Námávali-ácháraji. |
| 3. Krishna-premámrita. | 27. Bhujanga-práyn-áshtaka. |
| 4. Vithalesha-ratna-vivarna. | 28. Námávali Gusáiji. |
| 5. Yamun-áshtaka. | 29. Siddhánta-bhávaná. |
| 6. Bála-bhodha. | 30. Siddhánta-rahasya. |
| 7. Siddhánta-muktávali. | 31. Virodha-lakshna. |
| 8. Nava-ratna. | 32. Shrinagára-rasamandala. |
| 9. Antahkarana-prabhodha. | 33. Vaidhavallabha. |
| 10. Viveka-dhairá-shraya. | 34. Agni-kumára. |
| 11. Krishná-shraya. | 35. Sharana-upadesha. |
| 12. Chatura-śloki. | 36. Rasasindhu. |
| 13. Bhakti-vardhani. | 37. Kalpa-druma. |
| 14. Jalabheda. | 38. Málá-prasanga. |
| 15. Padeáni. | 39. Chita-prabhodha. |
| 16. Saniása-nirnaya. | 40. Pushti-dradha-váratá. |
| 17. Nirodha-laxana. | 41. Dwádasa-kunja. |
| 18. Sevá-fala. | 42. Pavitrá-mandala. |
| 19. Śikshá-patra. | 43. Purnamási. |
| 20. Pushti-pravaha-maryádá. | 44. Nitya-sevá-prakára. |
| 21. Gokul-áshtaka. | 45. Rasa-bhávaná. |
| 22. Madhur-áshtaka. | 46. Vallabh-ákhiána. |
| 23. Nin-áshtaka. | 47. Dhola. |
| 24. Janmavaifal-áshtaka. | 48. Nija-váratá. |

49. Chorási-váratá.
50. Baso-bhávaná-váratá
51. Nitya-pada.
52. Shriji-prágata.
53. Charitra-sahita-váratá.
54. Gusáiji-prágata.
55. Ashtakáviya.
56. Vanshávali.
57. Vanayátrá.
58. Lílá-bhávaná.
59. Svarupa-bhávaná.
60. Guru-seva.
61. Chitavana.

62. Sevá-prakára.
63. Múla-purusha.
64. Sata-bálaka-charitra..
65. Yamunáji-pada.
66. Vachanámrita.
67. Pushti-márga-siddhánta.
68. Dasa-marama.
69. Vaishnava-batrisa-laxana.
70. Chorási-sikshá.
71. Sadasatha-prádha. [kruta.
72. Dwárkesha-krata-nita-
73. Áchárji-prágata.
74. Otsava-pada.

# CHAPTER VI.

## WORSHIP AND PSALMODY.

THE doctrines of the Mahárájas we have laid before our readers in the last chapter. Of their mode of worship we have now to treat. The present ceremonial or ritual has of course been the growth of time, being formed, or added to as circumstances have occurred, or the prompting desires of the priests may have suggested. We shall endeavour to give as clear and distinct a statement as is practicable, premising that much of the information contained in this chapter is derived from the works of Mr. H. H. Wilson, and from the oral testimony adduced upon oath in the course of the trial for libel, as well as from other sources of a true and unimpeachable character. We hope to lay before our readers a complete picture, as graphical as such collective means will enable us to paint, so as to sustain the judgment we shall have to pronounce, after deliberately summing up the facts, in the few concluding words of this chapter.

A Vallabhácháryan temple consists of three successive compartments. The central one is larger and more open than the other two, being intended for the accommodation of the numerous worshippers who daily throng there. Of the remaining two, one is the residence of the Maháráj, and the other is dedicated to the worship of the image of Krishna.

The temples are numerous all over India, especially at Mathurá and Bríndában, In Benares there are two very celebrated and wealthy temples, one of which is dedicated to

Krishna under the name of Lálji, and the other to the same
god under the name of Purushottamji.  Those of Jagannáth
and Dwáriká are also particularly venerated; but the most
celebrated of these establishments is that at Śri Náthadwár,
in Mewár.  "The image is said to have transported itself
thither from Mathurá, when Aurangzeb ordered the temple
it stood in to be destroyed.  The present shrine is modern,
but very richly endowed, and the high priest, a descendant
of Gokulnáthji, is a man of great wealth and importance."*

The image of Thákurji, or the idol, in the different
temples, is either of stone or brass, and represents Krishna
in various attitudes, corresponding to those which he is supposed to have assumed in the several periods of his earthly
existence, either when performing uncommon feats or miracles,
or living at particular places, or engaged in any peculiarly
interesting scenes.  Each of these is worshipped under a
different name.  That of Śri Náthji, being the most important and most honoured, is at Náthadwár.  Krishna is
here represented as a little boy in the act of supporting the
mountain Govardhan on his little finger, to shelter his play-
mates from a heavy shower of rain which had suddenly
overtaken them while at play.  This image is always splendidly dressed, and richly decorated with ornaments, which
are often of the value of several thousand pounds.

Vallabháchárya, the founder of the sect, is said to have
distributed among his disciples more than thirty images,
under various forms and names.  These are still extant, and
held in more reverence than modern ones; and the Mahárájas, too, who possess them, are in consequence more respected than the other members of their fraternity.  But of
the thirty-five, the seven of *Navanita-priyáji* (literally, he
who is fond of fresh butter), *Mathureshji, Vithalnáthji, Dwá-
rikánáthji, Gokulanáthji, Gokulachandramáji* (the moon of

* H. H. Wilson's Works.

GOKULACHANDRAMAJI     MATHURESHJI

GOKULANATHJI     SHRI NATHJI     MADANAMOHANJI

DWARIKANATHJI     VITHALNATHJI

NAVANITA-PRIYAJI

Gokula), and *Madanamohanji* (the Lord of Lust-illusion)—these were procured by the seven grandsons of Vallabhá-chárya, each having one for himself, and are held in even greater reverence. The five first are now at Śri Náthadwár, Kottá, Kanoja, Kánkroli, and Gokula respectively, and the the two last at Jaypora. The Mahárájas are so covetous of possessing these, as well as the others distributed by the Vallabháchárya, that instances are related of their having endeavoured to possess themselves .of them by the meanest of actions. One of them, named Girdharji, was, about thirty-five years ago, convicted of having stolen one from a Vaish-ṇava at Damaṇ. The images are sometimes so small and overloaded with ornaments, that the votaries can see nothing but their lustrous embellishments, which have an attraction of their own, apart from that of the image.

The worship of the images is very sedulously performed, the most devoted homage being paid to them at fixed periods, eight times every day. There are also seasonal festivals, when they are worshipped with more ceremony. On these occasions the image is profusely decorated, and especially in the spring, when it is beautifully adorned with flowers arranged with much taste. According to the nature of the festival, the image is made to sit on a seat, or is placed in a cradle, or is so disposed as to recline in a swing. The cradles and swings and seats are either of wood or of brass or silver. Crowds swarm to the temples on these occasions, flocking to see the Thákurji in all his glory. At these times the Mahárájas ostentatiously decorate themselves in their gayest attire, that they may attract the attention of female devotees. The following are the eight regular daily services.*

1. "*Mangalá*, the morning levee: the image being washed and dressed, is taken from the couch, where it is supposed to

---

* In the intervals, or when no particular festival is being celebrated, that part of the temple in which the idol is placed is closed, and the deity is invisible.

have slept during the night, and placed upon a seat, about half an hour after (and during winter about three hours before) sunrise: slight refreshments are then presented to it, with betel and *pán*. Lamps are generally kept burning during this ceremony.

2. "*Śringára :* the image having been anointed and perfumed with oil, camphor, and sandal, and splendidly attired, now holds its public court : this takes place about an hour and a half after the preceding, or when four *gharis* of the day have elapsed.

3. "*Gwála :* the image is now visited, preparatory to its going out to attend the cattle along with the cowherd : this ceremony is held about forty-eight minutes after the last, or when six *gharis* have elapsed.

4. "*Rája-Bhóga*, held at mid-day, when Krishṇa is supposed to come in from the pastures and dine : all sorts of delicacies are placed before the image, and both these and other articles of food, dressed by the ministers of the temples, are distributed to the numerous votaries present, and not unfrequently sent to the dwellings of worshippers of rank and consequence.

5. "*Utthápaṇ :* the calling up, or summoning of the god from his siesta : this takes place at six *gharis*, or between two and three hours before sunset.

6. "*Bhóga :* the afternoon meal, about half an hour after the preceding.

7. "*Sandhyá*, about sunset : the evening toilet of the image, when the ornaments of the day are taken off, and fresh unguents and perfumes applied.

8. "*Shayan*, retiring to repose : the image, about seven in the evening, is placed upon a bed, refreshments and water in proper vases, together with the betel box and its appurtenances, are left near it, when the votaries retire, and the temple is shut till the ensuing morning."*

* H. H. Wilson's Works.

For the first of these services, in winter, the temple is opened at four o'clock in the morning, when it is quite dark, to give an opportunity to the Maháráj to communicate with his favourite female devotees, who much frequent it at this time. Upon all these occasions the ceremony is much the same, consisting of little more than waving a light, and presenting flowers, perfumes, and food to the image by the priests. At certain seasons the ceremony also includes rocking the swing or cradle of the image, or throwing *gulál* (red powder) over it. The votaries, on beholding the image or its lustrous embellishments, do nothing but repeat the name of the idol or Thákurji several times, with a variety of protestations and obeisances. This is the worship. There is no established ritual for general use, nor any prescribed form of worship.

Previously to the opening of the division of the temple where the image of the idol is placed, the Maháráj takes his stand near the image. Here, after the entrance of the votaries, he occasionally swings the image, or waves before it a small metallic lamp, in which burns a light, fed by clarified butter. The Vaishnavas, with their wives and daughters, having previously assembled in the passage, the door is opened, and the crowd rush to enter, crying out *Jaya! Jaya!* to prevent the doors being closed. The noise and confusion are immense. No time must be lost, for in ten or twenty minutes the doors are again closed. It is impossible all can get into the small room at once, and the weaker of the crowd have to await their turn to enter. To accelerate the devotions of those who have got in, and to induce them to make room for other devotees, who are anxiously waiting outside, one of the guardians of the temple mounts upon a rail, with a thick cord in his hand, to whip them along. Many of the devotees receive a very severe beating; and it has even happened that an eye has been lost, or other severe and permanent injuries inflicted. It is customary for these guardians of the temple to receive a considerable bribe in money to stay them from inflicting this castigation upon persons who can afford to be thus mulcted. But in the event of this douceur not being forthcoming, either from incapacity or unwillingness, the malice of the guardians is exasperated, and they are unmerciful in the application of the cord.

During the four periods of worship in the afternoon, females visit the temples in large numbers; and at these times the crush is fearful and shameful, for males and females are intermixed, and many men who have intruded for vicious and immoral purposes, assault the modesty of females with impunity. The crowd is so dense that, on extraordinary occasions, females are totally denuded of their slight and loose clothing in the crush. The practice, therefore, of permitting men and women to associate promiscuously in the room where the idol is worshipped is highly objectionable. Frequent applications have been made to the Mahárájas to put a stop to these indecent proceedings, but they appear to sanction them by their indifference.

The first duty of the Vaishṇavas who come to worship the image is to go to the Maháráj, who is found seated on a raised couch, and to prostrate themselves at his feet. The worshippers place their fingers on the toes of the Maháráj, and then apply them to their eyes. When females touch his toes, the Maháráj, who may have been attracted by one of them in particular, to indicate that he wishes for a further interview, presses her hand, and thus gives her the sign of solicitation. This is considered a high and distinguishing honour: it is fully understood and appreciated, and the favour is readily reciprocated. The parties avail themselves of the first opportunity to carry their purpose into effect, and we shall shortly see how readily such an opportunity is obtained. When it is understood that this distinction has a consecrating force, the excuse for infatuated compliance is at once found.

Upon the door of the temple being opened, the musicians and songsters placed there commence a succession of lascivious chaunts, descriptive of Krishna's amorous sport with the gopis. These choristers and musicians occupy a place opposite the image and the Maháráj, but behind the worshippers who throng through the open intervening space. The mode of solicitation by the Maháráj during this worship is the throwing upon the votaries of *gulál*, a red powder, made of a certain wood ground down; but this is done only in the spring and upon high festivals. In throwing this powder, which is often made up into small balls, the Maháráj aims chiefly at the breasts of the females. It is also customary for him to project a yellow extract obtained from flowers, from a syringe, at the worshippers, and particularly at the females.

Besides the adoration of the image, worship is performed to the Maháráj himself. There are generally eight or ten Mahárájas in Bombay, each having a separate temple, the dimensions of which vary according to the means and influence of the high priest. In one of the apartments of his residence, the Maháráj, during the time that divine honours are paid to him, seats himself on a raised seat. The Bháttiás, the Baniás, the Loháñás, the Multánis, and other persons, are the followers of his religion, and are known as *sevakas*, or servants. All of them, rich and poor, adore him by saluting his feet; and for a short time after these devotions, the rich or influential are accommodated in the hall, while persons of moderate means are left to shift for themselves in a large public room or courtyard. One apartment of the building known as the *zanána-kháná* (seraglio) is occupied by the Maháráj's wife and daughters, who never appear in the sight of men: their residence is considered sacred, and only the *sevakis* (female worshippers) have permission to enter it.

Next to the Maháráj himself, his wife (*vahuji*) and daughter (*betiji*) receive homage in the *zanána-kháná* from his female devotees.

The Maháráj can be otherwise worshipped at all hours of the day; that is to say, in the intervals of the worship of the idol, at which times his presence is required adjacent to the image of the god. It is at these times of his separate worship in his own residence that females are presented with the facile opportunity of showing their appreciation of the high honour of the selection he has made of them by throwing *gulál*, pressing their hands, or projecting on their breasts the yellow liquid extract of flowers.

Up to eight or nine o'clock every morning the Maháráj is engaged in performing ablutions and saying prayers, the rest of the day being whiled away at meals, in conversation, in repose, and in pleasure. After his meals, he seeks the privacy of his bedroom, which adjoins the *zanána-kháná*, and except on any urgent business—for instance, that of attending the worship of the idol—he does not leave this apartment until three or four o'clock in the afternoon. During the Utthápan period of worship, which begins at two p.m., the wives and daughters of the Vaishnavas visit the wife and daughters of the Maháráj in the *zanána-kháná*, from whence some of them proceed with presents of fruits, milk (in silver goblets), and other things, to the Maháráj's bedroom; and the most fortunate of them, according to their notions, comes out purer than before. If, while the Maháráj is in the sitting-room speaking to his followers, a female happens to come to the temple with her present of fruits, or whatever else it may be, he immediately retires into the *zanána-kháná*, and there accepts the present from her, and ministers to her lust.

The dust on which the Maháráj has walked is eaten by the votaries. Even his very wooden shoes are worshipped, as is also his *gádi* or seat. His feet are champooed, he is decorated with precious ornaments, he is frequently bathed by his votaries in saffron and milk : money and many precious articles are presented at his feet with humiliating prostrations, and the worship is directed not only to the Mahárájas personally but to their very pictures.

In the morning, when the Maháráj is at his ablutions, a number of Vaishṇavas collect at a short distance ; and as he stands up to wipe his body, one of the Vaishṇavas, or ministers of the temple, approaches him with reverence, takes into a vessel the water dropping from his *dhotar* (the cloth covering the lower part of his body). This dirty impure water is esteemed to be of high virtue, and is distributed among all present at the temple, who drink it with feelings of pride and satisfaction ! What remains is reserved for some hours for the purification of absent Vaishṇavas. The remnants of the Maháráj's meals, called *juhtan*, are preserved, being considered very precious, and can be had on a formal application by any Vaishṇavas who desire to eat them. In private banquets and caste feasts, given with the Maháráj's permission, these impure remnants are first served, and are eaten as though they were ambrosia ! The *pán-sopári* (leaf and betelnut) which the Maháráj throws out after chewing, is called *ogár*, and is collected and preserved to be distributed to males and females, who take a great pleasure in chewing it over again.

In the month of Shrávaṇ, the Maháráj takes delight in . sitting on the *hindolá* (a sort of swing), when his male and female followers move it backwards and forwards with their hands. This privilege of swinging his Holiness is purchased with presents to him. At the time of the Holi holidays (the saturnalia of the Hindus), the Maháráj stands in front of the temple and permits his followers to hail him with *gulál* (red powder). Some of the Mahárájas on these occasions throw the *gulál* in return on some especial favourite female worshipper, and indulge publicly in acts of impropriety and indecency.

The other occupations and amusements of the Mahárájas consist in social intercourse, in riding about and driving in their carriages, and in talking of the amorous sports of Krishṇa. In the intervals of their official priestly duties, they have recourse to every variety of amusement and pleasure; and not a few of them rejoice exceedingly in displaying indecent pictures to their female devotees, to excite them to amorous sports. The Mahárájas also undertake the settlement of caste disputes; they are usually solicited to be arbitrators in cases where the right of property is contested, and generally they subtly contrive that but very little of it shall come into the possession of the litigants. They are very great epicures, and consummate judges of every species of delicacy and good living, several of them indulging excessively in intoxicating drugs, such as *bháng* and opium. In the evening they are usually invited to the houses of the wealthy Vaishṇavas, whither they resort sumptuously attired, and fragrant with attar of roses and other luscious perfumes, in order that they may be the more attractive to those with whom they come in contact. Their visits are always of a semi-religious character; and therefore, upon these occasions, wives and daughters of the Vaishṇavas whom a Maháráj thus honours by visiting, entertain him with the songs which may be characterised as the psalmody of their religion. Ten or twenty minutes after he has taken his seat, all the members and friends of the family join in applying to him odoriferous stuffs, in offering him wreaths of flowers, in waving a light round him, in presenting him with money, and in prostrating themselves at his feet.

" The hymns, or sacred songs of a sect, are generally the most fervid exposition of their religious feelings. The hymns sung by the women of the Vallabháchárya sect, in honour of the Mahárájas and in their presence, are certainly no exception to this general rule. They are passionate with all the passions of the East, erotic pantings for fruition of a lover who is also a god. As it is said of the *gopis* in the *Vishnu Puránₐ*, 'every instant without Krishṇa they count a myriad of years, and, forbidden by fathers, husbands, brothers, they go forth at night to sport with Krishṇa, the object of their love,' so these hymns, sung at this day by the wives and daughters of the Vallabháchár․yans to their Mahárájas, express the most unbridled desire, the most impatient longing, for the enjoyments of adulterine love.'' *

These females yield themselves unhesitatingly to the ignoble task of exciting the gross passions of these priests, for whose pleasure, and to stimulate whose lusts, they, upon these visits, and also on festive occasions, sing songs which we quote as specimens of the lascivious poetry in which the Mahárájas find pleasure.

મોહન મલપતા ઘેર આવ્યા રે ॥
મેંતો લધને મોતીડે વધાવ્યા રે ॥
વાહલે મારે કરણની દૃષ્ટે જોઉં રે ॥
ખાધ મારે એ વર સુ મન મોહું રે ॥
પડ્યું મારે નંદના કુવર સાથે પાનુ રે ॥
હવે હું તો કેમ કરી રાખીશ છાંનુ રે ॥
દરી જન કેહવું હોય તે કેહેજો રે ॥
વાહલા મારા ૨દય કમળ વચે રહેજો રે ॥

[TRANSLATION OF THE ABOVE.]

Mohan merrily came to [my] house,
With pearls [by throwing them over him] I welcomed him ;
My beloved one looked with an affectionate eye :
O sister ! of this husband my heart is enamoured ;
[To marry] the son of Nanda I am destined ;
And how can I now conceal it ?
Let the wicked say what they may,
Darling ! let my heart be thy dwelling place.

* Judgment of Sir Joseph Arnould.

અતીરે ઉલટ ઘણો આવે મારે અંગે ॥
સામ સુંદર વર બેઠા છે સંગે ॥ ૧ ॥
મુખકું જોયા વના પાણી ન પીઉ રે ॥
રસીક સુંદર વર જોઈ જોઈ જીવું રે ॥ ૨ ॥
મુજને ન વારીશ માહારી રે માડી ॥
દરશાણ કરવાને જઈશ દાહડી ॥ ૩ ॥
સગપણ તો સાંમળીયાનું સાચું ॥
ખાકી સરવે દીસેછે કાચું ॥ ૪ ॥
કેહસે તેને કેહવારે દેશું ॥
આપણ સરવે સાંભળી લેશું ॥ ૫ ॥

[TRANSLATION OF THE ABOVE.]

An excitement, extreme and great, in my body is created;
The azure-coloured beauteous husband with me is sitting.    1
Without seeing [his] beauteous face, even water I will not drink;
The amorous and beauteous husband, by seeing oft and oft I'll live.  2
Restrain me not, Oh! my mother,
To pay my homage to him, daily I will go.    3
As to the connectionship, that of the Sávalyá* is the only true one
[And] all others appear to be but imperfect.    4
He who tells may tell, we will permit to do so,
And to them [with indifference] we shall listen.    5

પરદેશ જઈઓતો વલ્લભકુળ વેહેલા આવજો જો ॥
અમ્ભજાને સંદેશા કાહવજો જો ॥ પરદેશ૦ ॥ ૧ ॥
આપણી આજ્ઞાને આધીન અમે છઈએ જો ॥
આપે શરણે લીધાં અમને ચીત ધરીજો ॥ પરદેશ૦ ॥ ૨ ॥
સુંદર દ્રષ્ટી દયાળુ અમ ઉપર કરીજો ॥
તેથી તન મન લીધાં અમારાં હરીજો ॥ પરદેશ૦ ॥ ૩ ॥
આપ સાર મેં લોક લાજ નવ ધરીજો ॥
મુને આપના ચરણની ઈછા ઘણીજો ॥ પરદેશ૦ ॥ ૪ ॥
આવી વીનતી કરેછે દાસી ઘણી જો ॥
વેલા આવશો તો દાસી થેરો રાજી જો ॥ ૫ ॥

* An appellation of Krishṇa.

[TRANSLATION OF THE ABOVE.]

If to foreign lands you, the descendants of Vallabha, should go,
> Soon do you return.

And to [us] gentle women messages do you send.
> If to foreign lands. 1

To your commands obedient we are,
Us, the suppliant, you have accepted with all your heart.
> If to foreign lands. 2

A pleasant look, you the compassionate, by casting upon us,
Of our bodies and hearts have deprived us.
> If to foreign lands. 3

For your sake the sense of public shame I have not entertained,
A great desire I entertain for your feet.
> If to foreign lands. 4

Many such intreaties [your] female slaves are making,
If soon you will return, pleased will become [your] female slaves. 5

વલભકુળ છે કામણ ગારા કાનજે ॥
કામણીઆં કીધાંરે વ્રજની વાટમાં રે લોલ ॥ ૧ ॥
જેને એની સુખડું પુનમ ચંદ્ર જો ॥
અણીઆરી આંખેરે મનડાં મોહી લીધાંરે લોલ ॥ ૨ ॥
એ વાહલાની પાસે થઈને દાસી જો ॥
લોકોની લાજથી હવે હું નથી ખીહવાનીરે લોલ ॥ ૩ ॥
હવે એહની મેંથી ઘરનાં કામ ન થાયરે ॥
વાહલાને દેખીને મનડા મોહી રહાંરે લોલ ॥ ૪ ॥
વલભકુળ છે કામણ ગારા કાન જો ॥
કરડાને ઠણુંકેરે મનડા હરી ગયાંરે લોલ ॥ ૫ ॥
આપ છો પરમેશ્વર સરૂપ જો ॥
વલભ વર વરીને હું અતી પ્રેમથી રે લોલ ॥ ૬ ॥
વલભ વરને શરણે સુખીઆં થાશુરે ॥
તેઓની સંગતથી વઈકુંઠ પાંમસું રે લોલ ॥ ૭ ॥

[TRANSLATION OF THE ABOVE.]

The descendant of Vallabha is the amorous Kánú,
Enamoured, he has made [us], in the roads of Vraj.
> Bowing down? 1

See, sisters, the full moon-like face,
With his sharp eyes my heart he has enticed and attracted.

Bowing down ?   2

To that dear [soul] having become a female slave,
The public shame I will now no longer fear.

Bowing down ?   3

Now, sisters, the household affairs I cannot perform,
By seeing the dear [soul] my heart has become enticed.

Bowing down ?   4

A descendant of Vallabha is the amorous Káná,
The sound of the jingling of [his] toe-rings has deprived me of my
     heart.

Bowing down ?   5

The very personification of God you are,
Having married [or accepted] the Vallabha husband with extreme love.

Bowing down ?   6

By our submitting to the Vallabha husband, happy we shall become
By his association, the Vaikuntha* we shall obtain.          ·

Bowing down ?   7

મહેલે પધારો માહરાજ ॥ માણીગર મહેલે પધારો ॥
વાહલ વધારો વ્રજ રાજ ॥ માણીગર મહેલે પધારો ॥ટેક॥
કરી રાખીછે એકલી, ઘણા દીવસની ગોઠ ॥
રાજ મળે તો શ્રીજીએ, આવી રહીછે મારે ઓઠ ॥ માણી ॥
હું સરખી બહુ આપને, મારે તો એક આપ ॥
રેહવાતું નથી રાજવીન, કોને કહું પરીતાપ ॥ માણી ॥
સેજ સમારી ફુલડે, આનંદ ઉર ન સમાય ॥
પ્રાણજીવન તાંહાં પોઢયા, દાસી પલોટે પાય ॥ માણી ॥
હું પણ દાસી રાવલી, બાંહે અરબાની બાજ,
જોબન લેહેરે જાયછે, માનો મારા રાજ ॥ માણી ॥
પ્રીતમ દાસ દયા તણા, શ્રી વ્રજ રાજ કુમાર ॥
ઘણા દીવસની હાંસછે, પુરો પ્રાણ આધાર ॥ માણી ॥

[TRANSLATION OF THE ABOVE.]

May it please thee to visit my palace, lord;
Welcome be thou to my palace, charming lord.
Increase, O king of Vraj ! thy love [to me];

Welcome be thou to my palace, etc.

* The paradise of Vishṇu.

Many a story, and accumulated secrets
Of the heart I have to relate;
I shall narrate them, if you but meet [me],
Overflowed has it up to my lips.
Welcome be thou, etc.

You have many like myself,
But you are the only one I have;
I cannot live without you, my lord,
To whom shall I express my pangs?
Welcome be thou, etc.

Bespread with flowers is the bed,
The heart cannot keep the joy within itself:
Life-nourisher, thou liest there;
Thy servants shampoo thy feet.
Welcome be thou, etc.

Similarly I am also thy humble servant.
As thou hast held my arm, keep thou thy pledge:
The bloom of my youth is fading away;
Believe, my Lord, what I say.
Welcome be thou, etc.

Gallant of [your] slave Dayá,
Prince of Vraj, bestower of Life,
Satisfy the long felt desire;
Welcome be thou to my palace, charming Lord.

વ્રજના જીવણ કરે વીનતી, શ્રી વલભનંદ
શ્રી ગોકુલચંદ, વેગે તે આંખ્ય મોકલો ॥
તમારા દરશાણ વીના શ્રી વલભ રે, કોહો જી કેમ રહેવાય
મનડાં તે રાખ્યા કેમ રેહ, નૈણ નીર ભરાય ॥ વ્રજ૦ ॥
અરજ સુણો રે આદર કરી રે, શ્રી જમનાજી રે માય
બ્રેહ તણા દુખ દોહિલાં, કહો જી કેમ રહેવાય ॥ વ્રજ૦ ॥
દૂર રહે કેમ ચાલશે રે, કહો જી કાંહની રીત
આજ કાલનું કોઈ નહીં, છે જી પૂર્વની પ્રીત ॥ વ્રજ૦ ॥
હગી હૈયામાં રાખજને, રે છે પૂર્વ સ્નેહ
દયા કરો દીનાનાથજી, નહીતર તજશું આ દેહ ॥ વ્રજ૦ ॥

8

વ્રજ માલતી વાસ માંચુ, સદા રેહ શ્રી ગોકુલ ગામ
કાલીંદ્રાને કાંઠડે, શ્રી ઠકરાણી ઘાટ ॥ વ્રજ૦ ॥
નેણા ભરી કાહરે નીરખ્ચુ. શ્રી ઠકરાણી ઘાટ
અંતરમાં ઇચ્છા ઘણી, જોહુંછું વ્રજની વાટ ॥ વ્રજ૦ ॥
અમ્મે સુકાઇને તજ થયાં, રે શ્રી હલધર વીર ॥
ધીરજ રાખી નજ રેહે, ભરી ભરી આવેછે નીર ॥ વ્રજ૦ ॥
રાંક ઉપર શીયા રરાણા રે, પ્રભુ દીન દયાલ
દાસી જાણી પોતાતણી, કરજો સેવકીનો સંભાલ ॥ વ્રજ૦ ॥

[TRANSLATION OF THE ABOVE.]

O life of Vraj ! I pray thee,
Illustrious *beloved one* [*source of*] *pleasure*, Moon of Gokul,
An invitation send with speed.
Without seeing thee, O illustrious, beloved one,
Say, dear, how am I to live ?
How shall my heart be restrained ?
[My] eyes with tears are suffused [O Life of] Vraj !        1
Hearken attentively to [my] prayer, O revered mother Jamna !
The pangs of separation are unendurable.
Now, how am I to live ?   [O Life of] Vraj !        2
How shall I abide at a distance ?
Say, dear, whence this law.
Neither of us is of to-day or yesterday :
[Our] love is from the first [O Life of] Vraj !        3
O Hari, in thy heart retain
[Our] love [which] is of former times.
Be merciful, O Lord of the lowly and destitute !
Otherwise I will put off this earthly tenement.
O Life of Vraj ! an invitation send.        4
I want a resting place amidst the jasmine [bowers] of Vraj,
That always exist in the town of Gokul,
On the banks of the Kalindri,
At the landing place of Thakarani,
O Life of Vraj ! an invitation send.        5
When shall I satisfy my eyes with a full view
Of the landing place of Thakarani.
Inwardly I have a great desire,
I am longing to be called to Vraj,
O Life of Vraj ! an invitation send !        6

I am withered like [dried] cinnamon:
O Hari, brother of the plough-bearer,
I can have patience no longer.
[My eyes] are constantly filled with tears,
O Life of Vraj! I beseech thee!    7
What wrath is this against [me] an innocent person?
O Lord, [who art] merciful to the humble,
Regarding [me] as thy servant,
Protect [me thy] servant,
O Life of Vraj, I beseech thee!    8

ઉભા રોહો તો કહું વાતડી, શ્રીહારીલાલ૦
તમ માટે ગાળીછે મેં જાતડી, શ્રી૦
ને દાહડે મળીયાતાં વરંદમાં, શ્રી૦
તે દાહડાની તાલાવેળી તનમાં, શ્રી૦
વેદનાના વીરહેની તે ક્યાંહાં ભાંખીયે, શ્રી૦
ભીતરનો ભડકો ને ક્યાંહાં દાખીયે, શ્રી૦
કટકારી સરખી કરે વનમાં, શ્રી૦
કળ ના પડે પળ રજની દીનમાં, શ્રી૦
ઘેલી કરી છું સહુ ગામમાં, શ્રી૦
કેમ કેહવાય જેવું દુઃખ તનમાં, શ્રી૦
તાલાવેળી લાગી મારા મનમાં, શ્રી૦
ક્ષણે ક્ષણે બણકારા પડે કાનમાં, શ્રી૦
પ્રાણ પ્રોવાયો છે તમો તનમાં, શ્રી૦
વીકલતાની વાત કેહેવી, ના બને, શ્રી૦
ઘરમાં જાઉં ને જોઉં આંગણે, શ્રી૦
આતુરતા એવી કહાં લગી સહુ, શ્રી૦
છો ચતુર શ્રીરોમણી તાંહાં શુ કહું, શ્રી૦
પ્રીતડી કીધી તો હવે પાળીયે, શ્રી૦
આતુર શરણે આવ્યાને ન ટાળીયે, શ્રી૦
તમારે હું સરખી હજારો હશે, શ્રી૦
મારાં તો પ્રાણ તમ વીના નશે, શ્રી૦
ઓળીખું પણ ખીજલનું ગમે નહી, શ્રી૦
લાલચ લાગાં નધણા, તો જઈ એ કહી, શ્રી૦
નખશીખ લગીછો સ્વરૂપગુણ ભરીયાં, શ્રી૦

આવડા રૂપાળા તે કોણે કરીયા, ખી૦
હસો છો મધુર વાંકુ જોઇને, ખી૦
કટાક્ષ કટારીએ નાખ્યાં પ્રોઇને, ખી૦
વાંસળી વજાડે તેમાં વીરૈહે, ખી૦
અખ્ખાને જોતાં વીવેક કેમ રેહે, ખી૦
દરદી હોય તે જાણે દરદને, ખી૦
અવર દુખ એની આગળ ગરદમાં, ખી૦
કેહનાર કેહથે પણ છો ઘણી, ખી૦
ધ્યાના પ્રીતમ હું દાસ તમ તણી, ખી૦

[TRANSLATION OF THE ABOVE.]

Gallant Lord !

If you tarry a while, I'll tell you a tale.
On your account, I have wasted my body:
Since meeting at Vranda,
I have been suffering from anxious longing and hankering;
To whom shall I speak of the pangs of separation ?
How can I suppress the inward flame ?
Bewildered do I roam in the woods;
I do not feel a moment's rest day or night;
The whole village reckons me as mad.
How can I express adequately my agony ?
My heart burns with a longing and hankering desire;
Constant echo runs in my ears;
Our souls are threaded together.
I cannot express the uneasiness of my mind;
From window to window, to and fro, I run.
How long shall I suffer from such eagerness ?
Thou—the gem of [my] forehead, adept in all secrets,
                    What shall I say to thee ?

As thou hast loved me, now fulfil thy pledge;
Reject not one who has sought thy protection :
Thou mayst possess a thousand like myself;
[But] I cannot exist without thee;
The sound of any one pleases me not:
My eyes being enticed, now where can I go ?
From top to toe you are full of beauty and perfection.
Who could have made thee so beautiful ?
Thou smilest sweetly, glancing aside;

Thy wink as a dagger wounded my heart,
The sound of thy flute breathes woes of separation :
How can the weaker sex preserve their modesty ?
The diseased can only feel the agony of pain ;
Other diseases are nothing when compared with this.
Let people say what they may, but thou art my Lord ;
O Lord of Dayá, I am thy servant.

ઉભા રહોતો કહું એક વાત મારા વાહલા ॥
મરડી જયોછો શાને સુખરેજી ॥
વચન દીધું તે પાલીયું નથી રે વાહલા ॥
હું જાણુંછું લાગું તેનું દુઃખ રેજી ॥
મારી અરજ સુણો તો કહું એક મારા વાહલા
વીચારો નથી મારો વાંક રેજી ॥
હું વહુ વાર બાલે વેરા મારા વાહલા
અબખા માણસ ધણુ રાંક રેજી ॥
સાસરીયાં મુને સહુ સાચવેરે વાહલા ॥
પરણાીયો ના મુકે મારી પુંઠ રેજી ॥
સાસુડી ધણી સહેતાન મારા વાહલા ॥
નણદી આગળ ન નભે જુઠ રેજી ॥
જળ જઉ તો લોડે થાય માહારા વાહલા ॥
ગોરસ વેચતા સહીયર થાક રેજી ॥
માટે ટાહકું નાખ્યુંછે તક વીનારે વાહલા ॥
આપણ ડરવું રે દુરીજન લોક રેજી ॥
હરી મારે રૂપનું ગુમાન રખે જણતા રે વાહલા ॥
તે આપની આગળ તો નથી તેહ રેજી ॥
તન મન સોપ્યું છે તે દીવસનું રે વાહલા ॥
જારની દીધીછે નજર તેહ રેજી ॥
બાણે ભોજન નથી ભાવતું રે વાહલા ॥
નીદ્રા ન આવે કરે થેન રેજી ॥
હું ડાંકી ધીકું છું રાત દીવસ મારા વાહલા ॥
આપને વીયોગે નથી ચેન રેજી ॥
ખીજ કસરતો કાંઈ નથીરે વાહાલા ॥
સમો જો મળે તો સુખ થાય રેજી ॥
એજ વીચાર આઠે પેર મારા વાહલા ॥

મનડું રે માર ના કહું જપ રેજી ॥
પણ તે તો આવી છે તક આજ માહરા વાહલા ॥
પીયુડા પોહચેછે પરગામ રેજી ॥
મારી નણુદી વગાવી આજ સામેરે રે વાહલા ॥
ગોરસ વેચીવાનું અગત કામ રેજી ॥
માટે સંજાએ વેહલા આવજો રે વાહલા ॥
આપણે મળીસુ બંસીખટ ચોકરેજી ॥
સંગે સખા ન કોઈ લાવરો રે વાહલા ॥
હું પણ નહી લાવું સહી પર શોક રેજી ॥
તેજ પ્રમાણે મળ્યા એહ જણોરે વાહલા ॥
પુરણ અભીલાખ રમ્યાં રંગ રેજી ॥
પ્રસન થયા જીવન દયા તણોરે વાહલા
જીયો અજીત ને અનંગ રેજી ॥

[TRANSLATION OF THE ABOVE.]

If you stop a while, I'll tell you a tale.
Why do you turn your face from me?
I have not fulfilled the word I gave,
And this I believe has offended you:
I'll offer an apology, should you listen to it:
It's no fault of mine, do you see:
In my appearance I am a young married girl;
And being of the weaker sex, I am very meek.
My husband's relations all keep a watch over me;
My married one would not, if I go out, but follow me;
No false pretence would stand before my husband's sister.
If I go to bear water, or sell the products of the dairy,
My companions are in crowd with me.
Therefore, I have delayed for want of an opportunity:
We should dread the wicked people.
Do not think I am proud of my beauty;
It's nothing when compared with yours.
Since we have exchanged glances,
I have dedicated to you my body and mind;
I cannot relish food at dinner,
Nor can I get sleep when I lie down;
My heart burns within itself day and night;

I have no rest on account of your separation :
There is no other fault but this.
If an opportunity occurs happy we shall be ;
All the day this is the only thought engaging my mind.
But opportunity offers itself to-day ;
My husband leaves for a foreign town ;
My husband's sister is sent back to the house of her husband to-day;
To dispose of the products of the dairy is my important business.
Come, therefore, early at sunset,
To the grove of *Bansibatt*, where we shall meet ;
Take no companion with you,
And I too will not bring any.
Thus they both met
And sported to their complete satisfaction :
The cherisher of Dayá was delighted,
And conquered the unconquerable cupid.

It is the fatal result of the gross and indecent religion thus inculcated and practised by the Vallabhácháryans, that females are rendered callous to the moral degradation into which they are betrayed by their religious preceptors. These preceptors imbue their teachings with the idea that all emanates from the highest source of spiritual inspiration, they themselves being absolutely its full impersonation upon earth ; and their doctrines impressively inculcating that they are even superior to the Divinity himself, because, although ostensibly the mere medium of communication between him and the worshippers, they can save when it is beyond the power of the god, and can grant absolution and ensure pardon to the positive certainty of their votaries eventually enjoying the delights of paradise. The moral nature of the devotees being thus controlled and subjugated, they succumb slavishly to the infatuation, unconscious of the foul snare into which they fall ; and under the supposition that they obtain honour and spiritual exaltation by immoral contact with these incarnations of deity, lend themselves willingly to minister to their corrupt pleasures.

The Maháráj is invited to the houses of the Vaishṇavas when they are sick or on the point of death: in the latter case, he puts his foot on the breast of the dying person, with a view to free him from sin, and receives, in return for the blessings he thus confers, from ten to a thousand rupees.

In Bombay alone there are from forty to fifty thousand Vallabhácháryans. We may therefore form some conception of the manner in which the depravity of which we have spoken percolates through this community, which, as we have before seen, consists of the most wealthy and most intelligent inhabitants; and to how much greater an extent it may indirectly corrupt society by its contaminating influence. The Vaishṇavas are strictly prohibited from showing to the followers of other sects the book containing the amorous poetry, and, indeed, all the books issued by the Mahárájas.

The preliminary initiation of the Vallabhácháryans commences very early in life. The first instruction takes place at the age of two, three, or four years. The child is then taken to the Maháráj, who repeats to it the "Astákshar Mantra," or formula of eight letters, viz., श्रीकृष्णः शरणं मम

$$\underset{1}{श्री}\underset{2}{कृ}\underset{3}{ष्णः}\ \underset{4}{श}\underset{5}{र}\underset{6}{णं}\ \underset{7}{म}\underset{8}{म}$$

(*Śri Krishṇa sharnaṇam mama*), that is, "Śri Krishṇa is my refuge." This the child is made to repeat after the Maháráj, who then passes round its neck a string with *tulasi* (*ocymum sanctum*) or grass beads, called *kanthi* or necklace; and then the ceremony is complete. The second initiation, called *samarpaṇa*, which signifies consignment, takes place in the case of a male at the age of eleven or twelve years. He then becomes a full member of the sect, and is fitted for the duties of life. In the case of a female, it takes place upon her marriage, or shortly previous. This celebrated *samarpaṇa*, or absolute self-dedication to Krishṇa, and his incarnation, the Maháráj, is also known as *Brahm-sambandha*, which means connection with BRAHMA (the Supreme Being). The votary is required to repeat it daily, mentally and alone, after bathing, and it may not be recited to any one. It is in Sanskrit, and its form is as follows:—

॥ श्री श्रीक्रष्ण: शरणं मम सहस्रपरिवत्सरमितकालजातक्रष्णवियोगज
नितताप॒क्षेशानंततिरोभावोहंभगवतेक्रष्णायदेहेंद्रियप्राणांत:करणतद्व
मांश्वदारागारपुचाप्तविचेहपराख्यात्मनासह समर्पयामि दासोहं क्रष्ण
तवास्मि ॥ १ ॥

### TRANSLATION.

"Om! Sri Krishṇa is my refuge. I, who am suffering the infinite pain and torment produced by enduring, for a thousand measured years, separation from Krishṇa, do to the worshipful Krishṇa consecrate my body, organs of sense, life, heart, and other faculties, and wife, house, family, property, with my own self. I am thy slave, O Krishṇa." *

For the performance of each of these ceremonies, the Maháráj is paid a fee in money, which is not usually restricted to the prescribed amount, but is ordinarily accompanied with collateral presents, depending upon the opulence, position, or devotion of the votary. Its technical name is the *bhet,* or present.

This *samarpaṇa,* which professedly absolves from all sins previously committed, is deduced from the *Siddhánta-rahasya,* and incorporates the dedication there referred to. It is not a barren principle, it must bear fruit; as the preceptor says: "To each of us (himself a Krishṇa) you thus offer your body, your soul, your wives, your sons, your daughters, your body, mind and property. Before you enjoy any portion of *dhan,* you must offer it, him or her, to your god personified in us."†

The new full sectary thus goes forth, although disencumbered of his sins, yet heavily burdened morally, and without a claim to any possession; for in this formality he has renounced every possession to his Maháráj. He goes forth to repeat his

* Translated by Dr. John Wilson.
† Speech of Mr. T. C. Anstey in the Libel Case.

*mantra,* whilst numbering the beads of his rosary, which consists of one hundred and eight, made either of the stem of the *tulasi* plant or sandal-wood.  He is marked on his forehead with two perpendicular red lines, which converge in a semi-circle (with a red spot in it) at the root of the nose.  These marks are daily renewed after bathing.  He goes forth thus to be recognised by his brother sectarians, who mutually salute each other with hands raised to the face and the palms united, exclaiming, *Jaya Śri Krishna* or *Jaya Gopála,* Victory to Śri Krishna!  Victory to Gopála!  He goes forth with these marks upon him to be recognised as the enthusiastic devotee of the Maháráj, to whom he has desecrated the purity of his home, under the terrible threat of the denial " of the deliverance of his soul, and of its re-absorption into the divine essence;" under the threat here, also, of excommunication from all intercourse with his fellow devotees, and under the prohibition of enjoying food, or participation in the worship of his idol.  His contempt can be purged only by presents and submission, or by the strong act of renunciation of the sect, which few have the moral courage to resolve upon, chained as they are by the relations of life, or the artificial bondage of a conventional condition of society.

The woman goes forth a ruined victim.  She is undone by the obscenities which she has witnessed and practised, through the dissoluteness of the Maháráj, whom she has been taught to solicit by means of every possible artifice and blandishment, and by enticing presents.  She conceives herself to have been honoured by the approach of her god, to whose lust she has joyfully submitted.  Her whole nature is thus corrupted.

After receiving this initiation, it is incumbent upon the votary to visit the temples at Gokul and Śri Náthadwár at least once in their lives.  Having done so, the greatest devotees becomes *marjádis,** and can then be attended only

* Devoted to the worship of the god.

by such persons as shall have also visited the same temples. The mere performance of *samarpana* is not sufficient to attain this object, for "such disciples may eat only from the hands of each other. The wife, or the child, that has not exhibited the same mark of devotion can neither cook for such a disciple, nor eat in his society." *

The followers of these Mahárájas have usually in their houses an image of Krishna and a small book or wooden case containing portraits of Krishna in various attitudes. as well as of Vallabháchárya and some of his descendants, which they worship after the morning ablutions and bath. The image represents a young child, and the worship consists in playing before it with toys and childish trifles. But previously to this worship, the suppositious child must be aroused from the slumbers of the night by the ringing of a bell. It is then bathed and dressed, and offerings of fruit and other things are placed before it ; a lamp is waved before the image, the light being produced by the combustion of clarified butter ; a rosary of one hundred and eight beads is gone over, and with the numbering of each a repetition is made of the *mantra* of eight letters, as follows:—*Śri Krishna sharnanam mama* (Śri Krishna is my refuge). After this the *thákurji* (idol) is placed on his bed, and the votary takes his morning repast, and proceeds about the usual routine of his daily avocations.

These are the chief ceremonies of worship, and it will be seen that they are deeply impregnated with the vice inherent in the doctrines on which the ceremonial is framed. It must astonish every one that such debasing practices should proceed from the religious code of intelligent, if not educated, persons ; and those who are accustomed to think and to test everything by reason and common sense, can scarcely believe that such fanaticism can exist in an enlightened age. India was the centre of civilization for ages, while other portions of

* H. H. Wilson's Works.

the world were in a state of barbarism; and it is therefore
the more remarkable that it should be the *locale* of this
pestilential moral miasma, which the rapid and almost universal spread of intelligence has failed to dissipate.    The
existence of so foul a plague-spot would suggest that our
moral nature has its antithetical phases, and, like the lumi-
naries of the sky, is now at its zenith and now at its nadir;
and that the absolute progression of our race, without Divine
aid, is but an idle dream and a baseless hope.    It would
almost seem to be the duty of the rulers of the realm of
India to prohibit these practices, in the interest of our common humanity, leaving to public opinion the delicate task of
correcting mere social follies and aberrations.    Our govern-
ments may be legitimately held to be guardians of *public*
morals.    At any rate, the efforts of philanthropists for the
enlightenment and reformation of India should be increased
a hundred fold.

# CHAPTER VII.

## EFFECTS OF THE DOCTRINES AND WORSHIP OF THE VALLABHÁCHÁRYANS.

ALTHOUGH in the preceding chapters we have incidentally adverted to the natural effects of the dissolute teachings of Vallabháchárya and his immediate descendants, and of the commentators who have endeavoured to elucidate the tenets of the sect, we shall here briefly recapitulate them, and show at one view the tendency of the teachings themselves and the baneful effect of the ceremonial which has grown out of them.

One of the most conspicuous effects of the doctrines and ceremonial is to draw away the attention of the sectarians from the knowledge of the true God. The superstitions which the Mahárájas have introduced, to subserve their purpose of controlling the consciences of their adherents, lead them to see God only in their religious guides, and to worship them as absolute impersonations of the Deity. "According to the old Bráhminical tenet," developed in the philosophical Upanishads on which the Vedánta system is founded, "Brahma, the *all containing* and Indestructible, the Soul of which the Universe is the Body, abides from eternity to eternity as the fontal source of all spiritual existence : reunion with Brahma, absorption into Brahma, is the beatitude for which every separated spirit yearns, and which after animating its appointed cycle of individuated living organisms, it is ultimately destined to attain. This, then, is the pure and sublime notion of the reunion of all spirits that animate living but perishable forms with the Eternal Spirit, not limited by form, debased into a sexual and carnal coition with the most sensuous of the manifestations or '*avatárs*' of God. . . . . The religion which thus degrades the pure idea of spiritual reunion with God into the gross reality of carnal copulation with its hereditary high priesthood, appears to be sensuous in all its manifestations. Rás Lilá, or '*amorous dalliance,*' is held forth as the highest bliss here; Rás Lilá is the principal employment of Paradise hereafter: one of the many amatory names of the Maháráj is the ' Ocean of Rás Lilá,' and when a Maháráj expires he is not said to die, but to extend himself to an immortality of Rás Lilá." *

" If these things are sanctioned by the authoritative works of the religious sect; if reunion with God is figured under the emblem of sexual intercourse; if love for God is illustrated by the lustful longing of an adulteress for her paramour; if paradise is spoken of as a garden of amorous dalliance; finally, if the hereditary high priests of the sect are directed to be worshipped as gods and reverenced as the incarnations of God, it is not a matter of surprise that the ordinary devotees should make little practical distinction between Krishna and the Maháráj—that they should worship the Maháráj with blind devotion, and that their wives and daughters should freely give themselves up to his embraces, in the belief that they are thereby commingling with a god." †

Multitudes of the populace, therefore, servilely submit to all that these priests may chose to dictate; and they yield themselves passively to these delusions, which obtain an entire ascendancy over them. They are so subdued by this moral and intellectual paralysis, and so thoroughly debased by the apprehension of the consequences of thwarting their priests, that they have no will to exert in resistance to the debasing

---

* Judgment of Sir Joseph Arnould.         † Ibid.

practices which the Maháråjas have introduced, in supreme contempt of their abject and devoted followers. Were the Maháråjas, as the Jesuits were, an intellectual and highly educated class, we might conceive of such a subjection to them; but the instances of culture among these men are so extremely rare, and their spiritual ascendancy is so entirely maintained as a hereditary right, without any respect to their character or qualifications for the sacerdotal office, that there is nothing by which we can account for the influence they exercise. That men who, in the ordinary business of life, and in their daily intercourse with others, are acute and intelligent, quick to perceive their rights and persistent in maintaining them, should submit to be the victims and the dupes of these priests, and should adopt and allow the vile practices they have introduced, is a mystery which we are unable to solve, except by a reference to the power of superstition to enthral the mind. It may be laid down as an axiom, that we are more usually and effectively acted upon by what is near than by what is remote. In the daily and hourly agitations of society, we see men act both deliberately and impulsively, upon proximate instigations, without weighing the possibilities of distant consequences and contingencies .And, in this case, the threat of being born a thousand times as a dog, a serpent, an ape, or an ass, after passing from this life, makes the deluded followers of this superstition the serfs of the priests, whose wills they slavishly obey even to the extent of suffering the most hideous humiliation. Hope also comes to the help of fear; and the futile promise that they shall pass, without any intervening transmigration, direct to Goloka, excites in the minds of the Vaishṇavas a strong desire to give to their priests valuable presents, and blinds them to the degradation to which they are subjected in their families by their craft and lust.

Upon the females, who are entirely destitute of education, and who live in a climate which early developes the passions, and in a moral atmosphere in many respects unfavourable to purity and delicacy, the superstition has still more baneful effects. By it a door is opened to every tempting inducement, and for the outlet of a flood of evils. Where there is no knowledge of moral turpitude, the females of the country yield to their worst impulses, and think that they are doing right. They are taught by their parents and friends to obey their own natural promptings, and to submit unhesitatingly to those solicitations from without, compliance with which has the promise of both temporal and spiritual reward. The explanation here is easier than in the case of the man; for although woman, normally, has perhaps a keener perception of right and wrong than man, her intelligence is enfeebled by the want of education and enlightened society, and the force of example and the power of precept. Thus she almost necessarily becomes the victim of her own excited imagination.

Hindus! we exhort you to educate your females, that you may have a virtuous progeny from a pure and uncontaminated source; for, under the circumstances we have been compelled to narrate, often to our utter disgust, a man cannot be sure that his child is his own, and not the offspring of a licentious voluptuary. Virtue is inherent in the female breast, and if duly nurtured, like a fair tree properly cultivated and tended, will in its season yield its noble crop of cheering blossom and sustaining fruit. Abjure the degrading tenets that debase you; arouse yourselves to the dignity of manhood, and cast the chain from your necks. Trample down this vile priesthood into the mire they create around you, and raise yourselves to the position your intelligence fits you to hold. Divest your females of the notion that intercourse with the Mahárájas is an honour, and that amorous connection with them is bliss. Make them renounce this vile superstition. Claim them as your own only, and bind them to yourselves and your families by the strong and hallowed ties of conjugal, parental, and

affection. Let not your homes have the scent of the
:ities of the temple, whose odour should be disgusting to
nostrils.

other conspicuous result of the effect of the precepts
:ated by the Maharajas is the formation of the " Ras
.alis." These are " carnal love meetings." The institu-
if it may be so called, or rather the practice, is derived
the account of the Ras Lila, the ancient mythological
of the gopis, or female cowherds, mixing, dancing, and
ning passionately enamoured of Krishna. The meetings
:se societies are held privately at the residence of some
dox and rich Vaishnavas. They take place in the
ng, and at them are read stories from "The Tales
e Eighty-four Vaishnavas," and from " The Tales of
'wo Hundred and Fifty-two Vaishnavas," which pro-
:o relate respectively the histories of the converts of
bhacharya and of Vithalnathji. We have had occasion,
r chapter on the doctrines of the Maharajas, to quote
of these licentious narratives, to which we refer our
rs back for illustration, not choosing to cite any more
such prurient sources. The reading of these books
:s and stimulates the passions, and we may be prepared to
:t what must follow. Indeed, it is very questionable
er this stimulation is not the ostensible and main object
: meeting, rather than any religious motive. These read-
principally for the purpose of exciting concupiscence, is
cated by the religion. Friendly Vaishnavas take their
;, and possibly females of their acquaintance, with them to
meetings, and a discourse on matters of love and affection
d. It is not to be supposed that these societies have any
iblance to the Platonic concourse of the middle ages,
led the *Cours d'Amours*, a Parliament of Love, which pro-
ced its "*arrets*," or sentences determining cases of con-
ce, or propounded ingenious subtleties for discussion. No !

9

These meetings are of a practical character, with but a step
from word to deed. To them sweetmeats are taken, which
are consecrated to the books, after reading, and these
they put bit by bit into each other's mouth, each feeding
another's wife.

"The wife of one Vaishnava will put a morsel into the
mouth of another Vaishnava, who, in return, does the same
to her, with all the practical manifestations of the most ardent
love. After they have exhausted the sweets of these pre-
liminaries, the intoxication of delight so overpowers them,
and they become so enrapt with the ardour of the love that
inflames them, that, forgetting the earth and its platitudes,
they ascend to the very summit of celestial beatitude, and
blend together in the ecstacy of superlative bliss."

We have but given a paraphrase of what this passage says
in plainer and unmistakable language. We will proceed now
to some of the rules which regulate the Rás Mandali. These
direct that if one male Vaishnava wish to enjoy the wife of another Vaishnava, the latter should give him that liberty with
great delight and pleasure. Not the slightest hesitation is to
be made. It is a primary condition that a Vaishnava who
wishes to be a member of this Mandali should join it together
with his wife. The Vaishnava who has no wife, or who has not
been married, can also join the Mandali, and enjoy the wives
of other Vaishnavas. There are two or three such Rás
Mandalis in Bombay, and they are found in other parts of
India where Vaishnavas dwell. Capt. McMurdo, the Resident
in Kutch, has noticed the Rás Mandali. He says:—" The
well known Rás Mandalis are very frequent among them (the
Bháttiás) as among other followers of Vishnu. At these, persons of both sexes and all descriptions, high and low, meet
together; and, under the name and sanction of religion,
practice every kind of licentiousness."

It is not to be supposed that the Mahárájas permit their

votaries to have the exclusive enjoyment of these Rás Mandalis; for this would be an act of self-denial, not consistent
with their tenets. They themselves perform the part of
Krishna with the gopis, and represent the Rás Lilá. It
occurs in one part of the evidence in the Libel Case that the
enactment of this "amorous sport" may be witnessed upon
the payment of a fee, and one of the witnesses had actually
paid the fee to see it performed between the Maháráj, as
Krishna, and a young Bháttiá girl.

# CHAPTER VIII.

## PROFLIGACY OF THE MAHÁRÁJAS.

Our whole narrative has been scarcely anything but one continuous recital of the profligacy, debauchery, and licentiousness of the notorious Mahárájas. They find their infatuated votaries such willing victims, that their unresisting weakness tends to perpetuate and aggravate the evil; for all propensities, good and bad, by the very force of habit, become strengthened and confirmed. We cannot wonder, then, that these Mahárájas, accustomed from infancy to be treated with veneration, and to have every desire immediately and profusely met and gratified, should not desist from practices that have become bone of their bone and flesh of their flesh. Nurtured in indolence and sensuality, with the barest smattering of education, what can it be expected they should become but the precocious practitioners of every depravity? Accustomed to delicate nurture, the choicest viands, the richest habiliments, the smiles of women, and the abject and debasing servility of men, they unwittingly become gross sensualists; and the great wonder is, that, in the continuous practice of so much debauchery and dissipation, they should live even to the age of manhood. Comparatively few of them reach old age.

The Mahárájas must be often well-favoured, to inspire women with so strong a passion as to purchase intercourse with them at any cost, as they have sometimes done; for this surely cannot always be traced to a religious source, but must often arise from depraved sensuality. Women have been known to part with their personal ornaments to purchase intercourse with these priests; and, upon returning home, they have pretended to their husbands, or to the elders of the house, that the ornaments were lost in the crush of the throng which pressed to pay adoration to the image of the idol. The Mahárájas are solicitous to obtain the notice of all their female votaries; but only their particular favorites, or the exceptional charms of a beautiful female novice, specially allure them. That they may not lose any opportunity of fascinating, they go to the temple attired in the choicest raiment, from which streams the rich perfume of the unguents they have been anointed with: they are as odorous and as iridescent as a parterre of bright coloured and sweet scented flowers. Can we wonder, then, at the infatuation of the females, thus assailed through every sense, and whose imaginations are intoxicated by the desire and expectation of realizing sensuous connection with an incarnate god? Some females, in their impassioned devotion, dedicate themselves wholly to this sensual enjoyment; and are so strongly impressed with its beneficial and meritorious efficacy, that they dedicate their daughters to the same service. It has often happened, in the case of the sickness of husband or child, that, in order to procure their recovery, women have vowed to dedicate their daughters to the embraces of the priest. But it must be remembered that females, when young, are already initiated, as far as sight is concerned, in the alluring mysteries of this profligate religious frenzy: they behold from infancy all the processes of the atrocious superstition, and grow up to maturity in the pestilential atmosphere of moral impurity. They are thus prepared for what follows.

The profligacy, debauchery, and licentiousness which characterize the sect of Vallabháchárya have been noticed by several distinguished persons, two or three of whom flourished some hundred years ago. Dámodar Svámi, a dramatic writer, com-

posed a Sanskrit drama entitled *Pákhanda Dharma Khandan*
(The Smáshing of Heretical Religion), in the year of Samvat
1695 (about A.D. 1639), in which a distinct reference to Vallabháchárya and his sect is made as follows :—

आर्ये विद्तिमेव भवत्या वेदैः क्वापि पलायितं प्रियतमे वार्त्ता पि न
श्रूयते सांख्यं योग पुराण धर्म निचयः च्छांतर्गतो दृश्यते श्रीमद्वल्लभ-
विट्ठलेश्वरमुखैः श्रुत्यर्थबाधोयतैः प्रोक्तं खात्म निवेदनं युवतिभिः सं-
दृश्यते सांप्रतं

कंठे कर्णे च हस्ते कटितटविषये मस्तके काष्ठमालां वृंदायाः संद्धानो
मृगपदसदृशं चंदनं वै ललाटे राधेकृष्णेति जल्पन् श्रुतिपथविमुखो
वेदिकान् भर्त्समानः स्त्रीवृंदैः कामपूरैः मति पद्मिलितो वैष्णवी
चुंबमानः भो भो वैष्णवाः श्रूयतां आलिंगनं भुजनिबंधनमायताच्छः
सख्यं निपानमशनं खपराब्ध भेदः खात्मार्पणं युवतिभिर्गुरुषु प्रयुक्तं
धन्यंच वैष्णवमतं भुवि मुक्तिहेतुः

परस्परं भोज्यमहर्निशं रतिः स्त्रीभिः समं पानमनंतसौहृदं श्री गोकु-
लेश्वार्पित चेतसां नृणां रीतिः परा सुंदरि सार्ववेदिनां

यत्पादुका पूजन मुख्यधर्मः सुतास्नुषादार समर्पणंच न पूजनं ब्राह्मण
वैदिकानां नवा तिथेः आज्ञव्रतोपवासः

[TRANSLATION OF THE ABOVE.]

"The Sútradhára (says to the Nati):—O dear, the Vedas have
fled somewhere; no one knows the story of their flight (*i.e.* whither
they have gone). The collection of the Sánkhya, Yoga, and the
Puránas, has sunk into the bowels of the earth. Now, young
damsels, look to the self-dedication preached by Shrimat Vallabha
Vittaleshvara, who has conspired to falsify the meaning of the Vedas.
"Enters a Vaishnava, having on his neck, ear, hand, head, and
around his loins, a wreath made of the *Vrinda* (Ocymum Sanctum,

or Tulsi), having on his forehead *Gopichandana* (a substitute for sandalwood). He is one who repeats Rádhá! Krishṇa! Being opposed to the Shruti, he is the reproacher of those who adhere to the Vedas. He finds at every step crowds of females filled by *káma* (lust or cupid). He is the kisser of female Vaishṇavas. Ye Vaishṇavas, ye Vaishṇavas, hear the excellent and blessed Vaishṇava doctrine: the embracing and clasping with the arms the large-eyed damsels, good drinking and eating, making no distinction between your own and another's, offering one's self and life to gurus, is in the world the cause of salvation.

"Mutual dining, carnal intercourse with females night and day, drinking, forming endless alliances, are the surpassing, beautiful customs of the persons who have consecrated their souls to Sri Gokulesha. Charity, devotion, meditation, abstraction, the Vedas, and a crore of sacrifices, are nothing: the nectarine pleasure of the worshippers of the *Páduká* (wooden-slipper), in Sri Gokula, is better than a thousand other expedients. Our own body is the source of enjoyment, the object of worship reckoned by all men fit to be served. If sexual intercourse do not take place with the Gokulesha, the paramour of men is useless, like a worm or ashes.

"The chief religion of the worshippers of the *Páduká* is the consecration of a daughter, a son's wife, and a wife, and not the worship of Brahmaṇas learned in the Vedas, hospitality, the *Shraddha* (funeral ceremonies), vows, and fastings." *

Sámal Bhatta, a distinguished Gujaráti poet, who flourished in Gujarát about a hundred and fifty years ago, in his poem entitled Sudá Boteri (Seventy-two Parrots) makes the following remarks in the twenty-fourth story of the book :—

વૈષ્ણવ ધરમમાં કહું ॥ ઇનૈયે શીષું કાંમ ॥
સોળ રાહસ્ય સંતોષીયા ॥ નટવર જેનાં નામ ॥ ૨૩ ॥
ગોસાઈજી ગુરુ જેહના ॥ સમરપણી સરદાર ॥
તન મન ધન સોંપે તેહને ॥ નીરમળ પોતાની નાર ॥ ૨૪ ॥
વૈષ્ણવ વૈષ્ણવમાં આમરે ॥ રાસમંડળીની ગીત ॥
વંસંત રમેછે વૈષ્ણવો ॥ પરસપરે બહુ પ્રીત ॥ ૨૫ ॥
કો વૈષ્ણવ સામળા ॥ કો એક વૈષ્ણવ ભાંડ ॥
કેટલાક વૈષ્ણવ રાંડુવા ॥ કેટલાક રાંડી રાંડ ॥ ૨૬ ॥

* Translated by Dr. John Wilson.

છાપા કરેછે છેલજી ॥ બાંડ બાંડ ઘાલેછે ભાલ ॥
વ્યભીચારે વેસ વગોવતા કરે ॥ કામનિયોના કાળ ॥ ૨૭ ॥
ભિન્ને મારગ શ્રીજનો ॥ કેહવાય ધણીનો ધરમ ॥
નર નારો મળેછે એકઠાં ॥ કરેછે કુડાં કરમ ॥ ૨૮ ॥

[TRANSLATION OF THE ABOVE.]

In the Vaishṇava religion it is said
　　Kanayá (*i.e.* Krishṇa) did this business—
He gratified sixteen thousand (gopis),
　　Arch-actor is his name.
(They) whose high priest is Gosáiji,
　　The head of the Samarpaṇis (dedicators),
Make over to him their bodies, minds, and wealth,
　　(And also) their pure females (or wives).
The Vaishṇavas among themselves practice
　　The observances of the Rás Mandali:
The Vaishṇavas sport among themselves the spring sports,
　　Having great love towards each other.
Some Vaishṇavas are dark,
　　Some Vaishṇavas are indecent talkers,
Some Vaishṇavas are effeminate,
　　Some (are even like) widows.
(They) make foppish seal-impressions,*
　　(And) put on indecent brows;
They debase their appearance by adultery,
　　Being destroyer of female (virtue).
Another sect is that of Braj;
　　Their religion (is) called the husband's religion;
(Among them) the males (and) females mix together
　　And do wicked acts.†

Akha Bhagat, a man of distinguished piety, who flourished
in Gujarát about the same time, and who was once a follower
of the Mahárájas, used to recite a couplet which has since
become a proverbial saying among the Gujaráti people, and
which is as follows :—

'ગુરુ કીધો મેં ગોકુળનાથ, ઘરડા ખખડને ઘાલી નાથ ॥
ધંન હરે ધોકો ન હરે, એવો ગુરુ કલ્યાણ શું કરે ॥ ૧ ॥

---

　* On their persons with the *gopechandan* or white earth.
　† The attention of the author was directed to this passage by Kalidas.

[TRANSLATION OF THE ABOVE].

" I adopted Gokulnáth for my guru, and thus put a string in the nostrils of an old bullock: one who lightens wealth but does not lighten the pressure (on the heart),—what good can such a guru confer ?"

In the Kávya Dohan (the Cream of Poetry), or Selections from the Gujaráti Poets, we find the following piece, written probably about a hundred years ago, by Krishṇarám, a Gujaráti poet :—

વૈષ્ણવ થઈને વેષ, અભ્ળાને આરાધે ॥
કરે ધર્મનો દ્વેષ, શિવની નિંદા સાધે ॥ ૯૬ ॥
સમર્પણી થઈ સ્વાદ, શીરા પૂરી જમતા ॥
ગુરુનો લેઈ પ્રસાદ, રામા સંગે રમતા ॥ ૯૨ ॥
પરનારીને સંગ, પ્રીતિ મનમાં પેસે ॥
અળંકારથી અંગ, સરસ સમાવી એસે ॥ ૯૯ ॥
વેદ વિનાના ધર્મ, વાંચે નિત્ય વિખ્યાણે ॥
કૃષ્ણ ચંદ્રનાં કર્મ, જીવ સરીખા જાણે ॥ ૧૦૦ ॥
દંભી જનનો દાસ, થઈને શીરા નમાવે ॥
વિઠ્ઠલ તણો વિશ્વાસ, શુદ્રોને મન ભાવે ॥ ૧૦૨ ॥*

[TRANSLATION OF THE ABOVE].

Having assumed the appearance of a Vaishṇava,
    They worship the feeble sex.
They hate (the true) religion,
    And accomplish the defamation of Shiva.
Having become Samarpaṇi (dedicators) (they) indulge
    In (the sense of taste by) eating Sirá-pure.
They receive the consecrated food from their guru,
    (And) play with women.
(Thoughts of having) connection with other women
    Habitually occupy their minds.
Having decked up their persons,
    With ornaments they sit.

* Kávya Dohan, pp. 110, 111, 2nd edition.

(Their) non-Vaidik tenets
  (They) daily read and praise.
The deeds of Krishṇa Chandra
  (They) regard as (if they were their) soul.
They become the slaves of impostors,
  (To whom they) bow their heads.
The minds of (these) Shúdra (Vaishṇavas) like
  To place their faith in Vithal.

Sajjáuand Swámi, better known as Swámi Náráyan, who flourished in Gujaráti about sixty years ago, and founded a new sect, exposed the immoralities committed by the Mahárájas, and thus induced the intelligent portion of the Vaishṇava community to become his followers.

Mr. H. G. Briggs, the author of "The Cities of Gujaráshtra," in the eleventh chapter of his work, referring to Sajjánand Swámi, says:—

"No longer influenced by those dreads which had hitherto intercepted his career, he commenced his crusade against the *Vallabha Kula*, better known as the Gosáinji Maháráj. He boldly denounced the irregularities they had introduced into their forms of worship, and exposed the vices which characterized the lives of their clergy" (pp. 237, 238).

In the "Transactions of the Literary Society of Bombay" (now the Bombay Branch of the Royal Asiatic Society), vol. ii., published in the year 1820, Capt. McMurdo, Resident in Katchh, writing about Katchh and its people, makes reference to the Mahárájas as follows:—

"The Bháttiás are of Sindh origin. They are the most numerous and wealthy merchants in the country, and worship the Gosáinji Mahárájas, of whom there are many. The Maháráj is the master of their property, and disposes of it as he pleases; and such is the veneration in which he is held, that the most respectable families consider themselves honoured by his cohabiting with their wives or daughters. The principal Maháráj at present on this side of India is named Gopináthji, a man worn to a skeleton and shaking like a leaf, from debauchery of every kind, excepting spirituous liquors.

He is constantly in a state of intoxication from opium and various other stimulants which the ingenuity of the sensual has discovered. He was originally a Brahman" (vol. ii. pp. 230, 231).

Mr. Frederick Hall, formerly Professor of the Government College at Benares, published in 1854 Káshi Námah, one of the Persian works of the deceased Munshi Shilal Sheikh, in which the author makes a distinct reference to the sect of the Gokul Gosáins, or the Mahárájas. We give below the text and its English translation :—

دويم كوشائين كوكل بكوكلست مشهوراند بيشتر اوضاع ظاهر مثل

كوشائيان بندرابن و وضع قشقة علحده و مُريدان آنها بيشتر بقالان

گجراتي اند كه پيشه مهاجني دارند ديگر كسي كمتر به مريدي آنها

ميل ميكنند و مُريدان آنها از مرد و زن بوقت مُريد شدن تن من

دهن هرسه چيز گور آرپن مينمايند يعني درخدمت و براي خوشي

و از جسم و دل و زر دريغ ندارند و زن و مرد هر روزه بلاناغه و بعضي

سه مرتبه براي ديدار مرشد و بت معبود ميروند و سواي اين آن

قدر حُسن اعتقاد متحقق دارند كه بوقت شادي منكوح خودرا بلا

تصرف اوّل بخدمت پير دستگير مي فريسند بعده اُلش مُرشد كامل

بكام مُريدان غافل ميرسد و اگر احيانّا شخصي از مريدان در فرستادن

منكوح بطورند كورتالي و تامل نمايد برغم انها منكوح او عقيم

ميگردد و شوهرش را سود بهبود نمي شود چون خطره مرقومه از

مدت دماغ آن ابلهان را پريشان ساخت بترس و خوف درين عمل

منكر مي كوشند و سواي منكوح جديد نيز اگر بطرف زوج كسي

مُرید میلان مرشد می شود بہ مجرد استمزاج حاضر میسازند و
جمیع این ابلهان اعمال فسق و فجور مُرشدرا کرشن کریا می
شمرند و مرشدرا معبود خود دانست ارشاد اورا بمنزلہ وحي آسماني
میدانند و رازداري اعمال او می سازند خورد خورد نوش آنها نهایت
لطیف و فاخرہ و اکثر متمول می باشند

[TRANSLATION OF THE ABOVE.]

"*The Gokul Gosáinjís.*—They are generally known (by the name of) Gokulasth. In all their outward manners they are like the Bandrában Gosains, and they apply the Kasliká (mark made by the Hindus on the forehead) in a different way, and their followers are mostly Gujaráti grocers (or banians), who carry on the business of máhajans (or bankers). Few other people are inclined to become their followers. Their followers, whether men or women at the time of becoming their followers, make an offering to the guru (*i.e.* the spiritual guide) of these three things, namely, body, mind, and wealth,—that is, for (his) service and gratification; and they withhold not from him their bodies, hearts, and gold. Men and women unfailingly go once every day, and some of them three times (daily), in order to behold the face of their spiritual guide, or the adored idol. And, besides this, they are so firm in their good faith, that when they marry, they first send their wives to their spiritual guide without having made use of them; and the leavings of their accomplished guide are afterwards tasted by the ignorant disciples. Should any one of the disciples hesitate to send his wife as mentioned above, she becomes, agreeably to their belief, a barren women, and her husband will not benefit by her; and as this dread has disordered the brains of those foolish people for a long time, they, from fear, exercise this obnoxious act. Besides the newly married wife, should the guide desire the wife of any followers, as soon as they discover his intentions they produce her; and all these fools regard the wicked and sinful deeds of their guide as the gambols of Krishṇa, and, considering their adored guide as God, they respect his words as revelations from heaven, and conceal his doings. The food and drink of these (Gosáins) are delicious and luxurious, and most of them are wealthy."

The immoralities of the Mahárájas were proved before the Supreme (now High) Court of Bombay in the year 1862. Dr. John Wilson, who (in the words of Sir Joseph Arnould), "has studied the subject with that comprehensive range of thought—the result of varied erudition—which has made his name a foremost one among the living orientalists of Europe," says in his testimony as follows :—

"The sect of Vallabháchárya is a new sect, inasmuch as it has selected the god Krishna in one of his aspects—that of his adolescence, and raised him to suprèmacy in that aspect. It is a new sect, in as far as it has established the *Pushti-márga*, or way of enjoyment, in a natural and carnal sense. The sect is new in its objects, and new in its methods. The god Krishna is worshipped by its members in the form of images, and in the form of the persons of their gurus, the so-called Mahárájas. The Maháráj is considered by a great many of his followers as an incarnation of God, as god incarnate according to Hindu notions, which are peculiar on that subject. The Vallabhácháryans hold that Vallabhácharya and his official descendants are incarnations of the god Krishna, without holding that there is a complete embodiment of him in any one of them. According to Hindu notions, there have occurred nine incarnations of Vishnu, the last of them being that of Buddha. The orthodox Hindus do not believe in any incarnations which are said to have taken place between the time of Buddha and the present day. The Vallabhácháryans, on the contrary, hold that Vallabhácharya and his descendants are incarnations of Krishna. They view the Maháráj as intermediate between themselves and the god Krishna, in the sense of being entitled to have his *dicta* received as equal to those of Krishna himself. . . . *Tan, man,* and *dhan* (in the formula of Vallabhácharya initiation) are used in an all-comprehensive sense —*tan*, embracing the body in all its members and functions; *man*, referring to mind in all the mental powers and faculties; and *dhan*, comprehending all property and possessions, which have to be placed at the disposal of the god through the Maháráj, according to the doctrines of the sect. I have seen passages in works published by the Mahárájas of the sect, according to which the sectaries should make over their sons, wives, daughters, and every thing else before applying them to their own use."

We shall not dwell longer upon this subject than to recite

an extract from the judgment of Sir Mathew Sausse, in the Maháráj Libel Case:—

"It appears abundantly from works of recognised authority written by other Mahárájas, and from existing popular belief in the Vallabháchárya sect, that Vallabháchárya is believed to have been an incarnation of the god Krishṇa, and that the Mahárájas, as descendants of Vallabháchárya, have claimed and received from their followers the like character of incarnation of that god, by hereditary succession. The Mahárájas have been sedulous in identifying themselves with the god Krishṇa by means of their own writings and teachings and by the similarity of ceremonies of worship and addresses which they require to be offered to themselves by their followers. All songs connected with the god Krishṇa, which were brought before us, were of an amorous character, and it appeared that songs of a corrupting and licentious tendency, both in idea and expression, are sung by young females to the Mahárájas, upon festive occasions, in which they are identified with the god in his most licentious aspect. In these songs, as well as in stories, both written and traditional, which latter are treated as of a religious character in the sect, the subject of sexual intercourse is most prominent. Adultery is made familiar to the minds of all: it is nowhere discouraged or denounced; but, on the contrary, in some of the stories, those persons who have committed that great moral and social offence are commended; and, in one of them, the actors are awarded the highest position in the heaven of the Vaishṇavas, although for some attention paid on one occasion to the clearing of a temple of the god. The love and subserviency inculcated by the Hindu religion to be due in a spiritual sense to the Supreme Being, has been by those corrupt teachings materialised, and to a large extent transferred to those who claim to be his living incarnations. It is said to be ceremonially effected by a mystic rite, or dedication of 'mind,' 'property,' and 'body,' (or *man, dhan,* and *tan*), which is made in childhood by males, but by females in the ceremony of marriage; and a popular belief appears to exist to a considerable extent, that this dedication confers upon the Mahárájas absolute rights over the 'minds,' 'properties,' and 'bodies' of their followers. The Mahárájas, however, appear, upon the evidence, to have undoubtedly availed themselves of the existence of those impressions to gratify licentious propensities and a love of gain. These doctrines and practices are opposed to what we know of the original principles of the ancient Hindu religion, which are said to be found in the Vedas."

The observations we have been induced to make result from the impressions we have received in treating the subject; and we feel confident that our readers will concur with us in denouncing the flagrant abuses we have pointed out, and help us to hold them up to the indignation of the world. We sincerely hope that this public exposure of gross social evils will tend to their ultimate and speedy abatement.

# CHAPTER IX.

## OPPRESSIVE EXACTIONS OF THE MAHÁRÁJAS.

SINCE the Mahárájas exercise such unlimited spiritual authority over their adherents, it follows that they should possess
considerable temporal influence and power. Great personal
respect is paid to them; they are invited to sumptuous enter-
tainments by their votaries, are constantly in the receipt of
valuable and choice presents, are consulted upon most matters
of importance, and their sway over society is consequently
great. When a rumour reaches a town that a Maháráj is
approaching, a large throng of his devoted followers go forth
to meet him, and, forming themselves into a procession, he
enters the town with great pomp and jubilation. The most
influential and rich members of the sect think it no degradation to perform the most menial offices in his service.

Whoever displeases a Maháráj incurs the penalty of excommunication, which is thus carried into effect: The Maháráj
presses the most influential persons belonging to the sect to
interfere in the matter, and a meeting is convened, at which
the conduct of the offending Vaishṇava is discussed. As, in
all such cases, the voice of the wealthy and powerful pre-
ponderates; and as these have already been privately solicited
and won over by the Maháráj, the issue is never doubtful.
The person who has incurred the displeasure of the Maháráj
has no alternative but to endure all the pains and penalties of
excommunication, or to make the most abject submission, and
atone by the offer of costly bribes. Any one who resists the

imposition of a tax which the Maháráj desires to levy is punished in a lighter way, although one equally powerful in its consequences, for he is prohibited from worshipping the image, or the Maháráj, until he submit. It thus happens that even the rich and influential are often kept soliciting pardon, and fasting, at the door of the dwelling of the Maháráj, for they may not take even food or water until they have paid their adoration to the image and to the Maháráj, which they are not permitted to do until they have submitted to the imposition.

"After the Europeans and Pársis, the Gujarati community engross the largest portion of the commerce of Bombay. They include Bháttiás, Márwádis, Lowánás, and others. They may be characterised generally as a community of shopkeepers, and have always shown an instinctive aptitude for commerce. . . . By far the larger portion of this trading community acknowledge the Mahárájas for their spiritual guides. Our whole *Kapad Bazár*, cloth market, is almost exclusively monopolized by the devout Vaishnavas. They deal also very extensively in cotton, opium, sugar, spices, gold, silver, and in almost every important article of trade. The Mahárájas, taking advantage of the commercial character of their worshippers, have secured to themselves a permanent source of income, by imposing a tax upon every article or commodity in which their votaries are trading. How such a tax came to be imposed upon them is easily learnt from a little brochure published ten years ago by the special authority of Jivanji Maháráj, which furnishes information regarding the amount and nature of the tax that goes to him. It appears from this that, in 1811, when Gokulnáthji Maháráj, the ancestor of Jivanji, came to Bombay, all the Vaishnavas of the island of Bombay, collecting in a body, requested His Holiness to settle permanently with his family 'for the purification of their souls;' offering, at the same time, to build a temple for him, and to make arrangements to meet his expenses in connection with the temple. To secure permanency to his income, and that, too, in a way the least burdensome to his followers, the Mahá-ráj pitched upon articles of trade for taxation. Accordingly agreements were signed by Bháttiá, Baniá, and Lowáná merchants, in which they bound themselves to add to the price of every article they might buy or sell according to the following scale :—

| ARTICLES. | AMOUNT OF TAXATION. |
|---|---|
| 1. Silk, sugar, spices, metals, sack-cloth, cotton, and opium ......... | ¼ anna per every hundred rupees of sale effected. |
| 2. Cloth, silk, cotton, and every other species ............................ | Ditto. |
| 3. Bills of exchange, drafts, etc. ... | 1 anna per every thousand rupees transaction. |
| 4. Gold and silver specie ............ | Ditto. |
| 5. Bills and specie brokerage ...... | Ditto. |
| 6. Cloth brokerage..................... | ¼ anna per every hundred rupees transaction. |
| 7. Agency brokers ..................... | Ditto. |
| 8. Brokers to European houses ...... | Ditto. |
| 9. Grain brokers ..................... | Ditto. |
| 10. Pearls and jewels .................. | Ditto. |
| 11. Pearls and jewel brokerage ...... | Ditto. |
| 12. Insurance brokers ................. | Ditto. |
| 13. Muccadams ....................... | 8 annas per every hundred rupees of their income. |
| 14. Every *patimar* laden with goods from Malabar, and consigned to a Vaishṇava ....................... | Rs. 1½ per vessel. |
| 15. Every *padow* (native craft) from Rájápur, and of which the goods are consigned to a Vaishṇava ... | 9 annas per vessel. |
| 16. Grain of all kinds .................. | 1 anna per candy. |
| 17. Ghi (clarified butter).............. | ⅓ anna per maund. |
| 18. Oil ................................. | ¼ anna per maund. |
| 19. Rice ............................... | 1 anna per "mudá." |
| 20. Malabar cloth ..................... | 1 anna per every hundred rupees transaction. |

| ARTICLES. | AMOUNT OF TAXATION. |
|---|---|
| 21. Dealers in gold | Rs. 1¼ per every hundred rupees' worth of gold bought for trade. |
| 22. Cotton yarn | 2 annas per maund. |
| 23. Rope | 1 rupee per every hundred rupees' worth of sale effected. |
| 24. Iron | 1 anna per candy. |
| 25. Pepper, etc. | 1¼ anna per cwt. |

"It will be seen that there is not an important article of trade in which the Vaishnavas are engaged that has escaped the Maháráj's clutches. Small and inappreciable as the rate of *lágá* (tax) may appear on a superficial view, the proceeds of the whole, when collected together, amount to 50,000 rupees. This large sum goes every year to fill the coffers of Jivanji, the owner of the great temple in Bombay, and now one of the richest among the natives of our island.

"But this is not all. It is not enough that so much money goes to one Mahárái. Other high priests have come forward in succession to assert their several claims, and to have their need supplied by fresh impositions. For instance, there is a *lágá* on most of the other mentioned articles (the rate of which, however, is not the same as that of the first one), which goes to provide for the temple of Śri Náthji in Mewár. It would be tedious to mention the different rates on different articles. Suffice it to say that the proceeds of this second tax amount to 80,000 rupees a year, of which the tax on piece goods alone, which is one anna per every hundred rupees' worth of goods bought or sold, furnishes the important item of 42,000 rupees, Jivanji Mahárái deriving from this same source about 11,000 rupees. The *lágás* appear to have grown with the growth of the Mahárájas' number. Hardly two or three years pass but a fresh *lágá* is sure to be imposed. About three years ago Chimanlálji, Gopkeshji, and Lál Maniji Mahárájas imposed three *lágás* for their respective benefit on some of the above-mentioned articles, from which they derive 12,000, 5,500, and 4,500 rupees respectively every year.   The total amount of the six *lágás* we have now described is as follows :—

|  |  | RUPEES. |
|---|---|---|
| For Srí Náthji | | 80,000 |
| ,, Jivanji Maháráj | | 50,000 |
| ,, Chimanlálji ditto | | 12,000 |
| ,, Gopkeshji ditto | | 5,500 |
| ,, Lál Maniji | | 4,500 |
| ,, Bábu Rárjaji | | 10,000 |
| | Rs. | 162,000 |

" Perhaps some of our readers will be surprised to find that a tax of one anna or half an anna on every hundred rupees should produce so large an amount.   But the fact is that the rate of tax on every article is doubled, trebled, or quadrupled, as it passes from one merchant or shopkeeper to another, and from another to a third, and from a third to a fourth, and so on, for every Vaishnava merchant pays his *lágá* for what he buys or sells.

" Upon whom does this burden of 162,000 rupees fall ?   It is certain that it does not fall upon the orthodox Vaishnavas. It would be a different thing altogether were the taxes levied on the profit of his trade.   The Bháttiá merchant is at liberty to spend what he pleases out of his profits.   But it must be borne in mind that the *lágás*, or taxes of the Maharájas, are levied upon articles of trade, and the burden therefore falls upon the community at large.   The Vaishnava merchant pays not a farthing.   Let us see what he does.   He buys, say piece goods in lump from European merchants, and puts such a price upon them as will cover not only his profits but all he has to pay in the shape of *lágás* to the Maharájas.   He has no fear of his goods being undersold, for his brother merchants, who are alike Vaishnavas, are in similar circumstances. He is generally a retail as well as a wholesale dealer.   Mer-

chants who buy goods from him, in paying the increased price
(increased on account of the taxes), pay actually the taxes
themselves; but they lose nothing, since they must sell their
goods at a profit, however low. The consumers of the articles
are the real payers of the Maharajas' taxes. Thus Christians,
Zoroastrians, Mahomedans, and the non-Vaishṇava Hindus,
are called upon to make this little contribution to the Mahárájas. Again, merchants from Arabia, Persia, or Zanzibar, on
the coast of Africa, buy piece goods and other articles on a
very extensive scale from the Bháttiá dealers; and they, too,
pay for the Maháráj's imposition. These merchants, however, suffer nothing from it, for they charge it upon the price
of the articles they sell to the people of Arabia, Persia, and
Zanzibar, as the case may be. Foreign consumers, therefore,
certainly, though unconsciously, come in for a share of the
holy tax." *

Thus the power and influence of the Maharajas is col-
laterally aided by their wealth, which tends to increase the
respect in which they are held, especially by the populace,
with whom a poor priesthood is usually an object of ridicule
or contempt.

Men holding society by the throat with so powerful a grasp
as these Maharajas, for the gratification of their evil passions
and propensities, would be dangerous to society at large, were
there not firm laws which impose limits upon their power.
Of their misdeeds, so long as they are kept within the bounds
of their sect, and are limited to such acts as affect only their
devotees, the law takes no notice, for these are private wrongs
of which the law takes no cognizance, if the individual who
suffers chooses to submit to them. If, however, its protection
be claimed it will vindicate its supremacy. The Maharajas
are careful not to attempt to exercise authority in such a
manner as would bring them within the grasp of the law; but

* *Times of India*, February 1, 1862.

the private wrongs they inflict are nevertheless of sufficiently grave a character to be held up to public censure. Although all-powerful within their own area and pale, their sacerdotal character does not exempt them from the castigation of intelligent opinion.

We purpose giving a few instances of their misconduct, which might not otherwise come clearly to the knowledge of the public.

"About twenty-seven years ago, when Sir Henry (then Colonel) Pottinger, was the Resident at Katchh, a Maháráj from Katchh despoiled the houses of the Vaishṇavas of Sindh: this man had twenty-two Mussulman sepoys in his pay; and for disguise, we presume, he kept his beard like that of a Mussulman. After robbing the Vaishṇavas of some villages between Luckpat and Tera, he started for Katchh Mándavi, the inhabitants of which communicated the intelligence to the Resident through Deván Lakhmidás, mehtá of that place. Upon this the Resident sent a military guard, and directed that the Maháráj should not be permitted to enter the town. Accordingly, when he came to within two miles of the place, he was informed that he would be punished if he remained within the boundaries of Katchh. Upon this the Maháráj immediately fled."

"Another Maháráj (who died in Bombay about twelve years ago) went once to Katchh Mándavi. Here he found a person who had a claim against one Hansá Tilvánivállá. This claim was barred by law, and the man therefore made over the bond to the Maháráj, and told him so. The Maháráj immediately sent for Hansá Tilvánivállá and demanded the money from him. The poor man stated that he was not legally bound to pay the money, and that, besides, he was in impoverished circumstances, and could not. Hereupon, the Maháráj, without attending to what he had said, made him lie all day in the sun, and had a large stone placed on his breast."

"In another case, about three years ago, a subscription list was set on foot by Chimanji Maháráj for the purpose of constructing a great temple. In that list many Vishṇavas had willingly contributed large sums; but others, who had attached but small sums against their names, had a great deal of *zulum* (tyranny) practised upon them by the Maháráj. To extort large contributions from them, they were threatened with the closing of Chimanji's temple against them. Some were actually confined in the temple. The same Maháráj threw one of his worshippers from a staircase of his house, and thereby inflicted great personal injury upon him."

Authority has been exercised in other cases in a similar manner, for the purposes of extortion; but the personal injury inflicted in this case would have brought the Maháráj within reach of the law if the votary had chosen to claim its protection.

"In another case, Gokuleshadhishji Maháráj thought right to possess himself of the house of one Manikbái, widow of Kaliánji Okhai, late mukkadam to Messrs. Graham and Co. After confining her in his temple for some length of time, he forced her to deliver to him all the documents relating thereto, and extorted from her a writing to the effect that she had of her own free will made over the house to the Maháráj as a gift. Some time after, the widow sued the Maháráj in her Majesty's Supreme Court, and when the case was about to come on, the Maháráj caused a private settlement to be made, he making over to her the deed of the house (worth about 12,000 rupees) and receiving from her 1,500 rupees in consideration."

Here the religion of the votary did not shelter the attempted robbery; but it was a pity the action was compromised, as we have no doubt the Supreme Court would have strongly expressed itself upon the nefarious transaction. But we presume the plaintiff was induced by caste reasons to forego the pursuit, and was content to recover her own even at a cost.

"Again (and as the last instance we shall adduce, and to which we shall have occasion to advert in a subsequent chapter), about five years ago all the Mahárájas of Bombay framed a document which became subsequently celebrated as the 'Slavery Bond.' In this slavery bond it was stated that no Vaishṇava should serve the Mahárájas with summons to appear in a court of justice; that a fund should be raised for the purpose of trying to get an act passed in the Legislative Council by which no Maháráj could be summoned before a court of justice; and if, during the interval, a Maháráj were served with a summons by an outside party, the Vaishṇavas should undergo any expense to put a stop to it; that, if any Vaishṇava wrote against the Mahárájas, he should be punished by his caste people."

"The Vaishṇavas were not at all willing to sign such a rigorously framed document; but when, for eight days together, the Mahárájas closed the doors of their temples against them, and did not allow any Vaishṇava to see their faces, all the Vaishṇava *shets* signed the document. Some of the *shets* were altogether unwilling to do so, but they became afraid of the Mahárájas, and at last signed the 'Slavery Bond.' " *

The inference to be drawn from these instances is that the Mahárájas, if resisted in their tyranny, would be controlled; but while their infatuated votaries receive the dogma of the creed they follow, that these Mahárájas are the incarnations of Krishṇa, and adhere to the dedication of *tan, man,* and *dhan,* they must necessarily remain the victims of these artful, crafty, and dissolute priests.

* A pamphlet on the Mahárájas.

# CHAPTER X.

## THE MAHÁRÁJAS IN DIFFICULTIES.

IT might have been foreseen that power such as that exercised by the Mahárájas, resting on hereditary superstition of the most debasing character, and maintained by craft and cunning, must ultimately be overthrown. It was impossible that an authority having no other support could continue when the light of intelligence was thrown upon it. It must necessarily expire amidst the ridicule and scorn of those to whom its true character is shown. The impending fall of an illegitimate but long continued domination, arbitrary and tyrannous in its pressure on the consciences of men, is often accelerated by strange and unexpected circumstances. And thus it is with the power and influence of these Mahárájas. The circumstances that have conduced to hasten the deserved overthrow of their monstrous tyranny may be summed up as follows :—.

1. The religious disputes between them and the Brahmans.
2. Their objections to attend courts of justice.
3. The opinions of the press upon them and their deeds.
4. Their infatuated mistake in the endeavour to enforce the " Slavery Bond."

Let us first notice the religious disputes between them and the Brahmans.

In the year 1855, the Gujaráti Brahmans in Bombay, wishing to make the offering to Mahádeva, or Śiva, of Chhapanbhoga (which means fifty-six kinds of consecrated. food, and consists of as many different sorts of vegetables, grains, etc., and is very expensive from the quantity made), commenced a subscription for the purpose. This met with success, and the consecrated food was made and offered at the shrine of the idol, after which it was participated in by the Brahmans, and widely distributed.

The Mahárájas, seeking a pretext for disputing with the Brahmans, contended that what is consecrated to Śiva, is, according to the Hindu Śástras, *Śiva Nirmál* (which means holy to Śiva), and consequently ought not to have been partaken of by the Brahmans. The Brahmans in Bombay are, as a class, supported by begging; and throughout Gujarat and the adjacent parts, as well as at Bombay, they are wholly supported by Vaishṇavas, it being customary for all sectarians, without exception, to present gifts to the Brahmans, whose sect is considered the chief. The object of the Mahárájas in originating this dispute was to acquire the supremacy, thus virtually held by the Brahmans. To effect this, the Mahárájas urged upon the Vaishṇavas, and especially the Bháttiás, who were the chief supporters of the Brahmans, that, having committed this serious religious error of consuming the food consecrated to Śiva, they were unworthy of support and patronage, and urged that the customary gifts and supplies should be withheld from them. For a considerable time previous to this there had been much dissatisfaction among the Vaishṇavas on account of the conduct and practices of the Mahárájas; and as the latter prosecuted with great vehemence the scheme for withholding the supplies to the Brahmans, the Vaishṇavas thought it a favourable opportunity for obtaining some reform of the abuses they complained of, which consisted in the notorious adulterous intercourse of the Mahárájas with the females of their families (especially in the winter service at four o'clock in the morning), and the frequent ravishment of girls of ten or eleven years of age. These atrocities had only been submitted to with any patience by the most infatuated and devoted of the Vaishṇavas; for the Hindus generally set a high value on the chastity of their females, and the violation of it, as a point of doctrine, is severely reprehended as a sin in their ancient religious works. Profligacy is nowhere inculcated in the Sacred Books of the Hindus, and rests upon a corruption of symbolism from its true meaning, introduced by these infamous men to sanction their own misdeeds. Much dissatisfaction also grew out of the quarrels and disputes in families caused by the Mahárájas requiring the wives and daughters of the Vaishṇavas to make them presents of ornaments and jewellery; for the females, being willing to gratify the cupidity of their priests, urged their unwilling husbands to consent. Another ground of complaint was the treatment of the females in the thronged crowds of the temple, where they were indecently abused. The Vaishṇavas were also displeased on account of the large sums of money exacted from them in various ways, on pain of being exposed to the injury and annoyance which the Mahárájas always knew how to inflict on those who provoked their animosity. They were indignant that, in cases where private, commercial, family, or caste disputes were referred to the arbitration of the Maháráj, the dissatisfied party, against whom a decision had been given, because he had bribed the arbitrator less munificently than his opponent, was required to consent to the decision, under the penalty of incurring serious displeasure. These, however, were not the only grievances. The Mahárájas command the labour and services of their followers without giving them any remuneration, and even insist that, when busily occupied in their own ordinary avocations, they shall, when required, instantly quit them to obey the orders of the Mahárájas, by attending to the image of the idol, or wreathing its cradle, etc., with flowers. The practice of the guardian of the temples beating the worshippers, to hasten their passage through the temples, was another subject of complaint.

A favourable opportunity seemed to have arrived for the redress of all these grievances, and the Vaishṇavas collectively consented to the wishes of the Mahárájas in reference to the Brahmans, upon the condition that these abuses should be absolutely reformed. One influential person named Gopáldás Mádhavadás persisted in supporting the Brahmans in defiance of the Mahárájas; and two others, also of great weight in their different sects, named Rámbál Thákursidás and Sakhárám Laxmanji, supported the Brahmans. The Mahárájas yielded to the pressure put upon them, and consented to the demands made upon them, even to the minor reforms; but they required the respite of a year before carrying them out, and demanded complete secresy, conceiving that if they yielded to immediate execution they would be tacitly admitting the existence of evils, and putting a weapon into the hands of their opponents—the Brahmans.

The dispute between the Mahárájas and the Brahmans, however, led to newspaper controversy, and caused much bad blood. The Baniás and Bháttiás, the most devoted followers of the Mahárájas, were commanded not to salute either of the three gentlemen who sided with the Brahmans, and otherwise to withhold the respect they had always been accustomed to show to them. The Brahmans, convinced that they were perfectly orthodox in what they had done, convened several meetings, to which they invited the Mahárájas to discuss the matter with them; but the Mahárájas, knowing the weakness of their cause, and conscious of their ignorance of Sanskrit, abstained from attending the meetings, or taking part in discussions which they were aware must end in their defeat and disgrace. To obtain, however, the victory in the eyes of their votaries, they assembled a meeting of their own, which was attended by a beggar Brahman, whom they had previously bribed.

This man, who represented that he was deputed by the entire body of his brethren, publicly humiliated himself by asking pardon of the Mahárájas in their name. The pardon sought was, of course, graciously granted, and the Mahárájas thought they were restored to the good opinion of their followers. But, unfortunately for them, the trick was exposed, and the public discussed, and the native newspapers commented upon it. This was a heavy blow to the Mahárájas. But, as they had not succeeded against the Brahmans, they did not carry out the reforms they had consented to, and the affair terminated almost where it commenced, to the disgust of all parties. The power of the Mahárájas was, however, shaken.

It was at this period, an opportunity being afforded by these disputes, that the *Satya Prakásha* (Light of Truth), a weekly newspaper, was first issued. It was published by the defendant in the Libel Case, and its object was the advocacy of social, educational, and religious reforms. In consequence of the excited state of public opinion at the time, the newspaper immediately obtained a wide circulation.

The second circumstance conducing to accelerate the overthrow of the power of the Mahárájas was their objection to attend courts of justice. The Mahárájas conceive that their dignity is lowered and their persons polluted by attending courts of justice; but the Supreme Court of Bombay required them to obey the summons of the law, on the occasion of an action being brought by Srí Jivanji Maháráj against Ramdayál Motirám. The plaintiff's affidavit was to the following effect.—

"I, Srí Jivanji Maháráj, the plaintiff above-named, solemnly affirm and declare that on or about the 2nd day of August instant, I was served with a subpœna from the above-named defendant to appear and give evidence on the trial of this cause; and I further say that I am the chief Maháráj of a very large section of the Hindu community, consisting of Baniás, Bháttiás, Bhansállis, Márwádis, Lowánás, Khatris, and other Hindu castes; and that it is contrary to the religion of the said castes that I should appear in any public place, except our temple and in the houses of members of the said castes for religious and ceremonial purposes.  I therefore say that I cannot attend personally in the Supreme Court to give evidence at the trial of this cause; but that, if I did so attend, *I should subject myself to the liability of being deposed from my office;* and I further say that I have very little personal knowledge of any of the matters in this action; but my *mehtás* (clerks), who are fully acquainted therewith, will attend in court with all books and documents relating to the issues.  And I lastly say that my sole reason for not obeying the said subpœna is that given; and inasmuch as the defendant's advisers well knew that I could not attend, I verily believe they only caused the subpœna to be served in order to create annoyance and expense. If, however, the defendant think fit to do so, I am ready and willing to be examined at my own house and at my own expense."

The *Bombay Gazette* of August 12, 1856, says:—

" The application was opposed by the counsel on the other side, who contended that sufficient cause had not been shown to exempt Sri Jivanji Maháráj from the usage of the court.  The Maháráj, the learned gentleman was informed, was in the habit of attending public places and visiting the houses of other natives.  He once or twice took a sea trip in the steamer Phlox, travelled by railway along with low caste Hindus, inspected the Observatory, the Mint, the spinning machinery, equestrian exhibitions, native nautches, etc. etc.  Surely if his person were not polluted by these things, much less would it be by attending the Supreme Court.

The Chief Justice (Sir William Yardley) with whose view of the case Sir Mathew Sausse entirely concurred, expressed himself very strongly against the expediency of exempting any individual, however high or dignified his station might be, from the usual process of the Court, saying that once an exception were made in favour of any person, there would be no end of applications of the same nature.  The head of every petty sect and caste in the island would be calling himself a Maháráj, and demanding as a right that the Court should have him examined at his private residence."

The objection, which in a great measure was suggested by the fact that the Mahárájas feel it to be a degradation to sit lower than an European, whom they regard as only equal to the very lowest of their own caste, was thus defeated; and this defeat further tended to reduce their importance.

The opinions of the press upon the Mahárájas and their deeds have also tended to undermine their influence.

Owing to the circumstances just noticed, and the excited state of public feeling, the doctrines, worship, power, and influence, the ignorance and evil lives of the Mahárájas, became not only well known, but much talked of. The community was thoroughly aroused, and men began to think, to talk, and to act. The press, stimulated by this movement of society, gained courage to make its comments. There are about fifteen or sixteen Gujaráti papers printed in the vernacular idiom and three or four English local papers published at Bombay. All these made their comments, and severely censured the Mahárájas. The *Satya Prakásh*, which was conducted by the defendant in the Libel Case (who was himself a Baniá, and follower of the Mahárájas, and familiar with all their mysteries and evil practices), frequently denounced and exposed their immorality and corruption. This, in the ferment which continued to exist, greatly shocked the feelings of the public, which had no conception of the existence of the enormities thus exposed. The Mahárájas themselves were peculiarly sensitive to the censure of this particular paper, knowing that it was conducted by one of their own followers, and they therefore instinctively apprehended that it would have a most prejudicial effect. The body of the Mahárájas consequently resorted to every available means to endeavour to silence the writer, by holding out considerable pecuniary inducements, proposed through the medium of some of their most influential votaries. But they were thoroughly frustrated in this object; for not only were comments published in the various newspapers, but pamphlets and handbills were freely circulated, all tending to the destruction of their influence.

Extracts of the comments so made, and which will give an idea of how much the subject occupied public attention, are given in the Appendix, No. 2.

The Slavery Bond was another means of undermining their influence.

In consequence of the excited state of the public mind, resulting from the perusal of the several pamphlets and handbills, and the censorious comments of the newspapers, an advertisement appeared in the *Satya Prakásh* of the 25th of January, 1857, proposing for competition a prize essay upon the duties of Gurus (spiritual guides), and the rule of conduct of their female devotees. The object of the proposed essay was to show the line of conduct that ought to be pursued by the Mahárájas towards their female votaries, as well as how these were bound to act in return. Several essays were the result of this announcement, and one of them was crowned with approval. Whilst this was being printed for circulation, the Parsí editor of the *Chábak* newspaper wrote a series of articles in his issues of the 17th and 24th August, and 3rd September of 1858, advocating the cause of the Mahárájas, and criticising the conduct of the reforming party, no doubt stimulated to this by some interested motive. Some of this party he personally abused, and publicly named them; one of them, indignant at this proceeding, brought a civil action for damages, for it became well known that this editor had written at the instigation of a certain justice of the peace who strongly supported the cause of the Mahárájas, he being one of their most influential followers. This the editor himself made known through his journal of the 25th January, 1859; for, being cast in the action and disappointed in not receiving promised pecuniary assistance, he thus retaliated.

In justice to the *Chábak*, it is but proper to mention that the editor of this paper, before he was reduced to extremities, had advocated reform in the Parsí community, and had written ably and freely upon the subject, the *Chábak* then being one of the most popular and best vernacular papers in Bombay. Things unfortunately taking an adverse turn, he was induced, by the hope of bettering his interest, to veer round; but he was frustrated and disappointed. Whilst the action was pending in the Supreme Court, he was much pressed for money to make advances to his lawyers; and, to overcome this difficulty, it was suggested to him to subpœna some of the Mahárájas as witnesses. The Mahárájas, on this, took every care to avoid the service of the subpœna, and at the same time they closed their temples against their followers. This occasioned much commotion and great confusion in the community of the Vaishṇavas. When the temples were thus closed, the members of the sect, including the rich and influential, would not take their meals and water as enjoined by their religious duties, without first paying their adoration in the morning to the image of the idol and to the Maháráj. They were kept outside all day fasting. Upon the Vaishṇavas entreating the Mahárájas to open their temples, they refused to do so unless all the leading men in the sect would subscribe their signature to the document of which the following is a translation:—

" *To Bal-Krishnaji, greeting.*

"Samvat, 1915, month of Poushsood 12 (Sunday, 16th January, 1859) in Bombay to wit:—We Vaishṇavas, Bháttiás, and Vánias, and Lowánás, and Bhansális, and Márwádis, and Multánis, etc., (and) all conjointly, have made this agreement. Its object is to wit: that we must make arrangements in any way, by making a petition to the Government that our Gurus, all descendants of Gosáinji, should not attend the courts in case of any difficulty from Government or on being summoned. The fund subscribed by those who have framed this draft (agreement) for expenses that will be incurred by this, to be kept in some secure place. This business we all conjointly should conduct with Government, and (in this business) we should continue to join to the last, and spare nothing. Henceforth, if any Vaishṇava publishes or causes to be published a defamation of our religion, to that person his own caste men must certainly give punishment. And no Vaishṇava should summon the class of Mahárájas; and if a member of another caste summon, then all the Vaishṇavas conjointly must certainly make compromise about it.

11

This kind of agreement we all conjointly, with free faith, of our own will and accord have made. Every one must certainly conduct in this manner; any one acting contrary to the agreement is guilty of a crime against his religion and caste."

(Here follow the signatures).

" This document was signed by almost all the leading members of the Vaishṇava community, some of whom were her Majesty's Justices of the Peace and members of the Grand Jury. Its immediate object was to punish the editor of the *Satya Prakásh* by excommunication, and to make an appeal in the Legislative Council to pass an act which would secure a permanent exemption for the Mahárájas from attendance in courts of justice." *

This bond (a thorough "slavery bond," by the articles which thus stringently bound all who appended their names to it) the Mahárájas were eager to get subscribed by all the rich and influential Vaishṇavas without exception; and to fulfil the object of this bond it was further agreed :—

" 1st. That a barrister of first-rate talents should be sent to England with a view to secure a permanent exemption for the Mahárájas from attending in courts of justice. For this purpose 60,000 rupees are to be subscribed among the Hindus.

"2nd. That all cases in which the Mahárájas happen to be one of the contending parties should be referred to arbitration.

"3rd. That persons criticising the doings of Mahárájas, even in a spirit of fairness, should be punished with excommunication." †

The Mahárájas put every scheme into operation to compass their designs : they acted upon the females, who, beating their breasts and imploring with tears, solicited their husbands to yield to the wishes of these priests. They thus created considerable disturbance in the domestic circles of their followers,

---

* A pamphlet on the Mahárájas.
† *The Bombay Gazette*, January 26, 1859,

for it was not merely the willing whom they thus solicited, but even the unwilling, who were known to be the advocates of reform, whom they hoped to constrain by these strong and illegitimate measures. This was a period of severe trial to the editor of the *Satya Prakásh*, for the very friends who secretly approved and applauded the criticisms of his paper, subdued by these influences, appended their names to the " Slavery Bond." By this he was greatly perplexed, and for some time was at a loss to know what course to take, for he was fully conscious that those influential friends who had subscribed the " Slavery Bond" would be unable to assist him in caste matters. Calmly reflecting upon the line of action he should adopt, he saw that, if he yielded to the attempted tyranny of the Mahárájas, he would never again be able to put pen to paper in animadversion upon them, and that all the Vaishṇavas would be subjected to the full force of this despotism, and remain the slaves of the Mahárájas. Having, therefore, made up his mind not to submit, he wrote an article strongly reprehending the several clauses of the document, and the whole body of the Vaishṇavas became eagerly anxious for the next issue of the paper, to learn what the editor had said. We quote the translation of the *Satya Prakásh* in regard to the " Slavery Bond :"—

"The Mahárájas of the Hindus, having shut out their followers from Darshan, made them pass an important writing. The social and moral conditions of the Hindu followers of the Mahárájas is greatly dependent upon this writing. If, therefore, we omitted to bestow our own attention upon the document, we should at the same time be omitting to do what, as public writers, we ought to do. We consider it our bounden duty to lay our thoughts before our readers in an independent manner, and draw their attention to them. The following are the only principal articles inserted in that document :

"1. The people of each caste shall contribute what money the Mahárájas fix for their caste; and thus raising a large sum of fifty or sixty thousand rupees, send a learned and experienced barrister o England to get an act exempting the Mahárájas from the operation of a summons of a court of justice passed. If the above-mentioned sum be not sufficient, the Vaishnavas shall raise such other sum as may be required, and use their private means to the accomplishment of this undertaking.

"2. No Vaishnava from among the followers of the Mahárájas shall, for any cause or for any risk, issue a summons of a court of justice against a Maháráj.

"No Vaishnava from among the followers of the Mahárájas shall publish, either himself or through others, even a word tending to injure the Maháráj's feeling in any newspaper, pamphlet, or handbill. If any person infringe the second and third articles, their caste people shall inflict proper punishments upon them.

"4. If persons belonging to castes which do not believe in the Mahárájas issue summons against them, all the Vaishnavas shall combine, and come to an amicable settlement with the party or parties who summoned the Maháráj, submitting to the loss of any sum; and shall take such measures as shall not necessitate the attendance of a Maháráj at any tribunal or court of justice.

"The Mahárájas have taken a writing from their followers containing the above-mentioned four articles. It has been already signed by such Hindu Shetiás as . . . . . . and other Vaishnavas. Those who have not yet signed it are shut out by the Mahárájas from Darshan. It is reported that these will sign in a day or two.

"The fifth article which the Mahárájas had inserted in this writing, stated that no Vaishnava should buy or peruse such newspapers as contained anything likely to injure the Maharáj's feelings. But the Shetiás objected to this, and got it struck off. We publish below our own thoughts on each of the above-mentioned articles, and invite to them the attention of the Vaishnavas and other readers.

"About the first article. In this article the Mahárájas seek to claim exemption from the operation of a summons of a court of justice at an expense of the large sum of fifty or sixty thousand rupees. Those who are familiar with the technicalities of English laws, and tactics of English politicians, will at once pronounce that the Mahárájas will fail in the accomplishment of their desire, and that this large sum of money will be thrown into the water. Any barrister or European will undertake to be the champion of the Mahárájas with great pleasure and thankfulness, in order to fill his own pocket, and enjoy for a short time the sweets of his native land. But we hope the Mahárájas, and the Shetiás, their followers, will consider well before they incur such a large expense. They must know

that, under the just and equitable sway of the English, every subject
has a right to summons any person whatever to appear in a court of
justice in order to preserve his rights and liberties. Never will the
Mahárájas be exempt from the operations of this process. Even
great officers, whose time is extremely valuable, whose one minute
is sometimes equal to one month, are obliged, when necessary, to
wait for a long time in a court of justice. In consideration of the
value of their time, no act has been passed to excuse their attendance even for emergent business. It must, therefore, be fully considered upon what powerful grounds an act conferring such a privilege can be passed in favour of the Mahárájas, who spend a greater
portion of their time in jollity and pleasure, and make no objection
to see the dockyard and the Mint, and travel on railways. Let the
petition be signed by the greatest number of persons, however respectable they may be, the English politicians will neither pay
attention to the signatures nor to the persons who made those signatures. They will ponder over the request in the petition, and if
they find that it is likely to tarnish the fair fame of English justice,
they will in no case comply with it. We heartily wish that before
this large sum of fifty or sixty thousand rupees is thrown into the
water, the Gosái Mahárájas and their principal followers may consider this matter fully and seriously. On our part we advise the
Mahárájas and their leading followers, that, instead of throwing this
large sum of fifty or sixty thousand rupees into the water, they
should rather expend it on the Victoria Museum, by which means
they would be expressing affectionate and loyal regard towards her
gracious Majesty, and would be aiding an important undertaking.
We suggest an easy and plain way, that would be universally liked,
by which the Mahárájas might be exempted from appearing in a
court of justice. If it is adopted, we confidently say that the Mahárájas will have no need to appear any day in any court. What plan
is this? The Mahárájas should never interfere in any man's private
quarrels and concerns; they should win the love and affectionate regard of their friends and followers by upright and moral behaviour;
they should always aid such undertakings as will improve the cause
of their country's progress; they should cease all money dealings
with people of other castes; they should preach morality every day,
and observe no distinction between their rich and poor followers.
If they act in this manner, we confidently say that they will never
have to appear in a court.

"About the second article. This article suggests that no Vaish-

ṇavas shall for any cause summons a Maháráj to appear in a court
of justice.  We say, without fear of persecution, that this is hard
and oppressive.  If the Mahárájas do not interpose in a man's private concerns, and improperly wrong any Vaishṇava, it is plain that
no necessity would remain at all to take one's religious preceptor to
a court of justice.  Where, then, was the necessity of inserting such
a hard clause.  Any impartial thinker would at once honestly say
that the Mahárájas extorted such a hard clause from their followers,
simply that they might be free to interfere in one's private concerns
and administer arbitrary justice.  We say again, religious preachers
and preceptors ought never to make their followers to pass such a
hard writing to them.  Who can be so imprudent and rash as to summon his religious preceptor to a court of justice without any cause ?
After such a writing, it appears clear how the Mahárájas intend to
behave towards their followers, and how they wish their followers
to behave towards them.  We wish that the Mahárájas would look
to their respectability and position, and annul this article at once.

" About the third article.  This article suggests that no Vaishṇava shall write a word tending to injure the feelings of the Mahárájas.  With all due deference to the holy position of these religious
preceptors, we beg leave to say that we feel this to be a harder and
more oppressive article than the second.  The English Government
possesses such power and authority, that the native tyrants are too
feeble to cope with and encounter it.  Even this Government cannot peremptorily say to the newspapers, " Do not write anything
that would injure our feelings."  When even such a potent and
powerful Government cannot pretend to wield such an authority,
the Mahárájas, whose authority, when compared with the world,
extends over but a handful of Vaishṇavas, will never be allowed, in
this just and equitable reign of the English, to exercise this hard and
oppressive sway over the independent newspaper writers.  The
Mahárájas and their advisers have signally erred by inserting such
a hard article.  Had they exercised a little more discretion, they
would never have thought of inserting this selfish article.  We
heartily wish that this paper may not have to say ill of the Mahárájas.  But it is an error to suppose that this or any other newspaper will be backward in expressing just and proper thoughts, when
they find that public interests are at stake.  It is true that this, as
well as other respectable newspapers, will always refrain, as they
have done till this day, from publishing false slanders and un-
grounded stories about the Mahárájas; but no editor, living

under the shadow and protection of the English Government, will draw his pen backwards in denouncing any unjust act tending to jeopardize the weal of thousands. None will fear to publish anything just and proper. We are sorry to say that the Mahárájas and their followers have, by thus shutting the mouths of editors, ruined their own cause.

"About the fourth article. This article suggests that, if persons who belong to castes which do not believe in the Mahárájas summon Mahárájas in a court of justice, all Vaishṇavas shall combine, and at the cost of any sum come to an amicable settlement with them, or adopt such measures as will not necessitate the personal attendance of the Mahárájas to a court of justice. It appears that the Mahárájas and their followers have used no better discretion with regard to this than with the foregoing three articles. Any person who may have any money dispute about the Mahárájas will at once take advantage of this and issue a summons against them. Thus Vaishṇavas will be forced by this article to come to an amicable settlement with all the Mahárájas' creditors. If this necessarily becomes frequent, and involves the expenditure of large sums, the Vaishṇavas will find how feeble they are to bear the evils which they have themselves drawn upon their shoulders. These articles will then be annulled as a matter of course.

"Thoughts common to all the articles. It will be evident from this that not one of these four articles is just and harmless. Every one of them is as unjust and reprehensible as it is injurious to the social and private interests of all the Vaishṇavas. We are glad to say that their leading followers would not consent to the fifth article, which relates to the buying of newspapers. Had this been retained, they would never have progressed. But the Mahárájas and their followers will never be able to impede the sounding western torrent of civilization which has begun to flow with all its might towards this country. Those who inserted these four articles may insert fifty more, but no tyrants or their slavish followers will have power to impede the mighty torrent of civilization. We are sure that the current of civilization and liberty will in a short time overspread the whole of Hindustan, check the force of the opponents of civilization, and break the chains of oppression.

"It will not fail to excite both wonder and sorrow in any man of good sense to see that the very Shetiás who have been the foremost among the reformers, and thoroughly understand the beauty which the English rule affords, should have, by signing such a hard document, drawn the chains of despotism on their own hands. We wish, and pray to God that our wish may succeed, that these Shetiás may speedily look to their own respectability, to their own states in life, to the beauties of the benign and free government they are under, and boldly break off the shackles of despotism which they have worn. We have dwelt rather too long on the subject, and therefore we shall not say more, but conclude with the following prayer to God:

"O God! may the chain of despotism which the leading Shetiás, our companions in the cause of civilization, have worn round their necks, be quickly removed. O God! may the Shetiás who have temporarily lost their senses, and forgotten their respectability and position, recover their senses soon. O God! may the cloud of ignorance and doubt which has obscured the vision of our Shetiás be quickly dispelled, and may the faces of those who oppose civilization at once be covered with paleness. Amen." *

This article was followed by a succession of anonymous hand-bills, issued by various persons; and two prize essays were advertised in the *Satya Prakásh*, one upon the "Slavery Bond," and the other "Upon the Authority of the Mahárájas." These several attacks had the desired effect. The Mahárájas and their followers speedily discovered that, if the editor were excommunicated, he would file an action and drag the Mahárájas to the bar of justice. The funds the worshippers had been asked to raise were not realized; for the subscribers, seeing the drift of events, waited with impatience to ascertain if the conditions of that article of the "Slavery Bond" which threatens with punishment any one writing against the Mahárájas would be carried out. The timidity of the Mahárájas hindered them from taking this course, and their neglect to pronounce sentence of excommunication encouraged the Vaishnavas to withhold their subscriptions. The notorious "Slavery Bond," the object of which was to bind in still stronger fetters the patient Vaishnavas, thus fell to the ground, and the supreme Maháráj himself took flight from Bombay.

* *The Satya Prakásh*, January 23, 1859.

In the action brought against the editor of the *Chábak* by the Vaishṇava whom he had so conspicuously denounced, the editor pleaded not guilty, and that what he had published was not libellous. The court overruled this plea, after examining the plaintiff's witnesses, affirming it to be libellous, and entered a decree, with costs, against the Parsee editor, who thereupon solicited the "gentleman" by whom he had been specially instigated, to assist him. He was grossly disappointed by his refusal, and therefore published in his paper the name of the individual, and all the circumstances connected with the affair. This poor Parsee editor, being unable to pay all the incidental costs, died broken-hearted, in very distressed circumstances.

In the process of this "Slavery Bond," and all its adjuncts, we observe a further declension of the power and influence of the Mahárájas, to which the Libel Case, into the history of which we shall now enter, has given, we hope and expect, the fatal blow.

# CHAPTER XI.

## THE MAHÁRÁJ LIBEL CASE.

THE Mahárájas, being thus defeated in their attempts to prevent the public press from exposing their misdeeds, sought to attain their object by other means. Jadunáthji Brizratanji Maháráj, of Surat, upon arriving at Bombay in the middle of the year 1860, consulted with some of his followers with a view to ascertain whether an action for libel, brought by him against the publishers, could be prosecuted in his absence from the court, or whether, as plaintiff, his presence would be held to be necessary; for he wished to avoid appearing in a court of justice.

The editor of the *Satya Prakásh*, not being aware of the specific object of the Maháráj's visit to Bombay, but having heard that he had established a school at Surat, gave him a hearty welcome in his paper, and expressed a hope that he would render material assistance to the cause of education. This expectation seemed at first to be realised; for the Maháráj consented to be present at an exhibition of the Gujaráti girls' schools, and to distribute the prizes with his own hand, thus publicly expressing his approval of the education of females. The Mahárájas of Bombay, who had often been solicited to do the same thing, had always declined, and Jadunathji Brizratanji having accepted the invitation, the editor of the *Satya Prakásh* hailed it as a great victory in the cause of educational reform; for, owing to the populace being adverse to female education, the influence of the Maháráj's position gave it a strong and powerful support. The editor, unconscious and unsuspicious of the deception intended to be practised, was thus induced to speak of the Maháráj in terms of eulogy; but he soon discovered that the person whom he had praised was a wolf in sheep's clothing.

A friend of the editor, named Narmadá Shankar Lálshankar, a Nágar Bráhman, and, who was not a follower of the Mahárájas, invited the Maháráj to hold a public discussion upon the subject of the re-marriage of Hindu widows, to which the Maháráj was opposed. The invitation was by means of hand-bills, dated the 15th of August, 1860. The Maháráj accepted the challenge, and the meeting was held six days after the issue of the hand-bills, at a place selected by himself, where a warm discussion took place. Many Shástras (religious books) were brought forward as authorities, and a large number of persons assembled to hear the discussions. The Maháráj, feeling that he could not maintain his position by argument, entered into a desultory discussion with his opponent, who is a celebrated Gujaráti poet, and asked him whether he believed the Hindu Shástras to be of divine inspiration, saying that, before going into the question of re-marriage, he must first know the poet's opinion upon this point. The gentleman replied that he could not believe all the reputed religious works to be of divine inspiration, as they contained incorporated works on grammar and other miscellaneous subjects which had no religious bearing whatever, and which, therefore, he rightly maintained, could not be divinely inspired. The discussion did not pass beyond this subject, and the meeting broke up.

The Maháráj, doubtless stung with shame on account of his failure in the discussion, insidiously gave his followers to understand that the principles of the reform party were adverse to the ancient religion of the Hindus. Upon this, the editor of the *Satya Prakásh* took up the subject in the paper, and invited the Maháráj to discuss the matter through the medium of the press, and so give a wide circle of readers the opportunity of judging for themselves in the matter. This discussion was carried on in several issues of the paper. The Maháráj replied to the arguments, and simultaneously issued a monthly magazine, under his patronage, called *Svadharma Vardhak* and *Samshaya Chhekak* (meaning Promoter of our Religion and Destroyer of Doubt). In this magazine he carried on the discussion previously commenced; but not being able to give direct answers to questions put to him, he became annoyed, and charged his adversaries with entertaining heretical and mischievous dogmas and opinions. The question of re-marriage originally mooted having been transformed altogether into a religious question, the editor of *Satya Prakásh* wrote the following article, which originated the Libel Case, and became the subject of the judicial inquiries which followed :—

### *The Primitive Religion of the Hindus, and the present Heterodox Opinions.*

"In the Puráns and other Shástras of the Hindus, it is stated that in the Kali-yug there will arise false religions and heresies, and impostors and heretics will cause adverse persuasions and adverse religious systems to be established. According to the Hindu Shástras, five thousand years have now passed away since the commencement of the Kali-yug. From the Hindu Shástras themselves it is demonstrated that, during this period of five thousand years, as many new persuasions and religious systems as have arisen among the Hindus should all be considered spurious heresies. Now, four hundred years have not as yet elapsed since the birth of Vallabha, the progenitor of the Mahárájas. In the books of the Vaishnava persuasion it is written that the birth of Vallabháchárya took place on the 11th of Vaishak Vad, of Samvat 1535, the day of the week Sunday. Since this event three hundred and eighty-one years have elapsed to this day, and since the beginning of the Kali-yug five thousand years have passed. The sect of Vallabháchárya, then, originated within the Kali-yug itself. In the same way as the followers of Dádu, the followers of Sádhu, the Rámsnehi, the Rámánandi, the Shejanandi, and other sects arose, so the sect of

Vallabháchárya arose: all these sects have arisen in the Kali-yug; therefore, according to the declarations of the Hindu Shástras, they must be heterodox.

"Jadunáthji Mahárái says, that in the same way as some one goes from the gates of the fort to proceed to Wálkeshwar, and some one to Byculla, so exactly the original courses of the Veds and the Puráns, having gone forward, have diverged into different ways. What a deceitful proposition this is. Out of one religious system ten or fifteen byeways must not branch off. The course of religion and of morals must be one only. What necessity is there to quit the straight road by which to go to Wálkeshwar, ar-d take the circuitous road of Byculla? Each sectary has made every other sectary a heretic, and one has scattered dust upon the other; what, then, is the necessity for acting thus? But we have already made known that, as regards the weapons with which the Mahárái has come forth to defend himself, those very weapons will oppose the Mahárái and annoy him. The Mahárái considers the Hindu Shástras as the work of God; he cannot then assert that any particular statement of the Hindu Shástras is false. The said Mahárái cannot allege that the statement, that in the Kali-yug heretical opinions will arise, is false. Then, like several other sects, the sect of the Mahárájas has arisen in the Kali-yug; consequently it is established by the Hindu Shástras that it is a false and heretical one.

"The sect of the Mahárájas is heretical, and one delusive to simple people: this is proved by the genuine books of the Veds, the Puráns, etc., according to what is intimated above. Not only this, but also from the works composed by the Mahárájas it is proved that the Mahárájas have raised up nothing but a new heresy and disorder. Behold, with regard to *Bramha Sambhanda*, how Gokulnáthji has amplified the original stanza, what a commentary he has made:—

तस्मादादौ खोपभोगात्पूर्वमेव सर्ववस्तुपदेन भार्यापुत्रादीनामपि समर्पणं कर्तव्यं । विवाहानंतरं खोपभोगे सर्वकार्ये सर्वकार्यनिमित्तं तत्कायौपभोगिवस्तुसमर्पणं कार्यं । समर्पणं छत्वा पश्चात्तानि तानि कार्याणि कर्तव्यानीत्यर्थः ॥ ٧ ॥

"'Consequently, before he himself has enjoyed her, he should make over his own married wife (to the Mahárái), and he should also make over to him his sons and daughters. After having got married, he should, before having himself enjoyed his wife, make an offering of her (to the Maháráj); after which he should apply her to his own use.'"

"Alas! what a heresy is this, what a sham is this, and what a delusion is this! We ask Jadunáthji Maháráj in what Ved, in what Puráṇa, in what Shástra, and in what law-book it is written that one's married wife should be made over to a Maháráj, or to a religious preceptor, before being enjoyed. Not only one's wife, but one's daughter also is to be made over! Alas! in writing this, our pen will not move on. We are seized with utter disgust and agitation. To render blind people who see with their eyes, and to throw dust in their eyes, and in the name of religion, and under the pretence of religion, to enjoy their tender maidens, wives, and daughters—than this what greater heresy and what greater deceit? In the Kali-yug many other heresies and many sects have arisen besides that of Vallabháchárya; but no other sectaries have ever perpetrated such shamelessness, subtlety, immodesty, rascality, and deceit, as have the sect of the Mahárájas. When we use such severe terms as these, our simple Hindu friends are wroth with us, and in consequence of that wrath of theirs, we have endured much, and have much to endure. But when, throwing dust in the eyes of simple people, the Mahárájas write in their books about enjoying the tender maidens, the people's wives, and daughters, and they enjoy them accordingly—great flames spring up within our breasts, our pen at once becomes heated and on fire, and we have to grieve over our Hindu friends, and over their weak powers of reflection.

"Jadunáthji Maháráj has commenced issuing a small work, styled 'The Propagator of our own Religion.' We ask him, In what way do you wish to effect the propagation of religion? Your ancestors, having scattered dust in the eyes of simple people, made them blind. Do you wish to make them see? or, taking a false pride in the upholding of your religion, do you wish to delude simple people still more? Jadunáthji Maháráj! should you wish to propagate or to spread abroad religion, then do you personally adopt a virtuous course of conduct, and admonish your other Mahárájas. As long as the preceptors of religion shall themselves appear to be immersed in the sea of licentiousness, for so long they shall not be competent to convey religious exhortation to others. Gokulnáthji having composed the commentary above-mentioned, has attached to your Vaishṇava persuasion a great blot of ink. Let that be first removed.

Scorn the writer of the commentary. (Oh you) Mahárájas, acting up to that commentary, defile the wives and daughters of your devotees; desist from that, and destroy at once immorality such as that of the Rás Mandali. As long as you shall not do so, for so long you cannot give religious admonition, and propagate your own religious faith: do you be pleased to be assured of that."

This article was written on the 21st of October, 1860. The Maháráj maintained silence upon the subject, still carrying on the discussion of religious topics with the editor. On the 14th of the following May, however, seven months after the publication of the alleged libel, he filed an action of libel against both editor and printer.

The plaint was demurred to by defendant's counsel, and the case was argued under this bearing on the 2nd and 4th of July, 1861. Hereupon the plaintiff had to make certain amendments in the plaint, and the defendant then pleaded several pleas, on the 15th of August, 1861.

The first was a plea of not guilty, viz., that the article alluded to was not libellous; and the last plea was one of justification, viz., that what had been stated was true, both in letter and spirit. But this plea consisted of three portions—the first asserting that there were passages in the religious books of the Mahárájas which inculcated adulterous worship; the second, that the Mahárájas, as a body, committed adultery; and the third, that the plaintiff was not an exception to the general practice. The intermediate pleas were of inferior consequence.

When the pleas were filed by the defendant, the managers of the Maháráj's case knew from the nature of the pleas that the defendant was prepared to bring forward witnesses to corroborate the charges made. Upon this they communicated with the influential portion of the community, and made them aware of the danger that might result from the exposure that would necessarily take place in court. The leading men of the Bháttiá community convened a meeting of their caste on the 6th of September, 1861, and resolved that none of the caste should give evidence against the Maháráj; and they further resolved, that whoever did so should be subjected to the pains and penalties included in the comprehensive term, "excommunication." This resolution was clearly illegal, amounting, in fact, to a conspiracy. Indeed, it gave rise to two accusations of conspiracy. The special charge was, having concerted measures to obstruct and defeat the ends of justice, by dissuading and preventing others from giving evidence in the Libel Case, in which they had been summoned as witnesses. The defendants in the case were Gokuldás Liládhar and eight others. These were all highly respectable persons, who had been led to do what they did by the instigation of the Maháráj; but they were convicted of the offence on evidence which left no doubt of their guilt, and sentenced—the two chief culprits, Gokuldás Liládhar and Lakmidás Dámji, to pay a fine of a thousand rupees each; and the other defendants to pay a fine of fifty rupees each. In inflicting these penalties, Sir Joseph Arnould observed that the law empowered him to accompany them with a sentence of hard labour, but that, considering all the circumstances of the case, and the very high character the defendants bore, he should only inflict a pecuniary penalty.

This was the end of an abortive attempt to defeat the ends of justice, and a well-merited punishment of the offenders who yielded too weakly to the urgency of their abettors.

This conspiracy, in the course of its being tried, in the first place in the police court, and subsequently in the Supreme Court, created a very great sensation amongst the population of Bombay, but especially in the religious community, the defendants being leading men, and having extensive native and European connections of a superior class. The first day, when the preliminary examination took place in the police court, the defendant in the Maháráj's case, who was the prosecutor in this, was severely assaulted by the mob when he left the court, and, in consequence, solicited the protection of the magistrate. Had it not been for the energetic exertions of Mr. Forgett, the superintendent of the police, it is not improbable that he would have been killed by the populace. This excitement continued during the whole time that the case was pending, and threats of every kind were used, both against him and his witnesses, who, as well as himself, were obliged to seek the protection of the police.

The trial of the Maháráj Libel Case came on before the court on the 26th January, 1862. It was conducted by Mr. Bayley and Mr. Scoble, on behalf of the Maháráj, and by Mr. Anstey and Mr. Dunbar, on behalf of the defendant. The labours of Mr. Anstey in his client's defence exceed all praise. We should not be transgressing the limits of truth were we to ascribe the decision in the defendant's favour, in the greatest measure, to the very extensive legal attainments, the varied abilities, and the intense earnestness which this advocate brought to bear on the case. Those who attended the trial could bear witness to the skill and dexterity with which he turned the scales against the Maháráj, by arraying against him even the knotty points of Hindu theology; for, persuaded that his client's cause represented the truth and the right of free thought, as well as the liberty of speech, he spared no pains to study its complicated literature. The trial extended over forty days, but was before the Court only twenty-four days. In the Appendix will be found specimens of the evidence, and the entire judgment. About thirty witnesses were examined for the plaintiff, and thirty witnesses for the defendant, some of the latter of whom were learned and influential men.

Dr. Wilson's labours in this trial deserve special notice. He placed at the disposal of the defendant his rich and multifarious stores of learning, which proved of surpassing value. Throughout the whole trial this learned missionary ably sustained the character which he fills in the estimation of the natives of India—that of a philanthropist.

Much credit is due to Drs. Bháu Dáji and Dhirajrám Dalpatrám, for the disinterestedness of their evidence. They cast aside all consideration of self, when truth was to be established and morality to be vindicated.

The name of Lakhmidás Khimji, a leading member of the Bháttiá community, deserves honourable mention. Though nurtured from childhood in the filthy doctrines of the Vallabhácháryan faith, the moment the conviction flashed upon his mind that religion can never be a plea for immorality, he fearlessly lent his aid to the defendant, and gave, perhaps, the most damaging evidence against the Maháráj. Strenuous attempts were made to impeach his veracity, and impugn his evidence, on the ground of its intrinsic improbability. These efforts, however, proved fruitless, as he spoke the whole truth from his own personal knowledge.

It would be a very great omission if the name of Mr. Mathúrádás Lavji were passed over in silence. He furnished the sinews of war, so far as learning was concerned : his capacious mind and memory comprehends the whole range of vernacular literature, both ancient and modern ; and to his vast attainments he adds a rare tact in moulding the minds of others to his own opinions, an intimate acquaintance with the turnings and windings of the human heart, and a steady force of character and decision, dangerous to his enemies, but valuable for the advancement of truth.

Not a little credit is due to Mr. Nánábhái Rustamji Rániná, the printer and manager of the Union Press, for the honesty, integrity, and zeal with which he conducted himself throughout the case.

The names of the other following witnesses for the defence

also deserve notice for their evidence and their boldness in giving it. They are, viz., Messrs. Vishvanáth Náráyan Mandalik, Mangaldás Nathubhái, Khatási Makanji, Thakarsi Náranji, Ravji Sundardás, Dámodar Jethá, Narmdáshankas Lálshankar, Rámdás Bhánji, Káhndás Manchhárám, Kálábhái Lalubhái, Chaturbhuj Wálji, and Tribhovandás Dwárkádás.

A further remarkable feature in the character of this trial is the complete exposure of the lives and practices of the Mahárájas, and of the moral and social conditions of Western India. The large mob that thronged the court daily, during the course of the trial, spreading themselves throughout all the apartments of this large hall of justice, attested to the profound interest which it excited in the different communities of Bombay. When the judgment was given, there were several of the most respectable persons of Bombay present. In the opinion of both the judges, the justification of the libel was proved to the very letter, and the Court stigmatized the plaintiff and his witnesses as unworthy of belief even on their oaths. With respect to the defendant's first plea of not guilty, the Chief Justice differed from the Puisne, holding that a public writer could not make an attack upon the conduct of an individual in his private capacity, although he might be depraved and an adulterer; and, besides that the defendant, having no previous knowledge of the plaintiff's misconduct, was not justified in publishing an attack upon him, although the allegations subsequently turned out to be true. The Puisne Judge, on the other hand, held that it was not an attack on the private character of the plaintiff, but on his public character as a Maháráj, or religious preceptor, and that the defendant was quite aware of the existing practices in the sect.

The verdict was entered by the Court in favour of the defendant on the main issue of justification, and with costs, and for the plaintiff on the first plea of "not guilty," without costs.

The defendant incurred an expense of about 13,000 rupees in the action, out of which about 11,500 rupees were paid by the Maháráj, in addition to his own costs. The defendant, of course, incurred other private expenses incidental to the trial, as also in the trial of the Bháttiá Conspiracy, the expenses of which amounted to about 10,000 rupees.

The total expenses on both sides may be computed at about 60,000 rupees, of which about 50,000 rupees fell upon the Maháráj, that curiously being the identical sum for which he had sued the defendant as damages.

We cannot do better than terminate this portion of the subject with the close of the judgment of the learned Puisne Judge, Sir Joseph Arnould, who says in his admirable finding :—

"This trial has been spoken of as having involved a great waste of the public time. I cannot quite agree with that opinion. No doubt much time has been spent in hearing this cause, but I would fain hope it has not been all time wasted. It seems impossible that this matter should have been discussed thus openly before a population so intelligent as that of the natives of Western India, without producing its results. It has probably taught some to think ; it must have led many to enquire. It is not a question of theology that has been before us ; it is a question of morality. The principle for which the defendant and his witnesses have been contending is simply this, that what is morally wrong cannot be theologically right ; that when practices which sap the very foundations of morality, which involve a violation of the eternal and immutable laws of Right, are established in the name and under the sanction of Religion, they ought, for the common welfare of society, and in the interest of humanity itself, to be publicly denounced and exposed. They have denounced—they have exposed them. At a risk and at a cost which we cannot adequately measure, these men have done determined battle against a foul and powerful delusion. They have dared to look custom and error boldly in the face, and proclaim before the world of their votaries that their evil is not good, that their lie is not the truth. In thus doing, they have done bravely and well. It may be allowable to express a hope that what they have done will not have been in vain; that the seed they have sown will bear its fruit; that their courage and consistency will be rewarded by a steady increase in the number of those whom their words and their examples have quickened into thought, and animated to resistance, whose homes they have helped to cleanse from loathsome lewdness, and whose souls they have set free from a debasing bondage."

The history of the sect of Vallabháchárya, which has been here unfolded, reads like a chapter of romance. It is the history of a sect in which immorality is elevated to the rank of a *divine* law. The immutable distinctions of right and wrong, the sharp line of demarcation between virtue and vice, human personality and human responsibility, are lost and confounded in a system of theology which begins in lewdness and ends in the complete subversion of the first principles of our common nature. Such a system has, perhaps, no parallel in the annals of our race. Its effects can be more easily conceived than described. It has checked and arrested the healthy growth of all moral power. It has furnished its votaries with principles of action, which, if carried out in their integrity, must produce the dissolution of society ; for it treats holiness of life as a crime, and proclaims to " the world of its votaries" that man becomes acceptable to his MAKER *in and through sin.*

It would be strange indeed if the discussions awakened by the trial should bring about no tangible result. The sect, though to all appearance powerful in organization, is in an unsettled state. While the old and bigoted cling with pertinacity to the dogmas of their childhood, the young and the educated detach themselves more and more from its contaminating influences. Assailed from without, and racked by internal dissensions, the Vallabhácháryan faith must, sooner or later, be superseded by a more rational form of worship. The obstacles in the way of a thorough revolution are great, but not insurmountable. That the power of the Mahárájas for evil is not what it was fifteen years ago, is one sign of progress. Let us express a fervent hope that, by the combined exertions and the steady co-operation of all lovers of truth and moral purity, the Vallabháchárfrom the darkness of error and falsehood into the glorious light of day, and that the faith proclaimed by Vallabhá four hundred years ago may be crushed by the weight of its own enormities !

THE END.

# APPENDIX,

CONTAINING

## SPECIMENS OF THE EVIDENCE,

AND THE

## JUDGMENT IN THE LIBEL CASE,

WITH

## COMMENTS OF THE INDIAN PRESS.

# APPENDIX.

SPECIMENS OF THE EVIDENCE IN THE MAHÁRÁJ LIBEL CASE GIVEN BEFORE THE SUPREME (NOW HIGH) COURT OF BOMBAY.

## (*Evidence for the Prosecution.*)

(*Gopáldás Mádhavadás*, examined *January* 25, 1862.) I am the head of the Máhajans of the Banian caste of all denominations. They are numerous in Bombay. It is necessary to obtain my permission to hold meetings of the caste. I know the plaintiff Jadunáthji Brizrattanji Maháráj, who is about 40 or 42 years of age. He occasionally resides in Bombay at intervals of 10 or 20 years. He is a resident of Surat. The Baniáns and Bháttiás consider the Maháráj in a very good light, and respect him. The plaintiff is a Maháráj : he is our *guru* or spiritual guide, who worships our idols and performs divine service. The Maháráj is a Bráhmin, and is above the ordinary run of Bráhmins. Some Bráhmins regard him as a guru. The Bháttiás are worshippers of the Maháráj. The Bhátyá caste is different from the Baniá. They both respect the Mahárájás equally, as their gurus. A guru performs divine service and worships the images. The Maháráj may preach sermons, but I am in the habit of going to him only three or four times in the year. The Bráhmins read the Puráns and other religious books to the people. The Mahárájás occasionally read the Puráns, but are generally engaged in worshipping the images. The Mahárájás have temples in Bombay. There are sometimes two, sometimes five, and sometimes ten, and perhaps more Mahárájás in Bombay. Some permanently reside here, as, for instance, Jivanji Maháráj. In India, I believe, there are now about 60 or 70 Mahárújás. The Maháráj of Shriji is considered the chief; he has

1

a temple at Náthdwár, near Udeypor, in Northern India. The Mahárájás are spread over the cities of Hindustán. The Rájáhs and native princes respect the Mahárájás in the same manner as their devotees do. I have resided all my life in Bombay. I am a subscriber to the *Satya Prakásh* newspaper. I may have read the article upon which this action is brought. The *Satya Prakásh* is now amalgamated with the *Rást Goftár*.

(Cross-examined.) I have never been to the principal seats of the Mahárájás in India, nor have I seen the Mahárájás worshipped by the Rájáhs, and what I have said about the Mahárájás is what I have heard about them. I have recollection of an unpleasant controversy which was going on in 1911–12 (1855) between the Mahárájás and the Bráhmins. The controversy related to our religion. I was engaged in it against the Mahárájás. I don't remember Lálmaniji Maháráj issuing an order eight years ago, calling upon members of his caste to repair to his house and to give him presents; neither did Lálmaniji Maháráj give such an order ten years ago. I do not recollect incurring the displeasure of Lálmaniji for denying his right to ask for presents. I have not heard of the complaints among the Vallabhácháryas of the adulterous practices of the Mahárájás with their wives and daughters, but I have read some complaints of them in the *Satya Prakásh* and *Parsi Panch*, which I first began to read about five or six years ago. I have not signed a paper prepared by the Mahárájás, binding me to implicit obedience, especially with reference to these accusations; but many persons have signed such a paper, which I have heard was prepared by the Mahárájás. I have heard from the Baniáns, members of the sect, that an engagement has been entered into by Baniáns, Bháttiás, and all the sects to do their utmost to prevent the Mahárájás from being called as witnesses in a court of justice. This engagement has been designated the "slavery bond" by the printers and newspaper writers. I can't say whether others call it so. I have not signed this bond. It is true that to get the bond signed, the Mahárájás kept the temple closed eight days. This was about four years ago. I do not know of any attempt being made by the Mahárájás to get Karsandás excommunicated from the caste of Baniáns for writing articles against them. Such an attempt was made. Two persons

came to me and said that as the Bháttiás had made an arrangement we should make it also : this was but a day or two after
the signatures were obtained, to intimidate witnesses from giving
evidence in this case against the Maháráj. One was Parbhudás,
and the other Jaykisandás. They are both Baniáns, so am I, and
so is the defendant. Parbhudás is the person who is managing the
case for the plaintiff in this present action, and is sitting down in
Court behind the professional advisers on the part of the plaintiff.
He came to me once only about the business of excommunication. I said that if what Karsandás had published is false, the
Court will punish him. I refused to interfere, as the Maháráj had
brought an action against him. They went away. I can't say that
they knew whether I was going to give evidence for the defendant
in this action. The Maharájás are not the preceptors or spiritual
guides of all the Hindus, but only of the Bháttiás and Baniáns and
some Bráhmins. The majority of the Baniáns believe in the
Maharájás. Some of the Baniáns are Jains. Jain Baniáns don't
believe in the Maharájás. I have not heard of any Baniáns regarding the Maháráj as Almighty God incarnate in the flesh. I cannot
say whether Bháttiás regard the Maháráj as the incarnation of
the Deity, but some may believe in the Maháráj as the incarnation
of God, while others do not. [Mr. Anstey.—Do the whole sect of
Vallabháchárya regard the Maharájás as gods ?] I cannot say what
they think. Some people do say that they are gods, while some
deny that they are. It is the opinion of the Vallabhácháryans, that
the Maharájás and their descendants are incarnations of Brahma and
Vishnu, and deserve to be worshipped with the mind, property
and body of their followers. I believe it to be a sin of the gravest
character to neglect this worship. I cannot say if it is the duty of
female devotees (as stated in the plea) to love the Maharájás and to
be connected in adultery and lust with them. If such doctrine or
passage was shown me in any of the books I call Shástras, I would
take it as good and true. Referring to the "bandobast" (arrangement) I meant to refer to the Conspiracy Case of the *Queen* vs.
*Gokaldás Liládhar* and others. I heard the arrangement was to
prevent any person from giving evidence here on behalf of Karsandás : and the "bandobast" I was asked to sign was to the same

effect. The Mahárájás decide caste disputes, and also themselves fall into caste disputes. I do not know if some castes have had to complain of the Mahárájás seizing the property of widows and orphans; I have never heard such a thing. The Mahárájás have temples in Bombay: sometimes when there are marriages and such occasions, dancing and singing go on in the temples ; but not in the part where the idols are kept. Prostitutes are invited on such occasions to dance in the temple. Prostitutes are also invited to the party. In those temples the Mahárájás worship the idols, and men and women worship, sometimes, the Mahárájás. They prostrate themselves at the Maháráj's feet. By worshipping the Maháráj I understand applying to him scent and stuff, and offering him fruits and flowers, in the same way as the idols are worshipped. When we fall down before the Maháráj, he blesses us. One mode of worshipping the idol is by swinging it, and our women worship the Maháráj by swinging him in a swing. On certain occasions the Maháráj throws *gulál* (red powder) on the persons of men and women. It is thrown from a distance, and it may fall upon the necks and breasts of women. It is not considered among our people equivalent to adultery to throw gulál on the breast of a woman. If any person throw gulál on the breast of a woman our people don't consider it indecent or shameful. I do not know if other people consider it so. I have not heard of any Maháráj touching the breast of any of my relatives or of any other female. The *pán-sopári* thrown off by the Maháráj is taken in hand and eaten by his devotees. The water rinsed and wrung from the Maháráj's *dhotiá* (loin cloth) is drunk by his devotees and is known as *charanámrit, i.e.*, ambrosia or the nectar of the feet. Some portion of the remnants of the food eaten by the Maháráj is eaten by his followers. The water with which the Maháráj bathes is not drunk. I have been only three or four times in the year to visit the Maháráj. The Maháráj sees men and women in the same open space. I don't know if there are rooms of the Maháráj to which females only have access. If the Maháráj has a family, he keeps a separate " zenáná" in the temple. I do not recollect whether two or three years ago a meeting of the Bháttiás was held with a view to prevent females from going to the Maháráj in his private rooms.

(Re-examined). Plaintiff was not in Bombay four years ago. People of our caste follow the customs and usages of our ancestors; while some others follow the Shástras as religious instructors. They take their opinions from the gurus or Bráhmins. I have never been to a dance at the Maháráj's temple. The Mahárájás usually reside in the temple on one side, or in a separate dwelling-house, sometimes in a place within the compound, and sometimes in a house opposite to the temple. There are doors and entrances between the house and the temples. The dances take place in the house on one side, and sometimes in the compound of the temple. All nách-dancers in Bombay are prostitutes. Nách-dances are frequently given by respectable persons on occasion of the celebration of marriages and other events. The plaintiff is married and has children. The Mahárájás object to come and give evidence in courts. They would not incur anybody's displeasure if they came here; but as they might be detained two or three days, they would be prevented from the usual ceremonies and practices in the temple. When I say "worship the Maháráj," I mean that when we wish to invite the Maháráj to our house, we fetch him to our house, we offer him flowers, wave a light round him, present him with money, and prostrate ourselves at his feet. We do not worship the god; the Mahárájás do that. They bathe the image in several ways: they wash it in saffron, flowers, etc., dress it, wave a light round it, and then men and women go to worship before it. None touch the image except the Maháráj and particular servants of his, who are appointed to the office. The gulál is thrown about during the Holi festival: it is a kind of powder prepared from wood called "Patangi." It is usual among the Hindus to throw it: it is an ancient custom, and I cannot explain it. Now I am an old man, and I don't throw it: when I was young I used to do so.—(To Sir Joseph Arnould). When I said two people of the caste came to me and said, "The Bháttiás have made a 'bandobast,' and that we ought to make a 'bandobast' also," I intended "we" to mean the Baniá caste.—(To Sir M. R. Sausse). When I say "worship the Maháráj," I don't mean to say it is the same thing to worship the Maháráj just as he worships the image: there is a slight difference between the two. The image is bathed and dressed, and food is presented to it; but the same is not done to the Maháráj. The Maháráj eats of the food presented to the image, and also distributes it among the Vaishnavas.—(To Sir Joseph Arnould). When the Maháráj worships the image, I consider him to worship God. When I wave the light round the Maháráj and prostrate before him, I don't consider him as an incarnation of the Deity.—(To Sir M. R. Sausse). I have said there are some of the Bháttiás and Baniáns who consider the Maháráj as an incarnation of God. I cannot say if the majority or minority of the Baniá caste hold that creed. I cannot say if the number of persons holding such belief has increased or diminished within the last few years.

*(Jamnádás Sevaklál*, examined *January* 27, 1862.) I am a *Shroff* and a member of the Lád Baniá caste. I am not a shet of my caste. I know the plaintiff, who is our Maháráj. He instructs us in our religion. This is a copy of the *Satya Prakásh* of the 21st October, 1860, in which I see an article about the primitive religion of the Hindus. I observe in it the name óf Jadunáthji Maháráj introduced, the plaintiff in this case. I have not heard of any other Jadunáthji Maháráj.

(Cross-examined.) I give as much respect to this Maháráj as to any other; but the love of the people towards him, since the publication of this article, has somewhat diminished. I remember his arrival from Surat about two years ago. I have not heard of any complaint from Jadunáthji, since his arrival that people did not respect him and the other Mahárájás as they ought to do. don't remember to have ever read this paper before. I have not heard of Jadunáthji complaining of the neglect of his followers towards himself and other Mahárájás, previously to the year 1860, and before the arrival of plaintiff. I did not hear the Vaishnavas complain that the Mahárájás did not give them proper instruction and advice in matters of religion. We used to go before the Mahárájás, to prostrate ourselves before them, to go to the idol and to return. They did not give any other instructions except those connected with Brahma. Those instructions are given only once in a lifetime. Plaintiff used to say that if the Vaishnavas came to him and asked him any thing, he would answer them. Plaintiff did not, to my knowledge, complain that they did not come to him.

I have not heard him say so. I did not hear the plaintiff say that he would give instruction to those only who came to ask him. I have not heard the Maháráj say that, according to the Shástras, the guru should not give instruction without being asked by the pupil, nor that, giving instruction without being asked is to give food to one who is not hungry. The company or society of Vaishnavas, not the Maháráj, published a religious magazine. The Society is known as "the propagator of the Vaishnava religion." They inserted my name and sent me a message to the effect that I was made a member of the Society. Plaintiff is at the head of the Society. •I have not heard that Jadunáthji has called upon all the Vaishnavas to come forward and support the magazine, nor have I read a handbill to that effect. I do not remember the name of the magazine. I believe the name of the magazine is "Svadharma Vardhak" (propagator of our religion). The Vaishnava families in Bombay are numerous. I cannot say if they are ten thousand. The Marjádi (strict observers of ceremonies) are the Bháttiás. I have not heard of Jadunáthji complaining that, out of so many Marjádis, only one hundred have subscribed to the magazine, and that, out of so many Baniáns, only 120 have subscribed thereto. The Maháráj does not practise any tyranny. By connection with Brahma, I mean the chanting of a mystic verse relating to the worship of Brahma. I don't read Sanskrit. By God, I mean Krishna. The verse was not explained to me in Gujaráti. I believe the meaning of the verse was once explained to me by some Bráhmin. In my opinion, the Maháráj is a representative of Krishna. (This answer was, after much evasion, extracted from witness on the threat of a fine of Rs. 100 from the Bench.) It is not that I hesitate to answer these questions against the Maháráj, for the fear that I may be born again in the condition of a bird or dog. The sense of the Sanskrit passage is, that Krishna is my protector, and that I, who am destroyed by internal misery and pain, do surrender to Krishna my mind, body, my breath, my heart, my feelings, as also my wife, my house, my children, my relations, my wealth, and other worldly things, together with my soul. Some five or seven thousand Baniáns (in Bombay) assemble at a caste feast. Besides these there may be five or ten thousand Jains. It is true that about half the Baniá caste (the Jains) don't believe in the

Maháráj. There are two sects of Baniáns—believers and unbelievers.

Mr. Anstey.—Do some Baniáns believe the Maháráj to be a god?

Witness.—We consider him to be our guru.

Sir M. Sausse.—Tell witness if he does not answer the question, he will be sent to jail.

Witness.—What is the precise question? (Interpreter explains.) Some consider the Maháráj a god in the shape of a guru.

Mr. Anstey.—Is guru a god?

Witness.—Guru is guru.

Sir M. Sausse.—Tell him if he does not answer the question, most indubitably shall he go to jail.

Sir Joseph Arnould.—Tell him he is asked what others believe, not as to his own belief.

Witness.—I don't know if others believe him to be God; I consider him as simply a guru. I don't know under what name others worship him. There is no "bandobast" in my caste, to prevent witnesses from giving evidence in this case in behalf of Karsandás. I was not asked to join in such "bandobast." I am not a Marjádi. I don't know of my caste people going to the "Ras Mandali." I don't know what sort of thing it is. There is no festival among the Vallabhácháryans in which married men and women mix promiscuously in a room. I may have read in the libel article a reference to the Ras Mandali; but there is nothing of the sort in my caste. I do not know anything of the history of the Vallabháchárya sect. My only reason for believing the Mahárájás to be of high caste, is that even Bráhmins believe them. I don't know if those Bráhmins are few or many. The Mahárájás are originally Telingá Bráhmins. I don't know if the Mahárájás, on account of their practices, were outcasted by the Telingá Bráhmins for some hundred years. I don't know if they are so outcasted at present by the Telingá Bráhmins. I have never heard of a Maháráj intermarrying in a Bráhmin family. Males and females of my family visit the Maháráj. We worship him when he comes to our house: we don't go to his house to worship him. I have not at any time swallowed the spittle and leavings of pán-sopári thrown out by the Maháráj; but I have sometimes partaken of the remnants of his food. My family may have eaten the leavings of his food, but not the pán-sopári thrown out. In the month of Shrávan, the image is swung in a swing; the Maháráj also sits therein, we swing him. The females of my own and other families have swung him. The Maháráj has thrown gulál on thousands of females, not on the females of my family alone. By Thákurji I mean Krishna. I don't think that throwing gulál makes women pregnant. It is not the fact that young men throw gulál, and not the old. Throwing the gulál has no relation to sexual intercourse. I would consider it a great insult for any other person but the Maháráj to throw gulál upon my wife. Throwing gulál from a distance I don't consider as an outrage upon chastity. (Witness is fined fifty rupees for not giving a direct answer.) I cannot explain why it is an insult to throw gulál on a female at any other time but the Holi holiday. I have not heard any complaint of the Mahárájas handling the breasts or necks of females in playfulness. Complaints similar to this have been published in the *Satya Prakásh.*

(Re-examined.) I have been asked as to swinging the image and the Maháráj. It is a ceremony performed on certain religious and festival days. It is performed publicly, in the presence of men and women belonging to the Vaishnava persuasion. Throwing gulál is also part of our religious ceremonies during the Holi holidays. The gulál which remains after throwing over the idol, is thrown over the worshippers. If the Maháráj or Gosái handled the breast or neck of a female, it would be considered adultery—not so his throwing gulál on females from a short distance. I have been present at the marriages of Mahárájás. It is not lawful for a Bráhmin to marry out of his caste. (To Sir M. Sausse.) As we cannot touch and swing the image of the Deity, we swing the Maháráj. When we do so, we regard him as our guru. The Maháráj is the only guru of those of the sect who wear *kanthis* (necklaces of beads), and who are known as Vaishnavas.

(*Varjivandás Mádhavadás*, examined *January* 27, 1862). I am a justice of the peace of Bombay. I belong to the Baniá caste. I know the plaintiff. I have known the plaintiff these last two years since his arrival in Bombay. I am a shet in my caste, and one of the Mahájans. The Maháráj is a priest of the Bháttiás, Lohánás, and Baniáns.  The plaintiff is a guru or spiritual guide and Bráhmín by caste.  He is in a higher position than the ordinary Bráhmins. The Mahárájás are looked upon as descendants of Vallabháchárya. The plaintiff has no temple in Bombay.  Mahárájás are looked up to with respect by the Hindus, particularly by our sect.

(Cross-examined.)  I am brother of the witness Gopáldás Mádha-vadás.  I do not know whether my brother was in opposition to any of the Mahárájás, except to Jivanji Maháráj, in respect to a dispute between some Bráhmins.  I do not know the history of the sect of the Vallabhácháryans, nor whether he was the son of one Laksh-man Bhat.  Mahárájás were originally Telingá Bráhmins, but I have not heard that they are outcastes.  I have not heard that Bráhmins eat with them.  One half of my caste are Jains ; they do not worship the Maháráj ; they are Buddhists.  Some Baniáns wor-ship the Maháráj as well as Shiva, and those who worship Vishnu have a reserved worship for Shiva.  Some persons when they aban-don the worship of Shiva, worship the Maháráj.  I do not know whether the Rájá of Porbandar was disgusted with the worship of a Maháráj on account of his immoralities.  I do not know why a Maháráj was flogged by the Portuguese authorities at Daman.  An application was made for the release of a Maháráj who had been imprisoned at Jálnápatan.  The Mahárájás adopt sons from their own sects, and they become priests by adoption.  It may be criminal in the eyes of the Hindu religion to expose the vices of their parents, but I do not consider it so.  The Mahárájás wash their own bodies on their birthdays or religious days, and we throw saffron and other scent on their persons.  The image, too, is washed with saffron water on these sacred days.  The females also sprinkle saffron on the Maháráj's person, and they consider the touching of his feet as sacred.  I do not know if the dust on which he walks is regarded as sacred.  If a Maháráj dies, we do not say he is dead, but that he has joined play or amorous love in heaven between men and women.  I am not able to state whether it is a part of our belief that Krishna had intercourse with 16,000 women, and that they had salvation thereby.  I do not know that the Mahárájás are called the Avatárs of the Mahá Prabhu (the Great Lord).  The Mahárájás have imposed a tax on the gains of the Bháttiá and grain merchants that eventually fall on the community. There was a meeting held at the plaintiff's house for considering the re-marriage question and opposing it. I do not know when the *Vishnu Panch* was started. I have not drunk the water wrung out of the Maháráj's langotis after bathing, nor that with which his right toes are washed. Some people drink such water. I have not signed the "bandobast" against Karsandás in this action, nor do I know if my brother has signed it. I know only from the newspapers that my brother was asked to sign it. I signed a document by which we agreed that no members of the caste should call upon a Maháráj to give evidence in a court of justice; if they did so they would be expelled. We intended also to memorialize the Judges of the Supreme Court, and if this Court did not grant us exemption we would appeal to the Privy Council to be relieved. The temples were closed for eight days in order that the followers might sign the document. Mahárájás visit the steamers, shop, and nách parties, but do not like to come to this Court, as they have not done so from time immemorial. (Mr. Anstey.—Why do you say time immemorial, when your sect has been in existence only 400 years.) Our sect has been in existence only 400 years. Govardhanáthji Maháráj was a large trader; he received visits from and paid visits to Pársi and Mahomedan traders. I know nothing of the Mahomedan mistress of Vachháláji Maháráj. I do not know if there is a book containing verses written by the plaintiff. I have not read it. There is a separate zenáná where all the ladies go to visit the Maháráj's wives. The devotees are allowed to see the image eight times a day. I have sometimes heard that women's dresses are handled indecently in the crowd, and their persons disgraced. In the winter the men and women attend at so early an hour as four o'clock. I did drive the Maháráj's carriage as coachman; I do not consider it disgraceful to do so. I did not slight the late Governor, Lord Elphinstone, while driving in public in order to pay respect to our Maháráj. Before the publication of the libel I have read in some of the papers that the Mahárájás were in the habit of committing adultery. This was about four years ago. There was a talk amongst members of the Vallabháchárya caste. I do not know if any replies were made to this. There was a talk, I believe, among the Bháttiás that their females should go at proper hours to the temples of the Mahárájás. The women were to go only in the morning and evening. This was about ten months ago. I am not on bad terms with the defendant; I have been attacked by him in his newspaper. The attack was made on account of some caste disputes. I took no notice of the article. I do not read the doctrines of my sect; I learn them by hearsay from the Gujaráti Bráhmins.

(Re-examined.) The plaintiff said if the Shástras allowed him to support the re-marriage of widows he would allow it, but if they did not allow it, he would not allow it. There was some discussion, but I have not heard how it was settled. *Vishnu Panch* means Vishnu Assembly and not a caricature. These articles that I saw had no effect on my mind as to the character of the Maháráj. I frequent the Maháráj's temple. Several people are kept at the temple to keep order. They regulate the admission of people into the temple. They enter into one passage and go out of the other, The defendant attacked me three or four times in his paper, but I thought the attack too contemptible to notice it.

---

*(Evidence for the Defence.)*

(*Karsandás Mulji*, examined February 4, 6, 7, 1862.) I am one of the defendants in this case, and a Baniá, about 28 years of age. I was born in the Vallabháchárya sect. I am one of those who believe in the Maháráj as a guru; I never believed him to be a god. I was the Editor of the *Satya Prakásh* at the time the libel appeared: the paper is since amalgamated with the *Rást Goftár*, and is now known as the *Rást Goftár and Satya Prakásh*. The other defendant was merely the printer. I edited the Stri-Bodh (a magazine for the instruction of females.) I have also written several pamplets and books. I am somewhat familiar with the doctrines of the ancient Hindu religion. It is broken up into about a hundred sects, in some respects differing widely from each other. I am familiar with the distinction between the worshippers of Vishnu and those of Shiva: those distinctions are strongly marked. The Vallabháchárya sect are the followers of Vishnu. Both differ in morality; the creed of the Vallabhácharya does not inculcate self-denial; I think that of Shiva does. The ancient religion is one of self-denial, mortification, and penance. The Vallabhácharya religion commenced about 375 years ago. Vallabh was the founder of the creed and a Telingá Bráhmin. Lakshman Bhatt, the father of Vallabh, and Vallabh himself, were excommunicated by the Telingá Bráhmins, for founding a new sect. According to the doctrines of the sect, as mentioned in the Nij Vártá (written in the Brij Bháshá language,) Vallabh, on his death, ascended to heaven in a mass of flames. The Mahárájás marry among themselves: those, out of their body, who intermarry with them are outcasted. They intermarry by holding out large promises of money and other rewards. Those who intermarry with the Mahárájás are poor Telingá Bráhmins. In one instance of such marriage which came under my notice, I think the Telingá Bráhmin was poor. I am prepared to state that the Mahárájás are not Bráhmins of high caste, and that the creed of Vallabh is of a modern date. They are not the preceptors of the ancient Hindu religion to any body. As a general rule, the Vaishnavas receive religious instruction in their own peculiar doctrines from the Mahárájás. In respect to other opinions they receive instruction from the Bráhmins. The learned Bráhmins openly teach the doctrines of the ancient religion. The Mahárájás conceal their doctrines, there is a prohibition against revealing them. (Witness to Court.) I have given considerable attention to the Vallabhácharya sect, and am acquainted with the Brij Bháshá language. I am not acquainted with Sanskrit. (Witness continued.) Whoever divulges the secrets of (his) spiritual guide, or of the Shri Thákurji or the image, or the God, shall be born again in the condition of a dog. The number of doctrines taught by the Mahárájás are of such a nature that learned Bráhmins are not in a position to teach them. The doctrines which the Bráhmins teach our sect are the same that they teach to others. The sacred book of my sect, containing the doctrines of the Mahárájás, are named [witness gives the names of fourteen books, handing them into Court, with the translations of passages contained in them]. Three of these songs were printed at the Bombay "Union Press" the property of the co-defendant. It is said in these that Kahán or

Krishna (the Maháráj) is the descendant of Vallabh. That is the belief entertained by the sect. I am somewhat familiar with and know the history of Krishna. He is the subject of several avatárs (incarnations). God (Krishna) came to this earth in the shape of man; and 16,000 "Gopis" (female cowherds) obtained salvation by falling in love with Krishna. "Rás Lilá" means amorous and wanton sport with women. There is no sport imputed to Krishna, which is not amorous sport. When a Maháráj dies, he is said to extend his journey to the other world in amorous sport. The Mahárájás have neglected the instruction of the sect in their peculiar doctrines. In the strict sense of the word, they are not the pre-ceptors of religion. The kanthi is applied to males and females at the age of eight or ten. Both in the songs and in the vow, reference is made to *tan, man*, and *dhan* (body, mind, and property). A person who makes a vow to give all his "dhan," binds himself to give his property, his wife, his son, and his daughter to the Maháráj or Thákurji. I have heard of instances in which these offerings have been practically made by the most devoted followers of the Mahárájás. It is a matter of general reputation in the sect that all the Mahárájás have carnal intercourse with the wives and daughters of their more zealous devotees. Girls are sent to the Mahárájás before being touched by their husbands. I know of such instances. The knowledge of these practices, among the sect, does not in any way diminish the influence and respect of the Mahárájás. Within the period of my recollection, the Bháttiá caste, composed entirely of Vaishnavas, have taken steps to put a stop to these practices of the Mahárájás. In 1855 the Bháttiás convened a meeting of the caste, at which it was resolved that females should not be allowed to visit the Mahárájás unless at certain fixed hours, when they may not have any opportunities for carnal intercourse with the Mahárájás. According to the Hindu religion, the laws of God are unalterable, as regards morality, piety, etc. It is considered a sin to act contrary to them. Adultery is a great sin. Handling the breasts of females and throwing gulál on their persons is considered as a sin equal to adultery, according to the Shástras. "Red powder" (gulál) is a sign of a bad design, of an adulterous character. During the Holi holidays, the Maháráj throws gulál on the breasts of female and male devotees, and directs the current of some water of a yellow colour from a syringe upon the breasts of females. During the "Ras Mandali," wives and husbands collect promiscuously in a room, and have carnal intercourse promiscuously among them. The "Ras Mandali" is held about three or four times in a month. The Maháráj has actual sexual intercourse with many women, and is called the husband of many women. I used the passage in the libel, "You Mahárájás, acting up to the doctrines of that commentary," etc., in a hypothetical sense, and with no other meaning. I am not ashamed to say there was a time when I followed the doctrines of the Vallabháchárya religion more strictly than I do now. I and others have prosecuted enquiries on the subject of the religion of our sect. The views of our small party were directed towards the doctrines as well as towards the history of the religion. In my sect, particularly, our labours have been rewarded with abuse. I was an author and a journalist before I became a reformer. The tyranny and evil practices of the Mahárájás induced me to write against them. Besides my own works, there were pamphlets, books, placards, etc., published in different languages to expose the practices of the Mahárájás. They were published long before my time, and one of them was a drama written 250 years ago. There was no prosecution for libel by a Maháráj except this. My object in writing was to get the Mahárájás reformed. The plaintiff had organs to oppose us. One of them was the *Vishnu Panch* newspaper, patronized by plaintiff; another was the religious pamphlet edited by plaintiff himself. Plaintiff wrote several times letters to the *Chábuk* and *Satya Prakásh* and other newspapers. The communications were made to me through Govardhandás, plaintiff's secretary. Plaintiff has been in Bombay for some years past; he returned to Surat last year. He showed great interest on the subjects of female education and widow re-marriage. Subsequently, at a public meeting, plaintiff declared himself against re-marriage. From that time he became unfriendly to me, and discussed with me, through the publications, the questions of re-marriage and the creed of Vallabh. These are the pamphlets in which the discussion was conducted by plaintiff. Plaintiff wrote a letter which was published in the *Chábuk* of the 29th September, 1860. In the "Propagator of our own Religion," of about the same period, there was an attack upon the "reformers," that is, me and my friends.. I was challenged to review the plaintiff's lecture published in his pamphlet. That was after the article, containing the alleged libel, appeared. Plaintiff called my paper, named the *Satya Prakásh*, (Light of Truth,) the "Light of Untruth." From the measure of enlightenment in my sect, I do not think it likely that they are able to understand the nice distinction made in the concluding passage of that article, that is, the Mahárájás cannot be exculpated from the horrible doctrines mentioned in these documents, by the distinction in question. (To Sir M. Sausse.) That distinction is not the opinion of the less reformed of the Vallabháchárya sect. (Witness proceeded to say.) I think the plaintiff's power, influence, and respect, have in no way been affected by the controversy or the alleged libel. They are just the same. Before the commencement of the controversy, there was dissatisfaction in my sect at the conduct of the Mahárájás. The plaintiff had complained of such conduct in a handbill issued by him from the *Chábuk* press on the 19th September, 1860, and circulated among the Vaishnavas. Plaintiff complains therein of the carelessness of the Vaishnavas, as to religious instruction, and of there being only 100 subscribers to his magazine, the "Propagator of our own Religion," out of a population of 12,000 Vaishnavas in Bombay. The bad company, alluded to in the handbill, are the "reformers." The person whose signature appears at the foot of the handbill is Govardhandás, the plaintiff's secretary. The subscribers to the magazine are chiefly of the lower class. The *Vishnu Panch* is conducted by some Vaishnava, under the plaintiff's patronage ; and was so until the 8th November, 1860. (An article in a number of the *Vishnu Panch* is put in as an exhibit.) Attempts were made to injure me, and to put me out of my caste, but without success, as the castemen were afraid lest I should institute an action of damages. The plaintiff and his agents asked the Vaishnavas not to subscribe to my periodical. One Kánji told me so. These attempts were made before this action was filed. I received a notice of this action about the end of April, 1861. I replied to that notice in the *Rást Goftár and Satya Prakásh* of 5th May. It is the tyranny of the Mahárájás which makes the Vaishnavas

obedient : they don't allow a man who has incurred their displeasure, to visit the temple. Visiting the temple once in a day
is indispensable. I have seen Mahárájás put their feet on the
breasts of dying men, with the view of purifying them of sin. Rewards are paid for this, from Rs. 5 to Rs. 1000. A penalty is attached
to the breach of the kanthi vow. The general character of the
Mahárájás in my sect is adulterous and licentious. The plaintiff is
known to be debaucherous. The consequence of the Mahárájás'
practices has been general debauchery in the sect; and great
scandal and shamelessness prevail. The dedication or bowing of
maidens to the Mahárájás before marriage, has given occasion
to these practices. The Maháráj is called, also, "one whose sole
aim is amorous sport with women." Certain portions of the
sect, the Marjádis, consider these practices as meritorious, and
in no light worthy of blame. In addition to Marjádis, there are
the "Varkats," who are considered the most zealous of the Mahárájás' followers. They generally act as procurers of women for
the Mahárájás. Every Varkat is necessarily a pilgrim : they form
a distinct caste. The first thing in my studies, which arrested
my attention, was the commentary of Gokulnáthji. The "ten principles" are explained in a Maráthi book called "Kavi Charitra."
The Mahárájás, also promulgated a new set of doctrines called
"Pushti Márg." The Siddhánt Rahasya was written by Vallabh,
and his grandson Gokulnáthji has written a commentary on it. I
had my doubt excited as to portions of the Commentary, which led
me to studies and enquiries, the result of which was, that I believe
that these were the real doctrines of the sect. I announced in my
paper the result of my studies as soon as I had satisfied my curiosity.
I was aware that the females of my sect believed the Mahárájás to
be incarnations of Krishna, and that as the gopis obtained
salvation by falling in love with Krishna, our females were bent
upon adulterous love towards the Mahárájás. But I did not know
that such doctrines were contained in any of the sacred books of the
sect, until I learned the fact from personal enquiries and research.
The Maháráj is known by different names, such as Agni Svarup,
Achárya, Gosáiji, Vallabhakul, etc. The Maháráj pretends to be,
and is believed to be, the personification of God. In respect to

salvation of souls the Maháráj is superior to-God, for it is said that
when the Maháráj gets angry with any one, God cannot save him
from the Mahárájás' displeasure: but the Maháráj can save one from
God's displeasure. To believe the Maháráj to be merely a guru, is
to be born again in the condition of an animal or bird called
*sicháná*. The love enjoined to be cherished towards the Maháráj
means adulterous love. These horrid opinions are held wherever
members of the sect reside : they are not confined to Western India.
They prevail at Benares. I caused a copy of this book to be
procured from a press at Benares. I produce these papers as
specimens of the attacks made upon the Mahárájás previously to the
publication of the alleged libel. (Witness to Court.) These are
hand-bills, newspapers, and pamphlets published from 1855–59.
The purport of the attacks is similar to the purport of the libel, that
is, that the Mahárájás are adulterers. I saw and read these
different publications as they came out. I am able to say that these
publications were generally circulated and read. I read and
believed them to be true. To a certain extent they influenced my
mind, but I was already convinced. (Witness continued.) These
are only some attacks amongst many. I know what the "slavery
bond" was. The temples were closed for a week to force parties
to sign the bond, and the person signing it bound himself not to
write anything against the Mahárájás, nor attempt to procure his
attendance at the Supreme Court. One of its objects was to excommunicate me, in which they failed. The bond is still binding, and
I have read in it that persons not obeying it shall be guilty of a
crime against religion. I have seen the females bow to the Mahárájás, at the time of worship in the temples, and I have seen the
Mahárájás touch the toes of females of whom they are fond.
Touching the toe is indicative of a desire for carnal intercourse.
The females go into the zenáná, and the Mahárájás go after them.
I have seen the managers of the Mahárájás giving water to
Vaishnavas to drink, the water which fell from the Maháráj's
dhotiá. I have seen the leavings of the Mahárájás' food eaten
by some Vaishnavas. When the Maháráj walks on foot, males and
females follow him in the streets. I have seen the "ten principles"
in two other books, one in verse and the other in prose. (Mr.

Spencer Compton read English translations of passages from the sacred books of the Vallabhácháyra sect, which were put in as exhibits the previous day).

(*Karsandás Mulji*, cross-examined by Mr. Bayley). I first became acquainted with the plaintiff in the year 1860, but have never been in his company, nor even spoken to him in my life. He has no temple in Bombay. Mahárájás having no temples of their own, go to the temples belonging to other Mahárájás. I have no ocular knowledge of any improprieties committed by plaintiff, but have had in respect to others, when I used to visit the temples about ten or eleven years ago. I have observed the improprieties of Jivanji, the head Maháráj. I have not been to the temples, I believe, since 1848, because I knew that the Mahárájás' conduct was blame-worthy. I mean improprieties to the extent of pressing the toes of females by Jivanji Maháráj. I went once a week every Sunday, to Jivanji's temple. The temple consists of two parts, and I have seen both. I saw the toes of the females pressed three or four times when I myself went to touch the Mahárájás' toes. I did not mark this when I was young, that is, under fifteen. This circumstance, combined with their general reputation as regards adultery, made me secede from the Mahárájás. Jivanji is still my guru, but I stopped visiting him. I have a daughter round whose neck I put a kanthi myself, according to the ceremonial forms of my sect. Many Vaishnavas have put kanthis with their own hands round the necks of their children. There may be two hundred reformers among the Vaishnavas at the utmost. When I say all the Mahárájás have carnal intercourse with the daughters and wives of their devotees, and that maidens are first sent to the Mahárájás after their marriage, I say so from general reputation. Besides pressing the toes, I have seen the Mahárájás throwing gulál on the breasts of females during the Holi festival in different years, when all the men and women were in the temple. It was gulál which had been offered to the idol, and is considered holy by the people. The gulál was sometimes thrown in balls, which where pointedly thrown at the breasts of females. I received spiritual instruction from the Maháráj once in my life when the kanthi was put round my neck. These sacred books are the property of two of my friends and of Rámlál Thákorsidás. I found out the particular passages with the assistance of one Mathurádás. I was acquainted with these passages before the time of the alleged libel. I said there are about a hundred sects in India, but I don't think the old religion is represented by any one sect at present. Some of the sects follow the old religion more or less. The Vallabháchárya sect professes to follow the old religion, but I am not certain whether it does. It differs widely in its doctrines from those of the old religion, and conceives itself to be far superior to all other sects. The number of the Vallabhácháryans in Bombay may be thirty or forty thousand; they extend from here to the Ganges and to Agra, but not uninterruptedly. I heard six or seven years ago that the Mahárájás were excommunicated by the Telingá Bráhmins. It is the general belief in the sect that Vallabh was a Telingá Bráhmin and was outcasted. Telingá is a province in the Madras Presidency. The Telingá Bráhmins form a large body in Telingá as in other parts of India, and are the worshippers of Shiva. They are like any other Bráhmins in any other part of India. The Vaishnavas and the Shivas are "at daggers drawn." Lakshman Bhatt, the father of Vallabh, was excommunicated by his own castemen for founding a new creed. Manu and other books are considered to be of divine origin. The story of the gopis and the incarnations of Vishnu are believed in by several sects, but are opposed to the ancient religion. The Shaivites believe in the incarnations of Vishnu equally with the Vaishnavas. As far as I have read, all the sacred books do not contain amorous passages. I am not aware whether Sir William Jones has said that "Krishna is to this day the darling god of Hindu women." I have heard the story of Brahma coming out of an egg after remaining there millions and millions of years. I do not believe in the modern stories in books which are written after the Vedas, which I have not read. The stories are considered by most Vaishnavas as literally true. I was not present at any Ras Mandali; it is a matter of general reputation, and is described by Captain McMurdo of Katch, in his work on that province. Adultery is considered a crime whether committed by a Gosái or any other person. The instruction which Vaishnavas receive from the Mahárúj is only once in their life-time, when the kanthi is put round the neck. In certain respects the Maharájás are regarded as religious preceptors, but they don't teach more than once in a person's lifetime. Each family has its priest who gives instruction in religion. The plaintiff is not a Bráhmin of high caste; he is an outcasted Bráhmin, and no high-caste Bráhmin would dine with him or the other Mahárájás, under the penalty of being excommunicated. I collected and printed the licentious songs sung by females when the Mahárájás are invited to their houses. I have heard the songs sung within the last year or two. They are sung generally among the sect. What I printed are not exact words, but the substance of the songs, which I got printed for the purposes of this trial. There are many other songs of similar tendency; these are mere specimens. The Bráhmins are highly respected; they are not divine. The "amorous Kahán" plainly means the Maháráj; he is generally regarded as God, the Supreme Being himself. It is not possible that I can be mistaken as to the construction of the words "*tan, man,* and *dhan.*" "Dhan" means property, but the Vaishnavas have extended the sense. I differ with the Chief Translator as to the translation of the latter portion of the libel. The word *bigádo chho* simply means "defile." I had nothing to do with the article which appeared in the *Samáchár* : its editor was a Parsi. I had nothing to do with any of the articles which appeared in other journals against the Mahárájás. I don't know who wrote the article against the Mahárájás in the *Bombay Times.* I have seen Mahárájás follow females into their private rooms,—not the females of their own family, who are not allowed to be seen by strangers. Plaintiff pretended for some time to be a reformer. I have not read Gokulnáthji's commentary in the original, *i.e.* the Sanskrit. I have had no personal knowledge of the adulteries of plaintiff: it was a matter of notoriety that he committed a rape at Surat. I heard from a friend that plaintiff suffered last year from the venereal disease. (After discussion). Lukhmidás Kimji is the name of the friend. I know nothing of this, of my personal knowledge.—(To Sir M. Sausse). The females go to the zenáná, the place for the Maháráj's family. They go to the zenáná, and then into the Maháráj's bedroom. The zenáná has more than one room; but I don't know of my personal knowledge. At the time I wrote the article, I believed that the Mahárájás did defile their female devotees.

(Re-examined by Mr. Anstey). None of the sects does in itself represent the ancient Hindu religion. The adulteries of the Mahárájás are a matter of notoriety. Captain McMurdo has written on their adulteries and on the Ras Mandali, in the 2nd volume of the "Transactions of the Literary Society of Bombay," published in the year 1820. He says:—"The Bháttiás are of Sindh origin. They are the most numerous and wealthy merchants in the country, and worship the Gosáiji Maháráj, of whom there are many. The Maháráj is master of their property and disposes of it as he pleases; and such is the veneration in which he is held, that the most respectable families consider themselves honoured by his cohabiting with their wives or daughters. The principal Maháráj at present on this side of India is named Gopináthji, a man worn to a skeleton and shaking like a leaf from debauchery of every kind, excepting spirituous liquors. He is constantly in a state of intoxication from opium, and various other stimulants which the ingenuity of the sensual has discovered. He is originally a Bráhmin. . . . . The well-known Ras Mandalis are very frequent among them (the Bháttiás) as among other followers of Vishnu. At these, persons of both sexes and all descriptions, high and low, meet together, and, under the name and sanction of religion, practise every kind of licentiousness." (Witness here defines the grammatical construction of the passage containing the libel,—'You Mahárájás!' etc.) I am sure that the songs I have printed give exactly the substance of what I have heard women sing. Mahárájás are sometimes called by the name of Purushottam, "God or most excellent Being," or Purna Purushottam, "Perfect God," or "Perfect excellent Being."

(*Rev. John Wilson, D.D.*, examined *February* 8, 1862.) I was ordained to the office of the ministry by the Church of Scotland; and am a graduate of the University of Edinburgh. I came out to this country in the beginning of 1829. My professional duties as a missionary have led me to the study of some of the eastern and Indian languages. I have studied the Sanskrit, and with it the Zend, and to a certain extent the Pehliví. I am acquainted with some of the Prákrit (or provincial languages derived principally from the Sanskrit), and with the Brij Bháshá in both its spoken and written forms. I have presided at the examinations in languages of gentlemen of both the Civil and Military Services of India. I was offered the office of Oriental Translator to Government, but I declined it. I am a member of several learned societies. I am a Fellow of the Royal Society; and a Member of the Royal Asiatic Society of Great Britain and Ireland. I am a Member of the Bombay Branch of the Royal Asiatic Society; for seven years I was its President; and since 1842, I have been its Honorary President. I am a Corresponding Member of the Bengal Asiatic Society, and of the German Oriental Society. I am also an Honorary Member of one or two other foreign societies. I am the author of several works on the ancient Indian and Persian religious systems; and have long prosecuted the study of the literature of the East, which I commenced when a student at the University. I have heard most of the evidence in this case, up to yesterday, when I was absent from the Court. The Vishnu Puráṇa is a sacred book of the Hindus: it is a philosophical and legendary book, bearing the name of one of their gods, to the exposition of their views of whom it is devoted. I have read the translation of it, sometimes comparing it with the original. The most ancient books of the Hindus are the Véds. They and the other works associated with them are classified together under the denomination of *Shruti*, or what was heard, from their authors reciting them according to what was alleged in their behalf, their own vision. They are believed to be works of divine revelation in the highest sense of the term. I have read much of the Véds in Sanskrit and in the translations which have been made of portions of them. The Institutes of Manu, forming a judicial Code, were, I believe, with others, collected about the second century before the Christian era. The Hymns of the Véds were composed about three thousand years before the present time. There is now a pretty general consensus among orientalists about these dates. The law-books, such as Manu, belong to what is denominated the *Smriti*, what is remembered, or gathered from tradition. The literature of the Hindus bears evidence to the occurrence of great changes of belief in reference to their gods, and of moral and social practice in the Indian

community. It is a historical fact that the more modern religions
of this country are less pure in their morality than those which
prevailed in this land of old. Very great changes have occurred in
India in the concept and treatment of the gods, and positively for
the worse, as admitted by the Hindus themselves. I have heard
of the founder of a Hindu sect, named Vallabháchárya. He
flourished from the end of the fifteenth to the beginning of the
sixteenth century of the Christian era. I have read in Hindu
books of a visit made by him to Krishna Déva, king of Vijayanagar, when he is said to have received a large present of gold;
and I find Krishna Déva mentioned in the chronological tables of
his dynasty under 1524. I hold in my hand a Sanskrit Drama
entitled *Pákhanda Dharma Khanda,* or the Smashing of Heretical
Religion, bearing the date of Samvat 1695 (about A.D. 1639),
and which has the appearance of having been produced about that
time, in which I find distinct references to Vallabháchárya and his
sect. (To Sir Matthew Sausse.) I have not found any reference
to the drama in the books of authority in the sect. I don't know
if it has ever been acted; but it is the custom of the Bráhmins
to compose dramas, and circulate them among their friends, as
literary compositions, without reference to their use on the stage.
(Witness continued.) I have seen notices of the Vallabhácháryan
sect in the "Transactions of the Literary Society of Bombay" (now
the B. B. R. A. S.), vol. ii., by Capt. McMurdo, Resident in Katch
(given into Court by Karsandás Mulji); and in vol. xv. of the
"Transactions of the Bengal Asiatic Society," by Horace Hayman
Wilson, for some time the Secretary of that Society, and before his
death Professor of Sanskrit in the University of Oxford. (To Sir
M. Sausse.) From my personal study of the doctrines of the sect,
I believe that they are of an impure character. I agree with the
opinion expressed by Professor H. H. Wilson in the following
passage : "Amongst other articles of the new creed, Vallabha introduced one, which is rather singular for a Hindu religious innovator
or reformer : he taught that privation formed no part of sanctity,
and that it was the duty of the teachers and his disciples to worship
their deity, not in nudity and hunger, but in costly apparel and
choice food, not in solitude and mortification, but in the pleasures

of society and the enjoyment of the world. The *Gosáis* or teachers
are almost always family men, as was the founder Vallabha, for,
after he had taken off the restrictions of the monastic order to which
he originally belonged, he married, by the particular order, it is
said, of his new god. The Gosáis are always clothed with the best
raiment, and fed with the daintiest viands by their followers, over
whom they have unlimited influence : part of the connection between the guru and teacher, being the three-fold *Samarpan* or consignment of *tan*, *man*, and *dhan* (body, mind, and wealth), to the
spiritual guide." I agree also with what Professor W. says of the
eight daily times of worship of the sect; and of the veneration paid
to its superintendents, the Gosáis, the descendants of Vallabha.
"It is," he says, "not an uncurious feature in the notions of this
sect, that the veneration paid to their Gosáis is paid solely to their
descent, and unconnected with any idea of their sanctity or learning ; they are not unfrequently destitute of all pretensions to individual respectability, but they not the less enjoy the homage
of their followers." (To Mr. Anstey.) The drama to which I
have referred is, making certain allowances for scenic figures of
speech, a faithful and vivid mirror of the doctrines and practices of
the sect, as they prevail at the present day. I could not give a
more faithful picture of these doctrines and practices of the sect
than by reading some of the passages which I have extracted from
the drama and translated into English. They are as follows :—

The *Sútradhára* (says to the *Nati*) :—O dear, the Véds have fled somewhere ;
no one knows the story of their flight (*i.e.* whither they have gone). The collection of the Súnkhya, Yoga, and the Puránas has sunk into the bowels of the
earth. Now, young damsels, look to the self-dedication preached by Shrimat
Vallabha Vithaléshvara, who has conspired to falsify the meaning of the Véds.

"Enters a Vaishnava, having on his neck, ear, hand, head, and around his loins, a
wreath made of the *vrindá* (Ocymum Sanctum or Tulasí), having on his forehead
*Gopichandana* (a substitute for Sandalwood). He is one who repeats Rádhá !
Krishna ! Being opposed to the Shruti, he is the reproacher of those who adhere
to the Véds. He finds at every step, crowds of females filled by *Káma* (lust or
cupid). He is the kisser of female Vaishnavas ! Ye Vaishnavas, ye Vaishnavas,
hear the excellent and blessed Vaishnava doctrine—the embracing and clasping
with the arms the large-eyed damsels, good drinking and eating, making no distinction between your own and another's, offering one's self and life to gurus, is in
the world the cause of salvation." Mutual dining, carnal intercourse with females,
night and day, drinking, forming endless alliances, are the surpassing, beautiful customs of the persons who have consecrated their souls to Shrí Gokulésha. Charity,

devotion, meditation, abstraction, the Véds, and a crore of sacrifices, are nothing; the nectarine pleasure of the worshippers of the *páduká* (wooden slipper) in Shrí Gokula is better than a thousand other expedients.   Our own body is the source of enjoyment, the object of worship reckoned by all men fit to be served.  If sexual intercourse does not take place with the Gokulesha, the paramour of men is useless, like a worm or ashes.   The chief religion of the worshipper of the *páduká* is the consecration of a daughter, a son's wife, and a wife, and not the worship of Bráhmins learned in the Véds, hospitality, the *Shráddha* (funeral ceremonies) vows, and fastings.—Translated (from the *Pákhanda Dharma Khandana* of *Dámodarsvámi*) by John Wilson, D.D.

(Witness continued.)   The sect of Vallabháchárya is a new sect, inasmuch as it has selected the god Krishna in one of his aspects—that of his adolescence, and raised him to supremacy in that aspect. It is a new sect, in as far as it has established the *Pushti-márga*, or way of enjoyment, in a natural and carnal sense.   The sect is new in its objects, and new in its methods.   The god Krishna is worshipped by its members in the form of images, and in the form of the persons of their gurus, the so-called Mahárájás.   The Maháráj is considered by a great many of his followers as an Incarnation of God, as God incarnate according to Hindu notions, which are peculiar on that subject.   The Vallabháchárya and his official descendants are incarnations of the god Krishna, without holding that there is a complete embodiment of him in any one of them.   According to Hindu notions, there have occurred nine incarnations of Vishnu, the last of them being that of Buddha.   The orthodox Hindus do not believe in any incarnations which are said to have taken place between the time of Buddha and the present day.   The Vallabháchárya, on the contrary, hold that Vallabháchárya and his descendants are incarnations of Krishna. They view the Maháráj as intermediate between themselves and the god Krishna, in the sense of his being entitled to have his dicta received as equal to those of Krishna himself.   I have looked to the following passages in works in the Brij Bháshá, recognized by the Vallabháchárya, and given into the court, and have found them correctly rendered :—" We should regard our guru as God. For if God get angry, the Guru Déva is able to save from the effects of God's anger, whereas if the guru is displeased, nobody is able to save from the effects of the guru's displeasure."  (*Chaturshloki Bhágavata*.)   " When Hari (God) is displeased, the guru saves from the effects of Hari's displeasure." "The principal gurus are the Shrí A'chárji and Shrí Gosáijí and their whole family, the Vallabha family." "In this world there are many kinds of creatures. Of them all we are most fortunate that we have sought the protection of the illustrious Vallabhácháryají, Shrí Gosáiji, and their descendants, who are manifestly (incarnations of) God, the excellent being himself." (*Guru Sevá.*) "Whoever holds (his) spiritual guide and Shrí Thákurjí (or God) to be different shall be born a *sicháná*. Whoever disobeys the orders of his spiritual guide, shall go to *Asipatra* and other dreadful hells, and lose all his religious merits." (*Hariráyaji*, descendant of Vallabháchárya in the *Satsath Aparádha*, the Sixty-Seven Sins.) There are multitudes who believe the Mahárájás to be not only gurus, but more exalted beings in the sense indicated by the passages now quoted. The Mahárájás are certainly not preceptors of what is technically denominated the Hindu religion. They are not chiefs or heads of any single sect of Bráhmins. The descendants of Vallabha are considered as outcasted Telingá Bráhmins. To my certain knowledge caste intercourse properly so-called does not exist between the Mahárájás and the Telingá Bráhmins. According to the beliefs and practices of the Hindu religion, it is not possible for Bráhmins to hold such intercourse with the Mahárájás as members of one caste hold with one another. *Tan, man,* and *dhan* (in the formulas of Vallabhácháryan initiation) are used in an all-comprehensive sense—*tan* embracing the body in all its members and functions; *man* referring to mind in all the mental powers and faculties; and *dhan* comprehending all property and possessions, which have to be placed at the disposal of the god through the Maháráj, according to the doctrines of the sect. I have seen passages in works published by the Mahárájás of the sect, according to which the sectaries should make over their sons, wives, daughters, and everything else before applying them to their own use. In the *Virchita Bhakti Siddhánta Vivriti* (a commentary of Gokulnáthji on the *Siddhánta Rahasya*) it is said, "Therefore, in the beginning, even before ourselves enjoying, wives, sons, etc. (*putrádi*, comprehending daughters as well as sons), should be made over, (because of) the expression *sarva vastu* (i.e. "all things," occurring in the text). After marriage, even before using her ourselves, the offering of her (that is the wife) should be made with a view to her becoming usable (by ourselves). So, likewise, after the birth of a son, sons, etc., should all be made over. On all occasions (and) on account of all occasions there should be the making over. After making the things over, the different acts should be done." The translation of this passage (signed Vishvanáth Náráyan Mandalik), given in as an exhibit, is correct. In regard to a Bráhmin, it is said in the *Bhagavad-Gítá*, that his inherent qualities are "quiescence, self-control, devotion, purity, patience, rectitude, secular and sacred understanding, the recognition of spiritual existence, and the inborn disposition to serve Bráhma." The system of the Vallabháchár/ans has a relationship to this ideal somewhat analogous to that which Mormonism has to Christianity. The sense of shame and of decency is outraged by the doctrines and practices of the Vallabháchárans. There is no sense of shame recognized in the doctrines of the sect. I have heard that the translation of the Gujaráti passage containing the alleged libel has been disputed. (Directing attention to a passage pointed to by Counsel, the witness continued.) "Ye Mahárájás (in the vocative), on acting according to that commentary (or when you act according to that commentary), you corrupt the wives and daughters of your devotees, lift your hand from this." The passage is susceptible of the interpretation given of it by the defendant. All things considered, the alleged libel is a very mild expostulation, involving an appeal to the principle that the preceptors of religion, unless they purify their lives, cannot expect success to attend their labours. I do not think that the plaintiff is necessarily involved in what is said except in a general and inferential way. [Mr. Anstey then handed to witness a form of dedication in Sanskrit used by the members of the sect of the Vallabháchárans on receiving the kanthi (throat-ornament of the sect).] The translation of this formula is the following :—" Shrí Krishna is my refuge. I, who am suffering the infinite pain and torment produced by enduring, for a thousand measured years, separation from Krishna, do to the worshipful Krishna consecrate my body, organs of sense, life, heart, and other faculties, and wife, house, family, property, with my own self. I am thy slave, O Krishna."

(Cross-examined.) The passage containing the alleged libel is somewhat ambiguous; and its composition is loose. I think the Bháttiás who read it would connect the allegation of the corruption of their wives and daughters with the use of the commentary referred to. The effect of the participle *cháliné* is suspensive, making the whole read, " ye, on acting, or (when you act) according to the commentary," do so and so. The alleged corrupting is positive, but with this connexion. I am not prepared to state that Mr. Flynn's translation is incorrect, though it may be somewhat improved. I took no active part in getting up this case; but since it commenced, I have taken an interest in its advancement. This interest is founded not so much on professional as on moral grounds. I did not know the defendant personally till the action was commenced. I have not been inside any of the Mahárájás' temples. I have had no personal observation of the improper practices of the Mahárájás; but I have heard much of them from their followers, and I have seen great abominations practised by Vallabhácháryan sectaries, which I would much rather characterize to the court than minutely describe. From the books of the sect which I have examined, I conclude that both the Mahárájás and the idols are worshipped as gods. The Bráhmins, in general, have indeed very high and extravagant notions of themselves and their religious and social position. The Hindus worship cows and bulls; but not as personal incarnations of the Hindu deities. The Hindus according to their pantheistic teachings believe every object that exists to be in some form or other an emanation from deity, which they profess to believe to be the only entity. It is only of late years that European oriental scholars, such as Max Müller and others, have found any satisfactory indications of the age of the ancient Hindu writings. The codifying of the Laws of Manu, I think, took place about two hundred years before the Christian era, though many of the laws are doubtless considerably older. Sir William Jones thought that the Code of Manu received its present form somewhat under a thousand years before Christ (A.C. 880). (To Sir Joseph Arnould.) I would not call the Mormonites a sect of Christians. The Vallabháchárya sect, as such, is not properly speaking a sect of the ancient Hindu religion, though connected with the Hindu religion.

(To Sir Matthew Sausse.) I cannot say that any sect at present strictly follows the ancient Hindu religion. I know at least of one sect that holds immoral doctrines similar to those of the Vallabháchárya sect. It is that of the *Sháktas*, worshippers of the *Shaktis*, or female energies. (Mr. Scoble handed a Sanskrit pamphlet to the witness, when witness proceeded.) This pamphlet bears on its cover, that it has been published by the order of Shri Gokuládhishji Mahárájádhiráj. (!) It is a collection of various pieces. The sentence to which you point does not refer to adultery. *Vishayákránta* (occurring in it) is not equivalent to adultery; it means what is sensual. The connexion of the passage, however, has to be looked at.—I have heard of the sect of Svámi Náráyan at Ahmedábád. The high priest there is the third or fourth in official descent from its founder. His sect worships Krishna; but its priests, I believe, do not marry. I don't object to the marriage of priests. There are a number of sects in India as recent as that of Vallabháchárya. Words are symbols of ideas; and it is not with words themselves that fault is to be found, but with the application sometimes made of them. The words tan, man, and dhan are right in themselves; but they are badly applied by the Mahárájás. It is only of late years that tolerably successful attempts have been made to assign chronological limits to the different works of the Hindu literature. The intelligent members of the Hindu community are making researches at present about the foundations of their religion. The reform party is very much identical with what is called *Young Bombay*. I have read some of the works of the plaintiff and his associates, and have formed a very low estimate of them.

(Re-examined.) I have seen very obscene conduct on the part of the followers of the Mahárájás, and have turned away from it with disgust. I should have been pleased to have seen a better state of things in this country. Many of the passages given into the Court as exhibits were first shown to me by the defendant and his party. Some of them I myself first brought to their notice.—(To the Court.) The meaning of Rás Lílá is, etymologically and properly, "amorous sport." *Ras* alone, means juice, as the juice of the body, or the juice of fruits. *Átmá* means self, soul, spirit, and (in the Védánta) the Deity, supposed to be the universal soul.

(*Mathurádás Lowji,*\* examined *February* 13, 14, 1862.) I am a Bháttiá merchant, and a member of the Vallabhácharya sect. I know the Brij Bháshá, the Gujaráti, and the Maráthi languages. I am acquainted with the sacred books of my sect. I am not able to read Sanskrit or Persian. I have given these books to Karsandás for the purpose of being produced in Court. I consider myself skilled in the doctrines of my sect and the ancient religion of the Hindus. I have heard the ancient religion expounded from the Bhágavat and other two works. Our religion differs from the ancient religion. Idolatry is not enjoined by the Véds. It is mentioned in a book called Bálbodh that none would be able to read the Véds in the Kali-Yug, and that the acts mentioned in the Véds would not lead to salvation. In a work by Gokulnáthji it is stated that the Shástras are not to be followed which are opposed to the doctrines of the "Pushti Márg" of the Vallabháchárya sect. In our sect, "Puran Purushottam," and his incarnations Vallabhá-chárya and Vithal are considered as God. The Mahárájás are considered as those incarnations "and are known as the children of Vallabh," Puran Purushottam, Áchárya, etc. There are 108 names given to Vallabháchárya and his descendants, which names are similar to the 108 names of the Supreme Being. Mahárájás are called "Mahá Prabhu" (Great Lord) by several devotees at the time of worship. A part of the Bháttiá caste worships the Mahárájás as God, and also worships their portraits. Each Maháráj is also worshipped by his individual name, and is regarded as God from his birth, without reference to his subsequent character or qualifications. Vallabh is regarded as the incarnation of the head of the Supreme Being. In reality, he was the son of Lakshman Bhatt, a Telingá Bráhmin. The Telingá Bráhmins would not dine or associate with his descendants. The Mahárájás have about two lakhs of followers out of some twelve crores of Hindus. Except when putting the kanthi round the neck of a child, the Maháráj never gives religious instruction. The Maháráj, at the performance of the kanthi ceremony, makes a person repeat a *mantra* (incarnation)

---

\* Some portions of the evidence of this important witness, and of others for the defence, are given in a more correct form in the finding of Sir Joseph Arnould than in the report published.

tion) to this effect :—I have been separated from Krishna for a long
time. I dedicate my body, mind, wealth, organs, wife, children,
house, and all to Krishna." The Maháráj desires the person to
repeat it to him (the Maháráj.) Children are made to repeat this
mantra, as also young girls and lads on the occasions of their
marriage. The Maháráj is Krishna; and a Vaishnava dedicates to
him his tan man, and dhan. In practice all a person's wealth
is not given to the Maháráj; but as to women, he commits adultery.
Rás Lilá means amorous sport, carnal intercourse. This picture
(an indecent one) is a correct representation of the sport Krishna
had with women. There are many such pictures in the Mahárájás'
temples. This book is believed in by the sect; it contains this
picture, in which there are represented naked women and Krishna
at the top of a tree. One of the pictures represents the women,
shepherdesses, as coming out after bathing; the other represents
them as playing with gulál with Krishna, and of the colour of
Kesura flowers. *Buka* is a sacred powder called "abir," and is
used with gulál. The followers of the Mahárájás, males and females,
will, after death, become gopis, for the purpose of having amorous sport, Rás Lilá, with God, in which the Mahárájás will take
part and enjoy both as gods and as gopis. The Mahárájás, when
they worship the image, wear long hair because they regard themselves as gopis in this world. I had conversation with the plaintiff
to the effect that I should arrange with Jivanlálji Maháráj to write
and edit the "Propagator of our own Religion" during the time he
(plaintiff) would be away from Bombay. It was started by the
plaintiff in the name of a society, of which he is the president. I
received this hand-bill at the entrance of plaintiff's dwelling-house.
I have read it. I am known in my sect by the name of "Mathurá
Panth," because my opinions are opposed to the immoralities and
adultery of the Mahárájás, and as if I was the founder of a new
sect. This is not the case. From my infancy I was instructed by
my father not to believe in the practices of the Mahárájás, which,
he said, are immoral and adulterous. Many persons in my sect
know the fact, but refrain from avowing it for several reasons.
Since the last eight or nine years I have explained to my friends
these immoralities. I respected the Mahárájás outwardly; my friends

did the same. In the year 1912 (1855) a writing was prepared by
Bháttiás to prevent females from going to the Mahárájás unless at
certain hours, and with the view of preventing the adulteries. It was
resolved that the writing should come into force after a year. There
was a dispute at the time between the Mahárájás and the Bhuleshwar
Bráhmins, and it was apprehended that, if the document was made
public, the Bráhmins might obtain a triumph. The year elapsed,
but the agreement was not brought into force. Since this action
commenced, a hand-bill was issued from the press of plaintiff's
manager, Parbhudás, with the object of suppressing the agreement
and preventing its being produced in this Court. The Mahárájás'
adulteries were a matter of notoriety in the sect, and there has been
no improvement since 1855. I remember having been often to the
garden of Gokuldás Tejpál with Khatáo Makanji. About eight
years ago I went there with him, when at the entrance we were
informed by the *máli* that a Maháráj was inside with four women.
Seeing us go in, Lakhmidás Khimji followed us. Gokuldás was in
the garden opposite, knowing the Maháráj was in his own garden
with the women. We went in. Khatáo stopped in the dining-
room. I entered by another door, and saw two widows sitting outside. They told me something, but notwithstanding that, I pushed
forward. I found the door of a room fastened from inside, and
removed the latch with a knife. I saw there Maháráj Vachhálálji
in the act of connexion with a woman. The other woman was sitting
in the room. The Maháráj was ashamed on seeing me, and put on
his dhotiá (waist cloth). The woman was of the Bháttiá caste
and a member of the sect. She was about 25 or 30 years of age,
and was a married women. I paid my respects to the Maháráj on
seeing him commit the act! Gokuldás was sent for; the Maháráj
gave him some sweetmeat and pán-sopári. The women went away,
and a companion of Gokuldás struck one of them on the head. I
refused to conceal the act; I said I never would conceal such an
act. There is a club among the Bháttiás of my sect called "Ras
Mandali," of which the members are very much respected, as they
pay greater homage to the Mahárájás and commit more adultery.
The members would not admit a stranger. They go to the meeting
with their wives. I was a member. I have frequently seen females

3

approaching the persons of Mahárájás. I have seen ten or twenty Mahárájás worshipped by females. The females touch the soles of the Mahárájás' feet with their hands, and then apply them to their own eyes. I have seen females perform this kind of worship to plaintiff. Several Mahárájás press the toes of their female devotees. I have not seen the plaintiff do this. Pressing the toes is a sign of a desire for adultery. When the females look at the Mahárájás, the latter make signs with their eyes. Accordingly, the females take this hint and retire into a room. I speak this from my personal knowledge. The gulál is thrown on the occasion of the Vasant Panchami (which falls shortly before the Holi holidays). The gulál is thrown by the Maháráj on the persons of such females as he wishes to gratify his desire with. Gulál water is also thrown by means of syringes, and the Maháráj takes precise aim at the females. This is done with the same object and purpose. Females sing *garbis* (songs) of an amorous character in the presence of the Mahárájás; such as, "I was asleep and you awoke me," "You will ease my mind if you will take me," "You are my husband," and so on. The purport of such songs is evident as sung in the presence of the Mahárájás. It is notorious that the Mahárájás are adulterers. The plaintiff's reputation is no way better than that of the other Mahárájás. According to our Shástras, conduct such as this (throwing powders on females) is considered equivalent to adultery; and in fact, under the head of adultery in a religious book, it is so described. "Chuva," a sort of fluid, is thrown by females on the persons of the Mahárájás. Such conduct is witnessed quietly by the husbands of females who sing the "garbi" before the Mahárájás. I first became acquainted with Jadunáthji about sixteen months ago, when he paid a visit to the house of Jivaráz Bálu and sent for me. I am acquainted with about seven or eight Mahárájás in Bombay. They are Jivanji, the head Maháráj, Gokuleshji, Dhishji, Gokuládhishji, Chimanji, Maganji, Dwárkánáthji, and Jádunáthji. I have been out of Bombay, and have seen Mahárájás at Katch Mándavi, Beyt, etc. The Maháráj at Mándavi, is Ranchhodji, and I was also acquainted there with Máji Maháráj, the widow of a Maháráj. Eventually the Mahárájás refused to accede to my request not to admit females into the temple unless at certain hours. The refusal was made after some discussion. I am unwilling to reveal what private conversation I had with Jivanji unless forced to give it out. Jivanji said all persons are masters of their own houses, and adultery has increased very much, and it is difficult to stop it. He could not, he said, remonstrate with his elders or with those who were superior to him. If he attempted to remonstrate, he was afraid the other Mahárájás would not mind him; and he, therefore, suggested that I should secure the aid of Shrináthji and the Mathuresh-jiwállá Mahárájás. Without their co-operation, he said, nothing could be effected. As the females were the source of great income to the Mahárájás, it was rather a serious matter, he said, to stop that source of income, and thus deprive them of the means of defraying their expenses. He added that, like an opium-eater, a man could not give up the practice of lust, and therefore it was not possible to put a stop at once to the practices of the Mahárájás. He advised me to have patience in the matter of this desired reform. I had similar conversation with Jivanji on another occasion. I stayed for about four hours with plaintiff at the house of Jivráz Bálu. He also sent for me on other occasions. On the first occasion I had some discussion with him on the subject of female education, in the course of which he desired me to do as he or the Mahárájás directed. I said we are not bound to do so, unless what you say is good. He said you are bound to act according to what we say. I said I can show you precedents from the Shástras, upon which he desired me to see him at his house. I said the Mahárájás do not study the Shástras and instruct their followers, as it is their duty to do. He said that was not necessary, and that the followers must do what the Mahárájás directed them to do. I spoke of the desirability of establishing a library, when plaintiff said he had prepared a list for the purpose, and asked me to procure subscriptions. I said I would procure the subscriptions, but that the money could not be entrusted to him. He then said I and my friends might keep the money. This was subsequently to the publication of the libel. The Shankarácháryas do not allow women to approach them. I have read of the "ten principles" in the Brij Bháshá and the Maráthi languages. The doctrines mentioned in these correspond in substance with those of the sacred books. The doctrines propounded in plaintiff's works and Gokulnáthji's commentary, are to my mind productive of adultery in the sect, and lend encouragement to it. It is said in the "Propagator of our own Religion" that we ought to be in adulterine love with God; in another place it is said such love cannot be cherished in the Kali Yug. Of these two contradictory injunctions, the former, to my mind, would have effect over a person's mind much more readily than the latter. The adulterine love with God means something as the adulterine love between the Mahárújás and the Vaishnavas. The meaning of the dedication of the "tan" is that the wives and daughters of the devotees are dedicated to the Mahárájás. The seat or "baithak" of the Mahárájás, even, in his absence, is worshipped and respected by the devotees. I was myself present at the meeting of the Bháttiás in 1855, and took a part in the proceedings.

(Cross-examined.) I am not called Mathurá Panth because I have founded, or am about to found, a new sect; it is only because I have opposed the adulterous practices of the Mahárújás. I frequent at present the temple of Jivanji Mahárúj. I don't send my wife to that or any other temple, though it is the custom among the Vaishnavas to send their wives. The wives of very few Vuishnavas do not go to the temples. I do not worship Jivanji as God. The other Vaishnavas touch the Mahárúj's feet, swing him in a swing; a sacred necklace is put round the neck of the Mahárúj in the samo way as it is put round the neck of the image; they take up the dust of the feet of the Mahárúj and eat it or put it into their mouth. When worshipping, they call him Mahú Prabhuji, Purushottam, Vallabh Deva, etc. I can swear that the Mahárúj is addressed in these names of the Supreme Being, and not the image, which is in an inner room. The Mahárájás take their seat outside. At that time, the doors of the room containing the image are shut. I have been to the temples belonging to the other Mahárújás; the form of worship is the same in all. I went to worship the image only. I joined my hands to the Mahárúj, but did not worship him in any way. It is stated in the sacred books that the worship of the Mahárúj should be performed in the same way as that of God. The Mahárájás are Bráhmins, and are regarded as gurus. As Bráhmius they are not the preceptors of religion. A few of the Vaishnavas do not consider the Mahárájás as gods. I do not, but my brother does consider them as such. The dedication of "tan, man, and dhan" is not at present made by all Hindus. That after the dedication, the Maháráj can do what he pleases with females, is a matter of notoriety. I have not seen any act of impropriety by the plaintiff; I have heard of some. About four years ago, on the occasion of the marriage of my daughter, a Maháráj was invited by the father-in-law of the girl. A Maháráj then demanded a fine from me of Rs. 5-4 which I refused to pay; it was for my appearing in mourning. "Krishna Lilá" means amorous sport with Krishna, which commenced when he was six or seven years old, and lasted till he reached his eleventh year. Some four or five years ago, I saw dramas of this story of Krishna, which were performed in Mahárájás' temples before males and females. Pictures of this story are sometimes observed on the walls of some buildings, not on the walls of temples. The women, however, are not painted naked. This book, containing one indecent and some other pictures, was published at Ahmedábád five years ago: it is an abridgement of the Bhágavat. It is recognised among the Vaishnavas; there are some parts of it which are recognised by others. It is certainly indecent to observe naked men or women on the top of a tree. I have never appeared in that manner on a tree. I have never seen any pictures in the Véds. The Mahárájás wear long hair and consider themselves as gopis (cowherdesses) in this world. It is so stated in one of the sacred books. The hair on the head is worn by the Hindus not with the object that angels may hold us by it and pull us up to heaven: it is to be tied up at the time of worship. The plaintiff is a mere humbug when he pretends to encourage female education. I have heard that he opened a female school in Surat; and he collected subscriptions in Bombay for defraying its expenses. At the meeting of the Bháttiás held in 1855, several resolutions were passed, one of which was to prevent females from going to the temples at night during the cold season. The object was to prevent them being defiled by the Mahárájás. I have seen Gokuládhisji make signs to females two or three times about five or six years ago. From their dress I knew the women belonged to our caste. The place in which the Maháráj females reside is separate from the place where these acts are committed. I have been to his bed-room, and have seen females going into and coming out of his bed-room. I have been there only once, five or six years ago. He has sent for me, as there was a subscription list to be prepared. Widows are constantly near the Mahárájás' bed-rooms: it is their business. I have seen Dwárkánáthji Maháráj giving a signal to a female to go into his bed-room. On seeing me, he held back his hand with which he was making the signal. She was asking something of the Maháráj, and the latter said "take this"—(witness explains the very indecent attitude and signal made). The female was a married woman, about twenty years of age. I once threw gulál on the mother-in-law of my daughter, on the occasion of her marriage. This sprinkling of gulál was done with respect, not in the way in which Mahárájás throw it. On throwing the gulál, I made her a present of money. I remember one Matuji Maháráj held a meeting some years ago at Mahálakshmi, on which occasion gulál was thrown. In the island of Beyt, when the Mahárájás throw gulál, they touch the females. Licentious songs are sung by females on occasions of marriage; but when they are addressed to the Mahárájás, the females singing them wish for carnal intercourse with them (the Mahárájás). In some songs, on occasions of marriage, the women on one side wish those on the other side to exchange husbands, for the time being of course. Such a thing is never done; it is carried into practice only with the Maháráj. I have seen the seats of Mahárájás at Bombay, Beyt, and Mándavi worshipped by Vaishnavas. If the Bháttiás of Bombay were educated at all, such adulteries would not prevail amongst them. The report in the *Satya Prakásh* is not a full report of the Bháttiá meeting held in 1855: the resolution about the females and and the Mahárájás is omitted.

(Re-examined.) At the time of the Bháttiá meeting in 1855, I read the *Samáchár* in which the substance of the resolution about the females is given. It is also correctly given in the *Jámi-Jamshid*. The resolution was not embodied in the report published in the *Satya Prakásh*, because it was not come into force until a year afterwards. I think the singing of licentious songs on occasions of marriage is going out of fashion through the primary exertions of the *Satya Prakásh*. The Mahárájás sitting in conclave threatened to fine me once, because I had a controversy with them. They have committed many such extortions. The plaintiff said he had opened a female school at Surat : I had no further knowledge of its being a fact. There is a principal temple of a Mahárój at Beyt.

(*Dr. Bháu Dáji*, examined, *February* 14, 1862.) I am a Graduate of the Grant Medical College, and a private practitioner. I am a prizeman of the Elphinstone College. I won a prize on the best essay on Female Infanticide in Káthiáwár. I was a member of the late Board of Education, and am a Fellow of the Bombay University. I am a member of the Bombay Branch of the Royal Asiatic Society, the Bombay Geographical Society, and of several other Societies. There is a female school permanently endowed in my name. I am a Shenavi Bráhmin, and not a member of the Vallabháchárya sect. I have obtained a diploma of the Grant Medical College. I have taken a particular interest in the history and antiquities of my country. My practice extends amongst all classes of the natives, and I was the first Graduate employed by the Mahárájás of Bombay. I know the plaintiff, whom I first saw about a year and a half ago, once or twice professionally.

Mr. Anstey.—What was the nature of his disease?

Dr. Bháu.—Am I bound, my Lord, to name the disease which I came to know confidentially in the course of my profession?

Sir M. Sausse.—It is a proper objection on the part of this gentleman.

The objection was overruled.

(Witness continued.) The disease was syphilis, which is commonly known as the venereal disease. I did not treat him for it; he mentioned to me that he was suffering from "chándi," and would send a man to me the following day. "Chándi" literally means chancre, an ulcer. There were two friends present—Mr. Lakhmidás Khimji and Rao Sáheb Visvanáth Náráyan, who retired, as soon as the plaintiff began to describe to me the disease. So far as I remember I did not visit him again. He said the story of the case would be explained to me the next day. It was communicated to me by Govardhandás, plaintiff's secretary and disciple. Govardhandás came to me the next day, and said Mahárój Jadunáthji was suffering from chancre. I insisted upon an ocular inspection, and in the meantime prescribed simple ointment. He did not send for me again. I have attended three other similar cases connected with Mahárájás. I saw Jadunáthji's father at Surat in December, 1849. I went to his house. He lived on the second story of his house. There was a private staircase pointed out to me, by which a person could pass out without the knowledge of those in the rooms on tho first story. The plaintiff does not bear a good reputation; I have a very unfavourable opinion as to his character for chastity and morality. I have known only one learned Maháráj : the rest are not above the average of ordinary Bráhmins. The Mahárájas are respected for their descent, not for their learning. They are worshipped as in-carnations of Krishna. I have seen them so worshipped. After the visitors have paid their respects to the idol, they go to pay it to the Maháráj who sits outside. There is no order among visitors; there is great hustling and elbowing of men and women together. At the entrance to the inner room, there is a railing, at which two persons stand with large cords in their hands. Accidents have occurred from the striking of the cords. I have known an instance in which ornaments were lost in the crowd. I have seen the Maháráj's bath, and hundreds rushing to drink the water dripping from his langoti. The women apply their hands to the soles of his feet and eat the dust. In the compound of this (the Bhuleshwar) temple, there is a one storied house, to which the Maháráj repairs after he has done with the personal worship of the image. The devotees pay more attention to the Maháráj than to the idol. There are two rooms in the house and two staircases, one leading to the temple and one to the outer gate. There is an entrance from the zenáná into the Maháráj's bed-room. The inmates of the zenáná have their faces always covered, but the faces of the female devotees are uncovered. In this temple I have seen several pictures repre-senting the sport of Krishna with the gopis; I don't think they were indecent. About twenty years ago I saw a Maháráj exhibit-ing indecent pictures to men and women. His conversation was all about women: it was somewhat indecent. My opinion of the character of the Mahárájás for morality with women is very un-favourable. I have attended three Mahárájás (besides the plaintiff) for venereal disease. On one or two occasions a Maháráj applied to me for medicine which would prevent a woman from being pregnant I had conversation with Jivanji Maháráj about the immorality of the other Mahárájas, once publicly. I remonstrated with him; but he said he had no control over the adulterous acts of the Mahárájás. This was about three years ago. The Mahárájás are sectaries, and are not good Bráhmins. A Bráhmin has six duties to perform :—Sacrificing and assisting at sacrifices, taking charity and giving charity, etc. The Mahárájás only take charity. The great majority of them are not fit to be gurus. Their acts are inconsistent with the ancient doctrines of the Hindus. A guru is a person who initiates a child: it may be his father, his relative, or the family priest. There is no mention of "tan, man, and dhan," in our gáyatri, or verse of initiation, which is to be recited only mentally. It is not innocent sport to throw gulál on a female : it is considered one of the three forms of adultery. (Reads the translation of a passage from one of the Hindu law books called *Mitákshará*.)

The Law about Adultery is now told. [Adultery means the mutual connexion of a man with another's wife (or the means of bringing about the connexion).]

*Vyasa* describes three varieties of adultery, in order that the adulterer may receive the punishment for crime of the first degree, or for crime of the middle degree, or for crime of the highest degree.

*First Adultery.*—In uninhabited spots, or untimely occasions with (slang) language other than the current language of the country, casting lewd glances towards another's wife "or smiling" [(sporting) addition in the Maráthi translation]—this is called first adultery.

*Middle Adultery.*—Enticing [a woman] by good perfumes [(such as sandal, *Buká*, Argojá, etc.), addition in the Maráthi translation] flowers, incense, ornaments, clothes, food, and drink, is called middle adultery.

*Highest Adultery.*—Sitting in retirement and on one seat, and embracing each other, placing hands on [one another's] shoulders, and holding [each others'] hands and playing by taking hold of each other's hair is called highest adultery.

Whoever touches "the ends of the cloth passed round the loins," the cloth over the breast, the thigh or the hair, or who converses in a solitary place or at an improper time, or who occupies one seat (with another's wife,) is also to be caught (for punishment).

Manu 6. He who with pride or folly or flattery says, that he enjoyed this female before, that is also considered adultery.

*Note.*—The above is a translation of the Vyavahárádhyáya of the Mitákshará from the Maráthi translation of the Sanskrit original, published in Bombay by order of Government in 1844. I have compared this English translation with the original Sanskrit text published under the authority of the committee of

Public Instruction in 1829 at Calcutta. The brackets at the end indicate words in the Sanskrit Original but ommited in the Maráthi translation.

The word *lilá* means amorous sport. The dance called Rás Lilá is mentioned in Professor H. H. Wilson's dictionary and in the Bhágavata. I can best describe the way in which the Mahárájás wear their hair by showing a photograph taken by my brother (Dr. Náráyan Dáji). Except in one respect, the way in which they wear their hair is peculiar. There have long been public discussions and notices of the conduct and character of the Mahárájás. The earliest bitter notice that I saw was in the *Dhumketu* five or six years ago. I believe all the Mahárájás wear silver toe-rings. This passage at the end of the alleged libel I would read thus, according to my judgment:—Oh, ye Mahárájás, acting on that commentary, you spoil the daughters, etc., of your disciples: raise your hands from that, and destroy at once immoralities like the "Ras Mandali." I think that upon the whole "acting on that commentary" is quite positive. I think "desist from acting" is the most emphatic part of the passage. The passage is addressed to the Mahárájás generally. The plaintiff had a very bad reputation as to his chastity at Surat; but he was then equally revered as a Maháráj.

(Cross-examined.) In the course of my private practice, I have attended upon hundreds of different castes of natives, both high and low. I am sure the plaintiff used the word "chándi." It is possible patients may be mistaken in describing the symptoms of a disease. *Chándi* originally means silver; it is used as a slang term for chancre. (To Sir Joseph Arnould.) I was told the plaintiff employed another practitioner; he did not like to expose himself. (Witness continued). I think the plaintiff was not of a sanguine, but of a phlegmatic temperament. I know nothing of plaintiff's disease personally except what I was told by him and his secretary. I wish decidedly for a better state of things among the Hindus generally. I heard from plaintiff that he had established a female school in Surat; he wanted to train up the girls in the doctrines of his sect. I have never been present at "Ras Mandalis;" they are known to exist as secret societies. I think Krishna had no improper connexion with the gopis; they were in love with him.

(Re-examined). The story of the gopis and Krishna is not confined to the Vallabháchárya sect. Uneducated persons take it literally, but not so enlightened persons. (To Sir M. Sausse.) Some of the Mahárájás, as I have heard, are men of unspotted character, men of piety, and good men; and therefore I said the passage refers to the Mahárájás generally. (To Sir Joseph Arnould.) I think the passage in question is directed as an exhortation to the whole class of Mahárájás, not to the plaintiff personally. (To Sir M. Sausse.) From the context, I say the remark is not necessarily directed to the plaintiff, or necessarily implied against him. It is possible a reader may understand that it applies to the plaintiff. (To Sir Joseph Arnould.) I myself understand it as a general exhortation, and any reader of average intelligence would understand the main object of the writer to be, not to make a personal charge of mal-practices against the plaintiff, but to address a general exhortation to the class to which the plaintiff belongs, to desist from such mal-practices. (To Sir M. Sausse.) The expression "adopt a virtuous course of conduct," does not imply any imputation against the plaintiff; it is an exhortation to set a good example.—(To Sir Joseph Arnould.) The exhortation I think is carried on from the commencement of the paragraph to the words "desist from that." Nothing is imputed to the plaintiff distinctly. I think decidedly that the plaintiff is not singled out. Any imputation upon him would be inferential, not direct.—(To Sir M. Sausse.) I am of opinion that it is not intended against the plaintiff in a direct manner. The article in the original does not allude specially to the plaintiff. The English translation, now in my hands, tends that way. Reading the Gujaráti article, I don't think the plaintiff is intended to be included among the licentious Mahárájás. From my knowledge of his antecedents, I would include him.—(To Sir Joseph Arnould.) As a reader not acquainted with his antecedents, I would be doubtful whether I must include him or not.

(*Dr. Dhirajrám Dalpatrám*, examined, *February* 14, 1862.) I am a Graduate of the Grant Medical College and a private practitioner. I know the plaintiff, whom I first met in July, 1860, at the girls' school of Mangaldás Nathubhái. In consequence of something said to me, I called upon him at his house. In December, 1860, I attended on him professionally at his house. He was suffering from venereal affection; I made an ocular examination of it and found it to be an ulcer. He gave me the history of the case; he said he had suffered from it three or four months previously and had caught it and had it from an impure intercourse with a woman. I prescribed the blackwash externally, and mercury internally. Plaintiff said he had suffered some years ago from the same affection, and had taken a preparation of mercury, prepared by himself. Plaintiff asked me if I had read in medical works that the disease would go by having intercourse with a woman free from it. I said I had not. He then said he had twice tried the experiment at Surat. He succeeded once in it but not the second time, because he was then much reduced,

(Cross-examined.) The plaintiff, when I saw him in December, 1860, appeared to have been suffering for three months previously. My opinion as to the ulcer being syphilitic was confirmed by plaintiff's history of his case. I did make a personal examination. I treated the plaintiff for more than a month. I had seen him in Surat a good many years ago. There is a difference of opinion among doctors as to whether mercury is necessary in syphilis. The blackwash I applied externally was mercurial. I have treated a good many persons in high rank for this complaint. The plaintiff was alone in the backroom when I saw him: the room had more than two windows. In the commencement of the treatment, I told the plaintiff not to go out. I saw him sometime before I treated him. I have known the defendant for the last seven or eight years, but never communicated to him the plaintiff's complaint, nor even to Lakmidás Khimji, nor to anybody else. I never mentioned anything about this to anybody before appearing in the witness-box. I was born a Vallabháchárya, and am a Káyasth. I do not at present go to any of the Mahárájás' temples. I have been practising for the last three years. The plaintiff did not tell me he had prickly-heat.

(*Lakhmidás Khimji*, examined, *February* 14, 20, 1862.) I deal in piece goods and am a member of the Bháttiá caste. I am one of the twelve Shets of the Mahájans. I have known the plaintiff for the last ten or eleven years. I first became acquainted with him at

Beyt, whither I had been on a pilgrimage. Our acquaintance ripened into friendship. At Beyt I made some presents to him, when I invited him to my residence. I also made presents to him on another occasion. There is a temple dedicated to Lakshmi at Beyt, where I once saw Jadunáthji Maháráj. There were females present in the temple. After throwing gulál on the image, he threw it upon a number of persons, and in doing so, he pressed the breasts of a Bháttiá girl about fourteen years of age. As he squeezed her breast, she smiled. He threw the gulál upon the crowd, so that they might not see through it what he was doing. I used to visit him at the place where he had put up. My maternal uncle, Dámodar Devji, accompanied me. I went to the plaintiff about one o'clock in the day, when he was in his bed. My uncle went up and shampooed one of his legs. I went up and followed his example. It is a great mark of respect to shampoo the Maháráj's legs. The Bháttiá girl above alluded to came there with a widow, about a quarter of an hour after our arrival there. The widow whispered something into plaintiff's ears, upon which he desired us to go out. We obeyed the order. The widow came out with us and went in again. The girl was left in the bed-room. When I went outside, my uncle informed me of the visit of the females. Afterwards, the widow came out, shut the door, put up the chain and held it with her hand. The girl was inside all the time. In consequence of certain conversation I had with my uncle, we both went in again to see the Rás Lilá, *i.e.* the plaintiff's conversation with the girl. We were allowed to go in the moment we expressed a wish. I saw the plaintiff having carnal connexion with the girl. Several people are often anxious to see such Rás Lilá. Plaintiff asked my uncle what I would pay for seeing the Rás Lilá. My uncle said that I would serve him (plaintiff). I had to pay some money before I was allowed to see the Rás Lilá. I was then eighteen or nineteen years old. The followers who are allowed to see the lilá, as well as the female who is defiled, have to pay money for the indulgence. It is considered a pious act, and sure to lead to the paradise known as Gowlok. I left the room shortly afterwards from shame; my uncle remained inside. Two or three days subsequently, I saw another married Bháttiá female enter the plaintiff's bed-room.

When I went on a pilgrimage to Gokul Mathurá, about eighteen years ago, I first heard of a "Ras Mandali." I was present at a Ras Mandali at Beyt about the time I spoke of. There were twelve or thirteen men and thirteen or fifteen females. It was held daily for some days at the appointed place. On these occasions, after the persons had taken their seats, the stories of the 84 and the 252 were read from a book. Some offering is then made to the book, and sweetmeat, fruit, or parched rice is placed upon the book. The sweetmeat or fruit is then distributed among the meeting. The persons who are not members, and who came merely to listen to the stories, then left the room. I was a stranger at the meeting, and when I retired the men and women were in the room. [The witness then described the preparations which he saw made for the Ras Mandali.] My uncle was a member, and was desired by the other members to ask me to go out. The "Ras Mandalis" are a matter of notoriety; even a child of five years knows of their existence. . . . . . Each member must go to the meeting with his wife, except "Varkats," who are admitted without their wives. Those followers of the Mahárájás who are members of the society are reputed to be pious and staunch devotees. The Varkats are procurers of women for the Mahárájás. On one occasion, plaintiff told me "the Varkats are the persons who have corrupted us (Mahárájás)." On another occasion at Beyt, I was sitting near the plaintiff, when a female came there. . . . . I saw plaintiff on three or four occasions press with his toes the hands of females who worshipped him by touching the soles of his feet. Pressing the toes is the signal for adultery. I saw plaintiff at Byculla where he had put up, the second or third day after his arrival in Bombay. I am aware of plaintiff's arrival in Bombay in 1860. I saw him two or three days after his arrival. I was in the habit of seeing him frequently, two or three times a day. I was a friend of his. I invited him to my house, introduced him to. my friends, and induced them to invite him. I made him presents of furniture, lamps, chairs, sofas, etc. I know plaintiff was the editor of two pamphlets. I had a hand in getting them published. I made an arrangement with a printer named Ganpat Krishnáji, for the pub-lication of plaintiff's two pamphlets. I did so at his request. The pamphlets were edited by plaintiff: the Maháráj dictated, and Govardhandás, his secretary, acted as his amanuensis. I have seen the handbill issued by plaintiff, asking the Vaishnavas to become subscribers to the pamphlet. I recommended him to issue a handbill to gain more subscribers; the Maháráj dictated the contents of the handbill. Plaintiff caused a letter to be published in the *Chábuk* newspaper, in which there is mention made of the Wálkeshwar and Byculla roads, alluded to in the libel. Plaintiff, before the action, said to me:—"All the Mahárájás are running away from Bombay, in consequence of publications in the newspapers, and I have therefore come down to Bombay for the purpose of discussing and debating with the editors." He asked me if an action would proceed during his absence from Bombay. I said I did not know. Karsandás Nensi, who was present on the occasion, said the action would proceed even in his absence. Plaintiff then asked me if his evidence could be taken at his own house if he remained in Bombay. I said that that was impossible; that Jivanlálji Maháráj was summoned to Court some six years ago, but that all efforts failed to obtain for him an exemption from attendance. Plaintiff then asked whether, if he were to go to Court, he would get an elevated seat near the judge! I subsequently came to the conclusion that the plaintiff had not left off the practices he pursued at Beyt. For a few months I was misled by his professions for the promotion of female education, widow re-marriage, etc. One day whilst I was sitting at the plaintiff's temple, two females, one a married woman about 25 years of age, and the other a widow, came up. The former, when she approached the staircase, produced a silver goblet which she had concealed under her clothes. The Maháráj, on seeing her, made a signal to go into his bedroom. . . . . . I went down stairs to the veranda, but having had a suspicion in my mind, I went up again into the same room where I had been before. I found the widow sitting outside the door. I remained there about half an hour, when first the Maháráj came out and turned pale on observing me. I saw the young female come out. . . . . . She had not the silver goblet in her hand: it must have been given to plaintiff. The widow and the young woman then left. I told plaintiff I had some business and he had better send his own man to the printer. I left and visited plaintiff again in the evening, when he took me into an inner room for the purpose of private conversation. He opened the conversation by asking me what I had done with regard to opening female schools here. I said to him, "Maháráj, this is all a sham; you profess to be a reformer, while inwardly you commit such acts!" He denied the charge. He said he had been inside for the purpose of accepting sweetmeat or fruit. Plaintiff then adroitly changed the subject of conversation. On another occasion, I had conversation on the same subject with plaintiff. I said, "You told me that you accepted sweetmeats from female devotees openly, and how was it that you went inside the other day with the young woman?" Plaintiff said he did so at the desire of the woman. I then asked why he kept the widow out; to which plaintiff made no reply. I have seen male and female devotees touching the soles of the Maháráj's feet, and I have seen him press with his toes the hands of females, young and beautiful. About a week subsequently to what I have said above, I saw plaintiff taking some medicine. I had another conversation in the bedroom with plaintiff the same evening. He directed me not to fathom him and said, "What income do we derive from you, males? if you make arrangements for large profits to us, I'll undertake to root out adultery from the practices of the Mahárájás." Plaintiff's father or grandfather having committed a theft in Udayapur or the neighbourhood, he would not at any time be allowed to enter those territories without a pass. Plaintiff said he suffered from syphilis. I said, "Maháráj! I am now perfectly convinced you have not reformed your conduct as yet." Plaintiff said, "Do not fathom me. Our income is chiefly derived from females; if you make other arrangements for it, I will undertake to root out the practice of adultery from among the Mahárájás." He said it was impossible to give up at once such practices; but he had made some reform in his conduct. Plaintiff asked me to bring in Dr. Bháu Dáji. I took Dr. Bháu Dáji to the plaintiff's residence. Rao Sáheb Vishwanáth was with us at the time. (Witness describes what occurred then and in the evening.) Some days afterwards plaintiff informed me that he was under the treatment of Dr. Dhirajrám. He became pale and sickly. I took Dr. Bháu Dáji to plaintiff about the middle of September, 1860. The general reputation of the Mahárájás as regards adultery is very bad. I have personal knowledge of the licentious conduct of ten, twelve, or fifteen of them. After the meeting of the Bháttiás in 1855, I had conversation with Jivanji Maháráj on the subject of the conduct of the other Mahárájás. I as well as others were sent for by him. We said the printers were discussing, and he had been served with a summons. Dr. Bháu, Vináyikráo Wásudeva, and if I mistake not Náráyan Dinánáthji, were there. Dr. Bháu said to the Maháráj, "Reform your conduct, be pious, establish schools, preach to your followers, etc., and none dare publish anything against you." It was a long lecture that Dr. Bháu gave : I merely give the substance. Jivanji said he would not be able to control the acts of the other Mahárájás; as their principal income was derived from females. Khurshedji Cámá, who was present on another occasion, said a great deal to Jivanji Maháráj. The Maháráj said, "As regards myself, I am ready to give my signature to any arrangements; I will now leave off such practices." He offered to give, but did not give, his signature. Jivanji, on finding me on one side, accused me of, and reproved me for, divulging secret matters. No arrangement took place. I was invited to the general meeting of Vaishnavas held last year; my consent was not taken, as it ought to have been. I discontinued my visits to plaintiff afterwards.

(Cross-examined.) The plaintiff was about 28 years old when I saw him at Beyt; he is now about 40 years of age. At that time, I considered such acts as plaintiff was guilty of, as religious. My views have changed since the "slavery bond," to which I put my signature, as several Justices of the Peace put theirs. I knew from her dress that the young female I saw at Beyt was a married woman. Plaintiff presided in the year 1860 at an exhibition for the distribution of prizes to the female schools of Mangaldás Nathubhái. Plaintiff expressed an opinion against the system of education, saying the girls should have been taught religious doctrines only. Vináyak Vásudevji remonstrated against this. The subject of re-marriage was talked about everywhere at the time. A meeting was convened by plaintiff to discuss the question of re-marriage. It was largely attended. I discontinued going to the plaintiff on

4

account of his bad conduct. I am not acquainted with the two females who visited the plaintiff at his residence at Bombay. Plaintiff is said to be a guru of religion, but he does not act so; he never gives instruction. It is true he ought to do so. I signed the "slavery bond" unwillingly. By my coming here to give evidence I have forfeited that bond.—(To the Court.) I have spoken, five or six years ago, to my friend Mr. Dhanjibhai Frámji, partner in the house of Wallace and Co., about the immoral practices of plaintiff I saw at Beyt. I had also about a year ago conversation on the same with Khatáo Makanji, Mathurádás Lowji, and Narsi Jethá. The conversation took place in the garden of Gokaldás Tejpál when my maternal uncle Dámodar Devji was there. He is now at Zanzibár. I have also spoken to Mr. Mangaldás Nathubhái at Mátherán last year.

(*Kálábhái Lalubhái*, examined, *February* 20, 1862.) I am a Káyasth, and a student of the Elphinstone Institution. I know the plaintiff, whom I saw in Surat about three years ago. He was a friend of my father. I had a conversation with him on the subject of widow re-marriage. I visited him frequently and saw him in different rooms in his house. I used to receive from plaintiff folded pán-sopári when I went to him. I was sitting one day with him on the first story when a Banian girl came in company with a female servant of the Maháráj. She was about fourteen or fifteen years old. She passed across the hall into a side room, and a Banian who was sitting near us got up and went away. Plaintiff left the hall and went into the side room. The female servant sat in the hall. Four or five females came into the hall afterwards. I went to have my usual pán-sopári from plaintiff towards the side room, and on opening the door of it, saw plaintiff seated on a couch opposite the door, kissing and embracing the young woman. Plaintiff on seeing me left the female and came to the door and said, " Oh, I forgot to give you the usual pán-sopári;" so saying he came out with me and desired his attendant to get me the pán-sopári, which I received and went away. Plaintiff went back to the inner room. I used to visit the plaintiff in Bombay. On one occasion, I saw two or three "cháchiás" sitting near plaintiff, who advocated in their presence the adulterous doctrines of the sect. On another occasion, when I was standing in the house yard of plaintiff's residence, two or three Vaishnavas who were speaking among themselves, said, (pointing to a female) that Jadunáthji Maháráj was in love with her. Some days after, when I did not attend the school on account of a holiday, I saw the same female passing by the Kalkádevi road. I was going on some business; but on seeing her I followed her to plaintiff's. She went into the private room of the Maháráj; and I went to the visiting room where plaintiff was sitting. After a few minutes the plaintiff followed the young woman, and I remained sitting in the visiting room. About half-an-hour after, he came out and I smiled at him, when he asked me why I smiled. I told him, "You are effecting a great reform." He smiled at this and made no remark. The young woman came out after a time and went away smiling.... From the dress and the jewels she had on, I presume she was a respectable woman. I had some conversation with plaintiff about the "Propagator of our own Religion;" he said it was published on his behalf. One day at Surat I saw plaintiff refuse to allow some females to touch the soles of his feet; he told them to touch the feet of his wife in the zenáná. He explained to me afterwards, that allowing females to touch his feet might give rise to suspicions as to his chastity. After this, while at Bombay, I saw him allowing females to touch his feet. To my knowledge, the plaintiff tells lies. His general reputation in Surat was that he was immersed in adultery. My father is Sheristedár in the Sudder Adáwlat at Bombay. The respect paid to the plaintiff has not diminished since the publication of the libel.

(Cross-examined.) I am 16 years old, and am the nephew of Dr. Dhirajrám. I am acquainted with the defendant.

(*Chathurbhuj Wálji,* examined, *February* 21, 1862.) I am a Bháttiá of the Vallabháchárya sect. I know the plaintiff, whom I visited at his residence in Bombay. One day, a female having gone into the hall, entered an inner room. A female servant told plaintiff something in his ear, whereupon he left the hall on pretence of going to take his dinner, and entered the inner room. Plaintiff went inside, saying, "I am going to dine." About half-an-hour after he came out. The female came out soon after him and went away.

(Cross-examined.) I used to visit the plaintiff almost daily. I never saw the zenáná. I had once been into the inner room, to which there is only one door. I was asked to go in by the Maháráj, who wished to tell me a secret story. I presented him two or four books which he asked from me. I observed nothing in the hands of the female above alluded to. I studied for a year and a half in a school under the defendant Karsandás. I did not tell him anything about the female. I visit the great temple of Jivanlálji Maháráj. I had conversation with plaintiff about adultery. Kalábhái Lalubhái was present at the time. I asked plaintiff how it was that great men committed adultery, of which there is prohibition in the Shástras. To this plaintiff replied, "There is no sin in adultery."......

(Re-examined.) When I went into the inner room above alluded to, I saw a bed there. The books I presented to the plaintiff related to the Mahárájás. They were written against the Mabárájás, and I gave them to plaintiff within the month after his arrival in Bombay.

(*Damodar Jetha*, cross-examined.) I am a Bháttiá Shroff, and know the plaintiff, with whom I had a conversation once at the house of Karsandás Nepsi, about a year and a quarter ago. The Maháráj was sitting on a sofa, and we were sitting on the ground. The Maháráj spoke of the "Varkats." The owner asked him what was the explanation of the adultery committed by the offspring of Gosáijis. He said whatever evil is committed, it is through the Varkats. He did not say he was corrupted by them. The Varkats are at present in the habit of living in other persons' houses as a matter of charity; they commit bad acts, and go constantly to the Mahárájás.

(*Mungaldás Nathubhái*, examined.) I am a member of the Baniá caste of the Vallabháchárya sect. I am a shet of my caste, a Justice of the Peace, and a grand juror. I have founded a female school. I was present on one occasion with others at the house of Jivanji Maháráj. Dr. Bháu opened the conversation on the subject of the adulteries of the Mahárájás. Jivanji said he was unable to control the conduct and practices of all the other Mahárájás. He expressed a wish to do all he could. Dr. Bháu remarked that, if they adopted a virtuous course of conduct, none dare publish anything against them. At a private conversation with Jivanji (which witness divulged on being ordered to do so by the Court) he was informed that it was impossible to put a stop at once to the practices of the Mahárájás; their chief income was derived from females, and they could not be prevented from visiting the Mahárájás, etc.

(Cross-examined.) I invited plaintiff once to preside at an exhibition of the girls' school.

(*Thákarsi Náranj*, examined.) The plaintiff has a very bad reputation for his morality and chastity in Katch Mándavi for the last seven or eight years. (To Sir Joseph Arnould.) I heard that he had a bad reputation for his adultery.

(*Ravji Sundarji*, examined.) I knew the plaintiff in Katch Mándavi. He bore a bad character as to his morality.

(Cross-examined.) It is well known that all the Mahárájás are bad. In Katch I heard that the plaintiff's character was worse than that of other Mahárájás. I also heard that gambling was going on in his house.

(*Narmadáshankar Lálshankar*, examined.) I am a Nágar Bráhmin, and have taken an interest in the question of widow remarriage. I am the man who had a discussion with the plaintiff at a public meeting. He declared himself against widow remarriage. I furnished the manuscript to Janárdan for his notices of the Vallabháchárya sect. I have studied the books of the Vallabháchárya sect, and have no doubt as to the meaning of *tan, man,* and *dhan*; the dedication thereof includes wives, daughters, sons, property, body, soul, etc. The plaintiff bears a bad reputation everywhere, in Surat, Mándavi, Katch, and Bombay. I know the witness Kállábhái, who has communicated to me many things about the plaintiff.

(Cross-examined.) I have been a poet for the last seven years. I was delivering lectures at my house on the improprieties of the sect, to bring the devotees to their senses, and to make them shun the society of such nasty persons as the Mahárájás. I do not except Jivanji as being virtuous. I wrote my essay against the Vallabháchárya religion from materials furnished me by Shástris, from books, and by the devotees themselves. The dedication of *tan, man,* and *dhan* is addressed to the Mahárájás; I am quite sure of this from my study of several works. My version of the doctrines was approved of as correct by several Shástris. I informed the defendant of the plaintiff's bad character in Surat before the publication of the libel.

(Re-examined.) There is no morality of any kind whatever in the doctrines of Vallabháchárya. The Mahárájás are not preceptors of religion, much less of the ancient religion of the Hindus.

(*Nánábhái Rustamji*, examined.) I am one of the defendants in this case and managing proprietor of the *Union Press*. I was the printer of the *Satya Prakásh* newspaper, and the co-defendant was the editor. The paper was not started for profit to the proprietors, but in the cause of reform in the native community. The receipts fell far short of the expenditure. I printed some numbers of the "Propagator of our own Religion" for the plaintiff. The manuscript was brought to me by his secretary Parbhudás, who manages this case. I sent the bills to Dr. Dhirajárm, who paid them on behalf of the Maháráj.

------

## (*Rebutting Evidence for Plaintiff.*)

(*Velji Makanji*, examined, *February* 25, 1862.) I am a Bráhmin of the Sáchorá caste, and have been in the service of the plaintiff for the last fifteen years. I went with him on his travels, and was every moment with him. I accompanied him on his visits to the temples, when four of the Sirkar's sepoys and a Kárbhári attended him, as also his own sepoys and a number of Vaishnavas. At noon the females went to him for darshan. No darshan was allowed after six o'clock in the evening. During the plaintiff's residence at Beyt, women came on darshan up to the Maháráj's dinner time. They were always accompanied by some males. Males accompany females when the latter go to the temples at all places. Plaintiff had two rooms, one a bed-room and the other a cook-room, and he took his meals in the latter. There was a separate room to which only the followers were admitted. I never saw a female enter the bed-room. I did not see the plaintiff throw gulál upon any one at the temple of Lakshmiji.

(Cross-examined.) It is usual at the Maháráj's house to pay three rupees a month to servants of my class. I put in order the

Maháráj's clothes after he has taken them off. I did not leave him for five minutes. It is my custom to sleep outside the door when the Maháráj sleeps in his bed-room. I will not leave the Maháráj alone. Even if he told me, I would not go; not that we suspect him, but because some one must be constantly within call. I and the other servants are not procurers to the Maháráj. He is standing downstairs, and is watched by one Chobáji.

(Re-examined.) At Beyt, the Maháráj's wife was not with him; she was at her father's. He has two children, who, with his wife, reside in Bombay at present. He has a son of seven years and a daughter of four. If the Maháráj did anything wrong I would tell him that, and also inform the people of it. I never observed any impropriety in his conduct. I get three rupees a month besides board and lodging.—(To Sir Joseph Arnould.) The Maháráj travelled continuously for five or six years, during the whole of which time his wife was not with him.

(The name of Jadunáthji Brizratanji Maháráj, the plaintiff in this action, was here called out by the Crier, and all eyes were strained in every direction of the hall of justice to see His Holiness come in.)

(*Jadunáthji Brizratanji Maháráj,* examined *February,* 27, 28, and *March* 1, 1862.) I am the plaintiff in this action, and am above thirty-five years of age. I have never been in a court of justice in my life before. To my knowledge no other Maháráj has attended in a court of justice. Besides Gujaráti, I know the Panjábi, Márwári, and Hindustáni languages, Urdu more or less, Sanskrit for the most part, and the Brij Bháshá. I have seen those of the books of Vallabhácháryra sect which are necessary. I have opened a Sanskrit and Gujaráti school at Surat, the expenses of which are defrayed by me. One Shástri gives instruction in Sanskrit, and five or six teachers teach Gujaráti. Since I first came to Bombay I have taken an interest in female education. I first paid a visit about nineteen months ago to the "Mangaldás Girls' School." It is the duty of all Hindus to go on pilgrimages, the length of which varies with the kind of pilgrimage and the place. I set out on a pilgrimage, and arrived in Beyt in 1907. I visited twice a day the temple of Lakshmi. Gulál is thrown on the image in the temple. In the temple of Dwáskánáthji it is also thrown on the followers. I never threw gulál on the persons of the devotees at the temple of Lakshmi. How can I touch the breast of any female, when I regard all female devotees as my children? I never did so. I know Lakhmidás Khimji, with whom I first became acquainted about two years or two years and a half ago. I did not see him at Beyt in 1907. Any story he may have told against me is false. The last witness Velji is my personal attendant, and was so on my pilgrimage. He is daily in my presence. It is customary amongst all of my class to have at least three or four personal attendants constantly near them. I have visited Barodá, Gokul, Mathurá, Amritsar, two Mándavis, Multán, and other places. I saw Gokaldás Tejpal and Lakhmidás Khimji at Bycallá, where they came to me. I was married in 1905 or 1906 before I went to Shikárpor. I did not leave Surat because of a charge of rape against me. My wife was not with me on my pilgrimage to Beyt. I have been subpœnaed by the defendants to give evidence here; I was served by a Pársi. I saw Gokaldás Tejpál on my first visit to Bombay; he introduced me to Lakhmidás. I first put up at Bycallá when I came to Bombay two years ago. Lakhmidás invited me on one occasion when his brother was sick, and on another at the reading of the Bhágavat. I have some faint recollection of having authorized the publication of some articles in the *Chábuk* newspaper. I did not tell Lakhmidás that the Mahárájás were running away from Bombay in consequence of the articles in the newspapers, or that I had come to conduct a debate with them. I asked him if this action would proceed in my absence from Bombay. I have done nothing improper in respect to any female devotee in Bombay. I know Kálábhái Lalubhái, and remember having seen him in Surat and in Bombay. (Denies another allegation of immorality.) As to making "darshan," thousands of males and females used to visit me. Adultery is most distinctly prohibited in our religion. It never formed the topic of conversation between me and Kálábhái. He discussed with me about the authenticity and genuineness of the religious books. (Denies an allegation of immorality.) I don't remember having conversed with a doctor on the subject of adultery; I have never been guilty of it in my life. No female ever entered my bedroom whilst I was talking to Kálábhái. Many females daily visit my wife and children. I had no conversation at Surat with Kálábhái about touching the toes. He came and used to read with other boys a book for children which I caused to be written and printed at my expense. I assisted in its compilation. It is the universal custom for my followers to touch my feet; when I am sitting on a raised seat, the feet are touched from above and below, but when the foot is on the ground, it is touched at the top. Generally it is touched at the top. Kálábhái said to me that all the Hindu Shástras are false, and that he had become a perfect disciple of Narmadáshankar. As I maintain and am convinced that the Shástras are true, he perhaps thinks I am therefore guilty of telling falsehood. Narmadáshankar is a Nágar Bráhmin of Surat; he holds opinions contrary to mine. I had no conversation with Lakhmidás or any one else about the Varkats, nor did I ever say to any body that they had corrupted me. I don't know what is the meaning of Ras Mandali; I know Rás Mandali and have seen it too. The latter is a dramatic representation, and there is nothing indecent in it. When the deity is represented, we (Mahárájás) get up for the time; other spectators continue sitting. The Vaishnavas worship me and other Mahárájás as gurus,—those who cause happiness through God and are guides to him. I have not heard any one say that we are worshipped as gods. We are swung in a swing because we are gurus. When any money or present is given to us in the name of God, we take it. The devotees regard us as gurus, as guides to God: the Thákurji is God. We spend from three to eight or ten o'clock in the morning, and from four to six o'clock in the evening, in the worship of Thákurji. The idol in the temple is regarded as the image of God. In no book written by Vallabháchárya is it inculcated that the Mahárájás are to be worshipped as gods. I am acquainted with Gokulnáthji's commentary; I allowed Nandrám Shástri to copy it. It is considered a book of great authority by us and by all the Vaishnavas. The first Vallabháchárya is regarded as the incarnation of the head of God; he lived about 350 or 375 years ago. He was the disseminator of the opinions of Vishnu Swámi. Our faith is not opposed to the doctrines of the Veds and the Shástras. In my school at Surat, Sanskrit grammar is now being taught. The manuscript of the commentary referred to was found in my house, and was the property of my father, who died in 1908. It is more than a hundred years old. I have read it. The Purushottam referred to therein is the God of all gods, the Supreme Being. What is therein stated to be offered to God, is stated in the defendant's article to be offered to me and the Mahárájás. The sense of the original is perverted by the defendant. *Tan, man,* and *dhan* are directed to be offered to God. It is not inculcated in that commentary, or in any other book of the sect, that one should offer his wife and daughter to the Maháráj. I have not heard that any of my followers believe in a book containing such doctrines. I know Dr. Bháu Dáji. He came to visit me once, in company with Lakhmidás Khimji. I saw him on one occasion when I visited a girls' school. I was suffering from itches when Dr. Bháu visited me, because I had taken heating medicines when I was sick. I have suffered from eruptions occasionally. Some of the heating medicines were prepared by myself, and others by a native doctor. When Dr. Bháu came to me, I told him I was subject to itches, and told him I had taken heating medicines. The word "chandi" was not used at all by either of us. I asked him to prescribe some medicine for me. I never suffered from the venereal affection. The next day I sent Govardhandás to Dr. Bháu to get back a manuscript book for girls' schools, which I had prepared and given him for an inspection. I asked Govardhandás at the same time to bring any medicine which Dr. Bháu might give. I did not tell him (Dr. Bháu) that the story of the disease would be communicated to him the next day, and applied my own medicines. I know Dr. Dhirajram Dalpatrám, whom I saw at the exhibition of, I believe, Mangaldás Náthubhái's school. I described my case to him in the same manner as I had described it to Dr. Bháu. He prescribed some pills and a powder for me. The colour of the powder turned black when it was mixed with water. He came for six or seven days for treating me ; and also on other occasions. I convened a meeting to discuss the question of widow re-marriage in consequence of a note addressed to me by Narmadáshankar. I attended the meeting, but expressed no opinion on re-marriage, because other and irrelevant subjects were mooted for discussion and were discussed. The subject of re-marriage was not discussed. I said some Shástra must be fixed upon as an authority upon the subject of marriage. Narmadá-shankar said the Shástras may be followed when advisable. I said we must acknowledge all the Shástras; and my opinion was that, if the Shástras allowed, re-marriages might take place, but not otherwise. I have seen no authority in the Shástras for re-marriages. But I have no objection personally thereto. In my sect re-marriages take place; I don't prohibit them. Lakhmidás was present when Dr. Bháu visited me; he was sitting by and heard what I said. I had no further conversation with him on the subject of the disease. I did not confess to him anything prejudicial to my chastity or morality. I did not speak to him about the practices of other Mahárájás. I have seen no instance of improprieties on the part of any Maháráj. I did not tell Lakhmidás that I did not commit such enormities as I did before. I did not tell him that any improvement in the practices of the Mahárájás must be gradual, and cannot be made at once; nor that our income is chiefly derived from females. I told him I intended to go to Shriji Dwár, but not that I had fears of my life there. I have caused a plan of my premises to be prepared.

(Cross-examined by Mr. Anstey.) I am a man, and not a God. I am a man and a guru to my followers. I am not an incarnation of the Deity, and I am not aware that hitherto any of my followers has ever regarded me as a God or an incarnation of God. Our Ácháryaji is regarded as an incarnation of God, and we are regarded as his descendants and gurus. I do not remember whether Karsandás Nepsi once addressed me as "Ishwar," God. I and other Mahárájás are not addressed as Mahá Prabhu, or Purushottam or Deva; we are called the children of Mahá Prabhu. Vallabhá-chárya and his son Gosáiji are regarded as incarnations of God, but not so the sons of Gosáiji. The Mahárájás are styled Vallabh Deva. The words Agni-svarup (form of fire) is not applied to us. The title of Purna Purushottam (Perfect God) is applied to the Mahárá-jás. I held no meeting at 10 o'clock on Tuesday night to consider what answers I should make. Parbhudás did not tell me I should say, I don't recollect. The words referred to above are applied as titles to the Mahárájás in books inaccessible to such followers as understand Sanskrit. I have taught my devotees that they should regard us as gurus, not as gods. This book contains the names and pictures of Vallabháchárya and two of his immediate descendants. Vaishnavas worship these pictures. No Maháráj of the name of Dáudji is worshipped; he was the proprietor of one of the principal "gadis" (seats). In the garden in which I put up there is a seat to which the people resort for "darshan." I don't know if it is the seat of Dáudji. The name of Krishna occurs in a portion of the Veds. There is sin in telling lies, even for a good purpose. Untruth may be told to women in sport, on occasion of marriages, when life is in danger, when a cow is to be killed, etc.; any one who tells lies on such occasions is not to be despised, but he commits a sin nevertheless. Since the rising of the Court I had no consultation with Varjivandás and others. I believe everything mentioned in the Bhágavata. The Shástras of the Vaishnavas are in accordance with the Veds. I have not published any pamphlet: periodicals were published by the Vaishnava Dharma Sabhá, which were written by Govardhandás. I was the originator of the society. Hariráyaji was a Maháráj; I cannot say if he wrote any books in the Brij Bháshá. I cannot say whether a few Mahárájás only can read Sanskrit. The wives and daughters of the Mahárájás read books in the Brij Bháshá. I am unable to say whether this book (the Vachan-amrat in Brij Bháshá) is considered a religious book. I have not read up to this time any work in the Brij Bháshá relating to the Vallabháchárya religion, with the exception of songs in praise of the Creator. I mean to say that I have never in my life read a theological or philosophical work in the Brij Bháshá on the Vallabháchárya religion. I now remember I have read in Brij Bháshá one of Gokalnáthji's commentaries. I do not read books of my sect in the Maráthi language. I know Govardhandás wrote an essay in the "Propagator of our own Religion" on adulterine love, in the opinions expressed in which I agree in the main. I did not tell him to write that essay. It was written in reply to an article in a Maráthi magazine, but I cannot say if it was in reply to the libel in the *Satya Prakásh*. I cannot say whether it is the belief of my sect or not that the *gopis* loved God as their paramour, and that God loved them and made them happy. Whatever is stated in the Shástras is acceptable to me. Besides the sacred books of my sect, there are other Shástras, viz., the Bhágavat, the Puránas, etc. The young maidens of my sect swing Krishna in a swing. God Krishna is their father, husband, lord. They swing me and the other Mahárájas as gurus. We are swung by our fathers, mothers, sisters, and all devotees: but I do not recollect whether we are addressed as the amorous Káhan (Cupid). These amorous songs are addressed to the Mahárájás. Since the last two or three days, I have been subjected to surgical examination by two or three medical gentlemen. My face was not covered when one of them saw me. I don't know if one of them refuses to give evidence that there is no trace in me of the venereal affection. They examined me from a short distance. I don't know their names, and I have not been told that only two of them are coming to give evidence. Varjivandás Mádhavadás, J. P., and Kaliándás Mohandás, his nephew, who conducts this case, might have brought the doctors; I don't know. The examination took place in the shop of Rághu Shámji, one of the conspirators. Since my cross-examination yesterday, I have not been again inspected by a doctor. I did not ask Dr. Dhirajrám to send me calomel from time to time whenever I wanted it. Once I put calomel into *chunám* water and made a blackwash of it, and applied it. Dr. Dhirajrám told me to take a pill twice in the day, and I took five or six pills. I have purchased now a glass scale for use in taking photographs; I had none for measuring medicines. When my throat became sore, a preparation of borax was given me as a gargle. I had sent for some iodide of-potash and sarsaparilla. I tried the former; the latter I administered medically to another person. I have heard the name of the Brahma-vaivarta Purán; I have not read it; it is believed in by the Vaishnavas. (Witness is shown a passage in the book.) It runs thus : "Upon having seen the Rás, the mistresses of the God were tormented with the arrows of love; upon having performed the "rati-ras" Krishna, the perfect and perpetual, along with Rádhá, went to the waters of the Yamuna; with the 'gopis' went the magical forms of the exalted Krishna, which, tormented with the arrows of love, and pervaded with joy, performed sport with the gopis in the water." The translation is correct, but I am not quite certain of the meaning. I must collate the passage with other books. (Witness is shown another passage.)

It appears to be addressed to Rádhá, Krishna's principal Mistress, as follows: "Why dost thou weep, O Rádhá; remember the lotus feet of Krishna during the Ras Mandali night will fall: thou wilt perform with Krishna the desired uninterrupted *rati*." I know the Vishnu Purána; I may have seen a passage in it here and there. I don't remember having read the following passage (Vishnu Purána, p. 535):—"Whilst frolicking thus with the gopis, they considered every instant, without him, a myriad of years; and prohibited in vain by husbands, fathers, brothers, they went forth at night to perform sport with Krishna, the object of their affection. The Vaishnavas read the Vishnu and other Puráns, not because they contain the descriptions of the sports of Krishna with the gopis, but because they contain Vaishnava doctrines. We worship the image of Krishna with the faith that we are actually worshipping Krishna. He is brought into the images partly by ceremonies, partly by faith. The images of Krishna are represented as if he were in the infantile state. I have never seen him in the young or old state. (Witness is handed a picture of Krishna at the top of a tree with the naked gopis at the foot of it.) He is here represented between the ages of 5 and 11 years. When the Maháráj dies, persons say he is gone to his abode, or to the world of gods. Krishna, when he died, went to the Gowlok; religious and pious Vaishnavas go there also. He (Krishna) remains all day in joy; the Vaishnavas are present there in his service. I have not observed in any book if it is the doctrine of my sect, that true Vaishnavas, after death, become gopis and have amorous and improper intercourse with God. I do not believe in this doctrine, nor am I aware if any of my followers does or do believe in it. By *lilá* I understand sport, play. I believe it is impossible that Krishna should renew, in paradise, his amorous dalliance with the gopis; he may engage in Rás Lilá with them. The gopis are there in human form, but are not subject to early decay. I am forbidden to repeat here the "mantra" pronounced at the kanthi ceremony. The translation you give of it is correct. The dedication referred to in this "mantra" is caused to be made at the feet of Krishna not to the Maháráj. The guru at the ceremony is only the guide to Krishna. I asked Lakhmidás if an action might go on in the absence of one of the parties. When

I first arrived from Surat, I had no intention of bringing an action against those who published anything against the Mahárájás. The reason for the delay of six months in bringing the present action was that I am not acquainted with such matters in this island, and found it necessary to consult and take advice. (Witness is shown a passage of an article published in the *Satya Prakásh* of the 9th September, against all the Mahárájás.) ·When all the Mahárájás are libelled, how could I alone bring an action? I do not remember if I consulted Mr. Leathes about this article. I do not remember if I read it. I heard that all the Mahárájás were libelled., I cannot say if it was in consequence of this article or not that a hand-bill was published with my name to it; what is stated in the handbill as to the lessening authority of the Mahárájás accords with my view. The word "Asatya Prakásh" in one of the numbers of the "Propagator of our own Religion" refers to the defendant's paper; I think it is an error of the printer, or the letter "a" (not) may have fallen in by mistake near the word "Satya." I don't know if this article in the magazine was written in answer to the libel; I cannot say without reading over the whole of it.

Sir M. Sausse.—Now tell this witness the manner in which he has been giving his evidence latterly, is such as to impress the Court with an unfavourable view regarding it. He must be able to answer without reading over everything about which he is questioned.

Witness.—I cannot answer without reading it over.

Sir M. Sausse.—The man has too much intelligence and collected manner not to recollect or to know what he says he cannot answer.

Witness continued.—Then the article may be in answer to the libel. I have read part of the book called the "Debauched Guru." It refers to Ras Mandali. · I have read the article containing the libel; it reflects upon me. The article says, "You Mahárájás, acting up to that commentary, defile the wives and daughters," etc. This is libellous, though not directed against me individually. Being charged with the immoralities of the Ras Mandali, I do not consider it libellous, because I do not understand what Ras Mandali means. The book of Hariráyaji is in Sanskrit. I have never seen it in Brij Bháshá. I have heard of a work in Maráthi

by Janárdhan Rámchandraji entitled "Biographies of Eminent Men."
The story of the 252 and of the 84 is not considered a book of
authority in our sect. This book of songs was not published by me
nor do I know if it was published by Govardhandás. I don't know
if it is a libel on the defendant. The representation of a Maháráj
drawing a triumphant chariot over the prostrate bodies of the
reformers does not refer to me ; the printer must know who the
Maháráj is.

Maháráj.—No one should touch me.

Sir M. Sausse.—I saw one attempt to touch you.

Maháráj.—I am afraid some of the persons going from behind
might touch me.

Mr. Anstey.—Why should you not be touched? I am not going
to touch you. You are not a God. As for me I won't touch you
with a pair of tongs. Mr. Hastings touched you the first day.

Witness proceeded. The chief temple of our sect is that of Shrináthji at Kánkroli. An image thence was not stolen by my father
or grandfather, who sat on the *gádi* at Surat. I have never gone on
a pilgrimage to that temple, although I was seven years abroad.
The Maháráj receives presents and contributions from the Vaishnavas. Fines are also levied, the money received by way of fine
being eventually applied to the use of the Thákurji. I am not a
Brahmachári ; I was one before my marriage. I am not a Sanyási.
I believe in Purna Purushottam. Purna Purushottam (Perfect God)
is applied as a title to the Mahárájás, as " My Lord" is applied to
the judges. I don't know if the gurus of other sects are swung in
a swing like the Mahárájás. I have never seen the water from
a Maháráj's *langoti* rinsed and drunk by the Vaishnavas. The
*juthan* (remnants of food) left by the Mahárájás is eaten like that
of all other gurus. It is the custom in all sects of Hindus. It is
written that the Bráhmins should partake of the leavings of the
gurus' food. I don't know if there is a prohibition in Manu. We
give for the purpose of being thrown away the leavings of our
pán-sopári. They may be eaten by some persons. The Maháráj
applies his foot to the eyes of a dying person to relieve him from
sin ; no fee is paid for this. I don't know if the gurus of any
other sect do this. Males, females, and children apply and wash

with saffron water and scented oils the bodies of the Mahárájás. I don't allow my followers to eat the dust of my feet: I don't know if other Mahárájás allow it. Lights are waved round the Mahárájás' heads. All this is enjoined in the Shástras; I don't know what Shástra. The wooden shoes of my ancestors are worshipped, as also of other Mahárájás. My shoes are not worshipped. I do not go into private rooms to receive presents of fruit and sweetmeats from female devotees. I don't know if others do it. Vaishnavas bring them and present them to the Thákurji and we then receive them. I don't know if other Mahárájás go into private rooms for this purpose. Female devotees do not sing songs of a licentious character in the presence of the Mahárájás; songs of various kinds are sung. Gulál is thrown by the Mahárájás on the persons of all devotees, not expressly on the persons of females. The guru is to be worshipped in the same way as the image of Thákurji, which represents God. I have not read in the "Guru Sevá" that all the Vallabháchárya Gosáijis are to be considered as incarnations of God. Ever since I arrived at a proper age I have told my followers not to believe in this doctrine. Before my admonition, the doctrine was believed in by some persons in Bombay, not the majority. I cannot remember the names of any one person whom I instructed not to believe in the doctrine. Did I say yesterday that I did not know whether any one regarded the Mahárájás to be incarnations of God? Perhaps I did. I do not know if I swore to that effect.

Sir M. Sausse: Tell him the Court has taken down clearly what he said.

Witness: I don't recollect it.

Sir M. Sausse: Oh! his memory is very short; but the Court has taken down exactly what he said.

Witness proceeded: The Vaishnavas believe their obligations to their gurus to be greater than their obligation to God. The Vaishnavas are not allowed to touch the image; and they can make offerings through the Mahárájás or the Bráhmins who bathe or wash their bodies inside the temple. I believe that by Bráhma-sambandha the sins of the eleven organs (including those of ——) are washed away. I don't know if it is the doctrine of my sect that Vaishnavas should not divulge the secrets of the guru. It is good

5

among other things not to see the faults of others. I am a Bráhmin; you may think I have not the physical appearance of one. My ancestors were Telingá Bráhmins; they were not excommunicated. We take their daughters in marriage, but don't give any. With reference to Telingá Bráhmins in this country, we intermarry with them. I don't know if they are very poor; they are called Bhatji. They are not excommunicated for giving their daughters to the Mahárájás. Sometimes we find it necessary to give sums of money when the parents of the bride are poor. Manu prohibits the selling of daughters; I don't know of any prohibition against selling marriages. I believe the Mahárájás to be innocent of adultery; if they are guilty thereof, they don't deserve the rank of guru. Krashnaráyaji, my cousin, has married the daughter of a Telingá Bráhmin. I don't know of any scandals about him and a widow devotee. I don't know if his son Gokuluchhavaji was expelled by a Rájá from his territory. Vallabhji Maháráj was expelled by the other Mahárájás for interfering in a dispute between a father and his son. I don't know of any scandals connected with him. I was the first Maháráj to go to Daman; I went there through ignorance. There is a prohibition made by Mahárájás against going there. I don't know if the prohibition was, that a Maháráj was killed under the lash for larceny by order of the Portuguese government. Vithaleshji Maháráj was under surveillance at Patná; he was accused of sorcery. I don't know if he was accused of poisoning the Rájá. I don't know of Vrajpálji Maháráj looting the houses of his devotees at Lakhpat Bandar. I left Surat on a pilgrimage for seven years. There was no charge of rape ever made against me. I hear it this moment. I don't remember if I was asked about it the day before yesterday. I have heard of the daughter of Pitámbar Popá. There was no charge against me of having defiled her. I was not taken before the Surat magistrate on that charge twelve or fourteen years ago. I have no knowledge of such a charge having been compromised for me by the then Sheristadár of Surat. I have not summoned any brother Mahárájás to give evidence on my behalf. None of the Mahárájás intimated to me that he cannot deny the adulteries of the Mahárájás in this Court, because the fact is too notorious. The son of one Maháráj is at present in Bombay. Except myself, all other Mahárájás have left Bombay. I don't know of a disturbance near Jivanji's temple three months after my arrival in Bombay. I don't know Lakhmibái, the daughter of Thávar Mulji. I did not know her fifteen years ago. Up to the time of the discussion on the subject of re-marriage, I was on good terms with the defendant, who praised me in his newspaper. I did not prohibit the Vaishnavas from subscribing to defendant's paper. I don't know of having published any handbills against the *Satya Prakásh* being subscribed to. I have heard of the Bháttiá conspiracy case. I have not arranged with the other Mahárájás to shut the temples against those Vaishnavas who might give evidence against me in this case. I don't remember if Parbhudás told me that he managed the Bháttiá case. I either heard or read somewhere that Parbhudás took some message to one Gopáldás, and that the latter gave evidence of the visit and message. I heard also a rumour to that effect. I first spoke to Parbhudás on the subject during the trial of the Bháttiá conspiracy case. Parbhudás came to me to Surat to call me here. I spoke to him then. He told me of the "bandobast" which was made here. I said, "What is the necessity or object of making this 'bandobast?'" He said they must know. I did not authorise him to conduct or assist in the management of the case. There were no consultations between the nine conspirators at my house. One or two of them came to my house. The "bandobast" was in reference to the offering of virgin daughters, but I don't know for what case it was. I heard of the Baniá "bandobast" from a number of persons who came to me and said what they had heard in this court. I never reproved Parbhudás for his part in the making of the "bandobast;" he did neither right nor wrong. I believe what Lakhmidás has stated against me must be false; because if he saw me commit any immoral act, he would not have continued visiting me. I have never been guilty of adultery or immoralities. I took the heating medicines at Hyderabád, where I was sick. I took dry ginger, black pepper, chillies, etc., and these produced internal heat. With the exception of six or seven months, my wife was with me on my pilgrimage. About four or five years before 1909, I travelled without the society of my wife, who had then died. (To Sir Joseph Arnould.) Neither of

my wives was with me at Beyt. (To Sir M. Sausse.) I once travelled five years, in the course of which I went to Jaypor to call
my wife. I was away from Surat for two years, in the course of
which I proceeded to Beyt. I have married two wives. I married
before I set out for Beyt, and was away for two years from my second
wife, who was then of the age of nine or nine and a half years.
She came to live with me at the age of thirteen.

(Re-examined.) There was no meeting held at my house on
Tuesday evening for the purpose of a consultation. It is a common
form of salutation among Hindus to apply to each other, at a
meeting, the names of Rám and Purushottam, although they may
not be the real names of the persons addressed. There are two
seats of Dáudji, who established them and also worshipped them in
common with others. All the sacred books of my sect are in
Sanskrit; they are regarded as authorities even in Brij Bháshá, if
they correspond with the Sanskrit originals. All the Mahárájás are
*ex-officio* Presidents of the Vaishnava Dharm-prasárak Society, or the
Society for the Propagation of the Vaishnava religion. Since my
arrival from Surat, I have made exertions to propagate the Vaishnava
religion. I was asked in reference to the specific offence of several
Mahárájás. I heard them for the first time in court yesterday. I
have heard of those offences through several prints also; not of my
relatives in particular, but of the Mahárájás generally. I heard of
the charges for the first time yesterday brought against the Mahárájás generally. I heard of the charges for the first time yesterday
brought against the Mahárájás by name. The " Debauched Guru "
is not a book of authority in my sect; it is a lampoon. It is
believed in by persons who are our enemies. The Mahárájás have
authority to outcaste any one from the sect, with the approval of the
members of the sect. Without such approval, no one can be
excommunicated. The Maháráj has power to prevent a person from
coming to the temple over which he has jurisdiction. All the.
Mahárájás can combine to prevent a person from coming to any of
the temples. Such a combination, however, has not taken place
within my knowledge-

To Sir M. Sausse.—I have said that adultery is a great sin
according to the Shástras of my sect. The recommendation in the

essay, already referred to, which I approved of, is not to commit adultery, but to love God with love akin to what is called adulterine love.   Adulterine passion is intense love, and the same intensity of love should be shown towards God.   Such love towards God is very good; towards a strange woman, it is bad.   Such an illustration is given in the Bhágavat.   (Sir M. Sausse.)   Tell him that we are under the impression that, when asked before, he could not name any Shástra which contained such an illustration.   (Witness.)   I do not remember.   I believe it is stated in the Bhágavat that love should be entertained towards God akin to the love of the gopis. (To Sir Joseph Arnould.)   I said that God is to be gained by worshipping him in any form or manner.

Maháráj (on retiring).—"I bless your lordships!"

# JUDGMENT

-----

*(Judgment of Sir Matthew Sausse.)*

This is an action on the case for the publication of a false and malicious libel in the form of an editorial article that appeared on the 21st October, 1860, in a Gujaráti newspaper published in Bombay called the *Satya Prakásh* or the "Light of Truth."

The publication is as follows :—

"In the Puráns and other Shástras of the Hindus it is stated that in the Kali-yug there will arise false religions and heresies, and impostors and heretics will cause adverse persuasions and adverse religious systems to be established. According to the Hindu Shástras five thousand years have now passed away since the commencement of the Kali-yug. From the Hindu Shástras themselves it is demonstrated that during this period of five thousand years as many new persuasions and religious systems as have arisen among the Hindus, should all be considered spurious heresies. Now, four hundred years have not as yet elapsed since the birth of Vallabh, the progenitor of the Mahárájás. In the books of the Vaishnava persuasion it is written that the birth of Vallabháchárya took place on 11th Vaisákh Vad of Samvant, 1535, the day of the week Sunday; since this event 381 years have elapsed to this day, and since the beginning of the Kali-yug five thousand years have passed. The sect of Vallabháchárya then originated with the Kali-yug itself. In the same way as the followers of Dádu, the followers of Súdhu, the Rámsnehi, the Rámánandi, the Shejánadi and other sects arose; so the sect of Vallabháchárya arose; all these sects have arisen in the Kali-yug, therefore according to the declarations of the Hindu Shástras they must be heterodox.

"Jadunáthji Maháráj says that in the same way as some one goes from the gates of the fort to proceed to Wálkeshwar and some one to Byculla, so exactly the original courses of the Veds and the Puráns have gone forward, have diverged into different ways. What a deceitful proposition this is. Out of one religious system ten or fifteen by-ways must not branch off. The course of religion and of morals must be one only. What necessity is there to quit the straight road by which to go to Wálkeshwar, and take the circuitous road to Byculla? Each sectary has made every other sectary a heretic, and one has scattered dust upon the other; what then is the necessity for acting thus? But we have already made known that as regards the weapons with which the Maháráj has come forth to defend himself, those very weapons will oppose the Mahàràj, and annoy him. The Mahàràj considers the Hindu Shàstras as the work of God; he cannot then assert that any particular statement of the Hindu Shàstras is false. The said Mahàràj cannot allege that the statement that in the Kali-yug heretical opinions will arise is false. Then like several other sects, the sect of the Mahàràjàs has arisen in the Kali-yug, consequently it is established by the Hindu Shàstras that it is a false and heretical one.

"The sect of the Mahàràjàs is heretical and one delusive to simple people; that is proved by the genuine books of the Veds, the Puràns, etc., according to what is intimated above. Not only this, but also from the works composed by the Mahàràjàs, it is proved that the Mahàràjàs have raised up nothing but a new heresy and disorder. Behold with regard to the subject of Brahma how Gokulnáthji has amplified the original stanza, what a commentary he has made :—

तस्मादादौ खोप भोगात्पूर्वमेव सर्ववस्तुपदेन भार्यापुत्रादीनामपि स-
मर्पणं कर्तव्यं विवाहानंतरं खोपभोगे सर्वकार्ये सर्वकार्यनिमित्तं तत्का-
र्योपभोगिवस्तु समर्पणं कार्यं समर्पणं द्वात्ता पश्चात्तानि तानि कार्याणि
कर्तव्यानीत्यर्थः ॥ १ ॥

"'Consequently before he himself has enjoyed her, he should make over his own married wife (to the Mahàràj) and he should also make over (to him) his sons and daughters. After having got married, he should before having himself enjoyed his wife make an offering of her (to the Mahàràj); after which he should apply her to his own use.'

"Alas! what a heresy this is, what a sham this is, and what a delusion this is! We ask Jadunàthji Mahàràj in what Ved, in what Puràn, in what Shàstra, and in what law book it is written that one's married wife should be made over to a Mahàràj, or to a religious preceptor before being enjoyed. Not only one's wife, but one's daughter also is to be made over! Alas! in writing this, our pen will not move on. We are seized with utter disgust and agitation. To render blind people who see with their eyes and to throw dust in their eyes, and in the name of religion and under the pretence of religion to enjoy their tender maidens, wives and daughters, than this what greater heresy and what greater deceit? In the Kali-yug many other heresies and many sects have arisen besides that of Vallabháchárya, but no other sectaries have ever perpetrated such shamelessness, subtilty, immodesty, rascality, and deceit as have the sect of the Mahàràjàs. When we use such severe terms as these, our simple Hindu friends are wrath with us, and in consequence of that wrath of theirs, we have had and have much to endure. But when, throwing dust in the eyes of simple people, the Mahàràjàs write in their books about enjoying the tender maidens,—the peoples' wives and daughters,—and they enjoy them accordingly, great flames spring up within our inside, our pen at once becomes heated on fire, and we have to grieve over our Hindu friends and over their weak powers of reflection.

"Jadunàthji Mahàràj has commenced issuing a small work styled "The Propagator of our own Religion;" we ask him, In what way do you wish to effect the propagation of religion? Your ancestors having scattered dust in the eyes of simple people, made them blind. Do you wish to make them see, or, taking a false pride in the upholding of your religion, do you wish to delude simple people still more ? Jadunáthji Maháráj, should you wish to propagate or to spread abroad religion, then do you personally adopt a virtuous course of conduct and admonish your other Mahárájás. As long as the preceptors of religion shall themselves appear to be immersed in the sea of licentiousness, for so long they shall not be competent to convey religious exhortation. Gokulnáthji having composed the commentary abovementioned, has attached to your Vaishnava persuasion a great blot of ink. Let that be first removed. Scorn the writer of the commentary. [Oh, you] Mahárájás, acting up to that commentary, defile the wives and daughters of your devotees. Desist from that and destroy at once immorality such as that of the company at *Ras festival.* As long as you shall not do so, for so long you cannot give religious admonition, and propagate your own religious faith ; do you be pleased to be assured of that."

This publication may be divided under four heads :

1stly. So far as it characterizes the sect of Vallabháchárya, as heretical in respect of the ancient Hindu religion.

2ndly. As it attributes to the Mahárájás as the spiritual heads of the sect, the inculcation of heretical and immoral doctrines.

3rdly. As it charges the Mahárájás as a body with immoral practices under the pretence of religion.

4thly. So far as it charges the plaintiff individually with the practice of immorality with the females of his sect.

The plaintiff complains that these several charges are false and malicious, and that they have been published of, and injuriously affect, him,—in his individual character as a member of society at large, in his religious character and conduct as a Bráhmin, as a Maháráj, as a Hindu high priest and as a member of the sect of Vallabháchárya.

He claims damages for the injury done to him in these several characters which he claims to fill.

The defendants have pleaded several pleas.

*Firstly.* Not guilty.

*Secondly.* That the Mahárájás are not preceptors of the Hindu religion.

*Thirdly.* That they are not the heads or chiefs of the Bráhmins.

*Fourthly.* That the plaintiff was not a Hindu priest of high caste or a preceptor of the Hindu religion.

*Fifthly.* That the sect of Vallabháchárya is not an ancient sect, and that it holds doctrines repugnant to the doctrines of the ancient Hindu religion.

*Sixthly.* That the translation of the latter portion of the libel as rendered in the plaint, was not correct.

*Seventhly.* That the charges made by the defendants in the publication were all true.

*Eighthly.* The same plea in a general form.

The plaintiff joined issue on the first six pleas, and replied " De injuria," to the seventh and eighth.

The seventh plea was of very great length; it set out various points of doctrine, from books alleged to be of religious authority in the sect of Vallabháchárya and relied upon those passages as justifying the publication in charging heresy and immorality of doctrine against the Mahárájás and the sect. It also put in issue various facts and circumstances as proof of the evil reputation of the Mahárájás as a body for immorality, and it finally charged specific acts of personal immorality to have been committed by the plaintiff.

The Court have been thus compelled to receive evidence at great length upon controverted points of doctrine amongst the members of that sect, and to receive it in great part through the unsatisfactory medium of translations of isolated passages from works in Sanskrit or Brij-Bháshá, which are practically dead languages and not provided for in the translators' department.

For the plaintiff there were examined thirty-one witnesses and for the defendants thirty-one. The case was contested with all the obstinacy and acrimony which generally characterize caste and religious disputes, when they unfortunately force themselves into a court of law. The trial was thus prolonged to a most unusual length.

Publication by the defendants has been admitted. Upon the evidence, I entertain no doubt that the alleged libel has been correctly translated into English as it appears upon the plaint and think as so translated that the latter portion contains matter highly defamatory of the plaintiff. It substantially singles him out by name and thus directly charges him with leading a licentious and immoral life, and with defiling the wives and daughters of his devotees. It then calls upon the plaintiff to desist from those practices and ends by assuring him that unless he does so, he cannot give religious admonition or propagate his own religion. The applicability of that portion of the publication to the plaintiff has been controverted to some extent.

A very intelligent witness, Dr. Bháu Dáji, stated after some consideration that he understood the latter part as a " general expostulation" with the Mahárájás as a class and "that any intelligent reader would so understand it," and afterwards that "he did not think it alluded to the plaintiff." However he qualified that evidence in the end by stating to the Court " that he could not say that the plaintiff was excluded," that with his knowledge of the plaintiff's antecedents "he did include him amongst those who were charged with defiling the wives and daughters of his devotees," and his last answer was "that as a reader not knowing the plaintiff's antecedents he would consider it *doubtful* whether he was included or not." Now, if a writer expresses himself either through design or negligence in such a manner as to render it doubtful in the minds of one class of readers whether the defamatory matter applies to a person named; but leave no doubt whatever on the minds of others, that it does so apply, the writer must abide by the consequences, and if otherwise liable he must answer in damages for the injury he has done to the person so defamed. Libels are to be construed according to the plain and ordinary sense of the language in which they are written, and the suggestion of a possible construction by which the party complaining might not be included is not to relieve the libeller from responsibility.

The defence made at the bar, that the libellous matter was not intended to apply to the plaintiff individually is scarcely consistent with the reply which the defendants made to the complaint by the plaintiff in April, 1861 : when the latter called for a contradiction of and apology for the statements " so far as they relate to the alleged improper conduct ascribed to himself," the reply of the defendants was through the columns of their newspaper that they saw nothing to require " explanation, alteration, or apology."

Then holding the publication to be libellous and consequently malicious, I have next to consider the defence relied upon under the plea of not guilty, viz., That the defamatory matter was published under circumstances which formed a justifying occasion.

A " justifying occasion" has been defined in very clear terms by Baron Parke in *Toogood* v. *Spyring*, 1 Compton, Meeson, and Roscoe. He states it to be " the publication of defamatory matter, honestly made by a person in the discharge of some public or private *duty*, whether legal or moral, or in the conduct of his own affairs in matters where his interest is concerned." In such cases the occasion prevents the inference of "malice" and he goes on to say " that if *fairly* warranted by any reasonable occasion, or exigency, and honestly made, such communications are protected for common convenience and welfare of society, and the law has not restricted the right to make them within any narrow limits."

The effect of the existence of a "justifying occasion" is to negative malice both in fact as well as in law, either of which is necessary to maintain an action of libel. The difference between malice in fact and malice in law is laid down in *Bromage* v. *Prosser*, where the former is defined to be " *ill will* against a person," and malice in law " a wrongful act done, intentionally, without legal justification or excuse." And in *Duncan* v. *Thwaites*, 3 Barnwell and Cresswell, Chief Justice Abbot further defines the meaning of the word "malice," when he says the use of the word " malicious" in declaration of libel is " rather to exclude a supposition that the publication had been made in some innocent occasion, than for any other purpose."

In cases of this kind, when tried before a jury, it is their province to find whether the communication was made *bonâ fide* or not, and if in the affirmative, it becomes the duty of the judge, as a matter of law, to decide whether the occasion of the publication was such as to rebut the inference of malice, or, in accordance with the definition in *Bromage* v. *Prosser*, whether there was any " *legal* justification or excuse" for the " wrongful act."

I have thus to investigate and decide, first, whether the publication was made *bonâ fide* by the defendants, and next, if it were, whether then a legal justification or excuse is to be found in the surrounding circumstances proved in this case for the libel upon private character which the publication contains. In the present case I see no reason to doubt that the defendant entered into this controversy with the honest purpose of exposing to public reprobation doctrines which he conscientiously believed to be subversive of social morality, and so far as he has commented on these doctrines, I see no ground for complaint. I consider his strictures not to have in any degree exceeded the "licentious comment," as it has been termed, which is allowable upon matters more immediately affecting public interests, and I have no doubt that matters affecting the morality of a considerable portion of the public are undoubtedly matters of that description. But the question remains, whether under all the circumstances the defendants were justified in leaving the region of commentary altogether, and in making a direct charge upon the plaintiff's private character, by accusing him of having been engaged in the practice of defiling the wives and daughters of his devotees under the-pretence of religion. I thought the law on this subject was very clear, but in deference to some difficulty which my brother Arnould feels, I shall examine it at greater length than I would otherwise have considered necessary.

Now, so far as the plaintiff is concerned, the case stands thus: The plaintiff was practically a stranger to Bombay prior to July, 1860, when he arrived. At first he united in some reformatory views of the defendants and others with reference to female education and re-marriage of widows, but was supposed to have in part seceded from them after. He set on foot a pamphlet or periodical called "The Propagator of our own Religion," and invited extraneous or it may be hostile criticism and discussion upon the views it placed before the public. On the 21st October, 1860, the libel appears, and the plaintiff is charged in it with conduct which, if true, ought to deprive him of the respect of, and indeed communion with, the members of any civilized community.

The defendant, Karsandás Mulji, was not personally acquainted with the plaintiff, nor was he, according to his own admission, personally acquainted with any act of immorality committed by the plaintiff or any other Maháráj, but prior to the libel, one Lálshankar, an intimate friend of his, volunteered the information that the plaintiff bore a bad character for morality in Bombay, in Surat, and in other places in the Mofussil, where Lálshankar had been. Lálshankar was a native of, and an annual visitor to, Surat, where the plaintiff had a temple. So far as the plaintiff was individually concerned, that was all the information respecting his alleged immoral practices that the defendants possessed at the time of the libel. It does not appear that the defendants took any pains to make inquiries into the truth of these general charges, but rested satisfied with the statements of Lálshankar. The defendant Karsandás states that it was after the commencement of the action he began to make inquiries into the plaintiff's private life. In addition, the defendant, who was originally a member of the Vallabhácharya sect, appears to have entertained for ten or twelve years the belief that the Mahárájás as a body were guilty of adulterous practices amongst their female devotees. That belief appears to have been founded upon general rumours in the sect, and upon a resolution passed by the Bháttiá caste in 1855, to put a stop to such alleged practices, by preventing their females from going to the temple of the Mahárájás; and also upon reiterated charges of immoral and licentious conduct made against the Mahárájás, as a body, by newspapers, pamphlets, and periodicals, from 1855 until some months prior to the publication of the libel. The defendant's conviction appears to have been also influenced by the discovery in 1860 of a commentary by Gokulnáthji, which appeared to the defendant to give doctrinal sanction to the immoral practices which he had previously believed to be existing among the body of the Mahárájás. It appears, however, from Dr. Bháu Dáji's evidence, that he has personally known some few Mahárájás, whom he described as men of unspotted character and of piety, and good men. Apply then the test of Baron Parke in *Toogood* v. *Spyring* to these circumstances,— Were the defendants, in making this defamatory charge on the private character of plaintiff through the columns of a newspaper, discharging any legal or moral public duty, or any *legal* or *moral private duty;* or was the publication made in conduct of his own affairs in matters where his interest was concerned? There was clearly no *legal* duty, either public or private, cast upon the defendants to do so. Nor was there any moral duty, public or private, cast upon them to make that communication to the public beyond what might press upon any other individual who had heard a bad character of the plaintiff for morality and believed that report to be true. It would be a novel and a dangerous doctrine to lay down, that every editor of a newspaper, or any one who had the command of its columns, should be justified, even without inquiry, in making specific charges of a most defamatory character against the private life of individuals, simply because he had heard them and honestly believed them to be true, and that from their character it would be conducive to public morality to publish them. Were such a doctrine to prevail, it should be maintained independently of the actual truth of the charges; and property in private character, which the law protects so jealously, might be ruthlessly swept away without redress. In my opinion there is but one plea which can serve as a defence to a libel published as the present has been, viz.: that the charges contained in the libel are true. This principle is supported* by the view taken by Chamber J. in *Rogers* v. *Clifton*, 3 Bosanquet and Puller, 587, and is cited with approbation by Mr. Justice Cresswell in *Coxhead* v. *Richards*, 2 C. B., and I think it is further sustained by the decision and dicta of the judges in *Paris* v. *Levi*, 9 Weekly Reporter, which was cited to show that the doctrine of "justifiable occasion" has been extended to publications in newspapers as well as to those which come under the ordinary term of "confidential or privileged communications." But that case upon examination will be found to range itself under the class of cases which from *Tabbart* v. *Tipper*, 1 Campbell, down to the present time, have upheld the right of public comment and criticism, upon documents submitted to the public consideration. The plaintiff in *Paris* v. *Levi* published an advertisement calling the attention of servants to the fact that he was offering unprecedentedly high prices for articles that servants were in the habit of selling out of their masters' establishment; this advertisement was commented upon by a heading of "*Inducement to servants to rob their masters.*" There was no charge against the plaintiff of robbing any one, but simply that the tendency of his advertisement to the public was to lead dishonest servants to pilfer for the purpose of taking advantage of these unusually high prices. If made *bonâ fide*, the comment does not appear to exceed what might reasonably be allowed, and it was so held at the trial. It afterwards came before the full Court, principally on the ground of misdirection. With the direction of Chief Justice Erle, as reported in that case, I fully concur. Treating the case as one of comment, he said that the plaintiff was not entitled to recover unless he established that the defendant was actuated by malice; that the law, however, did not require that the plaintiff should show personal malice or ill will in the sense of private hatred; but that the defamatory publication was published without any of those causes which the law considers will justify them. "Such causes excuse the publication, because they shew the party was not actuated by any corrupt or malicious motives in saying that which tends to defame the character of another." But in criticism on matters which have been published by the complaining party, Lord Ellenborough laid down in a case where a journal had criticised books which had been published dangerous to morality, "that liberty of criticism must be allowed, or we should neither have purity of taste or of morality; that publication I shall never consider as a libel, which has for its object, not to injure the reputation of any one, but to correct misrepresentation of fact, or to censure what is hostile to morality." That if the jury found their verdict for the defendant, it must be on the principle so laid down. That had the defendant said one word against the plaintiff with reference to the plaintiff's private character, he would have felt himself bound to say "there was no excuse of the publication."

So Byles J. says: "The real question was, Does the comment go beyond what is sanctioned by law? was there a reflection on the plaintiff's private character?" And Keating J. states, "Now it is conceded that a newspaper is justified, nay it is rather incumbent on them to *comment freely* on any *publication*. I see no distinction between this handbill and any other publication for comment. Yet *that is not to degenerate into imputations of a personal character.* What was said at the trial was 'That though a fair comment could be privileged, yet if of a personal character it would not.' The direction was perfectly right." In *Carr* v. *Hood*, 1 Campbell, Lord Ellenborough said: "*Shew me an attack on the moral character of the plaintiff, or any attack upon his character unconnected with his authorship, and I shall be as ready as any judge that ever sat here to protect him;* but I cannot hear of malice on account of turning writers into ridicule." Thus from *Tabbart* v. *Tipper* and *Carr* v. *Hood*, from 1808 down to 1860 when *Paris* v. *Levi* was decided, defamation of private character in public journals, has been treated as ordinarily beyond the pale of "justifying occasion;" and I see nothing in the present case to take it out of that principle. The selection of a public news-

paper as the medium for matter defamatory of private character
is one of the strongest proofs of such malice and will withdraw the
protection of a "justifying occasion."

It was also contended that the defendant Karsandás Mulji was
justified in publishing the libel by reason of the private interest
which he had as a member of the sect of Vallabhácháryá in protecting it from the corruption of such immorality as was charged
against the plaintiff; but I much doubt on the defendant's evidence
whether he can be considered to be a member of that sect: whatever
force there might be in such an argument is taken away by the
mode of publication having quite exceeded the bounds suited to the
occasion. Had he taken means to have convened a meeting of the
sect, and so published to the members interested the defamatory
matter concerning one of their spiritual heads with a view to
investigation, perhaps he might have had some colour for the
defence; but the defendant selected a public newspaper, and without
any previous inquiry published the defamatory matter, not to the
parties interested only, but to the whole world. For the above
reason, I think the plaintiff is entitled to a verdict upon the plea of
the general issue.

I now proceed to consider the plea of justification. In commenting
upon the evidence I will avoid as far as practicable any reiteration
of its disgusting details, and deal with the credibility of the witnesses on general principles and in general terms. We are not now
called upon to express any opinion as to whether the plea of justification covers the charge in the libel. That plea, if proved, is on the
record admitted to contain a sufficient answer, and it is with it alone
we have now to deal.

The text upon which this libel was founded is a commentary by
Gokulnáthji Maháráj, upon a work composed by his grandfather
Vallabhácháryá, the founder of this sect. In the Sanskrit original,
the name of the person to whom an offering of wives and daughters,
etc., is to be made is not mentioned; and upon the evidence there
can be no reasonable doubt that the offering was to be made to
"Purushottam," which is a name for the Supreme Being. The
compiler of a small work in Gujaráti, entitled "Biographical
Sketches of ancient Hindu authors" (and in which he gives an

account of the various religious sects in India) acting upon his own knowledge of the Sanskrit language and upon his own construction of this passage, introduced the word "Ácharya" to represent the name of the person to whom this offering was to be made. That word appears to be one of very general and undefined application in various Hindu sects, but in the Vallabhácharya sect it is synonymous with guru or spiritual guide, and is one of the hundred and more names applied to the Mahárájás. The term "Purushottam," i.e., Supreme Being or Lord, is also one of the names by which they are addressed. The defendant took his text as it appeared in a Maráthi translation of the Gujaráti work, changing "Ácharya" into "Maháráj." He had no means of consulting the original, as he was not acquainted with Sanskrit, and there is no apparent reason to doubt that he relied on the accuracy of the compiler in introducing the word "Ácharya" into the text. It is not necessary to inquire, and it would perhaps be hazardous to offer an opinion upon, what the intention of Gokulnáthji was in making use of those words, but it appears abundantly from works of recognised authothority, written by other Mahárájás, and from existing popular belief in the Vallabhácharya sect, that Vallabhácharya is believed to have been an incarnation of the god Krishna, and that the Mahárájás, as descendants of Vallabhácharya, have claimed and received from their followers the like character of incarnation of that god, by hereditary succession. The Mahárájás have been sedulous in identifying themselves with the god Krishna by means of their own writings and teachings and by the similarity of ceremonies of worship and addresses which they require to be offered to themselves by their followers. All songs connected with the god Krishna, which were brought before us were of an amorous character, and it appeared that songs of a corrupting and licentious tendency, both in idea and expression, are sung by young females to the Mahárájás, upon festive occasions, in which they are identified with the god, in his most licentious aspect. In these songs, as well as in stories, both written and traditional, which latter are treated as of a religious character in the sect, the subject of sexual intercourse is most prominent. Adultery is made familiar to the minds of all; it is no where discouraged or denounced; but, on the contrary, in some of

6

the stories, those persons who have committed that great moral and social offence are commended, and in one of them, the actors are awarded the highest position in the heaven of the Vaishnavas, although for some attention paid on one occasion to the clearing of a temple of the god. The love and subserviency inculcated by the Hindu religion to be due in a spiritual sense to the Supreme Being has been by those corrupt teachings materialised, and to a large extent transferred to those who claim to be his living incarnations. It is said to be ceremonially effected by a mystic rite or dedication of - "mind," "property," and "body" (or *man, dhan,* and *tan*), which is made in childhood by males, but by females in the ceremony of marriage, and a popular belief appears to exist to a considerable extent that this dedication confers upon the Mahárájás absolute rights over the "minds," "properties," and "bodies" of their followers. The Mahárájás, however, appear upon the evidence to have undoubtedly availed themselves of the existence of those impressions to gratify licentious propensities and a love of gain. These doctrines and practices are opposed to what we know of the original principles of the ancient Hindu religion which are said to be found in the Veds. They recognise no incarnations, but the well known *avatár* and the Hindu code of law and morals equally inculcate chastity in females before marriage, and fidelity in the marriage state. Therefore, so far as we may be called upon to express an opinion upon this part of the plea, the defendant has successfully shown that the doctrines of the Vallabháchárya sect are in those respects contrary to those of the ancient Hindu religion. He has proved that the Mahárájás claimed to be and are considered and worshipped by a considerable portion of the sects as gods or incarnations of God; and he has, we think, established that this superstition has led to a lamentable want of moral feeling in the Vallabháchárya sect, and to the practice of gross immoralities. It is to the credit of the plaintiff, that in his evidence he has disavowed for himself any claim to be considered as an incarnation of God. He stated that he had so informed his followers, but was unable to remember when, or to whom he addressed such advice. There was no other evidence offered of his having done so, but it appeared to establish the generality or strength of such a belief amongst the followers of the Mahárájás, when it became necessary for him to thus disavow that character. The next branch of this plea of justification is that in which it is alleged that the immoral or licentious practices of the Mahárájás, as stated in the libel, were matters of notoriety in the Vallabháchárya sect as well as outside of it, that they had been denounced by their own followers, and by others in pamphlets, newspapers, and handbills published in all languages in Bombay. Several credible witnesses of the Vallabháchárya sect were examined, who deposed to the existence of that opinion in the sect, and in addition as evidence of the strength of that feeling, the defendants put in issue a resolution passed at a meeting of the Bháttiá caste in 1855 for the purpose of preventing the females going to worship at the temples, except at periods when the Mahárájás were personally occupied in the performance of the worship of their god. That resolution was proved to have been come to, in consequence of its being believed that immoral practices were taking place between the Mahárájás and their female Bháttiá devotees, under colour of the latter going at night to perform worship at the Vallabháchárya temples. Since that period, newspapers, pamphlets, and handbills, in various languages, in Bombay have very frequently denounced the pretensions of the Mahárájás to divinity, have charged them with the grossest immorality, have held them up as objects for public reprobation, and latterly, in 1859, have made use of the strongest and sometimes the coarsest terms, in describing their alleged profligacy of conduct and licentious vice. It also appeared in evidence that some Mahárájás had committed acts of immorality and licentiousness to the knowledge of witnesses who deposed to them, and whose testimony I do not see any reason to doubt. The plaintiff and Jivanji Maháráj in Bombay were stated in the plea to have admitted, in the presence of some of the members of the sect, the prevalence of the crime of adultery amongst their body, and also to have said, that great difficulty would be experienced in checking it, as the Mahárájás derived the greater portion of their incomes from female devotees, and that no other sufficient means were provided for their support. Jivanji Maháráj was not produced to contradict or explain these statements, although his name is mentioned in the plea in connection with that fact, and the plea had been filed for nine months before the trial. The plaintiff denied the admission, but we feel no difficulty in discrediting that denial, and in believing that the conversation took place. The credibility of the witnesses who deposed to it was not impeached, and the character of some of them was such, that we do not feel at liberty to doubt their truth. We have therefore no hesitation in arriving at the conclusion that this portion, also, of the plea has been satisfactorily proved.

We now approach the last division of this plea, which so vitally affects the character of the plaintiff, not only for immorality of conduct, but for truth on his oath in a court of justice. Any one who was present at his examination, and the lengthened cross-examination which he underwent for the greater part of three days, must feel that he is a man of great intelligence, and of considerable native attainments. Any contradiction to the testimony of other witnesses cannot have arisen from confusion or mistake; it must have been wilful and deliberate. He has contradicted in the most direct terms every charge of personal immorality made against himself, every conversation approaching to an admission of immoral practices upon his own part or of licentious conduct of other Mahárájás. In a conflict of evidence where there must be a wilful false swearing on one side or the other, it is desirable to select some one material fact upon which there is a clear and direct collision, and through it to test the credibility of the witnesses on one side or the other. The plea charged as evidence of the licentious character of the plaintiff, that in the year 1860, he was suffering from a malady contracted from immoral intercourse with females. The defendants produced two medical men who were consulted by the plaintiff—Drs. Bháu Dáji and Dhirajrám Dalpatrám. Both are Graduates of the Grant Medical College, and the first at least long distinguished for his scientific, literary, and medical attainments. It is but justice to those gentlemen to say, that they only gave medical evidence, upon the legal compulsion which it was the duty of the Court to apply. Dr. Dáji states that the plaintiff sent for him professionally, and in giving a description of his ailment, made use of a term of familiar and unmistakeable medical meaning, which, coupled with the history of its origin, left no doubt in Dr. Dáji's mind of the character of the disease. The plaintiff having then declined to submit to an ocular examination, informed Dr. Dáji that he would the next morning send Govardhandás to give more accurate details. Govardhandás was the confidential agent and manager for the plaintiff, and he next morning gave a description and history fuller but in substance and terms identical with that already given by the plaintiff. This agent and manager was in Bombay during the trial, and although several days elapsed between the evidence of Dr. Dáji and the close of the plaintiff's rebutting case, Govardhandás was not called to contradict or explain that evidence. Dr. Dalpatrám, who had been one of the Vallabhácharya sect, was consulted professionally by the plaintiff in about three months afterwards, and was in attendance upon him for more than a month. He treated the plaintiff for a similar disease, which was described by the latter as having been contracted by him from immoral intercourse with a female about the period when Dr. Dáji had been sent for. The plaintiff was cured by the treatment of Dr. Dalpatrám after salivation, and upon Dr. Dalpa_trám's evidence, there could be no doubt as to the character of the disease, or as to the mode in which it was described by the plaintiff to have been contracted. Dr. Dalpatrám had the opportunity afforded him of the necessary medical inspection. Lakhmidás Khimji, who is one of the leading men in the sect of Vallabhácháryans in Bombay, was at that time in the habit of daily intercourse with the plaintiff, and had been requested by the latter to bring Dr. Dáji (who is a Bráhmin) to visit him professionally. He fully corroborates these two medical witnesses. Through the medium of conversations with the plaintiff, the latter described his malady by name, and the mode in which it was contracted, together with other details which it is not necessary to mention. It was further elicited in cross-examination that the plaintiff had undergone a medical examination on the preceding evening by three doctors, with a view of sustaining his own denial of the existence of disease and of the truth of the statement made by Drs. Dáji and Dalpatrám and by Lakhmidás Khimji. None of these doctors were produced for the plaintiff to give an account of that recent examination. Upon this conflict of evidence between the plaintiff *alone*, and the three witnesses, Dr. Dáji, Dr. Dalpatrám, and Lakhmidás, coupled with the non-production of Govardhandás, or any of the three medical men who made the last examination, I feel myself compelled to come to the conclusion, that the plaintiff has allowed his personal interests to overcome his respect for truth, while on his oath in this court. And having reluctantly but confidently arrived at the conviction that he has in this instance wilfully forswore himself, I can place no trust or reliance upon any denials he has given to the personal acts of immorality with which he has been charged. The characters of the principal witnesses for the defendants have not been impeached. Many of them are members of the Vallabháchárya sect, and still frequent the temples of the Mahárájás. It has not been suggested that they entertain any personal hostility to the plaintiff. They have apparently no personal interest to serve, but much caste or sect obloquy to undergo for the part they have taken and the evidence they have given against a Maháráj. The account of Lakhmidás Khimji in support of the charge of the plaintiff's immorality at Beyt is a strange and almost incredible story, but I cannot believe it to have been invented for this trial. In answer to the Court, he stated the names of four persons, members of the sect, in whose presence several years before he had detailed the circumstances he narrated in the witness-box. None of those persons were produced to contradict him, and when all of those who were in Bombay, were produced by the defendants for cross-examination, the plaintiff shrunk from impeaching, through their testimony, the truth of the statement of Lakhmidás Khimji. The plaintiff produced evidence to his good character for morality at Surat, Beyt, and several other places in which it had been impeached. He also sought to establish the falsehood of the testimony of Lakhmidás Khimji respecting the act of immorality at Beyt, by calling witnesses to show that by night and by day, plaintiff had personal attendants waiting upon him, who never left him alone for an instant, and which rendered it improbable in the highest degree that he could have been guilty of the immoral act deposed to. That evidence is in itself contrary to all probability and is contradicted incidentally by the statement of Dr. Dalpatrám, who in his professional treatment always saw the plaintiff alone. On examination of those witnesses, it appeared that the greater number were followers of the sect of the Mahárájás. Some of them avowed that they believed the Mahárájás to be incarnations of the Deity. Others that they would not believe anything against the character of a Maháráj, that a Maháráj could not do anything wrong, that he could not be a bad man, and that it was a sin to give evidence against a Maháráj in a court of justice, and that any one who did, should not be spoken to and should be outcasted.

Bearing in mind the efforts that were proved to have been made to prevent evidence being given by his co-sectaries against the plaintiff in this case, and looking upon the description of that given for him, we cannot allow the negative character of the latter to outweigh the clear, strong, and direct evidence given for the defendant, under those difficulties.

We think that the essential points in the libel, as the record stands, have been sufficiently covered by the proof adduced in support of the plea of justification, and that there must be a verdict for the defendant upon that issue.

As to the minor pleas, a verdict for the plaintiff will be entered on the 2nd, 4th, and 6th; and for the defendants on the 3rd and 5th pleas, in addition to the 7th and 8th.

After having found a verdict for the defendants upon the issues raised by the plea of justification, the plaintiff can only recover a verdict for nominal damages on the plea of not guilty. As we have felt obliged to disbelieve the plaintiff on his oath and also the greater number of the witnesses produced to corroborate him, our verdict will be entered without costs.

The defendant to be entitled to the costs of the issues found in his favour.

---

## (Judgment of Sir Joseph Arnould.)

In this case I shall make no apology for stating at some length, the reasons for my judgment. In a matter of such general interest and importance the public have a right to be satisfied that the minds of both members of the Court have been actively engaged in sifting the evidence and arriving at a painstaking and conscientious decision. I have, besides, on one point not been able to come to the same conclusion as the Chief Justice; and though that point does not materially affect the vital question in the case, and relates not so much to the law itself as to the application of the law, it is yet too important to be passed over in silence.

I. On the first issue the question that arises is this : Is the article complained of a libel; or is it so far justified by the occasion, *i.e.* by the whole of the circumstances preceding and accompanying its publication, as to be, though defamatory, not *libellous ?*

The doctrine of "justifying occasion," as deduced from the authorities, is this : The essence of libel is malice. *Primâ facie* every publication containing matter tending to defame or criminate another is held to be libellous;—that is, malice, the essence of libel, is legally inferred from the mere fact of publishing of another that which tends to criminate or defame him. But this *primâ facie* inference may be repelled : it may be shown that the circumstances under which the publication took place were such as to preclude the legal inference of malice arising from the mere fact of publication and to constitute a *justifying occasion* for publishing that which tends to defame and criminate another.

If such a justifying occasion be made out, the only enquiry remaining, in order to ascertain whether a given publication be or be not libellous, is the enquiry whether the publication, *on the face of it,* shows what is legally called *express malice;* in other words, whether the virulence and bitterness of the language employed by the writer so far exceeds what the occasion warrants as to show that he was actuated by personal rancour, by a malignant and vindictive desire to criminate and defame. Unless this appears the publication, though defamatory or criminatory, is not libellous (see the whole current of authorities from *Rex* v. *Baillie,* 21 Howell's State Trials 10 (in A.D. 1778) down to *Harrison* v. *Bush,* 5 Ell. and Blackb. and 16 L. J. Q. B. 25 (A.D. 1855).

As to what will constitute a justifying occasion, the points principally to be attended to are these : *First,* The publication must be *bonâ fide, i.e.,* at the time of publication the writer must honestly and upon fair reasonable grounds believe that which he publishes to be substantially true. *Secondly,* The publication must be with regard to a subject matter in which the party publishing has an *interest*, or in reference to which he has a *duty*. *Thirdly*, Those to whom the publication is addressed must have an interest and a duty in some degree corresponding to his own.

The word *duty* (as the late Chief Justice of England declared the law in Harrison *v.* Bush) is "not to be confined to *legal* duties which may be enforced by indictment, action, or mandamus, *but must include moral and social duties of imperfect obligation.*" (*See the well-considered judgment of the Court of Queen's Bench as delivered by Lord Campbell in the case of Harrison v. Bush*, 16 L. J. Q. B. p. 20.)

As to the *extent of the privilege or the justification*, that varies necessarily with the nature of the subject matter of the alleged libel; if it be a matter like the character of a servant, etc.—in regard to which only one person or only a few persons have an interest or duty corresponding to that of the writer, then he is only privileged or justified in communicating to that one or to those few; if, on the other hand, it be a matter in regard to which the general public has an interest and a duty—if it be a great social scandal and a great public wrong—if it be a matter in the exposure of which all society has an interest and in the endeavour to discharge and put down which all society has a duty—finally, if it be a matter beyond the cognizance of any other tribunal except the condemnatory judgment of public opinion—in such cases, the writer, if writing *bonâ fide*, is privileged or justified in making the communication as public as he can.

Such, in my judgment, are the principles of law applicable to the present case. In applying them I propose to consider the following questions:—What was the defendant's professional and social position at the time the alleged libel was published? What was his consequent interest and social duty in reference to the subject matter of the alleged libel? What was his then state of knowledge and belief in respect to such subject matter? What or whom does he attack in the alleged libel? To whom does he address himself in publishing it? What was the immediate occasion of publishing it? Is the language in which the alleged libel is couched in excess of what the occasion warranted?

First then: *who or what was the defendant at the time of the pub-*

*lication of the alleged libel?* By birth and early initiation he was a member of the Vallabháchárya sect, but for some years before the libel was published, in consequence mainly of his disgust at the practices which in the libel he denounces, he had ceased to worship in the temples of the Mahárájás. For some time before the publication of the alleged libel he had been editor of the *Satya Prakásh,* a native newspaper published in the Gujaráti language, and principally read and circulated among the two wealthy and extensive castes of the Bháttiás and the Banians. Both these castes are devout followers of the Maháráj : of the Baniá caste the defendant was himself a member.

Such was the defendant's position; *what was his consequent interest and duty?*

As a Vallabhácháryan addressing his co-sectaries, as a Banian addressing his caste fellows—above all, as a journalist addressing his readers composed principally of followers of the Mahárájás, had he no interest, had he no duty, in denouncing the malpractices which it is the principal object of this alleged libel to expose? It appears to me that he had both an interest and a duty.

A public journalist is a public teacher : the true function of the press—that by virtue of which it has rightly grown to be one of the great powers of the modern world—is the function of teaching, elevating, and enlightening those who fall within the range of its influence.

To expose and denounce evil and barbarous practices; to attack usages and customs inconsistent with moral purity and social progress, is one of its highest, its most imperative duties. When those evils and errors are consecrated by time, fenced round by custom, countenanced and supported by the highest and most influential class in society, when they are wholly beyond the control and supervision of any other tribunal, then it is the function and the duty of the press to intervene; honestly endeavouring by all the powers of argument, denunciation, and ridicule, to change and purify the public opinion which is the real basis on which these evils are built and the real power by which they are perpetuated.

As editor of the *Satya Prakásh,* the defendant was, in my opinion, acting within the clear limits of his duty (as defined in the case of

Harrison *v.* Bush) in denouncing to a public principally composed of Bháttiás and Banians, the moral delinquencies of the Mahárájás.

*When the defendant published his alleged libel, what was his state of knowledge and belief as to the matters of which it treats?* To the defendant himself, a member of the Vallabhácharya sect, and of the Baniá caste, the profligacy of the Mahárájás had been known as matter of general reputation and universal notoriety from his earliest years.

" It is," says he, " the general reputation of our sect that when girls are married they are sent to the Maháráj to be enjoyed, before they are touched by their husbands. This has been the reputation as long as I can remember, and," he adds, " I have known instances."

When as a youth he had attended the temples, he had seen Mahárájás pressing with their feet the hands of their more favoured female devotees, and, though young, he knew perfectly well what this meant.

He was cognizant of the fact that, in 1855, those devout followers of the Mahárájás, the members of the Bháttiá caste, had held a caste meeting, at which a resolution was passed " to fix hours at which their females should visit the temples, *that they might not have carnal intercourse with the Maháráj.*"

With regard to the plaintiff himself the defendant was informed before the publication of the libel, on what he had every reason to consider good authority, that his conduct formed no exception to the general conduct of his class.

" The general character of the Mahárájás is that of debauchees; the plaintiff has also the reputation of a debauchee;" he was told this before the publication of the alleged libel by Narmadá Lálshankar, his intimate friend, and who, as being in common with the plaintiff a native of Surat and for some time a resident there, had the amplest means of information as to the plaintiff's character.

The result of all this as to his *state of belief* when the libel was published is thus stated in his evidence: " At the time I wrote the alleged libel, I believed the Mahárájás individually and as a class, to be guilty of what I call defiling the wives and daughters of their devotees."

Although thus fully informed of, and on good grounds firmly believing in the immoralities of the Mahárájás, it was not until a short time (some four or five months) before the publication of the libel, that he saw reason to believe that these immoralities were sanctioned by the sacred books of the Vallabhácháryans.

It was about that time that he fell in with a popular compilation in the Maráthi language, professing to give an account of the tenets of various sects, including those of the Vallabhácháryans. The portions of this Maráthi work relating to the Vallabhácháryans were supplied by defendant's intimate friend, the young Nágar Bráhmin, Narmadá Lálshankar, who had shown the MS. to the defendant before it was published.

In this Maráthi compilation the verse of Gokulnáthji, to which so much prominence is given in the alleged libel, is introduced thus :

"Besides this there are strict words of comment written in a book called the *Siddhánt Rahasya* (this is the book which forms the text of Gokulnáthji's commentary) to the effect that 'all things should be offered and presented to the Áchárya (*i.e.* the Maháráj) and then enjoyed.' It is then added, 'To offer everything means that even our wives, sons, etc., should not be brought into use without offering them.' "

From this publication the defendant would naturally infer that the commentary of Gokulnáthji enjoined the offering up of wives and daughters (for "daughters" are without dispute included in the expression "sons, etc,") to the Maháráj by way of carnal intercourse.

The defendant did not understand Sanskrit, but he could read Brij-Bhásh ; he forthwith began to study several Vallabhácháryan works in Brij-Bhásh. From these he derived the conclusion that the statement of doctrine in the Maráthi compilation was borne out by the authoritative works of the sect. As to the Sanskrit verse of Gokulnáthji, he satisfied himself, he says, from enquiry among those who understood Sanskrit, that its meaning is as set forth in the libel. That meaning is set forth thus :

"Consequently before he himself has enjoyed her, he should make over his lawful wife *to the Maháráj*, and he should also make over his sons and daughters ; after having got married he should, before having himself enjoyed his wife, make an offering of her *to the Maháráj*, after which he should apply her to his own use."

The friend to whom he applied for this translation would seem to have been Narmadá Lálshankar, the young Bráhmin who showed him the MSS. from which this part of the Maráthi work was printed; who represented himself as having a thorough knowledge of Sanskrit, and who strenuously maintained in the witness-box, that the meaning given in the alleged libel to Gokulnáthji's commentary was correct, that the dedication there spoken of was a dedication not to the Supreme Being for spiritual purposes, but to his personification, the Maháráj, for carnal purposes.

It has been elaborately and learnedly contended that this interpretation is incorrect—that Gokulnáthji never intended, nor do his words, in their literal sense, import the meaning thus put upon them. It may or may not be so : the question as to the precise grammatical meaning of the text, or the probable intention of the writer, does not go to the root of the present enquiry. It is not a charge of libel on Gokulnáthji that we are trying, but a charge of libel on the *plaintiff*. The question is not what Gokulnáthji originally wrote or intended, but what in practice, his text or other similar texts have been construed to mean and perverted to sanction. It is abundantly clear on the evidence, as it will presently be necessary to show more at large, that the Mahárájás have for a lengthened period been so far identified by their followers with Krishna—have been to such an extent regarded as gods and worshipped as gods, that it would be exceedingly difficult, if not absolutely impossible, to pronounce with any certainty, how far a text apparently contemplating a dedication to God, might or might not be regarded in the Vallabháchárya sect as authorizing a dedication to the Maháráj.

This, however, is not a question we are called upon to decide. The question for us, on this part of the case, is whether the defendant when he printed this alleged libel in his paper, had or had not justifying occasion for publishing that the class to which the plaintiff belonged, and the plaintiff himself, as a member of such class, acting on the supposed sanction and authority of certain texts, whether rightly or wrongly understood, whether wrested from their true meaning or not, defiled the wives and daughters of their devotees.

That the defendant when he printed his interpretation of the text in the alleged libel honestly and *bonâ fide* believed it to be the correct one is perfectly plain on the face of the evidence, and was not indeed seriously questioned by the learned counsel for the plaintiff. Ignorant himself of Sanskrit (the language in which Gokulnáthji's commentary is written) he applied for assistance to those whom he honestly believed to be competent authorities, and the interpretation with which they supplied him he made use of in sincere and undoubting reliance on its accuracy.

Such having been the defendant's position, consequent duty and state of knowledge and belief at the time he published this alleged libel, the next question is, *what and whom did he attack?*

Primarily he attacks a flagrant social enormity and scandal. For generations the hereditary high priests of his sect had, as he believed, committed whoredom with the daughters of his people. Like the sons of Eli, they had done this openly at the gates of the temple,—like the sons of Eli, they had done this under the pretended sanction, and in the abused name, of religion. This is the thing he denounces. It would be a waste of words to point out that in denouncing it—vehemently, bitterly, indignantly—he was within the strict limits of his duty as a public writer. The interests of society require that wickedness such as this should be sternly exposed and unrelentingly hunted down. If to write vehemently, bitterly, indignantly on such a subject as this be libellous, then were the prophets of old libellers,—then were the early fathers of the church libellers,—then have all earnest men in all time been libellers, who have published to the world in the fit language of generous indignation their scorn of hypocrisy and their hatred of vice.

Such is the *thing* the defendant attacks in this libel. *Who are the persons he attacks?* The class who do this wickedness, and the plaintiff as a member of this class;—the Mahárájás, and the plaintiff as a Maháráj. This is throughout the language of the alleged libel: "In the Kali-yug (or iron age) many other heresies, and many sects have arisen, besides that of Vallabháchárya, but no other sectaries have ever perpetrated such shamelessness, subtilty, immodesty, rascality, and deceit as have the sect of the Mahárájás."—"You, Mahárájás, acting up to the commentary, defile the wives and daughters of your devotees."

He attacks the class as perpetrators of this great wickedness; he attacks the plaintiff as one of the class. It is said that in so doing he inferentially also defames him as an individual. I admit it, but I say the occasion justified it. A case had arisen in which the possible injury to the individual was not to be weighed in the balance against the great countervailing benefit derivable to society from exposing and denouncing the evil deeds of the class: and the acts denounced were immoralities, not of the plaintiff as an individual in his private life, but of the plaintiff as a Maháráj in his public life.

Then *to whom does the defendant address himself in making the attack?* To the public at large :—the only power, the only authority, the only tribunal to whom in such a case as this the communication could be made, or the complaint directed. The Mahárájás, the hereditary high priests of the Vallabháchárya sect, are, in respect of the practices denounced in the libel, virtually amenable to no jurisdiction, spiritual or temporal, criminal or civil. As far as the evidence before us goes, they appear to constitute a co-equal brotherhood of sixty-five or seventy members, owning a vague and shadowy sort of allegiance to a nominal superior at Shri Náthji—a remote shrine among the deserts of Márwár. This nominal superior appears to be a careless and Epicurean sort of god: no instance of his interference was adduced before us : practically each Maháráj does as seems good in his own eyes, especially as relates to the abomination which it is the peculiar object of this alleged libel to expose.

From the tenor of the evidence I thought, at one stage of the enquiry, that Jivanji Maháráj (a high priest who appears honourably distinguished among his brethren for learning, piety, and comparative purity of conduct),—I was led to think that Javanji acted in Bombay as a kind of superior or principal over the other Mahárájás, who from time to time came down here to officiate. But I was wrong : Jivanji was merely an equal among equals. When appealed to by some of the most respectable Vallabhácháryans in Bombay to interpose and put a stop to these practices, his anwer was that he could do nothing. He admitted the alleged immorality; he deplored it; but he could not interfere with his brother Mahárájás to prevent it. "Every man," he said, "is master in his own house: all my fellow Mahárájás here are my equals in rank, some of them my superiors in age; what can I do?"

As there was no available *spiritual* tribunal, so neither was there any *criminal* or *civil* tribunal which could take cognizance of these immoralities of the Mahárájás. It was profligacy, it was vice, but it was not *crime*, it was not *civil wrong*, of which they were accused. There was no violence; there was no seduction. The wives and daughters of these sectaries (with their connivance in many cases if not with their approval) went willingly,—went with offerings in their hands, eager to pay a high price for the privilege of being made one with Brahma by carnal copulation with the Maháráj, the living personification of Krishna.

To what quarter then was a Vallabhácháryan in Bombay to look for redress or reform if he felt aggrieved at these misdeeds of the Mahárájás? He had one resource, and one only: to appeal to *public opinion through the Press.* This the defendant did; as a Vallabhácháryan it was his *right*, as the editor of a native journal it was his *duty* to do so; for if evils such as these were (in the language of Lord Ellenborough) "to exist for ever without public animadversion, one of the great uses of a free press is at an end." (1 *Campbell*, 117.)

And the public, which thus constitutes the only tribunal to which the defendant could appeal, had an *interest* and a *duty* in relation to the subject matter of the alleged libel corresponding to his own. No public can be conceived to exist which has not an *interest* in the discouragement and suppression of such wickedness,—upon which there is not imposed a *moral* and *social duty* of taking all legitimate means for its discouragement and suppression. The offence attacked in the alleged libel is an offence against the first principles of morality on which all society is based, and in the suppression of which the highest *interests* and the highest *duties* of all society, as such, are most intimately concerned.

If, while writing with a single purpose to discourage and suppress this evil, the defendant, in the course of reflecting on the class to which the plaintiff belonged, and on the plaintiff as a member of that class, published that which by inference was defamatory of the plaintiff *as an individual*, the occasion, in my opinion, justified him in so doing, and the defamatory matter so published is no libel, unless it can be shown either that he wantonly *singled out the plaintiff for attack*, or *unless his language was an excess of what the occasion warranted*.

Now did the defendant *single out the plaintiff for attack ?* On the contrary, it is clear *that the immediate occasion of the attack (if attack it can be fairly called) on the plaintiff arose out of the plaintiff's own act in having himself had recourse to the press for the purposes of controversy*. This is plain on the face of the libel itself, and is put beyond all doubt by the evidence. The plaintiff had for some time been publishing a series of articles of a controversial character in the Bombay press, in some of which the defendant as a writer on the opposite side was, or fancied he was, reflected upon. Some of those articles the plaintiff, through his secretary Govardhandás, had sent and caused to be inserted in the defendant's own paper, the *Satya Prakásh*; others had appeared in the *Chábuk*, and other native newspapers; others again were published in the *Sva-dharmavardhak* ("The Propagator of Religion") a monthly periodical of which the plaintiff was the originator and principal manager.

There can be no doubt on the evidence that the prominence given to the plaintiff among all the other Mahárájás in the alleged libel, is owing to two articles of the plaintiff's (or which the defendant supposed to be the plaintiff's), and which appeared, the one in the *Chábuk*, the other in the *Sva-dharmavardhak*, on the 16th and 29th of September, 1860.

" In these articles," says the defendant, " the Maháráj had spoken disparagingly of those reformers who write without quoting the Shástras. I, therefore," he goes on, " proceeded on that hint to write according to the Shástras, and produced the article which is the subject of the present action ' On the Primitive Religion of the Hindus.' "

The alleged libel was published on the 21*st October*, 1860.

The title is " On the Primitive Religion of the Hindus."

7

It commences by citing the Shástras ("the Veds and Puráṇs") to show that in the Kali-yug (or iron age) many heresies and false religions will arise; but the Kali-yug began 5,000 years ago, and the Vallabháchárya sect sprang up less than 400 years ago: it is therefore (the logic is somewhat at fault here) a heresy.

He then cites from one of the plaintiff's September articles a passage in which the plaintiff represents the different modern sects as so many extensions, not divergencies from the old religion, "just as some leave the Fort to proceed to Byculla, others to Wálkeshwar."

The defendant criticises this illustration, and then returns to his former point, that the recent date of the Vallabháchárya sect proves it, on the authority of the Hindu Shástras, to be heresy.

Then he adds, "Thus as regards the weapons with which the Maháráj has come forth to defend himself, those very weapons will oppose the Maháráj and annoy him."

Then follows Gokulnáthji's verse and the indignant comments on it, and then comes the conclusion of the article, *which, upon the evidence as presented by the plaintiff, and apart from the fresh light which has been thrown upon the case by the evidence for the defendant, the Court, on the application to nonsuit,* considered to be *primá facie* libellous.

"Jadunáthji Maháráj (the plaintiff) *has commenced issuing* a small work styled 'The Propagator of our own Religion.' We ask him, In what way do you wish to effect the propagation of religion? Your ancestors, having scattered dust in the eyes of simple people, made them blind: do you wish to make them see; or, taking a false pride in the upholding of your religion, do you wish to delude simple people still more?

"Jadunáthji Maháráj! should you wish to *propagate or to spread abroad religion,* then do you personally adopt a virtuous course of conduct, and admonish your other Maharájás that, as long *as the preceptors of religion shall themselves appear to be immersed in the sea of licentiousness, for so long they shall not be competent to convey religious exhortation.* Gokulnáthji, having composed the commentary above-mentioned, has attached to your Vaishnava persuasion a great blot of ink. Let that be first removed: scorn the writer of the commentary. You, Mahárájás, acting up to that commentary, defile the wives and daughters of your devotees. Desist from that, and destroy at once immorality such as that of the company at the Ras festival. *As long as you shall not do so, for so long you cannot give religious admonition and propagate your religious faith. Do you be assured of that.*"

Is it not plain that the whole of this portion of the alleged libel is addressed prominently and pointedly to the plaintiff, simply because the plaintiff had put himself prominently forward as the originator and the editor of the periodical called the " Propagator of the Faith ?" Is it not clear that the plaintiff's voluntary appearance appearance before the world in that capacity is the key-note to the whole of this part of the article ?

From the whole framework of the alleged libel as explained by the evidence, the unavoidable conclusion is, that the prominence given to the plaintiff throughout the article is not forced, groundless, and malicious, but is the natural result of his having himself entered into the lists of controversy as a champion of Vallabháchárryan orthodoxy, and a propagator of the Vallabhácháryan faith.

Then, lastly, is there on the face of the libel any evidence of *express malice*—is there personal rancour—is there an excess of bitness—is there an unfair singling out of the plaintiff with a hostile desire to defame, to criminate, to malign? I can see nothing of the kind.

The plaintiff is *not* singled out; he had voluntarily put himself forward as the champion and defender of the Maháráj cause.

The attack is primarily on the class to which the plaintiff belongs, incidentally the plaintiff bears the main brunt of the battle, as being the one amongst that class who had invited attack by making himself its representative.

The attack is on acts hostile to public morality done by the plaintiff, not in his private capacity, but as Maháráj. The main object is *not to attack at all, but exhortation*, earnest entreaties to lead a purer life and desist from licentious practices, and *that with a view to the more successful propagation of religion.*

The paramount motive, as deducible from the writing itself, is not personal rancour against the plaintiff; but an ardent desire to put an end to a flagrant and shameful licentiousness, in the suppression

of which the defendant and his co-religionists were vitally ?
ested, and in the practice of which he had honest and *bon(*
reason to believe that the plaintiff, like all the other members (
class, was implicated.

I agree with Dr. Wilson in thinking that "all things consi(
the alleged libel is a very mild expostulation," involving an "a
to the principle that the preceptors of religion, unless they ?
their lives, cannot expect success to attend to their labours."

I agree with Dr. Bháu Dáji that any reader of fair "av
intelligence would understand the object of the writer to be, ?
make a personal charge of malpractices against the plaintiff, 1
address a general exhortation to the class to which the pl(
belongs, to desist from such malpractices."

On these grounds I think there is no proof of *express malic*
the grounds previously stated I think there was a "*just*
*occasion.*"

I think the defendant, from his position and *status*, not onl
an *interest* and acted on a right, but also fulfilled a moral and
*duty*, in denouncing a great iniquity ;—I think he took reasc
sufficient care to inform himself of the facts before he publishe(
that what he published he at the time *bonâ fide* believed to 1
truth ;—I think that, in addressing himself to the public he ap}
to the right and, under the circumstances, to the only av{
tribunal ;—he appealed to those who, in relation to the su
matter of the alleged libel had an *interest* and a *duty* correspc
to his own ;—I think that in giving the plaintiff the prominer
has done in his article he was actuated by no malice, but {
dealt with the plaintiff as he found him, the representativ
champion of his class ;—I think that in the language of the {
itself there is no evidence of personal malice or malignity, but (
evidence of a public-spirited desire to denounce and put d(
crying scandal and wickedness which was a stain upon the cr(
the writer's caste—on the name of his nation—on the dignil
honour of human nature itself.

For all these reasons I am of opinion *that the article compla(
is no libel,* and therefore that on the first issue the verdict ou
be for the defendant.

II.   The other great issue—(for on all the minor points, on which I entirely agree with the Chief Justice, I shall add nothing to the reasons he has adduced in disposing of them)—the other great issue in this case is on the plea of justification.   On this issue I am of opinion that every material averment—every averment which in any way relates to the nature of the Vallabhárchárya sect, the character and position of the Mahárájás in general, and of the plaintiff in particular, is substantially proved.

I shall distribute the remarks I feel called upon to make on this issue under four heads.

*First :*—The evidence adduced as to the nature and tenets of the Vallabhácháryan religion.

*Secondly :*—The evidence as to the light in which the Mahárájás are regarded by the sect of which they are the spiritual chiefs.

*Thirdly :*—The evidence as to the general character of the Mahárájús for licentiousness.

*Fourthly :*—The evidence as to the personal immoralities of the plaintiff.

First.—As to the nature and tenets of the Vallabhácháryan religion. On this topic it is not my purpose to make any lengthened remarks : the passages cited in the plea of justification have been proved and verified : that is, they have been shown to be genuine extracts correctly translated from works received as authorities to a greater or less extent in the Vallabháchárya sect.   But it is obviously impossible to form anything like an adequate judgment of any religious system on any mere series of extracts, especially when selected with an avowedly hostile object.   It is only certain broad and general conclusions at which, aided by the very learned evidence adduced on this point, we can with any safety or satisfaction arrive.

Dr. Wilson, who has studied this subject with that comprehensive range of thought (the result of varied erudition), which has made his name a foremost one among the living Orientalists of Europe, Dr. Wilson says :—"The sect of Vallabháchárya is a new sect, inasmuch as it has selected the god Krishna in one of his aspects, that of his adolescence—and raised him to supremacy in that aspect."

"It is a new sect in as far as it has established the *puhshti márg,* or way of enjoyment in a natural and carnal sense."

This succinct statement seems to contain the essence of the whole matter. It is Krishna, the darling of the 16,000 gopis (or shepherdesses); Krishna the love-hero—the husband of the 16,000 princesses, who is the paramount object of Vallabháchárya's worship. This tinges the whole system with the stain of carnal sensualism, of strange, transcendental lewdness. See, for instance, how the sublime Bráhminical doctrine of unition with "Brahma" is tainted and degraded by this sensuous mode of regarding the Deity. According to the old Bráhminical tenet, "BRAHMA" the All-containing and Indestructible, the Soul of which the Universe is the Body, abides from eternity to eternity as the fontal source of all spiritual existence: reunion with Brahma, absorption into Brahma, is the beatitude for which every separated spirit yearns, and which after animating its appointed cycle of individuated living organisms, it is ultimately destined to attain. The teachers of the Vallabháchárya sect do not absolutely discard this great tenet, but they degrade it. I have no wish to wade through all the theosophic nonsense and nastiness of the plaintiff's own chapter on "Adulterine Love;" but one of the myths he thus cites on the authority of the *Brihad Váman Purán*, perfectly illustrates what I mean. For many ages the incarnations of the Veds prayed Shri Krishna, the most Excellent Being, for a sight of his form : the wish being granted, desire was produced in them and they prayed to Krishna to satisfy their hearts' desire, so that they might enjoy with him in the *form* of *women* : this desire also was granted, and the traditions under the form of women enjoyed Krishna as gopis with adulterine love in the mythical forest of "Vrij."

The comment of the plaintiff (for he is without question the writer or dictator of this article) upon this is, that if there were any sin in adulterine love, Krishna would not have turned these Veds into gopis for the purpose of enjoying them ; but there *is* no sin in such love when its object is God : for "God is all form. He is in the form of father, and he is in the form of husband; he is in the form of brother, and he is in the form of son. In whatever shape one may wish to love God, his wishes are complied with accordingly."

Thus, then, is the pure and sublime notion of the reunion of all spirits that animate living but perishable forms, with the Eternal

Spirit, not limited by form, debased into a sexual and carnal coition with the most sensuous of the manifestations or "avatárs" of God.

But it goes further than this. Unition with Brahma in the Kali-yug (or Iron age) being no longer possible through the medium of mystical intercourse with Krishna; it must be obtained in some other way.

The witness Mathurádás Lowji explains in what way : this is what he says :—

"The connexion with Brahma (necessary to the soul's becoming one with Brahma) in the Kali-yug is only possible through the Maháráj. The connexion is to be had by carnal intercourse betweeen the Maháráj and the Vaishnavas—the female devotees of the Vaishnava persuasion."

This, then, is the order of descent: spiritual unition with Brahma ; mystical coition with Krishna ; carnal copulation with the Maháráj. For, as Dr. Wilson says, and as we shall see more at large under the next head of evidence, "The Maháráj is considered by a great many of his followers as an Incarnation of God, as God incarnate according to Hindu notions, which are peculiar on that subject. The Vallabhácháryans hold that Vallabháchárya and his official descendants are incarnations of the God Krishna, without holding that there is a complete embodiment of him in any one of them."

The religion which thus degrades the pure idea of spiritual re-union with God, into the gross reality of carnal copulation with its hereditary high priesthood, appears from the evidence to be sensuous in all its manifestations. Rás Lilá, or "amorous dalliance" is held forth as the highest bliss here. Rás Lilá is the principal employ-men of Paradise hereafter ; one of the many amatory names of the Maháráj is "Ocean of Rás Lilá;" and when a Maháráj expires he is not said to die, but to extend himself to an immortality of Rás Lilá.

The hymns or sacred songs of a sect are generally the most fervid exposition of their religious feelings. The hymns sung by the women of the Vallabháchárya sect in honour of the Mahárájás and in their presence are certainly no exception to this general rule. They are passionate with all the passion of the East—erotic pantings for fruition of a lover who is also a God: as it is said of the gopis in the *Vishnu Purán*, "every instant without Krishna they count a myriad of years, and forbidden by fathers, husbands, brothers, they go forth at night to sport with Krishna, the object of their love." So these hymns, sung at this day, as the plaintiff admitted, by the wives and daughters of the Vallabhácháryans to their Mahárájas, express the most unbridled desire, the most impatient longing for the enjoyments of adulterine love.

"I have often," says Mathurádás Lowji, heard songs of an adulterous character sung by females before the Maháráj." "Improper songs in favour of adultery," says Khatáo Makanji, "very shameful and indecent."—"Your followers," such is the purport of the songs, "say that they are our husbands, but in fact you are our husband."

Several translations of these songs were before us, and they quite bear out the character thus given. I give a few extracts:—

> "An excitement extreme and great in my body is created."
> "The azure-coloured beauteous husband with me is sitting."
> "Without seeing his beauteous face even water will I not drink."
> "The amorous and beauteous husband by seeing oft I will live."
> "Restrain me not, oh my mother,
> "To pay homage to him daily I will go."
> "As to connectionship that of Krishna appears the only true one,
> "And all others seem to be imperfect."
> "He who tells, we will permit him to do so,
> "And to him in indifference we shall listen."
> "For your sake the sense of public shame I have not entertained."
> "The descendant of Vallabh is the amorous Kúná."
> "To that dear soul having become a female slave,
> "The sense of public shame no longer will I fear."
> "The descendant of Vallabh is the amorous Kúná."
> "The sound of the jingling of his toe-rings has deprived me of my heart."
> "The very personification of God you are,
> "Having married the Vallabh husband with extreme love."
> "By our submitting to the Vallabh husband happy we shall be.
> "By his association the Vaikunth (Paradise) we shall gain."

There is only one point left for consideration under this head, and that is, how far works regarded in the sect as authoritative, claim for the Mahárájás the attributes and the worship of Gods.

As to this there can be no doubt that the extracts proved at the trial fully bear out the correctness of those set out in the plea of justification.

"Whoever holds his spiritual guide and Shri Thákurji (or God) to be different and distinct shall be born a *Sicháná*" (a kind of bird).

" We should regard our guru as God, nay, as greater than God. For if God gets angry the Gurudev is able to save us from the effect of God's anger, whereas if the guru is displeased nobody is able to save him from the effect of the guru's displeasure." "Therefore God and the guru are necessarily to be worshipped." The "worship of the guru is to be performed in the same way as the worship of God." " In this world are many kinds of creatures. Of them all the most fortunate are we who have sought the protection of the illustrious Vallabhácháryans, Shri Gosáiji and their descendants, *who are manifestly incarnations* of God, the Excellent Being himself."

It is not necessary to go further; these passages claim for the Mahárájás the same worship as is paid to God; they claim for them also the character of incarnations of God.

If these things are sanctioned by the authoritative works of the religious sect,—if union with God is figured under the emblem of sexual intercourse; if love for God is illustrated by the lustful longing of an adulteress for her paramour; if paradise is spoken of as a garden of amorous dalliance;—finally, if the hereditary high priests of the sect are directed to be worshipped as Gods and reverenced as the incarnations of God,—it is not a matter of surprise that the ordinary devotees should make little practical distinction between Krishna and the Maháráj—that they should worship the Maháráj with blind devotion; and that their wives and daughters should freely give themselves up to his embraces in the belief that they are thereby commingling with a God.

Secondly.—It remains to be seen upon the evidence adduced at the trial how far these teachings are carried out in practice; and this brings me to the second head of enquiry, viz., *in what light are the Mahárájás actually regarded by their sectaries?*

On this point the evidence is ample. There is the evidence of the witnesses called in the first instance to launch the plaintiff's case; there is the evidence of defendant's witnesses; the evidence of the witnesses called by the plaintiff in rebuttal of the plea of justification; and the evidence of the plaintiff himself.

The witnesses called in the first instance for the plaintiff were much more candid and explicit in their disclosures on this point than those who were called in rebuttal of the defendant's case. The

latter, from the stereotyped uniformity of their answers on certain
points, and from the cautious restraint with which they spoke on
others, had evidently been warned and tutored against being surprised into admissions that might be damaging to the plaintiff's
cause. There was none of that caution about the earlier witnesses.
What says Gopáldás Mádhavadás, one of the most respectable of
these witnesses?

"We fall prostrate before the Maháráj, and offer incense and
flowers and money to him. Light is waved before him" (as it is to
the image); "the female devotees worship him by swinging him in
a swing:" "Some people in the sect say the Mahárájás are Gods;
others deny it: some Bháttiás and some Banians believe the Mahárájás to be Gods." Then follows admission of certain disgusting
and degrading observances:

"The devotees take pán-sopári after it has been chewed by the
Maháráj and swallow it."—"They drink the water in which his
dirty dhotiá has been washed." They call the water in which the
Maháráj has put his toe the 'nectar of the feet.' "

Varjivandás Mádhavadás (the brother of the last witness and
Justice of the Peace) says—"Some Banians believe the Maháráj to
be God as well as guru." "When the Maháráj dies it is said of
him, he is gone to (Rás) Lílá Bistárya—an extension of amorous
sport. When the Maháráj bathes himself I put saffron scent on his
body; this is on festivals." "The image is bathed on holidays with
the same ablution." "People in our sect perform menial offices for
the Maháráj." "I, though a Justice of the Peace, once sat on the
coach-box and drove the Maháráj among the shoutings of the
people."

So much for the witnesses called in the first instance for the
plaintiff; those called for the defendant brought forward a mass of
evidence on the same point, from which I will extract the more
important passages.

The defendant himself says, "The Mahárájás are considered by
their followers as incarnations of Krishna, as the very personification
of the excellent Being." "I have seen the devotees worship the
Maháráj as God by waving light, swinging, prostration, etc. I have
seen the managers of the Mahárájás giving water to the Vaishnava

to drink, in which the Maháráj had bathed. It is from these things, and from what they generally speak among themselves, that I infer they regard the Mahárájás as Gods."

Mr. Náráyan Dinánáthji, one of the principal interpreters of this court (but who, in the interpretation which he permitted himself to give of the words "Vyabhichár" and "Surat," was for the moment more mindful, I fear, of his admitted friendship with the respectable high priest Jivanji than of the strict line of his professional duty), Mr. Náráyan Dinánáthji was eager to establish that the Mahárájás in the Vallabháchárya sect were merely regarded as gurus, and that "like the gurus of all other sects, they are worshipped with the same forms and ceremonies as the image, but not as Gods." But in cross-examination this gentleman was compelled to allow that "no other sects besides the Vallabhácháryans have *hereditary* gurus by natural descent or adoption;" that "in other sects gurus are sexually ascetic;" that "eating chewed pán-sopári, drinking the nectar of the feet; swinging, rubbing, and bathing the body with oils; eating the dust on which they have walked; are not practised towards the gurus of other sects."

I shall only add the evidence of two more witnesses for the defence,—that of Mathurádás Lowji and that of Dr. Bháu Dáji.

Mathurádás Lowji, a grave and reputable person, earnest, of considerable reading, and unimpeached honesty; a Vallabhácháryan by sect and a Bháttiá by caste; gave the following evidence as to the point now under consideration:—

"Purna-Purushottam is worshipped as God who is in paradise; his incarnations are Vallabh, Vithalnáthji, and their descendants. Vallabh was the incarnation of the head of God." [In this apparently extraordinary statement of doctrine this witness is borne out to the letter by the plaintiff.] "The Mahárájás are regarded as the incarnation of God; the terms Purna-Purushottam and Mahá Prabhu (Supreme God—Mighty God) are applied to the present Mahárájás, especially in the act of worship. The major part of the Bháttiá caste do worship the Maháráj as God, and worship the pictures of each of the Mahárájás and repeat their names, as 'Jivanji,' 'Jadunáthji!' in the act of worship, and worship them in a variety of ways. It is such worship as is enjoined in our

books, for the most part it is the same worship as that of God in
paradise; there is no such worship in any other sect; they touch
his feet; they swing him in a swing; there is a necklace put round
his neck as there is round the neck of the idol; they take up the
dust on which he has trod and put it into their mouths : when they
worship they cry "Mahá Prabhu," "Shri Prabhu," etc.   "In
doing all this I will swear they worship the Maháráj, because the
image is inside.   Some members of my own family, my brother for
instance—believe the Mahárájás to be Gods.   The Mahárájás obtain
their godship from birth, without reference to qualities of body or
mind, or whether they may afterwards turn out to be ignorant,
debauched, or otherwise."

The last evidence for the defence I shall cite on this point is that
of Dr. Bháu Dáji—a gentleman who in learning, freedom from
prejudice, and general superiority of mind is among the foremost,
if not *the* foremost of the native citizens of Bombay.   This gentleman,
by caste a Bráhmin, is not a Vallabhácháryan by creed, but he has
a very extensive medical practice among the more wealthy members
of the sect, and has attended all the Mahárájás who for the last ten
or twelve years have visited Bombay.

Dr. Bháu Dáji says :—" The majority of their followers regard
the Mahárájás as incarnations of Krishna; they are worshipped as
such; I have seen them worshipped.   After the Maháráj has worshipped the image his followers worship him : more time is devoted
to the Maháráj than to the image.   I have seen women put their
hands to the soles of the Maháráj's feet and then apply them to their
eyes; I have seen the water of the bath of the Maháráj distributed
to his followers; and I have seen them crowding in hundreds to
drink it."

Such are a few of the passages from the evidence of the witnesses
originally called for the plaintiff, and of the witnesses for the defendant, as to the light in which the Mahárájás are regarded by the
devout majority of their followers.   To oppose this we have the
evidence of the witnesses called by the plaintiff to rebut the plea of
justification, and the evidence of the plaintiff himself.

As to the evidence of these witnesses, I may say generally that,
except when it consisted of admissions indiscreetly made, it produced

very little effect on my mind. These witnesses all knew perfectly well that they had to deny certain specific allegations, amongst which was the allegation that the Mahárájás were regarded by their followers as Gods, or as incarnations of God. The mode in which they gave their testimony as to this point—the uniform and set styles of their answers to certain evidently expected questions, necessarily led to the inference in my mind, accustomed carefully to scrutinise testimony, that they had been tutored and trained as to the evidence which on this point was expected from them. That evidence was to the effect that they regarded the Maháráj *as guru, not as God.* In their examination in chief they kept pretty steadily to the mark; but on cross-examination, they were more than once incautiously betrayed into the expression of their real feelings and their genuine belief, I say real feelings and genuine belief, because it was impossible not to draw this inference from the spontaneous earnestness of the one set of replies when contrasted with the forced, parrot-like manner of the other set of replies. "I love my guru," said one of these witnesses—Purushottamdás Dayárám—"I worship him as I should God." "It is not possible," said another—Gokaldás Kessavadás —"It is not possible for a Maháráj to commit sin." "I regard the Maháráj as my guru" said Bháichand Kevalchand—"we regard him in the place of God; I regard him as an incarnation of God."—"I regard the guru" said Mansukhrám Narrotam "as an incarnation of God; the guru would not commit sin; I cannot say whether what would he sinful in other men would be lawful in the guru." If we turn from the evidence of his witnesses to the evidence of the plaintiff himself on this point, what do we find?—a series of categorical negations absolutely neutralized by an important admission. "I am not," he says, "an incarnation of God. I do not know that any of my followers regard me as an incarnation of God: I know they ought to regard me as a guru: they worship me as a guru: as those who cause happiness through God;—as guides to God: I have heard no one say we are worshipped as God! but because we give religious instruction they worship us as gurus."

Such are among the principal of the plaintiff's positive denials of the imputation that any of the sectaries worshipped the Mahárájás as Gods or as incarnations of God. But he too, with all his craft and caution, was compelled, under the pressure of cross-examination, to make an admission entirely fatal to the position thus taken up: the admission, viz. that till he taught them better some of the sectaries even in Bombay did believe in the doctrine which he had previously denied that any of the sectaries ever believed in, anywhere, or at any time.

"I have instructed my disciples," he says, "that except two of the Mahárájás, Vallabh and Gosáiji—whom I regard as incarnations of *Ishvar* (God) they should regard us as gurus and not as gods." As to Vallabh, the founder, the plaintiff agrees verbatim with Mathurádás Lowji in the apparently extraordinary statement of doctrine, that "he is regarded *as the incarnation of the head of God;*" but as to all his other descendants, except Gosáiji "I have taught the people," says the plaintiff, that "they should regard us as gurus only. *I prevented all persons from believing such a doctrine* (as that *all* the descendants of Vallabh were incarnations of God); *until I prevented them they did believe it. When I came here some persons believed it and some did not;* the majority did not, the minority did."

What then on this point is the result of the whole evidence? In my opinion it is this:—

1st.   That many passages in the religious works of these sectaries authorize the doctrine that the Mahárájás are incarnations of God and ought to be so regarded and worshipped by their followers.

2ndly.   That in practice they are regarded and treated, at all events by the less reflecting portion of the Vallabhácháya sect as a sort of God-like, powerful, and mysterious beings who cannot commit sin, who are to be worshipped with divine honours, and whose persons are so sacred that the observances which with reference to mere mortals, would be infinitely disgusting, become pious and meritorious acts when done towards the Maháráj.

The two next heads under which I propose to examine the evidence in support of the plea of justification, are,

Thirdly.—*The evidence as it relates to the general immoralities of Mahárájás.*

Fourthly.—*The evidence as it relates to the particular immoralities of the plaintiff.*

Before going into this, a few general observations must be made on the comparative value and credibility of the three principal classes of testimony with which we have to deal, viz., 1, the testimony of the witnesses for the defendant; 2, that of the witnesses for the plaintiff; 3, that of the plaintiff himself.

First, as to the witnesses for the defendant, it is impossible to have presided at this lengthened trial without becoming aware, not only by the positive evidence tendered, but by the demeanour and bearing of the crowds by which from day to day the court was thronged, that the defendant and his witnesses gave their evidence on the unpopular side. The religious animosities of the sect, the social prejudices of the caste, the personal hatred and alienation of former friends, were all arrayed against them. They had to face sectarian obloquy and caste exclusion. They were not free even from the risk of personal assault. I will take two passages from the evidence given by the witnesses for the plaintiff to show the nature of the feeling that was arrayed against them. "Two persons came to me," says Gopáldás Mádhavadás, "on the subject of outcasting the defendant for writing about the Maháráj in the newspapers. They said 'as the Bháttiás have made a bandobast, we (Banians) should make one also.' This was one or two days after the Bháttiás had put their signatures to a paper got up to intimidate people from giving evidence in this case—the bandobast I mean which was made a subject of prosecution for conspiracy in the court last Criminal Sessions. The two persons who came to me were Parbhudás and Jaykisandás: they, I, and the defendants are all Banians."

Dámodar Mádhavaji said:—"If any member of the Vallabhácháryan sect is found to entertain opinions adverse to the rest of the sect, we should not believe him: we should have no intercourse with him; he would be isolated in his own house; we should remain aloof from him. I would regard persons who think the Mahárújás guilty of wicked practices as *outcastes: I would not speak to Lakhmidás Khimji and Mathurádás Lowji, because they have given evidence here against the Maháráj*."

To those who consider how little the Hindu is accustomed to independent thought and independent action—how his whole life is

circumscribed within the sphere of the family or the caste—
entirely the whole social happiness, not only of himself but of
nearest and dearest to him, is blighted by that terrible pena
outcasting (equivalent to the excommunication of the middle ag
those who think of these things will probably be of opinion
nothing but a strong belief in the truth of what they have s
and a firm conviction of the duty of stating it, could have im]
the witnesses for the defendant to come forward as they have
on his behalf. For the majority of these witnesses are not stud
or editors, or non-believers ; they are grave, reputable middle
family men, having a firm belief in the teachings of their ar
religion and a profound reverence for the authority of their ar
scriptures.

Lakhmidás Khimji, one of the twelve leading Setts of the B
caste ; Mangaldás Nathubhái, the Banian Justice of the Peac
well-known founder of Hindu Girls schools; Khattáo Ma
Mathurádás Lowji, and other witnesses of that stamp, are l
likely to have come forward to give evidence they did not be
in order to encounter general odium in the sect and determine
like in their caste. Dr. Bháu Dáji is not indeed a member (
sect or caste, but he has enjoyed an extensive and lucrative pr
among the wealthy Vallabhácháryans, and for the last ten or t
years has attended every Maháráj who, during that period
visited Bombay. It is scarcely probable, on the ordinary prin
of human nature, that Dr. Bháu Dáji, by the evidence that l
given, should risk the loss of such a practice, except from a
conviction that what he had to say was true, and that, being
he ought to make it public. On the whole the fair inference
the evidence for the defendants is, that being given at consid
risk and at considerable sacrifice, it would only be given ur
sense of duty founded on a firm conviction of its truth and
public importance.

The evidence of the witnesses for the plaintiff stands on a 1
different footing. It is true these witnesses, with the same
with which they denied all knowledge of the fact that the Mah
were ever regarded in any way except as gurus, were sedul
declare their conviction that if they ever saw or heard of an

doings of a Maháráj, *it would be their duty* to tell the truth openly
and not scruple to reveal the secrets of their guru.  But the value
of these declarations was considerably impaired by the circumstance
that several of these witnesses swore that till they came into court
they had never heard the morality of the Mahárájás called in question, and that others declared that even if they had heard such
reports they would not have believed them.  " It is not possible for
a Maháráj to commit sin," says Gokuldás Kesavadás.  " Every
Maháráj is a good man," says Hargovandás Mulchand; " a Maháráj
cannot be a bad man; if I heard any report against the moral
character of a Maháráj I would not believe it, nor could a Maháráj
be guilty of bad conduct."  " If," says Narotamdás Haribhái, " I
heard a report of the licentiousness of a Maháráj, I should not
believe it.  A Maháráj would not do bad acts."

It is important to bear these expressions in mind when we consider
the *nature* of the evidence given by the plaintiff's witnesses as to
the part of the case now under consideration.  It is all purely *negative*
evidence.  It amounts to this: you, the witnesses for the defendant,
say the Mahárájás generally bore a bad character; we, the witnesses
for the plaintiff, say we never heard of it.  Again, you, the witnesses
for the defendant say the plaintiff himself bore a bad character at
Surat, at Beyt, at Dwárká.  Well, we are witnesses for the plaintiff
—some of us came from Surat, some from Beyt, some from Dwárká,
one or more of us from every place in which you have proved affir-
matively that the plaintiff bears a bad character; and we say that
we never heard of such bad character.  In any case this negative
evidence amounts to very little, for it is obviously quite possible
that the negative and affirmative evidence may both be true.  It is
obviously no contradiction of a man who says of another that he
bore a bad character at such a place to bring forward a third man,
or (if the place be a large one) half a dozen other men to say they
never heard of such bad character.  But when amongst those
called to give this species of evidence you find a variety of persons
who admit they would pay no attention to, nay, would disbelieve
the bad character if they even heard it, then this species of evidence, at the best singularly inconclusive, becomes for all practical
purposes of absolutely no value whatsoever.

There is another consideration, if another were wanting, to show
how little weight is to be attached to the evidence on this part of
the case, of the witnesses for the plaintiff.  They came forward at
the call of what they and the great majority of their co-sectaries
regarded as a sacred duty of religion, to give evidence in favour of
their guru.  They asserted indeed that it would be their duty to
give evidence against their guru, if he was in the wrong, but it was
never alleged or pretended that it was not a duty to give evidence in
favour of the guru, if he was in the right.  And this was a duty,
the neglect of which would expose them to the reproach, the due
performance of which would entitle them to the applause of their
sect and of their caste.  Accordingly there was an obvious eagerness
and alacrity on the part of the plaintiff's witnesses to come forward
and give their evidence on behalf of the Mahárájás—their gurus if
not their gods—whom their opponents the reformers have had the
profane hardihood to attack.  It is not to be denied that this feeling
is an intelligible one, that it is even in some degree a creditable one ;
but it is too obvious to need remark, that it materially detracts from
the value and reliability of the testimony that is mainly given under
its influence.

If we now turn to the evidence of the plaintiff himself, it is too
clear to admit of a doubt that the peculiar position in which he
stands most materially affects the value of the evidence he gives,
especially in repelling the personal charges that have been made
against himself.  It has been urged, and with substantial truth, by
the counsel for the plaintiff, that, in repelling the charges made on
this plea of justification, the plaintiff is in the same position as if he
were a defendant, endeavouring to clear himself from a criminal accu-
sation.  He is so, except in one respect ; he can be examined on his
oath in his own defence, which the defendant in a criminal trial
cannot.  The law of England, which allows no evidence to be given
except on oath, recognises the existence of cases in which the sanction of an oath ceases to be any effectual guarantee for truth.
Where a man's life and liberty are at stake, it considers, and rightly,
that his mere oath, as a sanction for truth, would be utterly valueless, and therefore, as it admits no evidence except on oath, it prohibits the defendant in a criminal case from giving any testimony at

all as a witness on his own behalf. It is not so in cases which involve a man's reputation, though it is obvious that in all cases where the imputations on character are grave and serious, and in precise proportion as they are grave and serious, *the value of the plaintiff's oath as a sanction for the truth of his testimony* becomes almost infinitesimally small. The plaintiff, as the old phrase runs, "gives his evidence with a rope about his neck:" he has an interest in denying the charges made against him, which becomes stronger in the exact proportion in which those charges become graver, until, in cases of very serious imputation, it may well be doubted whether, even in the most truth-loving of countries, the sanction of an oath, as such, is practically of any value at all as a guarantee for truth. The truth in such cases must be tested by other means than those of mere oath against oath.

With these general observations I pass on to consider the evidence *under the third of the proposed heads of inquiry, viz., as it affects the general character of the Mahárájás for licentiousness and debauchery.*

The evidence on this head is exceedingly voluminous, and I shall only select some of the more prominent passages. I will pass by the evidence of the defendant, to which reference has already been made, in considering the question of libel or no libel, and go on at once to that of Mathurádás Lowji, a well-informed and highly respectable witness, Vallabhácháryan by sect, and Bháttiá by caste. "From childhood," says Mathurádás Lowji, "when my father used to tell me that the practice of adultery by the Mahárájás was not in accordance with the old religion, I have had my attention turned to those practices. Many persons know of those practices; but they don't avow them, for many reasons. I began to explain to my friends about eight or ten years ago that the Mahárájás practising adultery is wrong. In the year 1855 my caste took measures to prevent the adultery of the Mahárájás, and I joined them: they made a writing and gave it. They proposed to put a stop to it by preventing the women from going at night to the Mahárájás' temples. The Mahárájás issued a handbill lately to prevent that writing from being brought forward in evidence in this court. It was resolved at the time that writing should not be brought into force till after the lapse of a year. This was lest the Bhuleshwar Bráhmins should say something against the Mahárájás if the writing were published."

In cross-examination, he says, "I was present at this meeting. I will swear a resolution was passed about adultery, a resolution prohibiting females from making *darshan* at night through the cold season. That was *not* owing to the danger of their being in the streets at night: *the reason was to prevent their being defiled by the Mahárájás.*"

The witness then goes on to describe the particular acts which he has himself witnessed. "Several Mahárájás press the hands of their female devotees with their feet: this is a sign for the purpose of committing adultery. When the woman looks towards the Maháráj, he makes signs with his eyes and smiles, and minding these smiles, the woman goes accordingly into an inner room if the signs indicate that she should. I know this of my own knowledge." The witness then mentioned the names of two Mahárájás whom he had often seen making signs to women, and, in one case, a grossly indecent gesture capable of only one meaning. He swore that he had frequently seen women going into and coming out of the bed-rooms of the Mahárájás, and related with minute detail a scene of actual sexual intercourse between a Maháráj and a Bháttiá female, which he, in common with several respectable witnesses whom he named, had seen going on in the garden-house of the Gokuldás Tejpál.

With regard to the dedication of "tan, man, and dhan," he said, "This dedication does not take place with females till they are going to be married: it is made to Krishna. The Maháráj represents Krishna as stated in the Siddhánt Rahasya; there is no difference, as far as the dedication is concerned, between Krishna and the Maháráj. As to the women, after the dedication the Maháráj does as he likes: he commits adultery with them; there are names of the Maháráj indicating this; one is, 'Rás Lilá—Mahodadhi,' 'the ocean of amorous sport,' meaning that he can have intercourse with many women like Krishna. It is notorious among our people that, after dedication, the Mahárájás do what they like with our wives and daughters. It is notorious through the whole world that the Mahárájás are guilty of adulterous practices. Though this is notorious, they retain their influence in the sect."

The witness then goes on to relate the result of an appeal to Jivanji Maháráj, to put a stop to these scandals. Jivanji said, "All persons are masters in their own houses; adultery has increased very much; it is difficult to put a stop to it. I cannot say anything to my elders nor to my equals. If I were to attempt to say anything to any one, he would not mind me. *All the Mahárájás derive a great part of their income from women: how can they keep up their expenses if their incomes suddenly cease?* Like an opium eater, a man cannot suddenly give up the practice of lust to which he is addicted: it is difficult to abolish such a practice at once; have patience, and I will endeavour to have it abolished gradually."

This evidence, entirely uncontradicted and unshaken, corroborated as we shall see directly by other unimpeachable testimony, is to my mind conclusive as to the generally known existence of such practices. Jivanji does not attempt to deny the evil; he admits and deplores his own powerlessness to suppress it.

Dr. Bháu Dáji says,—"My opinion of the character of the Mahárájás for morality with women is very unfavorable. I have attended three Mahárájás (besides the plaintiff) for venereal disease. I personally, once almost publicly, remonstrated with Jivanji on the subject of these immoralities. He said he had no control over the others to prevent them from committing acts of adultery."

Lakhmidás Khimji says—"The general reputation of the Mahárájás is very bad as regards adultery; to my knowledge that bad reputation is well deserved. *I know of my own knowledge of adulterous acts and general licentiousness on the part of Mahárájás— of ten, twelve, or fifteen of them. The plaintiff himself described to me the acts and conduct of other Mahárájás, naming eight or ten of them. He said they committed adultery; that he had spoken to several to dissuade them; and that, with the exception of one Mahárái whom he named,* the others promised to desist from such practices. He said, 'Do not press me now; what income do I derive from you males? Most of my income is derived from females. If you make arrangements by which we may receive large dues, we will give up these things.' After the Bháttiá caste meeting of 1855, I had a conversation with Jivanji on the subject of adultery. Dr. Bháu Dáji was there. He said, 'Reform yourselves; establish schools; make arrangements to prevent the Mahárájás from committing adultery, to which they are addicted.' Jivanji said, 'The other Mahárájás will not obey me; the arrangement is difficult, the income of the Mahárájás being principally derived from women.' "

Mr. Mangaldás Nathubhái, referring to the same occasion, says, "Jivanji expressed regret at the existing state of things, but said some of the Mahárájás get all their maintenance from women, and it would be very difficult for them to give it up."

Such are some passages from the evidence on this point given by witnesses of the highest character and credit; it was evidence not in any way shaken on cross-examination. How was it met on the other side? What is there in the case of the plaintiff to set against this mass of positive, varied, and yet concordant testimony? Nothing but blank denial; the assertion of absolute ignorance or total incredulity.

Take the plaintiff's own evidence: he positively denies the conversation with Lakhmidás Khimji. As to the general subject, he says:—"I don't know whether any Mahárájás have committed adultery. I have never seen them acting immorally with women. According to the prints, they are immoral; I believe them to be innocent; if guilty, it is contrary to the Shástras."

The witnesses called by the plaintiff to rebut the plea of justification went much further; they had never heard a word against the moral purity of any of the Mahárájás till a few months ago; till they saw the imputations in the Bombay papers; *till this trial commenced; nay, till they came into the court and heard those imputations for the first time suggested by the questions of counsel.*

This proves too much; it is absolutely incredible, except on the supposition that these people obstinately refused to see, or hear, or believe anything unfavourable to the character of their gurus; that, like Gokuldás Kissordás, Hargovandás Mulchand, Narottamdás Harribhái, and others of their number, they believed it impossible for a Maháráj to be a bad man, or to commit sin; that, therefore, if they heard any reports against the conduct of a Maháráj, they would steadily refuse all credence to them.

Applying, then, to this part of the case the most familar rules established in the science of jurisprudence for the sifting and weighing of testimony, I find it wholly impossible to come to any other conclusion than this, that the Mahárájás as a class were, and for years notoriously had been, guilty of the immoralities imputed to them by the defendant in the alleged libel and in the plea of justification.

The fourth and last head under which I propose to review the evidence was that of the *personal acts of immorality charged against the plaintiff in the plea of justification.*

Under this head the testimony mainly relied on, in rebuttal of the charges, is naturally and necessarily that of the plaintiff himself. It is obviously, therefore, very desirable to obtain, if possible, some test or measure of the value and credibility of the plaintiff's evidence when relied on in contradiction of the evidence adduced by the defendant. Such a test of credibility presents itself—clear, decisive, not to be explained away. It is unfortunately connected with one of the most repulsive parts of the case. It is alleged by the defendant's witnesses—it is denied by the plaintiff, that on two occasions in the year 1860, one shortly before and one shortly after the alleged libel, he was affected with syphilis. It is, moreover, alleged on one side and denied on the other, that he admitted having had similar attacks on previous occasions, when he had resorted to a supposed mode of cure, not unheard of by those who have practised in the Criminal Courts of Europe.

Now what is the evidence on this point? Lakhmidás Khimji states that the plaintiff requested him to bring Dr. Bháu Dáji to see him, as he was suffering from chancre (chándi) and had been so for seven or eight days; that the plaintiff said that he caught it from an abandoned woman in Bombay; that he had once tried to cure himself of a similar attack by connexion with an untainted woman, but that, although allowed by the Shástras, he did not like to try that mode of cure again, as the woman had caught the disease from him. So far Lakhmidás Khimji.

The plaintiff, in his rebutting evidence, admits that Dr. Bháu Dáji was called in at the suggestion of Lakhmidás Khimji, but that it was with reference to the management of some girls' schools. He denies categorically that he ever told Lakhmidás Khimji that he had "chándi," or that he had any conversation with him in reference to

his complaint; or that he ever admitted having had connexion with
impure women in Bombay, or that he ever said a word as to having
formerly tried to cure himself by connexion with a second woman to
whom he communicated the complaint.

Then comes the evidence of Dr. Bháu Dáji, who has medically
attended all the Mahárájás who, for the last ten or twelve years, have
visited Bombay, and who, before his visit to the plaintiff, had attended
three of the number for the venereal disease. Dr. Bháu Dáji says
that, about the 20th of September, 1860, he went to the plaintiff's
house with Lakhmidás Khimji and Vishvanáth Náráyan Mandalik.
On the retirement of these two witnesses, the plaintiff said he had
"chándi:" he ascribed it to heat; he said, "The full particulars of
the case would be communicated to me afterwards. Next morning,
the full particulars were conveyed to me by Govardhandás, his
secretary; Govardhandás told me plaintiff was suffering from
'chándi.' I told him I must examine before I could prescribe. He
wanted me to prescribe. I prescribed a simple ointment." In
cross-examination, Dr. Bháu Dáji says,—"I understood the plaintiff
to say he had a discharge from the ulcer. I can say positively he
used the word 'chándi.' 'Chándi' has other meanings besides
syphilitic ulcer: it is the slang term for chancre. A common ulcer
would not be described as 'chándi.' "

In answer to this evidence the plaintiff says that when he consulted Dr. Bháu Dáji, he said he was subject to itches caused by
heat (this agrees with Dr. Bháu Dáji's statement). He admits that
at the time he had sores on the private parts; he denies that they
were venereal; he denies that he ever used the word "chándi," the
word he used was "cháthá" (a Gujaráti word for sore or eruption).
He declares that he never told Dr. Bháu Dáji that he would send a
person the next day to describe his symptoms; he admits that he
sent Govardhandás the next day to Dr. Bháu Dáji, but that he so
sent him in order to bring back a manuscript. "I said to Govardhandás, Bring any medicine he may give you, and bring back the
work." Govardhandás brought back the prescription.

Now, apart from the use of the word "chándi," which Dr. Bháu
Dáji positively affirms and the plaintiff positively denies—the important contradiction here is the denial that the plaintiff ever pro-

mised to send, or did in fact send, Govardhandás to communicate to
Dr. Bháu Dáji the history of his case. There was one person who
could set this point at rest, and that was Govardhandás himself.
Was he called as a witness? No. Was any excuse offered for not
calling him? None. What is the legitimate inference? Why,
that if called, he would have been compelled, under pressure of
cross-examination, to admit that he was sent by the plaintiff to
relate the history of his symptoms, and that those symptoms were
what Dr. Bháu Dáji stated them to be.

This was on or about the 20th of September: about three months
later, in December, 1860, Dr. Dhirajrám Dalpatrám is called in.
"The plaintiff," says this witness, "told me the nature of his complaint; I ocularly inspected the part; it was a syphilitic ulcer on
the *glans penis*. The history of the case given by my patient quite
confirmed my opinion as to the ulcer being syphilitic. I personally
inspected the parts six or seven times. I attended him for a month.
Externally blackwash was applied, internally mercury. He continued the mercury treatment till he was salivated. The sore disappeared within a month. He told me he had suffered in the
same way about three months before, in consequence of impure connexion with a woman. I am sure he did not tell me he had eaten
a great many chillies, nor that he had prickly heat. In the course
of my visits, I remember his asking me whether the disease could
be removed by intercourse with a fresh female? I said 'No.' He
said he had tried it twice with fresh Banian females; it had succeeded the first time, not the second, because he was then somewhat
out of condition. He said he had tried these experiments at Surat."

Such is the positive evidence of Dr. Dhirajrám. What does the
plaintiff say in reply?

"I consulted Dr. Dhirajrám, and took the medicines he prescribed.
I described my case to him; it was of the same character as when
Dr. Bháu Dáji came; it had recurred. I described it as I did to Dr.
Bháu Dáji; I said it was caused by heating medicines and scratching. I did not describe it as syphilitic '*chándi;*' he did not inspect
the parts. I had had no impure connexion with a woman. *How
could I? It is contrary to our religion to have such intercourse.* I did
not tell him I had such intercourse. I did not tell him 'chándi'

would be removed by intercourse with a clean woman; I did not ask whether it could. I did not tell him I had tried the experiment twice, and that the second time it had not succeeded."

With regard to the medicines prescribed, and the effect of them, the plaintiff says:—"He gave me some powders which were mixed with water; the liquid was dark. I used this blackwash; the lime water for it was prepared in my own place. I put the powder into it and so made blackwash, which was applied. I took five or six pills. *After I took the medicine for four or five days, I suffered pain in the throat and left off. After the pain in the throat came on, I did not go on taking a pill a day; he gave me a preparation of borax and water to be used when the throat became sore. My gums pained me slightly. When this took place, the sore had been cured.*"

Now what is the result of this evidence? Why that plaintiff admits he was mercurially treated, both internally and externally, till salivation was produced; that when salivation was produced, or shortly after, the sore was cured, that that sore was an ulcer on the glans penis—and yet that that ulcer was not syphilitic. An ulcer on the glans penis, mercurial treatment, a doctor who, after six or seven inspections, declares the ulcer to be syphilitic—this is the evidence on the one side. The mere denial of the plaintiff, who has a life-and-death interest in making that denial, is the sole evidence on the other. If the matter rested here, could any person accustomed to weigh evidence, have the shadow of a reasonable doubt left on his mind as to where the truth lay? But it does not rest here: it was elicited from the plaintiff that the part affected had been subjected to minute and microscopic observation by three medical gentlemen in the course of the trial; *and yet not one of those medical gentlemen did the plaintiff venture to put in the witness-box.* It would be idle to comment on such a circumstance as this: even in a doubtful case it would have turned the balance against the plaintiff; in a case like this, free without this circumstance from all reasonable doubt, it renders it absolutely impossible to come to any other conclusion than that the plaintiff was affected with syphilis, both in September and December of the year 1860.

And this conclusion is all-important in its bearing on the value and credibility of the plaintiff's evidence; it is not only that having deliberately perjured himself on this one occasion, his oath where he stands alone in contradiction to credible testimony, is utterly valueless for all purposes and on all occasions—it goes further than this : the fact, as to which doubt is impossible, that the plaintiff had syphilis on two occasions in the year 1860, shakes to pieces the whole framework of his evidence and shows it all to be conceived in a spirit of hypocrisy and falsehood.

With great tact and plausibility, the plaintiff assumed, throughout the whole of his very lengthened evidence, a tone of parental piety, and outraged purity.  When asked whether he had toyed with the bosom of the young lady in the temple at Beyt, his answer was " How can I commit such an act as touch the breast of a woman, *when I regard all women as my children.*"  Again, when questioned as to his still closer intimacy with a young married lady in Bombay, he repeats the expression "I regard all women as my children." Again he says, " Would I have told Kalábhái Lalubhái that there is no harm in adultery when adultery is strictly prohibited in our religion?  How could I invent such a new thing" (as to say that illicit intercourse is good for the health) " when I had no experience, never having committed adultery in all my life; it is a thing I hate. Amongst us these things are strictly prohibited; it is laid down that intercourse with one's own wife is lawful, but that intercourse with any other woman is unlawful.   That includes intercourse with *kasbins,*" he said in answer to a question of mine, and we have just seen how in denying that he ever had intercourse with an impure woman, he exclaimed, " How could I, it is contrary to our religion to have such intercourse."

Convinced as I am on evidence the most clear and conclusive that this man laboured under an attack of syphilis, the result of impure connexion, about the very time this alleged libel was published, I am constrained to regard these expressions of simulated purity as the offensive language of hardened hypocrisy.

There is another respect in which a material, but to me a most incredible, part of his evidence is utterly shattered by the conclusion at which I have been compelled to come, as to his having been under treatment for venereal disease in 1860.  The plaintiff himself most positively swore, and his personal attendant swore quite as positively, that while a young man in the prime of life, for the space of four years, all of which were spent without a wife, and two of which were spent on pilgrimage—the plaintiff never on any one occasion had carnal intercourse with any woman of any rank or class whatsoever.   The statement upon the face of it seemed in the highest degree improbable.   Here was a young Hindu—a Maháráj— no ascetic—the hereditary high priest of a religion of enjoyment, with the amorous Krishna for its god, and an ocean of Rás Lilá for its paradise—in the vigour of early manhood, without a wife, on pilgrimage, never once in the space of four years having sexual intercourse of any kind with a woman.   A less probable story was hardly ever sworn to in a court of justice; but what shred, what rag of probability is left to cover the nakedness of this transparent lie, when we find this alleged purist in matured life, in the city of his enemies, with a wife and family in his dwelling-place, so little capable of controlling his sexual passions as to purchase pleasure at the price of disease!   It has been said that if the plaintiff had an unlimited command of pure women he would not have resorted to those who were impure: there is no force in the remark—polygamy and courtezanship are always found to flourish side by side; it requires but a very moderate knowledge of the world and of history to be aware, that the women who make pleasure a profession are not least patronized by those for whom immoderate indulgence has rendered the sexual act at once a necessity and a weariness.

For the reasons indicated, I find it utterly impossible to treat the plaintiff's mere oath as of any value at all, when it stands alone in opposition to the evidence of credible witnesses.

Then, are the witnesses who depose to the particular acts of immorality with which the plaintiff is charged in the plea of justification credible witnesses?   In my opinion they are thoroughly so. These witnesses are Lakhmidás Khimji, and the two young men, Kálábhái Lalubhái and Chathurbhuj Wálji.   As to Lakhmidás Khimji, his credibility is beyond suspicion; a grave, respectable, intelligent man, of the highest position in his caste, animated by an earnest desire to purify the practices of his sect; he gave his evidence in a quiet, calm, straightforward manner, eminently calculated to conciliate belief; nor was he betrayed into a single inconsistency or self-contradiction in the course of a very long and searching cross-examination. The young Káyasth, Kálábhái Lalubhái, a son of the Sheristedár of the Sudder Adáwlut, gave his testimony with extreme intelligence and in a frank, artless, natural manner, which unavoidably created the impression that he was honestly speaking the truth. The young Bháttiá, Chathurbhuj, was a less intelligent person, but he too gave his evidence calmly and clearly, nor was he shaken in a single particular.

It was said that the testimony of these two young men was open to suspicion, because both were great friends of the defendant; because one had also been his pupil for some time at the Elphinstone Institution, and the other was the nephew of Dr. Dhirajrám. If they had told a less plain and unvarnished tale, if they had been shaken in cross-examination, if they had become confused or hesitating, if they had shown any eagerness of partizanship, I might have felt there was something in the suggestion; though even then it might fairly have been said that, in a case like this, no motive but one of friendship for the defendant, or earnest zeal for the reform of the sect, could induce people to brave odium (and, if members of the sect or caste—worse than odium) by coming forward to relate in open court what they knew of the malpractices of the Maháráj. But considering the mode in which these young men gave their evidence, the fact that one is a relation of Dr. Dhirajrám and that both are friends of the defendant, though it may have supplied a reason for watching their testimony more closely, affords none for discrediting in any way the testimony which in fact they gave. And that testimony was wholly uncontradicted except by the mere denial of the plaintiff—a denial which, for the reasons already more than sufficiently indicated, may be regarded for all purposes of evidence as practically worthless.

Kálábhái Lalubhái, who seems to have been on very intimate terms with the plaintiff, speaks to two instances, one in Surat and one in Bombay, in which he witnessed facts that can leave no reasonable doubt of illicit intercourse between the plaintiff and two ladies of the Baniá caste. The first took place at Surat about three years ago: "I was sitting," says the witness, "with the plaintiff and a male Banian in his 'diwánkháná.' A Banian girl, about 14 or 15, came in with a female servant of the Maháráj. She passed through the 'diwánkháná' where we were sitting and went into the side room: the Banian man immediately got up and went away; the plaintiff left the room and went into that into which the female had gone. I was a boy at the time" (he would have been about 13). "I attempted after some time to go into the room which the Maháráj had entered: I expected folded pán-sopári, and I went to get it. I entered the room. I saw the Maháráj sitting with a girl on a couch embracing and kissing. I did darshan (reverence) to him: he got up, took me by the arm, and took me out; he then gave me some pán-sopári; I then left and he went into the inner room again."

That is the first case: the second took place in Bombay, where the youth had renewed his intimacy with the plaintiff, and was well aware from conversation that had passed between them that his friend was acting in public the part of a reformer. Kálábhái had his suspicions as to the genuineness of these professions. "In consequence," he says, "of what I heard about the plaintiff, I once watched a lady to his house. I heard people say, pointing to her, 'that is a lady with whom the Maháráj has fallen in love.' I followed her to the plaintiff's house; she entered a doorway inside the 'diwánkháná.' I went into the 'diwánkháná' and sat there; the plaintiff was there; the plaintiff went inside, into the room the lady had entered. I did not go away. I remained sitting there about half an hour. The plaintiff came out; he had only his waist-cloth on. I began to smile; he asked me 'why are you laughing?' (he was laughing too). I said, 'You are certainly effecting a very great reform.' He laughed and said nothing. Presently, the lady came out; her dress was disordered. I looked at her and laughed. She laughed and went away. From her dress I can say she was a Banian: from her dress and jewels, I concluded she was a respectable woman."

That is the testimony of Kálábhái,—testimony given with a simplicity of manner and naturalness of detail, which it would be difficult to surpass; testimony which, unshaken as it was by cross-examination, and uncontradicted except by the bare denial of the plaintiff, I have no difficulty in believing to be substantially the truth.

Chathurbhuj, who also appears to have been a good deal about the plaintiff's house, deposes to have seen a third young lady introduced into the plaintiff's bedroom, and both he and Kálábhái concur as to the fact of those conversations between themselves and the plaintiff in which he maintained the doctrine, and confirmed it by the results of his own experience, that illicit intercourse with women is favorable to the health and vigour of the human system. These conversations are of course denied by the plaintiff, but it is also urged that they are intrinsically improbable. I do not think so. In this country, youths of 16 or 17 are often husbands and fathers : in no country do we find that lads of that age are indisposed to enter into such discussions. As to the improbability of the plaintiff's taking part in them, would there, it may be asked, be anything strange in a Mormon elder taking up such a topic in defence of polygamy, if pressed hard in argument by a couple of young unbelievers in the merits of that patriarchal institution ?

And now as to the evidence of Lakhmidás Khimji. I shall consider first that part of his testimony which relates to the plaintiff's conduct in Bombay, reserving to the last the consideration of that which relates to his earlier immoralities at Beyt. Lakhmidás Khimji, like many others, believed in the professions of reform with which the plaintiff introduced himself to the Vallabhácháryan public of Bombay. He was come to promote female education; he was open to argument on the question of widows' re-marriage. It was known —and this is a fact which should be borne in mind to the plaintiff's credit—that he had opened, and that he contributed to support, a flourishing boys' school at Surat, where instruction was given, amongst other things, in Sanskrit. These things more than counter-vailed with Lakhmidás Khimji the scandals of the plaintiff's youth; and he appears, from the moment of his arrival in Bombay, to have entered into warm and friendly relations with the new Maháráj. " I called on the plaintiff," he says, " the second or third day after his arrival. I was on friendly terms with him, saw him twice or thrice a day, invited him to my house, asked friends to meet him. I did this because he was making promises of effecting reform, abolishing these bad practices, and getting girls to be permitted to learn. I formed an opinion subsequently that plaintiff continued his former bad practices, and that for three or four months I had been misled. One day I went to his house and was sitting conversing when two females arrived; one of them had a silver goblet in her hand; she was about twenty; the other was a widow about forty; the young woman was a Cutchee Bháttián, a married woman."

The witness then goes on to state that the young lady having been conducted by a female servant into the bedroom, the plaintiff sent him off to the printer's to make immediate arrangements for the publication of some article. "I went downstairs," says the witness, "but some suspicion crossed my mind, and after a short time I went upstairs again into the same room; no one was there except the widow, who was standing beside the door; I continued sitting there till they came out. First the Maháráj came out: on observing me, he grew pale. Then the young lady came out; she was smiling and laughing; her rose-coloured 'sári' was in a confused, rumpled state; it had been all right when she went in. She had not the silver goblet. I presume she had given it to the Maháráj. Both the ladies shortly left. I remained. Nothing was said on the subject at that time, but in the evening," says the witness, "I went again. The Maháráj took me into an inner room to have some private conversation with me. He began: he said, 'What have you done with regard to the opening of female and other schools? Speak to Mangaldás and others; request their aid; get up a subscription list.' I said, 'Maháráj, this is all a sham; you profess to be a reformer, and to wish to open female schools; and in private you commit such bad acts, such adulteries.' His answer was, 'Yes, you might have suspected me, but I have not committed any bad acts; I only went in to accept food from the female.' To this I replied, 'You told me that when females came for that purpose you did not take them inside; if you went in to accept food, why did you leave the widow outside?' He did not answer that, and changed the conversation."

Such is the evidence of the defendant's witnesses as to the immoralities of the plaintiff during his recent residence in Bombay. I have reserved for the last the consideration of the scene which Lakhmidás Khimji deposes to having witnessed fifteen years ago at Beyt. Here, again, I shall let witness speak for himself:—

"There is a temple at Beyt dedicated to Laxmi ; the plaintiff threw gulál there. There were females present; he threw the gulál on the females, then on a number of persons near the gate. When the gulál was thrown in two or three handfuls, persons outside the inclosure could not see what was going on inside. Immediately after throwing the gulál, he squeezed the breasts of a young girl, a Bháttián, who was near the gate. She smiled. A few days after this, I and my uncle (Dámodar Devji) went to the plaintiff's house at Beyt; it was about one or half-past one o'clock in the day; he was lying in his bed. I and my uncle went up and began shampooing his legs. It is usual to do so when the Maháráj is lying down : regarding him as a God, shampooing his legs is considered a pious act. While so employed, the girl, whose breasts the Maháráj had squeezed, came accompanied by a widow. The widow came up and whispered to the Maháráj. He said, 'Go out.' I and my uncle then left the bedroom and went outside. The girl was left there; afterwards the widow came out and shut the door, and held the chain. The widow smiled, and asked my uncle if I would like to see Rás Lilá. We went in. The plaintiff was in the act of having carnal intercourse with the girl inside. The plaintiff said to my uncle, ' What will he (meaning me) give for seeing this?' My uncle said, 'He will do you service.' Before I went in I had agreed to give 100 Cutch cowries (about 30 rupees) for seeing the sight. I made my respects (darshan) and came out. I was then about 18 or 19 years of age. It is considered," continues the witness, "a pious act by Vaishnavas to witness the Rás Lilá of the Maháráj ; it is a custom in the sect to pay for witnessing this act; both the sectary who sees, and the woman who is enjoyed, pay. To have connexion with the Maháráj is considered to lead to 'Gowlok' (the paradise of the 16,000 gopis)."

Such is the sworn testimony of this very respectable witness, given with the most perfect simplicity and candour,—given as though he was relating nothing extraordinary—absolutely unshaken in cross-examination. The plaintiff, in answer to questions put by his counsel, contradicts absolutely and categorically the whole story. As to the value of that contradiction standing alone, nothing further need be said ; but on this part of the case the plaintiff attempted to

9

go beyond mere contradiction, and called three witnesses to throw doubt on the statement of Lakhmidás Khimji, by showing that in the temple he specifies at Beyt (the temple of Laxmi), gulál is never thrown on the worshippers, but only on the image, it being the temple of female divinity. The first of these witnesses, Devidás Hansráj, formerly superintendent for the Guicovár of the temples at Beyt, proves very little as to the point for which he is principally called. "Gulál," he says, "is thrown on the *images* in all the temples; but not on the worshippers when the image is female." But having thus laid down the rule, he admits there may be exceptions, for he adds, "a witness may have seen it thrown on the worshippers at Laxmi temples; I have not, that is all I mean."

Mithárám Purushottam, a Bháttiá from Rájkot, whose duty it was nine or ten years ago to follow the Mahárájás round the temples of Beyt and collect the tax due to the Guicowár from the devotees, gives the following evidence:—"Gulál was only thrown *on the worshippers* in the temple of Dwárkánáthji at Beyt: it is thrown *by the Mahárájás and the Brahmacháris.*

Premji Pujá, the third witness, a Pokarná Bráhmin, who has come down to Bombay to act as cook, but who previously for twenty years had been a servant in the temple of Rádháji, another female divinity at Beyt, contradicts witness No. 2 in two important particulars. Agreeing with him that gulál in Laxmi temple is only sprinkled on the image, he swears that even in the temple of Dwárkánáthji, it is only thrown *on the* musicians, *not on the worshippers;* thrown *not by the Mahárájás* at all, only by the Brahmacháris.

Even if the point were a material one, it is clear that this evidence of contradiction wholly fails: but the point is not a material one; the evidence of these very three witnesses shows this temple of Laxmi at Beyt to be one of five small shrines dedicated to different gods and goddesses, all of which are in close proximity. Lakhmidás Khimji, without any serious impeachment of his accuracy, may easily have mistaken one of these small shrines for another; or the plaintiff, to serve a particular object, may have done an act which was not strictly regular.

There is another objection to this whole story founded on the proposition that it is incredible in itself, as involving a violation not only of the most universally observed laws of decency, but of the very principles on which our common human nature is built up. This is a very inconclusive objection : it is not an objection likely to have any weight with those whom reading and experience have carried beyond the circle of home manners and home opinions. It is difficult for an Englishman of the nineteenth century to believe in the existence of such a state of manners as is depicted by Petronius or Martial, and yet we know that these two writers were the most fashionable and favorite authors among their Roman contemporaries; the very essence of their popularity consisting in the general truthfulness of their social portraitures. So in order to put ourselves in a position for judging adequately of the probable truth of such a story as this, we must endeavour to realise as best we can the state of feeling habitual among those whose corruptions it exposes. We must suppose the case of a weak and blinded people; a rapacious and libidinous priesthood ; a god whose most popular attributes are his feats of sexual prowess; a paradise whose most attractive title is that of "a boundless ocean of amorous enjoyment." But there is one plain fact which on this matter is worth a world of speculation. So little did Lakhmidas Khimji suppose that there was anything incredible in the story, that at a large party at Gokuldás Tejpál's, he made it the subject of an attack half-jocose, half-earnest against his uncle, who has now for some years been absent in Zanzibár. He mentioned the names of several highly respectable members of his caste and sect in whose presence the alleged attack was made : those witnesses were put into the box and tendered for cross-examination, but no question was put to them tending in any way to impugn the statement of Lakhmidás Khimji.

Such is the evidence in support of the charges made against the moral character of the plaintiff in the plea of justification ; on my mind that evidence leaves not a shadow of doubt; the charges made are, in my opinion, fully substantiated. Jadunáthji Maháráj is conclusively shown to have been in no degree superior in morality to the average of his brethren, and principally to have differed from them in the tact and cunning with which he employed public professions of zeal for reform as a convenient cloak for uncleanliness.

Having thus gone through all the observations I proposed to make on the evidence, there is only one other point on which I wish to say a few words.

This trial has been spoken of as having involved a great waste of the public time. I cannot quite agree with that opinion. No doubt much time has been spent in hearing this cause, but I would fain hope it has not been all time wasted. It seems impossible that this matter should have been discussed thus openly before a population so intelligent as that of the natives of Western India, without producing its results. It has probably taught some to think; it must have led many to enquire. It is not a question of theology that has been before us! it is a question of morality. The principle for which the defendant and his witnesses have been contending is simply this—that what is morally wrong cannot be theologically right—that when practices which sap the very foundations of morality, which involve a violation of the eternal and immutable laws of Right,—are established in the name and under the sanction of Religion, they ought, for the common welfare of society, and in the interest of humanity itself, to be publicly denounced and exposed. They have denounced—they have exposed them. At a risk and at a cost which we cannot adequately measure, these men have done determined battle against a foul and powerful delusion. They have dared to look custom and error boldly in the face, and proclaim before the world of their votaries that their evil is not good, that their lie is not the truth. In thus doing they have done bravely and well. It may be allowable to express a hope that what they have done will not have been in vain—that the seed they have sown will bear its fruit—that their courage and consistency will be rewarded by a steady increase in the number of those whom their words and their examples have quickened into thought, and animated to resistance, whose homes they have helped to cleanse from loathsome lewdness, and whose souls they have set free from a debasing bondage.

# THE INDIAN PRESS

ON THE

# MAHÁRÁJ LIBEL CASE.

## I.—*The Times of India.*

*Serus sed Serius,*—late but in earnest, must be our motto in commenting upon the judgment given last week in the great Maháráj libel case. The arrival of the English mail and other causes, have compelled us hitherto to defer the consideration of an event which must be regarded as having the most important bearing upon the interests of native society. It is true that the progress of reform and enlightenment may be looked on as ultimately safe, and beyond the influence of any particular events; but such events, if inauspicious, might retard the progress, though they could not arrest it. If, in the present case, the Maháráj's party had gained a triumph,—that circumstance would really have given them no protection or safety against the tide of enlightened ideas which is advancing irresistibly, and which is destined in a few years to change the entire surface of Hindu society. But such a triumph would have tended to conceal the real state of affairs; it would have given fresh hope to the reactionary spirits; and it would have had the undesirable effect of damping the courage of a very excellent and estimable set of men, whose main defect is not any want of intellectual discernment to see what is best, but a want of moral resolution to carry out what they know to be right in the face of opposition.

We are happy, however, to be able to congratulate the Reformers upon a substantial victory, which sets them quite above their adversaries, and which must necessarily fill them with confidence as regards the work which still lies before them in the future. The judgment, it is true, was a mixed one, and a verdict on the first plea with nominal damages was recorded for the plaintiff. This the Maháráj's party have endeavoured to avail themselves of, by adroitly announcing that the sum of five rupees was fixed by the Court in compassion to the poverty of the defendant, and that the smallness of the mulct merely shows the contemptible position of the person condemned. But this attempt to brave out the matter has been utterly unsuccessful. "The bazaar," however easily it may be gulled as to the probability of Russian invasions and the like. is sufficiently keen in judging of matters that are really brought home to itself, The natives know perfectly well the true meaning of the judgment. And the plaintiff's supporters who had prepared sweetmeats to be distributed among the caste on the evening of the decision, in celebration of the triumph which they hoped to win, were observed to refrain from any demonstration of the kind and exhibit a crestfallen demeanour.

We cannot of course deny that we wish the verdict had been otherwise. We wish that a complete victory, nominal as well as real, technical as well as substantial, had been awarded to the defendant. But there is consolation to be found even in the present result. The confidence which all sections of the natives feel in the Supreme Court, will surely be confirmed by observing the entire absence of partizanship which characterises the recent judgment. And, on the other hand, it becomes still more damnatory of the Maháráj, if after the the most equitable willingness to allow all points in his favour, it is found that neither of the judges is able to exonerate him from a single one of the charges laid against him, and that both of the judges unanimously declare that he must have deliberately perjured himself in almost every part of his evidence. Can any one believe that after this public revelation and exposure of his real character, Jadunáthji Brizrattanji will be able to maintain his position as a sanctified teacher, and an incarnation of God? The *Satya Prakásh* has in reality verified its name. Through a long night of superstition and darkness, vile creatures like this Maháráj have been able to make their dens of vice and debauchery seem to their spell-bound followers to be the holy temples of God. But as soon as the morning light comes, the place is found full of corruption and uncleanness; magical spells lose all their effect; and all men of a better sort rise disgusted, and at any cost break loose from such a haunt. We have no doubt that the greatest of all public services has been performed by the excellent and intelligent Karsandás Mulji for his countrymen, a service that must for ever bear fruit. And to commemorate their achievement and the glorious battle that they have fought, we think that the Reformers might well set up in their houses in golden character the noble and impressive words of Sir Joseph Arnould :—

"The principle for which the defendant and his witnesses have been contending is simply this—that what is morally wrong cannot be theologically right—that when practices which sap the very foundations of morality, which involve a violation of the eternal and immutable laws of right,—are established in the name and under the sanction of religion, they ought, for the common welfare of society, and in the interest of humanity itself, to be publicly denounced and exposed. They have denounced—they have exposed them. At a risk and at a cost which we cannot adequately measure, these men have done determined battle against a foul and powerful delusion. They have dared to look custom and error boldly in the face, and proclaimed before the world of their votaries that their evil is not good, that their lie is not the truth. In thus doing they have done bravely and well. It may be allowable to express a hope that what they have done will not have been in vain—that the seed they have sown will bear its fruit—that their courage and constancy will be rewarded by a steady increase in the number of those whom their words and their examples have quickened into thought and animated to resistance, whose homes they have helped to cleanse from loathsome lewdness, and whose souls they have set free from a debasing bondage."

We shall now turn from the moral and social aspects of the case, to say a very few words on the verdict as a legal decision. We are told that if the defendants had not pleaded "not guilty"—that if they had contented themselves with the plea of "justification" they must have got a simple verdict in their favour, with costs. The first question then that arises, is this, were the defendants to blame for entering a plea which they could not support? Was the flaw in their victory caused merely by a piece of technical imprudence,—in short by a false move on the part of the defendants' legal advisers? We think that the answer to this question depends entirely on the purpose with which the plea was entered. If it was entered with a view to some technical advantage possibly arising out of it; if it was put in with any intention of evading the real grounds of the issue,— we should then feel the less regret that a defeat had been suffered on the plea. But if, as appears more likely, the defendants considered the plea to be *bonâ fide* defensible, though at the same time they did not propose denying the publication of the so-called "libel," it then remains to be asked,—What was the view of their case, which caused a verdict to be given against them? Now it is always allowed that pleas in a defence need not of necessity be congruous and consistent with each other. They may resemble the excuses of the washerwoman in the case of the broken mangle, who said, *first*, that she had sent back the mangle quite sound, and *second*, that it was broken before it was lent to her. But it does not appear that there was even that allowable amount of incongruity in the pleas of the recent libel case. Libel stands on a different footing from other things. In a case of homicide, if the accused person pleads *first* "not guilty," and *second* that the homicide was justifiable, those pleas are inconsistent. But in a case of libel the affair is different. For the plea of not guilty is not a mere question of fact, but a question of *animus*. The essence of a libel is not defamation, but defamation accompanied by malice. And thus, as a matter of fact, the "libel" may have been published, but the publisher of it may obtain a verdict on the head of "not guilty" if his *animus* was proved to be devoid of malice; and again he may obtain a verdict on the plea of justification if the defamatory accusations were proved to be true. In the opinion of the puisne Judge, the defendant was entitled to a verdict on both those pleas; in the opinion of the Chief Justice he was entitled to a verdict on the plea of justification only. The point of difference between the judges turned on the view taken of the defendant's position, and we must confess that the views taken by Sir Joseph Arnould appear to us broad, penetrating, and just, while those of the Chief Justice were narrow in their scope, and too much limited by an exclusive reference to technical precedents. Sir Matthew Sausse refused to acknowledge any public duty in the editor of a newspaper to expose abuses : he refused to consider the *controversial* article written by Mr. Karsandás Mulji as having any but a merely personal character : and he, as we think, mistakingly refused to consider the atrocious acts of the Mahráj, committed in his priestly and official character to have anything of a public import. To all these views we think the replication of Sir Joseph Arnould to be overwhelming ; and, as in duty bound, we wish to place on record our appreciation and admiration of the following passage :—

" Such was the defendant's position. *What was his consequent interest and duty ?*  •

" As a Vallabhácháryan addressing his co-sectaries, as a Banian addressing his caste fellows—above all, as a journalist addressing readers composed principally of followers of the Mahárájás—had he no interest, had he no duty in denouncing the malpractices which it is the principal object of the alleged libel to expose ? It appears to me that he had both an interest and a duty. ·

" A public journalist is a public teacher : the true function of the press—that by virtue of which it has rightly grown to be one of the great powers of the modern world, is the function of teaching, elevating, and enlightening those who fall within the range of its influence.

" To expose and denounce evil and barbarous practices ; to attack usages and customs inconsistent with moral purity and social progress, is one of its highest, its most imperative, duties. When those evils and errors are consecrated by time, fenced round by customs, countenanced and supported by the highest and most influential class in society—when they are wholly beyond the control and supervision of any other tribunal—then it is the function and the duty of the press to intervene, honestly endeavouring by all the powers of argument, denunciation, and ridicule, to change and purify the public opinion which is the real basis on which these evils are built, and the real power by which they are perpetuated.

" As editor of the *Satya Prakásh*, the defendant was, in my opinion, acting within the clear limits of his duty (as defined in the case of Harrison *v.* Bush) in denouncing to a public principally composed of Bháttiás and Banians, the moral delinquencies of the Mahárájás."—*Times of India, May* 2, 1862.

## II.—*The Bombay Gazette.*

Shortly after the Coup d'Etat of Louis Napoleon, a law was issued in France against the liberty of the press. Almost simultaneously, a Napoleonic *sic volo, sic jubeo* was issued to the editor of a journal in Paris, to the effect that, if he continued to remain totally silent on political matters, he would incur the displeasure of the Powers. The Paris editor had an article next day, headed "The Liberty of Silence." No enlightened man can doubt that a government or a country must suffer incalculably more by imposing a constrained silence on the press, than by granting an unrestricted liberty to it. The "Maháráj Libel Case," on which the judgment of the Supreme Court was delivered yesterday, was one of paramount importance in its bearings upon many vital interests, upon none more than upon the liberty of communion. What is society without this liberty? If earnest men in society have not the liberty of communion with one another respecting the vilest conceivable abuses that prevail in their midst, that society is in degraded bondage. There was but one opinion in the community as to the nature of the judgment that would be pronounced in this case. It was universally expected that it would be one which would vindicate the liberty of the press, the justice of English law, the cause of progress in this land, and more especially the moral reform which is struggling to make headway in this community against the most powerfully antagonistic influences. The judgment delivered by the Puisne Judge, Sir Joseph Arnould, has fully realized and justified the public expectation. In his judgment, Karsandás Mulji is not guilty of libel; there was the most fully justifying occasion for his exposure of the scandalous practices of the Maháráj, and the justification has been completely established. We regret that we are not able to characterise in the same terms the judgment of the Chief Justice, Sir Matthew Sausse. In his judgment Karsandás is guilty of libel, and there was not justifying occasion for his accusations against the Maháráj. At the same time, the Chief Justice considered the justification established. His judgment, therefore, was for the Maháráj on the plea of libel,— damages five rupees, without costs. This will go forth as the judgment of Her Majesty's Supreme Court in this important case. We greatly wish that Her Majesty's Judges had been of one mind in this matter. We need not say that we fully agree with the Puisne Judge; if we did not, we believe that we should stand alone, in an inglorious isolation from the public of Bombay, European and native, unconnected with the case. "The greater the truth, the greater the libel." Yes; but only when the libellous truth is uttered in malice. The justice of the legal adage depends, not upon the mere fact of the libellous character of certain allegations, nor upon the fact that the libellous allegations are founded in truth, but upon the fact that the true libellous allegations have been prompted by envious, selfish, and malicious feelings. When there is no evidence of such prompting, nothing to warrant the suspicion of it, a libel is not greater, but less, the greater its truth. There are cases where it is proper and necessary to expose the character and design of the base, as a safeguard to the public good, or a warning to the innocent when they are exposed to danger and suffering. It certainly could not be said with any truth—the greater this propriety and necessity, the greater the libel. Such a proper and necessary exposure has nothing in it which partakes of the nature and character of a libel. We have said that there are such cases: we must guard our meaning against misapprehension, by adding that such cases are probably comparatively rare. When they do occur, however, and are conducted with becoming tenderness and self-denial, the one who makes the exposure must be regarded as in every sense of the word a public benefactor. Such a case certainly is that of the exposure of the Maháráj; and such a public benefactor is Karsandás Mulji. This "Maháráj Libel Case" has convinced the public that immorality is no name for the debauched, adulterous lives led by those satyrs the Mahárájás under the name of religion, nay—of divinity. If it ever could be proper and necessary to expose the character, designs, and practices of the profligate and libertine as a safeguard to the public good, it certainly was so in the case of these Mahárájás. In the exposure that has been made, every intelligent person must be struck with the temperate, judicious, and conscientious tone and character of it. The only wonder is that Karsandás, with so much knowledge of the evil practices of the Maháráj, and so much knowledge of the injury to public morals from those practices, could have exercised such moderation and self-denial in exposing them. The efforts he first made to persuade the Mahárájás personally to renounce those practices of which it is a shame even to speak, evinced a becoming tenderness and desire to avoid exposure : the efforts he then made to move the sect to exert its united authority or influence for the same purpose evinced a real sincerity, an honesty of intention, and a freedom from selfish motives : the efforts which he finally made, after all others had failed, to try the virtue of a public appeal to the Mahárájás through the press, which he knew would put enmity between his caste and himself, and raise up a storm of foul-mouthed reproach against him, evinced a firmness, self-denial, and determination to effect the necessary reform, which are admirable in themselves, and which would have had the desired effect upon any but those sunk in the sottishness of lust. Karsandás has done his duty. We are very far from viewing him in the character of a thorough reformer; but he has probably acted up to the light and convictions which he has received, and we trust he will receive more light and stronger convictions. He has done his duty. And although he has met with opposition in the discharge of it, he has not yet, like many a more thorough reformer, "resisted unto blood, striving against sin." We trust, therefore, that his good intentions and his courage will not fail him,—that he will not draw back in dismay, now that he has "put his hand to the plough." He has done his duty. The European community and the more enlightened members of the native community, who desire the civilization and improvement of their fellow-subjects, should consider this fact, and should give him the support to which he is justly entitled. Let no one feel himself justified in withholding his support from the consideration that Karsandás has not gone far enough, or that he has gone too far. In so important a matter, such objections would be most flimsy, and would belie any show of interest in native improvement. The matter is a really important one in itself and in its bearings ; and it will argue the want of a sense of responsibility on the part of our own countrymen, if they refrain from doing what they legitimately may do to countenance, encourage, and support Karsandás and his associates : it will argue the want of moral courage on the part of the more enlightened members of the native community, if they refrain from giving their countenance, encouragement, and support.  The cause is one of public morals.  We are not viewing it in a religious point of view at all.  We suppose that few of our own countrymen in Bombay had any suspicion that such gross immoralities as those which this "Maháráj Libel Case" has publicly exposed were countenanced and practised by the men with whom they have daily intercourse in the way of business; or that they had any idea that they were living in the midst of a people whose social customs and religious observances were of such a debased character as they have now publicly been shown to be.  If the natives have any respect for the opinions of their European acquaintances and friends, the knowledge on their part that the latter are now aware of the disgusting and abominable things that are done of them in secret, must have a salutary effect upon them.  We call upon them to renounce these hidden works of darkness : to protect their wives and daughters from the vile designs of adulterers : to behave themselve like men, and not like beasts.  If one thing more than another proves the besotted character of these Mahárájás, it is the fact that they have been so infatuated as to provoke this exposure and drag their own filthiness before the public—"raging waves of the sea, foaming out their own shame."  If these men are your gods, what must your devils be!  The judgment delivered yesterday will be published in a few days.  We wait with impatience for that of Sir Joseph Arnould, one of the most eloquent, impressive, and just ever delivered from the Bench of the Supreme Court in Bombay.  We shall return to the subject on the publication of the judgments.—*Bombay Gazette, April* 22, 1862.

## III.—*The Bombay Satarday Review.*

The moral effect of the judgment of the Supreme Court of Bombay in the cause which for so many weeks has engaged public attention, and upon the issue of which may be said to have depended the fate of reform and reformers in our Presidency, has been unfortunately marred by the disagreement of the two Judges on a question of great legal, but no substantial importance.  While freely admitting the dignified impartiality of Sir Matthew Sausse's judgment, and the care and labour he has used to work out a conscientious verdict, we cannot but think it a matter to be deeply regretted, that, although the learned Chief Justice agreed with his colleague in stigmatizing the Maháráj as one guilty of the foulest adultery and the most deliberate perjury, and although he therefore decided that the defendant who was accused of libelling this man had justified that libel on every point by proving that he only spoke the simple truth, Sir Matthew nevertheless found himself compelled to come to the conclusion that the plaintiff is entitled to a verdict with nominal damages on the plea of "not guilty."  The argument of the Chief Justice is that there was no "justifying occasion" for the publication of the libel by the defendant. He says to the defendant: "Whatever you alleged is true; but you have failed to show that the plaintiff gave you any provocation to publish this truth; and the English law so tenderly respects the sacredness of private character, that I am bound to declare your article a libel in the eye of the law." If we read the judgment aright, Sir Matthew contends that no "justifying occasion" can be said to have arisen, except in cases in which the parties accused of publishing libels have a strong interest in the matter concerned, or have commented on written or printed documents which challenged public discussion. This may be good law—that is to say, if a judge should always cling to the letter instead of being guided by the spirit of the law—but to a layman at least it certainly appears that the larger sympathies and more liberal views of Sir Joseph Arnould have brought him to a verdict more consistent with justice and common sense. Not the least convincing passage of a judgment as eloquent and as impressive as we ever heard in a court of justice was the argument of the Puisne Justice in support of the position that there had been "justifying occasion" for the publication of the libel. Sir Joseph Arnould showed first that it was the interest of the defendant as a member of the Baniá caste to expose the filthy practices by which the Mahárájás and their followers disgraced the community to which he belonged, and that it was his duty as a public journalist to denounce immoralities which, under the sacred name of religion, were corrupting the very heart of society. To whom then, the Puisne Justice next asked, was the defendant to appeal? The courts of law were not open to him, for the Mahárájás, however vicious they might be, had been guilty of no crime in committing adultery with women whose husbands and fathers presented them for that purpose to priests whom they believed to be incarnations of the Deity. He could not hope that, if he appealed to those who were formerly his fellow-sectaries, they would support him; he knew, on the contrary, that they would cast him out from their midst as one accursed, and persecute him with unrelenting hatred. To whom could he turn, or in what way could he satisfy his righteous indignation and do his duty as a teacher of the people, except by appealing at the bar of public opinion? But, even although this was the only resource left him, the defendant contented himself with attacking the Mahárájás generally and the doctrines of the Vallabháchárya religion; and it was not till Jadunáthji Maháráj himself offered provocation by starting a journal of his own in which he constituted himself the champion of the faith, that the editor of the *Satya Prakásh* at last singled out this Maháráj by name, and charged him personally with practising the very vices he affected to deplore in others. All these circumstances seemed to Sir Joseph Arnould to furnish the "justifying occasion" for the publishing of the libel, and we do not know what can be said in answer to his exact and luminous reasoning. But the Puisne Justice was overruled by the Chief, and in consequence a verdict has been given which enables the partizans of the Maháráj to hold up their heads, and to proclaim through the bazaar that their master has gained the day, and that the Court has awarded him nominal damages solely out of compassion for the poverty of the defendant. The natives, of course, do not care to understand the technicalities of the law courts; the only fact plain to their comprehension is that there has been an apparent compromise; and it is deplorable that such should be the result of a merely technical difference of opinion between the Judges. In a case of this sort, in which the verdict could not fail to exercise a wide influence on the popular mind, it was allowable for Sir Matthew Sausse to look beyond the limits of the Court, and to consider what would be the effect of a judgment in which the slightest inclination in favour of the Maháráj would be sure to be misconstrued.

The mischief, however, is done; and it remains for the press to point out, as clearly as possible, that with regard to the only substantial plea, the plea of justification, the opinion of the Chief Justice as to the guilt of the Maháráj is quite as decided, and the language in which he expresses that opinion quite as strong, as Mr. Justice Arnould's. There was not the least shadow of hesitation left on the mind of either of the Judges as to the truth of the evidence given for the defence, and the worthlessness of the evidence offered on behalf of the plaintiff. It had been distinctly proved, both Judges were agreed, that the Mahárájás in general are in the habit of committing adultery with the wives and daughters of their sectaries, and that the conduct of the plaintiff Jadunáthji has been as filthy and abominable as that of any of his colleagues. Both the Chief Justice and Sir Joseph Arnould, too, emphatically declared the plaintiff to be a man utterly unworthy of credit, and that he had come into Court with an affectation of purity which his craft and intelligence enabled him to assume, for the purpose of upsetting, if he could, by systematic and deliberate perjury the strong evidence given to prove that he had led a horribly dissolute life. With unblushing countenance he had sworn in the witness-box that he knew not what it was to have connection with strange women, and that it was impossible for him, the priest and leader of his people, to commit impure or immoral acts; yet the testimony of respectable medical witnesses established beyond a doubt the fact that he had suffered from a disease which could only have been brought upon him by his immorality, and to this testimony he had nothing to oppose but his simple denial, his counsel prudently declining to call as witnesses medical men who had been asked to examine him in the hope that they might find he had been afflicted with some other complaint. Since he had lied thus shamelessly on one important point, it became impossible to put faith in a word he said; and were the man not utterly hardened against exposure, he would, after the publication of the judgment of the Court, shrink from the light of day, throw away the mask of religion, with which, like the veiled prophet Mokanna, he has concealed the features of the satyr beneath the appearance of the god, and so save his deluded followers from further misery and degradation.

But, if repentance and reform are not to be expected from the Maháráj, if all that can be done with him is to bring him as a criminal to the bar of the Supreme

Court, and have him punished for his perjuries, we may at least hope that some of those who have believed in him most firmly will be driven by the storm of public ridicule and public indignation to renounce a creed of which perhaps for the first time they have had the impiety and bestiality laid bare to their view. Henceforth, it will be impossible for any respectable Banian or Bháttiá to frequent a Vallabháchárya temple without exposing the honour of his family to suspicion. Many amongst them, no doubt, have been as ignorant as the public in general were before this trial took place of the debauched habits of the Mahárájás; or, if they knew what was done, they considered such practices to be sanctioned by their religion. The whole truth has now been revealed to them; they have learnt that their faith is a foul and wretched superstition unknown to the founders of the Hindu religion, and that all intelligent men look upon them with amazement and with scorn as votaries of a creed which sanctifies the worst passions of our nature and deifies the most degraded of mankind. Knowing how strongly entrenched in each man's heart are the superstitions which he has been taught to lisp in his childhood, and which have grown with his growth and strengthened with his strength, we fear that the ignorant mass of the Vaishnavas will still cling to their former faith; but at least the exposure the Mahárájás have had the folly to provoke will encourage the more thoughtful and enlightened amongst them to throw off their allegiance to the abject creatures they have worshipped as gods, and their example may in time effect a revolution. To all such we cannot say anything in the way of exhortation so effective as the bold and earnest words with which Sir Joseph Arnould fitly concluded his judgment:—"It is not a question of theology that has been before us; it is a question of morality. The principle for which the defendant and his witnesses have been contending is simply this—that what is morally wrong cannot be theologically right—that when practices which sap the very foundations of morality, which involve a violation of the eternal and immutable laws of Right,—are established in the name and under the sanction of Religion, they ought, for the common welfare of society, and in the interest of humanity itself, to be publicly denounced and exposed. They have denounced— they have exposed them. At a risk and at a cost which we cannot adequately measure, these men have done determined battle against a foul and powerful delusion. They have dared to look custom and error boldly in the face, and proclaimed before the world of their votaries that their evil is not good, that their lie is not the truth. In thus doing they have done bravely and well. It may be allowable to express a hope that what they have done will not have been in vain—that the seed they have sown will bear its fruit—that their courage and constancy will be rewarded by a steady increase in the number of those whom their words and their examples have quickened into thought and animated to resistance, whose homes they have helped to cleanse from loathsome lewdness, and whose souls they have set free from a debasing bondage."—*Bombay Saturday Review, April* 26, 1852.

## IV.—*The Indian Banner.*

TRIUMPH OF CIVILISATION.—There is a pleasure to watch the triumph of truth and progress in this world of probation. Whatever the trials and turmoils that human insanity inflicts at the onset upon a man righteously devoted to the cause of truth and progress, we recognize in his *ultimate* triumph the protecting hand of Providence, disposing events to march up to their destined goal of success. We have watched the indictment, the prosecution, the trial and the sentence pronounced in our Supreme Court on the recent case in which was involved the weal or the woe of a large and by no means an unimportant section of the native community, and we have not failed to recognise this grand moral maxim. Mr. Karsandás is triumphant; his cause is triumphant; and we think not so much of it as interesting as the moral effects which that triumph is calculated to produce upon the minds of his ignorant fellow countrymen.

\*          \*          \*          \*          \*          \*

A man just like ordinary men, in many respects far less in mind and heart, claims descent from the Beneficent Creator—nay holds himself a part and parcel of that Awful Being. Hundreds and thousands of men put implicit faith in his arrogant pretension and worship him. But how? to our shame, let the following extract speak for it :—

"In the morning when the Maháráj is at his ablutions, a number of persons collect at a short distance, and as he stands up to wipe his body, one of the Vaishnavas, approaching him with reverence, takes into a vessel the water dripping from his *potíd* (the cloth covering the lower part of his body). This dirty, impure water is esteemed to be of high value and distributed among all present at the temple, who drink it with feelings of pride. Some of it is reserved until the next day for the purification of absent Vaishnavas. The remnants of the Mahárájás' meals are called *juthan;* they are preserved as very precious stuff, and can be had on a formal application by any Vaishnava who desires to eat them. At private banquets and caste feasts, given with the Maháráj's permission, these impure remnants are first served, and are eaten as though they were ambrosia. The pán-sopári which the Maháráj throws out after chewing, is also collected and preserved, to be distributed to males and females, who alike take a great pleasure in chewing it over again.

"In the month of Shravan, the Maháráj takes delight in sitting on the *hindollá* (a sort of swing) when his male and female followers move it backwards and forwards with their hands. This privilege of swinging His Holiness is purchased with presents to him. At the time of the Holi holidays, one of the Mahárájás stands in the street near the temple in the Fort, and permits his followers to hail him with gulál (red powder). Some of the Mahárájás on such occasions, throw the gulál in return on some favourite female worshippers, and indulge publicly in indecent and improper scenes. On sad or joyful occasions, the Maháráj is invited to private residences, and for his trouble receives a present of from ten to one hundred rupees. He is often asked to visit a *sevak* or death-bed, when he puts his foot on the breast of the dying person with the view to free him of his sins, and receives for his blessing from ten to one thousand rupees."

In no region of the world was man ever degraded so low. The water that comes dripping from his potiá corresponding to our pijámas for the lower part of the body, when the Maháráj is bathing, is collected into a vessel with all the dirt and impurities which—oh! it shocks our feelings to speak more particularly of the impurities coming from the filthy flesh—distributed among all present at the temple and drunk with feelings of pride and exhilaration! The pán-sopári is chewed by the Maháráj, and the insipid remnant that is thrown out from the mouth, collected most reverentially, and distributed among the followers of the dismal faith—males and females alike—and chewed over again as ambrosia from their gods! But our terrible charge against the monstrosity of the Mahárájás yet remains. It is said they call in females to worship them; and it is something too much for wild human nature—and the nature of these Mahárájás is such from the want of a previous systematic development of the mind—to resist the evil temptation, when they hear the footsteps of the beauties of the first water tripping on their floors, with soul and heart entirely yielded up into their hands. This, an Elphinstone Scholar, Mr. Karsandás, then editing a vernacular journal, loudly complained against; and the especial victim of his caricatures brought an action of libel against the writer. We confess the latter had in his zeal allowed himself to be betrayed into much extravagant vaporing against the Maháráj—who, whatever the faults of men of his class—was one much above the orthodox views. . . . . . (But) the bitter tone of our friend spoke terribly on the Maháráj and his followers. The former instituted a suit for libel, and the latter combined to give any evidence against the practices of their religious head, so as to throw our poor editor singly upon himself into the arena of the Court of Justice. The result of their combination was very ably calculated—*the writer was to be ruined*. But in an evil hour for themselves, Mr. Karsandás brought an action of conspiracy against the chief instigators of this illegal measure of the Hindu community, and the prosecution ended in triumph. It has been the triumph of the glorious liberty of the Press as well as the triumph of progress in Western India. Generally speaking, the Bháttiás and the Banians, who make up the agitation community of our Presidency, are ignorant and unthinking, and the moral effects of their defeat will never be lost to them. The conspiracy case arose out of the Maháráj libel case; it was condemnatory on its very face and hence the defendants suffered; but in the rude simplicity of their mind our Hindu brethren will ascribe this their defeat to their advocacy of the Maháráj cause, which, with their proverbial timidity, they will henceforth astutely eschew to espouse openly. They might passively oppose all reforms; but their effort at active opposition being thus nipped at the very onset, they are not expected henceforth to puff themselves into importance on any measure against the Reformers, and if a native Guizot were to compile at some future period a work on the "History of Civilisation in India," we believe the raciest chapter in the book will be that which will treat of " Mr. Karsandás and his Prosecution." March on, Progress, thine is the day! Glory, Reformer, thine is the VICTORY!—*Indian Banner, December 22, 1861.*

## V.—*The Bámdád or Dawn.*

We beg to acknowledge with thanks receipt of the Report of the great Libel Case both in English and Gujaráti. We are glad to find that the proceedings of this important case are preserved in these forms. They will ever remain as witnesses testifying to the vile and debasing nature of the Vallabháchárya system of religion; and also to the immoral and beastly character of its teachers, the Mahárájás. Our space being pre-occupied, we are prevented from making any lengthened remarks on the Report. We must, however, make room to say a word on the decision of the Court. We have read this decision with great satisfaction, and our satisfaction would have been altogether complete had the Chief Justice taken the same view of the case as his colleague. The technical objections he took to the plea of not guilty, and the enforcement of nominal damages of five rupees, have somewhat marred the effect of his otherwise most able and weighty judgment. Looking at it in a legal point of view, we are constrained to say that it is a judgment that will ever do honour to the name of Sir Matthew Sausse, and will place him among those eminent men who have adorned the English Bench in this or in their own native country. The judgment of Sir Joseph Arnould is all that could be desired. It is to say in a single sentence the most eloquent, powerful, and satisfactory judgment that was perhaps ever pronounced in any of the Indian courts of justice. We happened to be present in the Court on the day the decision was given by the Judges, and we shall never forget the earnest tone of Sir Joseph. He seemed to have felt that he had a great duty to perform, and he certainly performed it well. Being convinced by the evidence produced in the Court that the Mahárájás and their tenets were of immoral and debasing character, he did not shrink from denouncing them in language, the force of which will ever remain unabated. We admire Sir Joseph for the breadth of his thought, for his strong sense of justice, for his perfect honesty, for his love of liberty, and for his legal attainments.* He has shown himself a thorough Englishman by upholding and vindicating the cause of truth and humanity.

We shall now say a word or two about the principal parties concerned in this case before concluding. The first and foremost is the Maháráj Jadunáthji himself. It must be confessed that he showed great courage and independence of mind by appealing to the Supreme Court for what he considered defamation of character. Hardly any other Maháráj would have done such a thing, and certain

10

we are that no other Maháráj would have appeared in the Court, as he did, to give evidence. But by so doing he has worked out his own and his brother Mahárájás' ruin. It is well that he took refuge in the Court, otherwise we should not have known half the truth concerning these gurus and their religion. Their immoral character has been incontestibly established, and we would advise them to leave off the evil of their ways and to seek the knowledge of that truth which by its renovating influence will change them for the better. The counsels of both sides did their duty to the best of their capacity, but it were ungrateful not to notice that the success of the case in favour of the defendants is very much owing to the great skill, the legal acumen, the immense researches, and the unwearied efforts of their witnesses' counsel, Mr. Anstey. The name of Chisholm Anstey, the successful barrister, will not easily be forgotten in the Bombay community. The witnesses whose evidence seems to have decided the case are the Rev. Dr. Wilson, Drs. Bháu Dáji and Dhirajrám Dalpatrám, and Messrs. Mathurádás Lowji and Lakhmidás Khimji. Dr. Wilson's clear and comprehensive evidence did much to throw down the wicked pretensions of the Vallabháchárya religion. Mr. Bayley seemed to have felt the weight of this evidence, as is obvious from the manner in which he spoke of Dr. Wilson in one of his addresses. Dr. Bháu Daji's and Mr. Mathurádás's evidence clearly established the bad character of the Mahárájás in general, and of the plaintiff in particular. The evidence of Dr. Dhirajrám and Mr. Lakhmidás left no doubt as to the fact that the plaintiff is a monster of wickedness in human form. These have laid the friends of native improvement under the greatest obligation. We thank them for the bold, uncompromising, and intelligent way in which they gave their evidence. The last, but the most important, party we have to name is Mr. Karsandás Mulji, the chief defendant in the case. We do not know in what words to express our admiration of this gentleman. For years past he has fearlessly denounced their errors, superstitions, and immoralities: and has laboured unweariedly to enlighten them by the light he possesses. There is no pride or vanity about him; but he is sincerely desirous of the welfare of his brethren. It was from the purest motives to do good that he penned the article, which raised such a storm in the Vaishnava community as was never witnessed before. The Maháráj Jadunáthji and his blind devotees used every way and means in their power to induce him to offer an apology to his offended holiness; and an apology from Mr. Karsandás Mulji would have seated Jadunáthji and his fellow Mahárájás on their gádis seven times more firmly than before. But this naturally timid gentleman, when he perceived that efforts were being made to make him succumb to the authority of the Maháráj, boldly stood out as a lion, and refused to listen to any compromise. During the proceedings of the case in the Court, promises and threatenings were addressed to him that he might come to some understanding with the Maháráj, but all to no avail. He felt that he had truth on his side, and that it would be unworthy to yield to any improper influence. He had very few friends to stand by him at first and of these few there were some who, had the Bháttia Conspiracy Case been decided against him, would have, like genuine Banians, with one hand on the *págri* and the other on the *dhotar* ran away from him, and joined the ranks of the Maháráj. He made up his mind to go on with the case at all risks, and his consistency and perseverance have been rewarded. The cause of truth has at last prevailed. A most degrading superstition is exploded : the teachers and propagators of this superstition are in the estimation of enlightened men cast down to the lowest depths from that proud, high position which they enjoyed for three hundred years : and the way of reformation thrown open. Mr. Karsandás Mulji has the honour of being the chief instrument in bringing about these results. His name will descend to posterity as that of a brave, genuine Reformer. It will ever be associated with the cause of reformation in this country.

Before concluding these remarks we have a suggestion to make to our educated young men, and to all the friends of native improvement. Our suggestion is this, that considering the toils and troubles Mr. Karsandás has undergone in connection with the Libel case, and the services he has rendered to the cause of morality and humanity by his disinterested and manly conduct, some acknowledgment ought to be made of these services. We shall feel very much disappointed if something is not done towards this object. Many persons have received testimonials from the people of Bombay, but we question very much if any of those gentlemen was more entitled to a testimonial than our friend Mr. Karsandás. The amount of suffering and pain he has undergone in the last twelve months for the good of his fellowmen, no one can tell ; and it will not redound to the honour of Young Bombay and others who have the welfare of the country at heart if they allow this opportunity to slip without giving an expression of their sympathy with the person who endured so much in doing good to his fellowmen.

We are not done with this Libel case. It suggests many important questions, and serious considerations. We have neither space nor time to touch upon these in the present number of the *Bámdád*. We hope to return to this subject soon. In the meanwhile let our friends the Reformers and the whole body of the Vaishnavas ask what are they to do now? The Vallabháchárya religion which they professed is no religion at all, but a system of lies and delusions,—a system wholly opposed to the glory of God, and the wellbeing of man. It is clear that a religion like this no man who has a particle of good sense or right feeling will ever follow. What are you, friends, then to do? Some of you may perhaps reply, we shall take leave of it, and have nothing to do with it. Very good, but what next? You cannot do without religion. You cannot acquit yourselves as rational men without the aid of true religion. Your enquiries, therefore, should be directed to ascertain the religion which is of God, and not of man.—*Bámdád or Dawn, for April.*

## VI.—*Oriental Christian Spectator.*

EDITORIAL NOTE.—We have now, with considerable exertion,—though in the matter we have received the kind assistance of some friends,—completed the article on the Maháráj Libel Case which we promised to our readers some time ago. It contains the official documents laid before the Supreme Court; the substance of the evidence adduced on both sides (which we have taken principally from the report printed at the *Gazette* Press and published at the office of the *Times of India*); and the elaborate and searching judgments of Sir Matthew Sausse and Sir Joseph Arnould. Many of our readers, who will admit the necessity, in the present circumstances of India,—with other systems of corruption defiling the land but partially explored,—of a record being made in this periodical of the great contest for truth and purity in which that most amiable and promising reformer, Karsandás Mulji, and his associates have been lately engaged, will decline to read the disgusting details of this remarkable trial. Their entire avoidance of them may be altogether expedient in many cases, while the study of them, with some attention, may be incumbent on the philanthropist, the reformer, and the statesman. The apostolical advice of Paul to the Gentile converts at Ephesus is applicable to all in a case of this kind: "Have no fellowship with the unfruitful works of darkness, but rather reprove (or expose) them. For it is a shame even to speak of those things that are done of them in secret. But all things that are reproved (or exposed) are made manifest by the light: for whatsoever doth make manifest is light." Even though shame must be felt in the very imagination, or expression in conversation, of the deeds of darkness, they must, to bring about their cessation, be both laid open and reprobated. Light must be thrown on the darkest places and darkest deeds of iniquity, that they may be brought to a speedy termination. There is often a moral power even in disgust, which, in some important quarters, cannot be dispensed with. There is a great difference between writing of evil to entice to its commission, and showing its existence, to deter from its commission.

We should have been glad to have given a report of the pleadings of counsel on both sides of this case; but our space, on which we have much encroached by devoting to it considerably more than the number of pages contained in any two issues of our periodical, forbad us to make the attempt. This is the less to be regretted, as of these pleadings but very imperfect notes have been preserved. They were of an able character, particularly in behalf of the defendant. Mr. Anstey's efforts, both in his searching examinations and impassioned exposures of the evils with which he had to deal, will never be forgotten in Bombay.

The *Friend of India* has proposed that Sir Joseph Arnould's admirable judgment should be translated into the various languages of India, and published as a tract. With a general view of the evidence, it has already appeared in Gujaráti. It is intended, we believe, to give it in the Brij-Bháshá, as soon as practicable.

Some notices in the Indian press of this extraordinary trial, we hope to give in an early issue.—*Oriental Christian Spectator, for July and August,* 1862.

## VII.—*The Deccan Herald.*

The judgment in the great Maháráj libel case has at length been made public; curiosity has been satisfied, and the verdict of Her Majesty's Judges is now a topic of general conversation. It is to be regretted that the opinion of the two Justices is divided, as it is feared that the apparent difference in their decisions will give rise to a considerable amount of litigation. That the plaintiff will appeal to the Privy Council, cannot reasonably be doubted, and indeed, we have heard that special counsel has already been retained in England for this purpose. Substantially, the verdict is in favour of the defendant, who has successfully vindicated the right of free discussion. No public writer need now be afraid to appear before Her Majesty's Judges, if their cause is good, and their evidence unimpeachable. Sir Joseph Arnould has, in his judgment, placed the liberty of the Press upon a basis of security which it never previously occupied. Only a very few years ago, to be called upon to defend an action in the Supreme Court, for libel, was one of the most perilous positions in which a journalist could be placed. We remember upon one occasion, the counsel for the defendant, in an alleged libel case, advising the adoption of a compromise, at all hazards, on the grounds that having the ear of the Court, he knew that a determination existed in the mind of one of the Judges to make an example of the first Indian Editor— who had the misfortune to be cast in damages—that came before him. His Lordship's decisions had provoked the criticisms of the press, and he, therefore, awaited in grim expectancy the advent of the first victim. Fortunately for his reputation, the opportunity, so eagerly desired, never arrived, and Bombay was spared the humiliation of seeing the ermine spotted by individual animosity. In the case under notice, few will venture to deny that both Sir Matthew Sausse and Sir Joseph Arnould have exhibited a degree of patience and research, in endeavouring to arrive at a knowledge of the true merits of the discussion, rarely equalled in judicial investigation. For more than a month they had to listen to a mass of evidence as conflicting, as it was disgusting, and for upwards of another month they appear to have been assiduously analysing the whole depositions— separating the few grains of truth from the mountain of falsehood, with such discrimination and precision, as will entitle them to the lasting respect of the native community. It will be borne in mind that, in the Maháráj case, they sat in the capacity of both jurors and judges, and their responsibility was consequently all the greater, especially as their legal training would incline them to lean to the law of the case rather than to its equity. It seems a singular anomaly, that in India actions of this nature are not referred to a jury, for decision, as they are in England. If they were, the judges would be relieved from a good deal of anxiety, and a feeling of security would be engendered, which the public do not at all times feel. With judges like Sir Matthew Sausse and Sir Joseph Arnould, no apprehension need be entertained that their verdicts would at any time not be in strict accordance with justice; but, unfortunately, as we have already mentioned, there are sometimes men elevated to the Bench who cannot submerge the prejudices of the individual in the impartiality of the judge. Into the merits of the alleged libel, it is not our intention to enter, until we have perused the written judgments, which we have been informed will shortly be published. The European public can take but little interest in a question of Hindu immorality, the more especially that the priesthood of the heathen have ever been noted for their profligacy and hypocrisy. The plaintiff in this case is, we dare say, no worse than the generality of the brotherhood, and we cannot help thinking that the good which the cause of christianity is expected to derive from the exposure, is extremely questionable. The followers of the Maháráj will be inclined to regard him as a martyr, and it is not unlikely that his influence, instead of being diminished, will be greatly increased. The sterling benefit which will result from the investigation of the case, consists in the right which the judgment guarantees the people, to indulge in the legitimate discussion of all questions, affecting the civil and religious liberties of the subject. The veil of superstition, which has for such a length of time deadened the senses, and darkened the intellect, has been ruthlessly swept away, never more, it is to be hoped, to disgrace the humanity which it held in fetters. That India is in a state of transition both politically and socially, cannot be for a moment doubted. The people are beginning to despise the darkness, in which they have so long dwelt; their delusions are passing away, and in the succession of organic changes, which we see constantly taking place around us we recognize the dawn of a glorious day. The starless night of ignorance and error is rapidly passing away; the sun of knowledge is nearing the horizon; and before many years have swept by, we trust to see the millions who people this land, standing free and emancipated from every vice that degrades, and every belief that enslaves. In some parts of India, a native press may be dangerous, but in the Presidency of Bombay it has ever been found one of the strongest levers which progress possesses. The triumph which the editor of the *Satya Prakásh* has just achieved is not, by any means, the first of its kind, although it is perhaps of more importance than any that have preceded it. The native journalists of Bombay have ever been distinguished for ability and independence; and the calm manner in which all manner of questions are discussed, is often quite equal to the tone of the English press. We congratulate Mr. Karsandás Mulji on the victory he has gained and trust that his courage will be duly appreciated by his countrymen.—*Deccan Herald, April 25, 1862.*

### VIII.—*The Poona Observer.*

We have to acknowledge with thanks the report of the Maháráj Libel Case, and of the Bháttiá Conspiracy Case connected with it. We are also informed that it is intended to put all the notices of this famous case in the various newspapers and periodicals, in the form of a pamphlet, and circulate them among the followers of the Mahárájás,—a very desirable object.

The aspect of this case, which perhaps gives it its greatest importance is this:—the fact that the plaintiff, Jadanáthji Brizrattanji Maháráj, should have thought it necessary to deny the doctrines of his sect, when they were imputed to him.

It must strike his followers that this is not the conduct of a teacher of a true religion. Persecution is always taken advantage of by teachers of truth as an opportunity of asserting the heavenly nature of their creed. Why did not the Maháráj, a high priest of the sect he belongs to, take advantage of this public opportunity, and using the witness box for his pulpit proclaim from it the truth he believed in? Why did he not declare that it was the duty of all true believers to give up their wives and daughters to his embrace and that of his colleagues; that carnal intercourse with him on the part of a woman was equivalent to her communion with the Infinite; that eternal happiness in another state is of the same nature; and that holiness and sanctity consists in making this world a foretaste in this respect of the next?

He did nothing of the sort. He disclaims the imputations to him of the doctrines held and the practices countenanced by the Vallabháchárya sect as an injury and insult, to be atoned for by a fine of five thousand rupees. A newspaper publishes what has since been proved in open court, and at a fair and careful trial, to be nothing more than a true picture of the proceedings of the sect; and he knows no escape from the infamy which he well knows it will bring upon him, than to denounce the imputation as a false, scandalous, malicious, infamous, and defamatory libel, wickedly, maliciously, and designedly printed and published with a view to bring him into disrepute, and injure his good fame; and when it was proved that the alleged libel was only sober truth, he is said to have fled from Bombay in fear of a prosecution for perjury.

It is such conduct which is likely to produce so wide an effect upon the native population. It is not so much the scandalous nature of the revelations made as to the deeds of this false and licentious priest, which seem to us so important. There have been false and licentious priests of other religions. Mahomet used his pretended prophetical office to excuse his licentiousness; and even Christendom, we grieve to say may be reproached with its Borgias and its Achillis. But it is that when when the creed of the sect of the Mahárájás was brought before the public, one of their high priests denied it just at the time he was expressly called upon to confess and proclaim its truth. Who will believe in a religion which the priests themselves are the first to repudiate with pretended horror and disgust?

The religion of the Vallabháchárayans will not survive this blow; at least we hope so for the honour of human nature. But the effect of it will be felt still farther. It will resound throughout the Hindu world. For in truth, though this particular sect is said to have originated only three hundred years ago, it has derived its doctrines and practices by not illegitimate deduction from the old theology of the Hindus.   The worship of Krishna is certainly much more ancient; and the worship of Krishna is indirectly but most decisively struck at in the judgment of the Supreme Court of Bombay.

That the consequences of this case will be very important, there can be no sort of doubt; it must occasion a great revulsion of religious feeling among a large part of the population.   And we should hope there can be little doubt in what direction this will take place.

We are not among those who regard the exposure of the falsehood of the old fables of the Hindu books with much apprehension.   It has been said that to exhibit to a Hindu the falsehood of the pretension of these books to infallible truth—which the knowledge possessed by Europeans as to geography and so forth must necessarily do—is to leave him without any religion at all; and that it is better he should retain his old belief than fall into scepticism.

We might perhaps reply that no religion at all is better than a religion of which the principal end and object is sensuality and vice.   But speaking generally, we believe there is on the whole no real truth in the theory.   We believe that to deprive most men of their former theory would be, not to reduce them to infidelity, but to drive them to seek a new one.—*Poona Observer*, *May* 20, 1862.

## IX.—*The Sindian.*

The Maháráj libel case dragged on so slowly during the time it was before the Supreme Court, and such a long period was allowed to elapse before the judgment was delivered, that it is not surprising if the public interest in this remarkable trial has rather fallen off.   We have postponed making any remarks upon the subject until we had received and perused the judgment *in extenso*.   Two issues back we presented our readers with an abstract of it taken from the Bombay papers.   The extended text has now come to hand, but is of such great length as to preclude us entirely from reprinting it.   There cannot be a doubt that the evident conscientious care with which this document has been prepared, the rigid attention to forms of law which it displays, and the substantial justice which it deals forth, will add largely to the general respect with which the Supreme Court is regarded.   The public at large, if we except the Maháráj and his deluded votaries, have every reason to be satisfied with the verdict.   It would certainly have been pleasanter had the Chief Justice been able to take the same view of the legal technicalities of the case as his colleague, but his decisions show so clearly his determination not to allow his knowledge of the law to be overborne by the sympathy which every honest man must have felt with the defendant, that it is hard to take exceptions to it.   On the other hand it is eminently gratifying to find a lawyer of Sir Joseph Arnould's well known attainments able honestly to declare his conviction that in this instance at least, a strict legal award is thoroughly compatible with our preconceived notions of what was just and right. If the man who so fearlessly exposed the abominable superstition which had gradually become engrafted upon his creed,—without malice, as malice is understood by the world at large, but honestly and with becoming indignation—if this man had been cast in damages for his pains, the liberty of the press might indeed have been set down as a thing of the past. On this point Sir Joseph Arnould's own words will be read with pleasure, and will find an echo in the heart of every one who desires the reformation of society and the prompt exposure of abuses. "For generarations" says the learned judge, "the hereditary high priests of his sect had, as he (the defendant) believed, committed whoredom with the daughters of his people. Like the sons of Eli they had done this openly at the gate of the temple—like the sons of Eli they had done this under the pretended sanction and in the abused name of religion. This is the thing he denounces. It would be a waste of words to point out that in denouncing it—vehemently, bitterly, indignantly—he was within the strict limits of his duty as a public writer. The interests of society require that wickedness such as this should be sternly exposed and unrelentingly hunted down. If to write vehemently, bitterly, indignantly on such a subject as this be libellous —then were the Prophets of old libellers—then were the early Fathers of the Church libellers—then have all earnest men in all time been libellers, who have published to the world in the fit language of generous indignation, their scorn of hypocrisy and their hatred of vice." For this bold exposition of the law Sir Joseph Arnould deserves the thanks of the whole press of India. It is a matter of no small moment to have it so clearly laid down that a public writer is not exceeding his duty in the fearless exposure of abuses, when he does it in good faith, and without malicious exaggeration. And yet it causes us considerable solicitude to find that Sir Matthew Sausse seemed to consider the mere publication of a defamatory statement as *prima facie* evidence of malice in law, and that there was no "justifying occasion" for the libel in question. He admits that the defendant entered into the controversy "with the honest purpose of exposing to public reprobation doctrines which he conscientiously believed to be subversive of social morality"—(surely there could be no room for doubt as to the tendency of the abominable doctrines of the Maháráj)—and that he did not exceed the "licentious comment" as it has been termed, which is allowable upon matters more immediately affecting public interest; but the argument of the Chief Justice appears to be that the defendant before publishing the alleged libel had not made proper enquiries into the truth of the grave charges which he urged against the plaintiff, and that these only came out in evidence afterwards. Further, that in singling out by name, a man with whom he had had no previous acquaintance, and who had given him no direct cause for hostility, he laid himself open to the charge of having published a "malicious" libel. We are of course satisfied from Sir Matthew Sausse's assurance that this view of the case is in strict consonance with law and precedent; but Sir Joseph Arnould's arguments are those which will be most appreciated by the public, and they appear to us to deal more fairly with the broad features of the case before him. He points out that if the plaintiff was singled from the rest of his sect for the animadversions of the defendant, it was because he had put himself prominently forward as an expositor of their quasi religious doctrines, and was thus to some extent a marked man amongst them. In other words the strictures of the defendant were directed against a class, which by common repute held the most atrocious doctrines, and the argument which he addressed to the plaintiff simply was, "You have come forward as the defender of the antiquity of your sect, and as a propagator of religion ; would it not be more consistent with propriety for you and your co-religionists to devote yourselves primarily to the repression of the abuses which have become so notorious ? Desist from your evil practices and you will then have some claim to be considered fit teachers of religion."

So much for the legal technicalities of the case. It is gratifying that both judges are unanimous in declaring that the practices alleged against the Mahárájás have been fully proved, and that looking at the question in this light, the man who so fearlessly exposed them, and has in consequence been subjected to such an amount of persecution and intimidation, in order to force him from his purpose, is entitled to a substantial verdict in his favour. The false prophet has been remorselessly exposed. The man who was so solicitous that no one in court should so much as touch him, lest his godship should be defiled, has been publicly shown up as stained with the foulest excesses, and it has been proved that he—the leader of his people—had perjured himself shamelessly and unblushingly in a court of justice. It has been proved beyond a possibility of a doubt that the horrible creed, which it is impossible even to particularize without offence to modesty, is practically believed in by a modern sect of Hindus,—and that the dedication of their bodies and property to the men whom they regard as the incarnation of the Deity is no mere form of words but is taken advantage of to the utmost by one at least of their religious teachers. So far as a thorough exposure is concerned, the editor of the *Satya Prakásh* has accomplished his object;—it remains to be seen whether the deluded votaries of this false creed will be induced thereby to return to the comparative purity of Brahminism, or whether they will show themselves deaf to remonstrance, and cling more closely than ever to the priest who has now some claims to be considered a martyr. The strong feeling which from the first has been directed against the defendant, is but too conclusive evidence of how the current is likely to turn ; but whatever may be the result of this remarkable trial, the gratifying fact remains, that this effort for reform has come from within, and as such is entitled to our highest respect and sympathy. There is yet hope for the degraded idolators of this country, when we find that there are men amongst them who are not afraid to stand boldly forward as social reformers ; and we have no reason to fear but that the good work inaugurated by Karsandás Mulji, will in the fulness of time bear its legitimate fruits. It is to be hoped that his investigations into the history of the Vallabháchárya sect, may have the effect of convincing him that a creed which could develope such a bastard offspring as this, must in itself be intrinsically false. Leaving the followers of the Maháráj to wallow in sensuality and to call it religion, he and his adherents may yet be able to advance a little further in their onward progress towards a purer faith, and to recognize the fact that the tendency of an idolatrous worship is ever to degenerate into something even more degraded.—*Sindian*, *May 7, 1862.*

## X.—*Our Paper.*

THE MAHÁRÁJ LIBEL CASE.—The judgment and verdict in the cause of *Jadunáthji Brizrattanji Maháráj* v. *Karsandds Mulji and another*, which of late has excited as much attention as it has disgust, under the title of the "Maháráj Libel Case," are now before us unabridged, and afford the opportunity for which we have waited, to pronounce upon their justice and merits, from that point of view under which a subject of this nature and magnitude presents itself to the public journalist. From the brief abstract which we gleaned a week ago from the Bombay newspapers, we hastily formed the opinion that the Chief Justice, Sir Matthew Sausse, had founded his decision too religiously upon the law of the issue, greatly to the prejudice of equity, and the cause of public morality. Now that we have carefully perused his judgment, we feel confirmed in that first opinion, and regret that such should be the case. We are indeed positive that in all the annals of the British judiciary, there is not such another trial which in its results better exemplifies the danger and the actual wrong of bowing scrupulously to the dictates of sheer abstract law, than this revolting case of that brutal man the Maháráj. To precedent and technicality we do not hesitate to say that the Chief Justice has sacrificed principle and the best interest of the community. Under the folds of a laboured plea, assisted by an ostentatious display of impartiality, Sir M. Sausse, with an eye single, it appears, to the establishment of his reputation as a shrewd and profound lawyer, has dealt a heavier blow at the progress of morality and civilization in this country than any other hand so well armed could ever have dared to aim. Although he himself admits—and how could he do otherwise with the overwhelming mass of testimony reeking before him, with the evidence of lecherous abominations incredible if they were not solemnly sworn to by the outraged followers of the infamous priest,—he admits, we say, that the Maháráj has been guilty of the vilest outrages upon public morality, and invoked in their perpetration the prestige of sanctity, with which his poor dupes invested him ; the Chief Justice further admits that, in the positive denial which the plaintiff made under oath of those shameful practices, he had grossly perjured himself; and yet in the next breath, Sir Matthew pronounces that this perjured, adulterous wretch has been libelled, and awards him a nominal verdict, it is true, but one which among the deluded victims of this man, and his designing coadjutors, may be fraught with the most deplorable consequences. The Chief Justice has decided that, although the Maháráj was guilty of all that was brought to his door, of adultery with the wives and daughters of an influential class of the native inhabitants of no less a place than a presidential town, it did not belong to the editor of the *Satya Prakásh* to expose his misdeeds: he had no business to libel that disgustingly lewd and perjured man. The judgment even goes the length of denying to the press the exercise of one of its most sacred duties, the duty of stigmatizing vice wherever it may flaunt itself, and crime by whomsoever, be he high or low, it is committed shamelessly, openly in the face of all mankind, and before high heaven. He argues that because Mr. Karsandás Mulji had no earthly direct interest in stirring up this loathsome filth-pit, he ought to have left it alone: in other words, because the editor who so nobly came forward had neither wife whom the infamous Mahárág had defiled, nor daughter whom the same individual had for ever lost to shame, he, the editor, should have kept silent and passed on to the performance of some less disagreeable duty. This is the law of libel narrowed down to its straightest application, and it proves plainer than argument can establish, that the suspicion with which the masses look upon the law as a subterfuge which defeats the ends of justice, which screens the guilty and blasts the innocent, is but too well founded. The object of the law, in its abstract sense, is the interpretation of enactments, and its task is to sift their meaning so thoroughly that in their application no misconception may arise, and no wrong be done; but as all minds do not possess the same analytical powers, and as they are not all endowed with the same logical capacity, it will happen, as it does but too often in our courts of justice, especially those where causes are not submitted to the decision of juries, that the wily pleader wins the day over his less clever adversary, and the very best and purest cause is thus lost. We do not mean to insinuate here that Sir Matthew Sausse has been argued into the decision he has given by the adroitness of the plaintiff's counsel. We maintain that he has even gone beyond: he has assumed the place of those gentlemen, for they too know as well as he, that the Mahárág is guilty of all the gross actions charged against him, and that he has perjured himself in swearing that he had never committed them  From this view which we take of the case, it will be perceived that we disagree with the great majority of our contemporaries if not all of them, in the significance we attach to the Chief Justice's decision; but we must not be mistaken as anxious to impute unworthy motives as his guides in aiming at such a decision; far be it from us to hint at such a possibility,  But we cannot deplore too deeply the error into which his *esprit de classe* has evidently betrayed him: and had we not Sir Joseph Arnould's able judgment to accompany Sir Matthew's side by side, correcting at every step the insidious effects which the latter might have wrought; had it gone forth to the world alone and uncontradicted, we should have anticipated evils too great to be estimated to their full extent. Yet this timely antidote can only operate among the more enlightened members of the native population. With the lower orders, those upon whom villains like Jadunáthji Brizrattanji fatten and thrive, no hope can be entertained that a similarly beneficial result will follow the Puisne Judge's able decision. It is among these poor people that the Mahâráj will exhibit the *five rupees* he owes to Sir Matthew Sausse's legal acumen, as an invaluable token of his righteousness, and his power to triumph over the enemies of the "Ocean of *Rás Lilá*," and as a homage to his godship from the hand of a Christian judge !

Notwithstanding the disheartening aspect which this case assumes in the eyes of a conscientious press, which does vastly more than is expected at its hands towards the support of the judiciary in the repression of crimes and abuses, and yet so often gets spurned in return for zeal which its duty bids it exercise in the cause of the common weal, we still cherish the hope that there is yet left a remedy for the evil wrought by the Chief Justice's *devotion to his profession.* This remedy is the attitude which every enlightened native should adopt in conjunction with Karsandás Mulji, towards the Mahâráj and his followers. But if they fail to extend a cordial support to the *Satya Prakásh ;* if they look on supinely at the commission of bestial acts at their very thresholds; then the task will devolve upon the Christian community of Bombay to punish the perpetrators of those deeds and all who may tolerate them, by refusing to hold any communion, be it socially or otherwise, with them. The man of honour, be his creed what it may, should recoil with loathing and disgust from the contact of beings so vile, so lost to all sense of shame, as to countenance the prostitution of their own wives and daughters to debauched men veiled under the cloak of sanctity. Then, if this still fails, if the persisting influence of the governing race fails to root the dreadful evil out of their neighbourhood, it will remain for the authorities to indict the Mahârájás as they do keepers of houses of ill-fame, and bring the Mahâráj himself to the criminal's dock as a perjurer ; on this point at least the Chief Justice is clear and there would be the chance of obtaining a conviction. If we do not consider this as the best step to be adopted even while the case is yet fresh in the minds of the people, it is because a prosecution of this description may invest the Mahâráj with a semblance of martyrdom, in which event his cause would push fresh and deeper roots in the bosoms of his deluded and debased disciples. These alternatives, and these only, do we think, will effectually remove the nuisance to which Sir M. Sausse has lent the sanction of the law. It remains to be seen whether the community of Bombay are prepared and willing to embrace them in vindication of the fair fame of their city and the cause of morality at large.—*Our Paper, May* 9, 1862.

## XI.—*The Friend of India.*

Some time ago our news columns contained from week to week the record of a suit in the Supreme Court of Bombay known as the Mahâráj Libel Case, in which the whole system of Hindu Idolatry was practically on its trial. The decision of the judges has now reached us, and we proceed to put our readers in possession of the facts of a lawsuit much more remarkable in its character and important in its consequences, though less exciting in its attendant circumstances, than the "Nil Darpan" trial in Calcutta.

On the 21st October last Karsandás Mulji, Editor of a Gujaráti newspaper called the *Satya Prakásh*, or "Light of Truth," published an article in which he charged the Mahárájás or high priests of the Vallabháchárya sect with teaching immoral doctrines and indulging in adulterous practices with their female devotees; and accused Jadunáthji Brizrattanji, a high priest in Bombay noted for his opposition to religious and educational reforms, as especially guilty of the grossest immorality. The Maháráj brought a civil action against the editor, whose leading counsel was the well-known Mr. Chisholm Anstey. The Maháráj complained that the article characterised the sect of the Vallabhácháryans as heretical, attributed to its high priests the inculcation of immoral doctrines, charged the whole body with immoral practices, and brought definite accusations of adultery against the plaintiff individually. After a vain attempt on the part of the Maháráj to prevent his devotees from giving evidence against him, the case came on, the editor having fortunately the moral courage to brave the penalties of excommunication and social persecution. The defendant pleaded justification among other pleas, and on this the case virtually went to trial. Thirty-one witnesses were examined for the plaintiff and thirty-three for the defendant, the latter embracing some of the most distinguished native reformers and men of science in Bombay, like Dr. Bháu Dáji, and oriental scholars like Dr. Wilson. The plaintiff himself, whose sanctity had never been defiled by a court of justice, appeared in the witness-box, only however to make the most self-contradictory admissions of the truth of the charge, and to call forth from both of the judges the declaration that he had deliberately perjured himself.

In spite of the excitement among the native community of Bombay, of the crowded state of the court and the long continuance of the trial, never was a case conducted with more fairness, or so as to reflect more credit on the judges, the counsel, and all parties concerned except the plaintiff and his witnesses. The evidence was of the most revolting character from the depths of moral pollution which it revealed. The sacred books of the sect written in Sanskrit or Brij Bháshá were necessarily laid before the judges, in the shape of translations of leading passages, and they were required to pronounce upon the doctrines very much as Dr. Lushington does on the Thirty-nine Articles. But the point at issue was so much more one of the grossly immoral life of the plaintiff than of the theological tenets of his sect, that the court were not required to lose themselves in the mazes of Hindu theology. As Sir Joseph Arnould put it, the principle contended for was "that what is morally wrong cannot be theologically right; that when practices which sap the very foundations of morality, which involve a violation of the eternal and immutable laws of Right, are established in the name and under the sanction of Religion, they ought, for the common welfare of society, and in the interest of humanity itself, to be publicly denounced and exposed." The conclusion to which both judges came was that the essential points in the libel were proved, and a verdict was accordingly given for the defendant on the main issue. The Chief Justice should not have weakened the moral effect of this decision by entering a verdict for the plaintiff on three purely formal pleas, and giving him five rupees of damages. The judgment of Sir Joseph Arnould is a noble and dignified protest against that idolatry which saps the very foundations of society, and in favour of that freedom of public opinion through the press, by which such practices as those of the Vallabhácháryans can alone be exposed. The judgment should be translated and widely circulated among the natives. We only regret the case could not have been tried under that chapter of the Penal Code which deals with offences relating to religion. The clauses are so vaguely worded and a recent trial in Calcutta shows them to be so dangerous, that a precedent such as the Maháráj's defeat would have been of inestimable value to the cause of true religious liberty and morality.

The light let into the hideous recesses of Vallabháchárya obscenity by the evidence in this case far more than confirms all the statements of such scholars as Ward and H. H. Wilson. It is a fact that the wealthiest and largest of the Hindu mercantile communities of Central and Western India worship as a god a depraved priest, compared with whom the filthiest satyr is an angel, and that their females apply to amorous dalliance with a diseased debauchee the sacred principle of the love of God and of self-dedication to his service. From such profanities the reader recoils appalled. It is no less true that three-fourths of the people of Bengal are devoted to the adoration of the Shakti or female principle, which in many cases is attended with midnight orgies, even to hear of which pollutes the imagination. To this has Hinduism come, and lower than this must it sink. Every century as it rolls on steeps the people and their priests in deeper defilement, and removes them from the comparative purity of those Vedic days, to which some youthful reformers are striving to return. The last bond of society is the family : when that is corrupted the end is at hand. It was so with ancient heathenism, with the society which Juvenal lashes, and such writers as Petronius and Martial depict. If only all the Shakta and Vaishnava sects of the Hindus—that is almost the whole of them—could be dragged to the light of heaven as the Vallabhácháryans have been, what revelations would not be made ! Here we find it established in a court of justice that the wives and daughters of the wealthiest Hindus in the Presidency of Bombay, the Banians and Bháttiás, are at the disposal of a wretch, who as God daily commits crimes from which Tiberius would have shrunk. When lust is deified and adultery adored, not as in Corinth and Cyprus by a special caste but by the matrons of a whole community, and when this is done with the sanction of their husbands and brothers, there can be little hope of a people. It remains to be seen if any shame is left in the Vallabhácháryans, if Jadunáthji Maháráj will still pursue his career in Bombay, and fathers will still permit the females of their families to frequent his temple.

Hinduism will never reform itself. Slowly the process of mortification is beginning. The light which our missionaries, our schools, our courts, our railways and all that is English is letting into the land makes it seem only the more hideous. A religion which makes proselytism impossible must perish of inanition. Caste may keep it for a time in a sort of life-in-death existence. A new generation, influenced by the secular instruction imparted in state schools and the civilizing agencies everywhere at work, may for a time find peace in such a compromise between truth and error as Vedantism is, and may even show the moral courage of Karsandás Mulji and Dr. Bháu Dáji, the defendant and principal witness in this case. But all compromises are temporary, all scepticism fails to give permanent satisfaction. Vedantism will as inevitably rise in time into the region of a higher faith, as Hinduism must degenerate till it expires under the weight of such corruption as this case has revealed. Meanwhile we trust this decision will give the honest native reformers of both Bengal and Bombay new courage to expose the evils of a superstition which bears such fruit, boldly to come out from among a people who so worship such gods and so adore such priests, and "to seek the Lord if haply they might feel after him and find him, though he be not far from every one of us."—*Friend of India, May* 8, 1862.


## XII.—*The Hindu Patriot.*

THE MAHÁRÁJ LIBEL CASE: ITS MORAL.—We have received a thick octavo volume of two hundred and thirty-four pages, being a full report of the great Maháráj Libel case of Bombay and of the Bháttiá conspiracy case connected with it. The history of the libel and of the trial of the libeller is the history of a strong religious movement in the Western Presidency. Conservatives though we are, we need still hardly protest that we have no sympathy with the demoralizing superstitions of our country. The Hinduism of to-day is not the Hinduism of our forefathers three thousand years ago; an avaricious and licentious priesthood has engrafted on a simple system doctrines of which we find no trace in the beautiful and spirit-illumining texts of the Veds, and which by the immorality they inculcate and the bondage of degradation in which they yoke the people, are precisely the very reverse of what the great teachers of a nation of Rishis, as Max Müller calls the Hindus, taught in the golden age of the creation. When we advocate the conservation of Hindu society; when we battle for the preservation of our national individuality, as marked out by religion, customs, and manners; when we rebuke the irreverent spirit of our young countrymen, and call upon them to moderate their novel zeal for go-ahead reform; we do not intend by any means to perpetuate the vile course of error and degradation which Bráhminical dominance has forced into existence. We are proud to confess that we yield to none in our desire for true reform; in fact, we consider every day of the present epoch is pushing us on a step nearer to that goal which is justly the ambition of every right-minded and patriotic Hindu. English education is destined, we believe, to effect a greater change in the moral and social constitution of India than the revival of letters did in Europe, and none can rejoice more at this glorious result in *prospectu* than we do. Such movements as the Maháráj libel case of Bombay are great helpers of the great end in view, and we rejoice at the termination which has attended this vitally important moral question. The report before us gives a detailed account of the proceedings of the trial, and none who has the patience to read it, which we believe will not be wanted by any that takes an interest in India or looks forward to its future, will fail to be struck with a deep impression of the earnestness and energy of the Reform Party represented in the trial. "To those (to quote the eloquent words of Sir Joseph Arnould, one of the presiding Judges) who consider how little the Hindu is accustomed to independent thought and independent action—how his whole life is circumscribed within the sphere of the family or the caste—how entirely the whole social happiness not only of himself but of those nearest and dearest to him is blighted by that terrible penalty of outcasting —(equivalent to the excommunication of the middle ages)—those who think of these things will probably be of opinion that nothing but a strong belief in the truth of what they have stated, and a firm conviction of the duty of stating it, could have impelled the witnesses for the defendant to come forward as they have done on his behalf. For the majority of these witnesses are not students or editors or non-believers; they are grave, reputable, middle-aged, family men, having a firm belief in the teachings of their ancient religion, and profound reverence for the authority of their ancient scriptures." The circumstance mentioned in the last sentence carries a graver meaning than the bare words import. It is not students or lads, idle talkers without any stake in society, or dreamy speculators, that have raised the cry of Reform at Bombay. They were, as Sir Joseph Arnould observes, followers and supporters of the Vallabháchárya sect, and they have recanted their faith after personal observation, enquiry, and sincere conviction. Remembering the tremendous influence which the Mahárájás wield in the Western Presidency, and the strong hold which religious bigotry has over the minds of the people even in the most enlightened parts of that region, it was indeed no homœopathic moral courage, to use the words of a contemporary, which he directed against a band of youthful reformers in Calcutta, that led the Bombay Reformers to undertake their crusade against their quondam faith, a faith in which they were originally brought up, which they followed like other devotees, and which we believe many a member of their families still follow. Men of substance, position, and of mature years, they are precisely the men to inaugurate a reform movement, and we congratulate Bombay on the happy conjuncture which has attended her march in the path of progress and enlightenment.

It is difficult in the compass of a newspaper article to discuss satisfactorily the merits of the libel suit. We can, however, testify that the defence could not have been placed in better hands than those of Mr. Anstey. The barrister did not for one moment lose sight of the real character of the case,—of the pregnant issues which were at stake. He battled with the same energy and vigour with which the advocates of the Lutheran Reformation directed their thunders against the

11

Vatican. The judges who tried the case were, as their judgments testify, eminently qualified to preside over a tribunal investigating into such momentous issues as the case involved. We cannot too highly praise the rigid impartiality of Sir Matthew Sausse displayed in his judgment. In a country like India, the religion of which is split into different sects and divisions, and where the law is administered by a foreign race, widely differing in religion and customs, it is of the greatest importance that the judge should maintain the utmost neutrality in matters of religion. Sir Matthew Sausse has not only preserved that neutrality, but has even gone so far as to rouse a suspicion of a leaning to the other extreme. If, however, Sir Matthew has given cause to the orthodox party for some confidence in their power, the bold and emphatic words of Sir Joseph Arnould must have chilled that momentary feeling. The two judges have taken two standpoints of view: Sir Matthew Sausse has mainly confined himself to the legal question; Sir Joseph Arnould has taken the loftier view by surveying also the moral aspect of the question. While Sir Joseph justifies the libel on high moral and public grounds, Sir Matthew does it on purely legal grounds duly established by evidence. Taking a broad view of the two judgments, no man, whether an illiberal bigot or a large-minded reformer, can have cause for complaint. Law has been respected, justice has been upheld, and the cause of morality duly conserved. The Maháráj cannot say that he has been victimized by partial judges; nor can the Reform party complain that enlightened Christian judges have arrested their good work by a discouraging verdict.

Now to the moral of the trial. It has a double bearing; it bears upon the problem of social and moral improvement of India, and also upon freedom of speech and freedom of opinion. As Sir Joseph Arnould justly observes, this great libel case has probably taught some to think; it must have led many to enquire: "it is (as the learned judge adds) not a question of theology that has been before us, it is a question of morality. The principle for which the defendant and his witnesses have been contending is simply this—that what is morally wrong cannot be theologically right—that when practices which sap the very foundations of morality, which involve a violation of the eternal and immutable laws of right—are established in the name and under the sanction of religion, they ought, for the common welfare of society, and in the interest of humanity itself, to be publicly denounced and exposed. They have denounced, they have exposed them. At a risk and to a cost which we cannot adequately measure, these men have done determined battle against a foul and powerful delusion. They have dared to look custom and error boldly in the face, and proclaim before the world of their votaries that their evil is not good, that their lie is not the truth. In thus doing they have done bravely and well. It may be allowable to express a hope that what they have done will not have been in vain—that the seed they have sown will bear its fruit—that their courage and consistency will be rewarded by steady increase in the number of those whom their words and their examples have quickened into thought and animated to resistance, whose homes

have helped to cleanse from loathsome lewdness, and whose souls they have
ec from a debasing bondage."

e above are words of high import, and coupled with what the learned judge
aid regarding the defendant's position, his consequent interest and duty,
have a most impressive significance. As a public journalist we quote with
ire and pride the following words of the learned judge.—

.s a Vallabhácháryan addressing his co-sectaries, as a Banian addressing his
fellows—above all as a journalist addressing his readers, composed princi-
of followers of the Maharaj, had the defendant no interest, had he no duty
iouncing the malpractices which it is the principal object of this alleged
:o expose? It appears to me that he had both an interest and a duty.

. public journalist is a public teacher; the true function of the press, that
:tue of which it has rightly grown to be one of the great powers of the
:n world—is the function of teaching, elevating and enlightening those who
ithin the range of its influence.

'o expose and denounce evil and barbarous practices; to attack usages and
ns inconsistent with moral purity and social progress, is one of its highest,
st imperative duties. When those evils and errors are consecrated by time,
i round by custom, countenanced and supported by the highest and most
ntial class in society, when they are wholly beyond the control and sup-
on of any other tribunal, then it is the function and the duty of the press
ervene; honestly endeavouring by all the powers of argument, denunciation
:dicule, to change and purify the public opinion which is the real basis on
. these evils are built and the real power by which they are perpetuated."

: feel an unqualified satisfaction to see a member of the Native Press afford
i notable illustration of the noble definition of the duties and responsibilities
Press, so nobly expressed by Sir Joseph Arnould.—*Hindu Patriot, June* 9,


## XIII.—*The Indian Reformer.*

are not at this time of day about to delineate the features of the Maháráj
Case. With the details of that extraordinary trial our readers must be
.y acquainted. And, certainly, whether we consider the deep sensation
. it created in all sections of the Indian community, the length of time over
it extended, the varied character of the witnesses whose depositions were
the able pleading which it called forth, and the abler judgments which were
red, or review the exposure which it made of a fearful amount of depravity
rofligacy existing in Hindu society under the cloak of religion, the Bombay
Case must be confessed to have been perhaps the most extraordinary of any
ied in any of Her Majesty's Courts in India. Neither is it our object in this
: to hold up to public reprobation the practice of the so called Maháráj.
practices are of so diabolical a nature, that a simple description of them is

sufficient to excite the disgust and the horror of any man who is not absolutely devoid of every virtuous emotion; and we should almost conclude that Hindu society was incapable of amelioration, if after the exposure of such appalling immorality, the Vallabháchárymns continued to respect the Maháráj as before.  Our object in this article is entirely different.  We wish to commend to the youth of Bengal, the spirit which animates that class of the educated people of Bombay, who have deservedly won the proud appellation of " Reformers."  It would be superfluous to remark that Young Bengal is a better English scholar than Young Bombay; but it seems that the latter is a truer patriot and a more earnest reformer than the former.  A Bengali patriot, in the ordinary acceptance of the term, is one who dabbles in politics, makes longwinded speeches in florid language on liberty, equality and fraternity, writes caustic letters against the non-official Anglo-Indian community, hates everything Anglo-Saxon except pantaloons and iced champagne, and defends everything Hindu, good, bad, or indifferent.  He sees no evil in the pernicious social, moral, and religious institutions of his country, and has therefore no wish to reform them.  In Bombay it is different.  There is not there so much of patriotic declamation, of fine writing, and of empty talk.  But there is more of substantial work done there.  Young Bombay is by no means a stranger to politics, yet he bestows a large share of his attention on the discussing of questions pertaining to social reform and moral improvement.  He loves his country as much as Young Bengal, but he does not blindly admire everything belonging to his country.  He boldly declaims against the vices of his countrymen, and is of opinion that the man who admires every social or moral institution of the land of his birth, however pernicious in its tendency, is an enemy to his race and a traitor to his country.  In Bengal, vernacular editors have been prosecuted, but only for libelling or indulging in filthy abuse.  In Bombay they are prosecuted for declaiming against the profligacy of their countrymen.  All honour to Mr. Karsandás Mulji for so boldly, so patriotically exposing the enormities of a most licentious priesthood.  In Bengal, they screen the faults of their countrymen; and the man who has the boldness to lay them bare, is regarded as an enemy in disguise.  We put it to our countrymen whether such a method of procedure will ever result in national reformation.  Let them be persuaded of the truth that he is a traitor to his countrymen who flatters their prejudices, and thereby confirms them in their errors and their evil practices.

To the Bombay Reformers we will just say one word.  You have done well in exposing a vile practice; but remember that the practice is essentially connected with the system of religion which is yet dominant in the land.  Lay the axe at the root of that system itself; uproot it, and plant in its stead the tree of true religion.  And then, but not till then, will you witness the dawning of your country's regeneration.—*Indian Reformer,* June 6, 1862.

## XIV.—*The Indian Mirror.*

The Maháráj Libel Case, the proceedings of which have occupied for some time past the columns of the Indian journals, has been finally decided. Seldom was a trial conducted amid an unusually excited public with more calmness and dignity and manly respect for the cause of truth and humanity. Never did both judge and counsel discharge their high duties more creditably and honourably. Nor can the importance of the decision arrived at, considered in its social and moral bearings, be over-rated. This great trial may well be styled the Trial of Superstition *versus* the Nineteenth Century ; and the triumph of the latter over the former is beyond doubt a matter for congratulation to all who are interested in the progress of truth, and especially to the enlightened community of India. Honour, all honour to Karsandás Mulji, Editor of the *Satya Prakásh,* who so manfully and in bold defiance of the penalties of excommunication, disclosed the immoral doctrines and practices of the Vallabháchárya sect, and to the worthy Judge, Sir Joseph Arnould, whose vigorous denunciations against idolatry constitute a lasting monument of the harmony of law and religion. Thanks to English court and English law, the awful sore which had been for a long time eating into the vitals of native society has at last been probed to the depth, that the horrors of the exposure might procreate a desire to forthwith find out a restorative and root out the malady. Is there a heart that does not recoil from the repulsive disclosures made by the trial of the frightful extent of corruption to which Hinduism has driven the souls of thousands of God's children ? Who beholding these pernicious corruptions will not instantaneously ejaculate :— " Oh! for the day when Hinduism shall be no more !" Is it not astounding that in one of our most enlightened Presidencies, in the teeth of so many civilizing agencies, such flagrant profligacies should have been perpetrated with impunity by crafty and immoral hierophants, and the wives and daughters of respectable families allowed to frequent their temples to learn adultery in the name of sacred religion, making lust and sensuality a virtue and a passport to heaven!! Assuredly the most callous heart will be inflamed with righteous indignation against such profanities. For the good of India and humanity however, the den of Vallabháchúryan wicked- ness has been penetrated by the keen-eye of the law, and the depraved culprit has been dragged out of it, and visited with condign punishment. Who can say that there are not abominations yet more hideous than these lurking in some secret corners of Hinduism not yet exposed ; yea, which years to come will not be able to expose—abominations which, if revealed, would shake the stoutest heart that looks hopefully to India's future. Let our educated country- men rise as one man and demolish the stupendous edifice of Hinduism, and save millions of their fellow countrymen from the horrors of idolatry. A constant struggle and an heroic warfare—not by means of pen or lips—not a wordy warfare of arguments and empty sounds—but an earnest moral struggle. We can assure

them that their highest conceptions of Hinduism's horrors will fall far short of the
reality, and that half measures will never avail to exterminate them.   If our
educated countrymen will not allow themselves to be aroused by such horrid
exhibitions! alas for the millions of our daughters, and wives and mothers and the
poor peasantry groaning under the oppressions of relentless and infatuated priests.
We require not arguments, but a heart to feel, to be moved to immediate action,
and we entreat young India with all the earnestness we can command to rise in a
crusade against the evils of idolatry—that national curse of our country.   It is a
pleasure to observe the attempts that are making here and there to gain this
object; but we want a broader association and a more extended community of
feelings and co-operation of hands to ensure success.—*Indian Mirror*, May 15,
1862.    .

## XV.—*The Indian Field.*

KNOWLEDGE *v.* SUPERSTITION.—There is no doubt that obstructionists make
heretics and heretics make obstructionists.   The former are represented by men
of the past and the latter by men of the future.   The one fights for precedence,
the other for progress.   Dogmatic and presumptuous, Hinduism is no longer
allowed to trample on reason and conscience.   Its strongholds have already
become untenable.   Its high priests are no longer permitted to assume infallibility
and wallow in vice with impunity.   True that ceremonies are performed and
mantras are mumbled, but they mean no more than an oath "by Jove."   The
colleges and schools have been too strong for the *Shástras*, and the geographical,
astronomical, and historical truths inculcated there have left behind Manu's
dogma of Bráhminic supremacy and demolished the tortoise upholding the earth.
The beginning of the end is approaching.   A spirit of enquiry and progress has
worked its way among the educated natives.   Every part of British India is now
witnessing and tolerating a searching investigation and severe scrutiny into those
institutions and opinions which had for ages marked the peculiar character of her
inhabitants.   Liberties in thought and action are now fearlessly assumed, which
would have scandalized Viás and Válmik.   Progress is the law of God and
obtains alike in the religions of the races and the sects of the provinces and
presidencies.   No wonder therefore that the educated native in all parts of India
will not submit with implicit faith to the pilotage of their spiritual guides, but
summon Bráhminism to the bar of their own reason.

The Bombay Libel Case which has suggested these remarks has given a substantial victory to Hindu reformers.   It has set them far above the opponents of
progress, and should instil into them confidence in respect to the great work which
lies before them in the future.

The particulars of the case are briefly told.   Karsandás Mulji, the courageous
editor of the *Satya Prakúsh*, in his issue of the 21st October last, preferred
charges of gross immorality against the principal Porohits of the Vallabháchárya
sect, corresponding to the Bamachári sect of Bengal.   Jadunáthji Brizrattanji,

the Maháráj and the arch-offender, instituted an action for libel against Karsandás Mulji. He availed himself of the ruling of Sir Mordaunt Wells in the *Nil Durpan* case, and complained that the leader in the *Satya Prakásh* libelled the whole sect of the Vallabhácháryans as heretical and immoral. But the plea of justification set up by the defendant was fully supported by the evidence not only for the defence but for the prosecution. The *Chelás* or disciples of the Maháráj were obliged to testify to his adulterous practices with female devotees, under the fire of cross-examination. Thirty-one witnesses were examined for him, and thirty-three for the Editor; but the preponderance of the evidence was in favour of the latter; the Reverend Dr. Wilson, Dr. Bháu Dáji, and several other distinguished men bore their weighty testimony to the infamous character and conduct of the Maháráj and his co-religionists.

The judgment was virtually in favour of the plaintiff, and a verdict on the first plea with nominal damages was recorded for the Maháráj. The following words of Sir Joseph Arnould are very impressive and encouraging to all Hindu reformers :—" The principle for which the defendant and his witnesses have been contending is simply this—what is morally wrong cannot be theologically right— that when practices which sap the very foundations of morality, which involve a violation of the eternal and immutable laws of Right,—are established in the name and under the sanction of Religion, they ought for the common welfare of society, and in the interest of humanity itself, to be publicly denounced and exposed. They have denounced—they have exposed them. At a risk and at a cost which we cannot adequately measure, these men have done determined battle against a foul and powerful delusion. They have dared to look custom and error in the face, and proclaimed before the world of their votaries that their evil is not good —that their lie is not the truth. In thus doing they have done bravely and well. It may be allowable to express a hope that what they have done will not have been in vain—that the seed they have sown will bear its fruit—that their courage and constancy will be rewarded by a steady increase in the number of those whom their words and their examples have quickened into thought, and animated to resistance, whose homes they have helped to cleanse from loathsome lewdness, and whose souls they have set free from a debasing bondage."—*Indian Field, May 10, 1862.*

## XVI.—*The Phœnix.*

THE BOMBAY MAHÁRÁJ LIBEL CASE.—This case has formed a prolific subject of comment for almost every journal in the country, and a printed circular on our table informs us that it is intended to republish in book form all that the journals have said thereon. We have further within the last day or two received from Bombay, the report of the trial, which in small print, and large octavo form, makes a stout book of 284 pages. There can be little question that this remarkable case is destined to exercise a powerful influence for good on the Hindu population of the Western Presidency. It has let in a flood of light on a terrible system of the most corrupting immorality hitherto carried on, and concealed from the knowledge of the general public, under the cloak of religion. The history of the case dates from the 21st October, the day on which the editor of a Gujaráti newspaper called the *Satya Prakásh*, or Light of Truth, published an article in which he charged the Mahárájás or high priests of the Vallabháchárya sect with inculcating immoral doctrines, and under the pretence of religion, practising adultery with the females who visited the temple as devotees. Jadunáthji, a Bombay high priest, was especially charged with these evil practices, and in consequence brought a civil action against the Editor of the Light of Truth, Karsandás Mulji, who has since published the trial, and now proposes to publish the comments thereon. Neither Karsandás Mulji nor his journal were, however, the first to make open assault on the bad practices of the Mahárájás. Other journals of the native press had for some time previously warned against them, and though the denunciations seemed to be productive of little immediate effect, they so frightened Jadunáthji that he came in person to Bombay from Beyt, the site of the Chief Temple of the Tribe, to take legal measures to put a stop to the attacks on his order. He evidently depended on wealth and influence procuring a judgment in his favour, and counted on deterring any Bháttiás from giving evidence against him. He was egregiously mistaken, for the result of his going to law has been the exposure to the world of vile practices hitherto only suspected by the great body of the Hindus themselves. It was established at the trial that the wives and daughters of the highest of the Bháttiá caste used to frequent the temple to prostitute themselves to the high priest, and seemed to consider that in so doing they were doing what would procure them favour with the Deity. The details of the case are of too gross a character to bear more than allusion to them. They all tell of a debased, diseased, debauchee priest dishonoring the wives and daughters of his flock, and teaching as a sacred tenet that it was the desire of God he should do so! Worse still, the presents made by the women thus dishonored appear to have formed a chief source of the revenue of the temple. These daughters of Vallabháchárya piously robbed their husbands and fathers that they might dishonor them in the name of God! The trial created a very great sensation in Bombay. Every art of inducement and intimidation was resorted to in order to prevent parties from giving evidence. Those efforts most signally failed, for bold estimable men, who set prejudice and caste at defiance, prosecuted with a will, and in the future history of Indian civilization the names of those men will rank as reformers of the highest type. Some miserable followers of the depraved priest essayed to disprove what these gentlemen had established, and drew down on themselves in open court the reprobation due to perjury.

Looking over the report of the case we find that almost all the witnesses who spoke in justification of the articles in the *Satya Prakásh* were "educated natives," that is natives who had imbibed the knowledge and undergone the training of the English schools and colleges, some of them being Medical Practitioners who had graduated at the Grant Medical College. Who after this will say that English schools and colleges are doing no good in the country, doing nothing towards the growth of a purer morality? Had those men been of the old school, taught but the false learning of the Bráhmins, it is not too much to say they would never have been witnesses against the Maháráj. They themselves fully appreciate the advantages of knowledge and education for their countrymen, for it appears in the evidence that could the Maháráj Jadunáthji but have been induced to forego his secret opposition to religious educational reforms, and to sincerely exert his influence in their furtherance he would not have been denounced. We are not competent to estimate the good effect this case will have on native society in Bombay. That effect cannot, however, be other than most beneficial. The prosecutor could not brook exposure and assault in the columns of the native journals, and made a desperate effort to beat them down, by ruining by money damages the publishers and writers. Evidently alive to the power of the press he sought to muzzle it. The result has been that instead of mention in the native journals of Bombay his ill practices are now bruited throughout the whole country by every European journal and by many of the native journals, to boot. That this will be effectless none need fear. If it were likely to be so the Maháráj and his friend would never have exerted themselves to extinguish their vernacular tormentors. They dreaded the power of publicity, and would risk all to prevent that power being brought to bear on their own infamous doings. They failed, were exposed, and the result of that exposure will every day become more and more beneficially apparent. It has been urged by some of our Bombay contemporaries that the local Government should take action on the case, and erase from the list of Justices of the Peace and from Government employ, the names of those who put themselves forward prominently as supporters of the Maháráj. We think this would be a most mistaken course. Government may interfere with individuals for their actions, but not for their opinions. If it can be shown that a native Justice of the Peace deliberately permits the prostitution, to a priest, of the wives and daughters of his household, let his name be struck off forthwith as unworthy to remain on the roll. But that he is a follower of the Maháráj, or a Vallabhácháryan of the old school, is no sufficient reason why he should be considered ineligible for municipal distinctions by Government. Mahomedanism recognises conversion by the sword, but so long as a Mahomedan does not attempt to carry the doctrine into practice, he is considered as eligible for public distinctions as the members of any other sect. There need be no fear that the Maháráj case will be otherwise than productive of a full crop of the most beneficial consequences.— *Phœnix, June* 3, 1862.

## XVII.—*The Delhi Gazette.*

One of the most important trials that has taken place for many years has lately been concluded, after a lengthened judicial enquiry extending over a year and a half, at Bombay. The principles involved are of the utmost possible consequence to the people of this country. Indeed it is difficult to overrate the weight which the decision of the Judges of the Supreme Court have come to, must, if fairly dealt with by the Hindu nation, bear upon the mind and morals and religion of the people. We allude to the famous case, familiar we doubt not by name to many of our readers, as the case of the Mahárájás of Bombay.

We propose to describe briefly what the case was, how it was decided, and why we consider the question of so much importance.

There is a sect of Hindus in Bombay denominated the Vallabháchárya, who are styled unorthodox by those who call themselves orthodox Hindus. Dr. Wilson, the best authority probably in India, who was examined before the Supreme Court on these points, says, the sect is a new sect, inasmuch as it has selected the god Krishna in one of his aspects, that of his adolescence, for its peculiar object of worship ; and it is a new sect inasmuch as it has established as the road to eternal happiness the injunctions contained in the holy books of the Hindus in a carnal and material sense. Or, as Sir Joseph Arnould in his very able judgment more plainly puts it, "by selecting Krishna in his character of the love-hero, the husband of the 16,000 shepherdesses, for the especial object of worship, the sublime Brahminical doctrine of 'unition' with Brahma is tainted and degraded by this sensuous mode of regarding the Deity." And Sir Matthew Sausse, "the love and subserviency inculcated by the Hindu religion to be due in a scriptural sense to the Supreme Being, has been by these corrupt teachings" (the teaching of the plaintiff in this case, the high priest of the sect or the Maháráj) " materialised and to a large extent transferred to those who claim to be his living incarnation."

The Bombay judges, and as far as we know of their opinions, the Bombay press too, appear to look on this materialized Hinduism as exceptional. They speak of the Veds as if they were now the accepted scriptures of the Hindus according to whose tenets they endeavour, as they profess, to live. This view of the case is new to us. We have always looked on the Veds as the sacred book indeed of the Hindus, but with the mass of the people to all intents and purposes an unknown book. The writings that regulate, so far as any sacred writings do regulate, the lives and actions of the mass of the Hindu nation, are the Puráns, a much more modern compilation than the Veds, and very different to them, inasmuch as in them the original and undoubtedly pure spiritualized system of the Bráhminical faith has been sadly degraded and materialized. No one who has read the Prem Ságar for instance can have much idea of the spiritual nature of the system inculcated in it. The sports of Krishna with the 'gopis' and the very questionable (to use a very mild term) sort of connection between them, may indeed by a great stretch of language or imagination, be construed in a mystical sense signifying the spiritual union of a god with his worshippers, but to say that the mass of the people regard it so is to utter nonsense. The really learned and religious Hindus themselves will tell you how they regret the degradation of their spiritual system to one of sense and matter. And as for the masses they will not seek to conceal the real nature and objects of their sensual philosophy. Ask them to produce authority from the Veds for their ceremonies and festivals, the orgies and indecencies of the Holi for instance, and they will, if they think at all about it, look on it as an implied desecration to their holy books, to suppose there is anything in them to sanction such rites at all. Any one who had studied these books and had opportunities of learning the views of Hindus with regard to them, would have expected as soon to have seen a chief justice announcing that the earth went round the sun as a new thing, that people in general were unacquainted with, as gravely devoting time and labour to elucidating the fact that the Hinduism of the present day, was not the Brahminical philosophy of the Veds.

What we want to find out is, in what points do the Vallabháchárya sect differ from the Hindus in this or the greater part (perhaps the whole) of India who have selected the god Krishna as an especial object or worship. The Hinduism of the Western Presidency may be pure, and less corrupted by what we may call *puranism* than that of the Hindus of Oude, and the Upper Provinces of India, from whence our Hindu sepoys were mostly enlisted; but certainly no judicial officer in this part of the world, who had the least practical acquaintance with Hinduism as it is, would have ever thought it necessary to announce that the Hinduism of the present century was not the religion of the Veds.

One peculiarity we observe in the Vallabháchárya sect, and that is the extraordinary reverence, amounting indeed to worship, paid to their priests, or high priests, or Mahárájás as they call them. To them they appear to pay divine honour, to them they make the offering of *tan, man,* and *dhan,* or body, mind, and property required by the tenets of the Brahminical faith to be made to the Deity. Great as is the respect paid to priests, and Brahmins in general, in this and other parts of India, and to certain ones in particular, we never heard of a sect before in which the divine character and the claim to divine worship were so openly and unblushingly assumed as by the Mahárájás. Most undoubtedly, however, the stories told of the Mahárájás, out of which this famous action arose, are by no means without their parallel in other parts of India and among other Hindus. They are of a nature that we cannot allude to them specifically in a public journal like this. Any one whose knowledge of the subject even is confined to reading "Ward's Hindus" must be quite familiar with these views.

The editor of a native (Gujaráti) paper in Bombay, to whose honour his fellow countrymen ought to erect a statue as large as Government House, published an article in which he denounced the practice and system of religion as carried on in this sect. He denounced the practice of the Mahárájás receiving the worship in a material and sensual form, in their own persons, intended according to the pure religion of the Hindus to be paid to the gods, and that only of course in a spiritual sense. He accused the Mahárájás of the most disgraceful and immoral acts, of public indecencies and breaches of the laws of the land, too obscene and disgusting to be enumerated here— our reader's imagination will easily supply the filthy details, especially if they are familiar with the words of holy writ, and recollect that the heart of man is "desperately wicked" and call to mind the painful picture delivered by the Apostle Paul of the state to which in his days human nature had been brought, by the influence of an impure religion among men, " who changed the glory of the uncorruptible God into an image made like to corruptible man and to birds and fourfooted beasts and creeping things, for which God also gave them up to uncleanness through the lusts of their own hearts."

The Maháráj chiefly aimed at it in this article (a high priest who had published writings in a sectarian controversy justifying these immoral doctrines), replied by an action for libel; the defendant pleaded justification, and hence the exposure, and the defeat of the Maháráj's party. For the defendant there were thirty-three witnesses examined, for the plaintiff thirty-four. The former gave positive, the latter negative evidence. The disclosures made by this evidence, as we had said before, we cannot detail—our readers will readily understand its nature when we tell them the result of the trial, that the libel was considered to be justified.

Sir Matthew Sausse (for both judges delivered judgment, as, though they agreed in the main points they differed on a minor one that did not materially affect the vital question in the case), considered that "the essential points in the libel, as the record stands, have been sufficiently covered by the proofs adduced in support of the plea, that there must be a verdict for defendant on that issue." Sir J. Arnould said, "On my mind the evidence leaves not a shadow of doubt: the charges made are, in my opinion, fully substantiated."

The reason why we think this trial so important is that it must surely strike forcibly every educated Hindu in the country who reads it. Indeed we cannot but think that it will lay the foundation of a reformation analogous to that in which the great Luther took a lead after the exposures of the practices and morals of the priesthood in the sixteenth century. Accordingly we learn from the Bombay papers that so great has been the revulsion of feeling among their fellow-country-men in Bombay that the Maharájás have been forced to leave the place.—*Delhi Gazette, May* 22, 1862.

## XVIII.—*The Oudh Gazette.*

There has just been tried a case at Bombay, which discloses a state of facts so horrible, that it is hard to conceive otherwise than that a numerous, wealthy, and most influential caste of men, who live there are brutes by choice, and bestial from sheer love of bestiality.

The Bháttiá caste are second to no class in the world, in the force and constancy of their adherence to all the forms and customs of their religion, and in the ex-ceeding reverence they pay their priests; but, strange to say, the claims which their religion has upon their regard, and the nature of the adoration they render to their spiritual superiors, are so utterly the opposite of reasonable or tolerable that the sect presents the curious problem of an entire race of men who solemnly ignore right because it is right, and diligently worship evil because it is evil. In the selection of the strange peculiarities which form their creed, they seem to have been actuated by the most perfect system of unreason. Their tenets are impossible of observance without the outrage of every ordinary human passion and feeling. The grossest, foulest, and most degrading of all matters imaginable constitute their ritual; and the vilest brute among them is worshipped for his vileness, as an incarnation of the godhead.

A native newspaper editor exposed this state of things in a temperate remonstrance on behalf of the community against the existence of so foul a blot, protected by law. The Bháttiás met their antagonists boldly enough, but after their own unreasonable fashion. They at once prosecuted their asperser for libel, and called a caste meeting, at which every member pledged himself to belie their own doctrines, and deny their own customs. This conspiracy was, however, discovered, and the police forthwith procured evidence of it, which, in the fearless hands of counsel for the Crown, has resulted in a trial that has convicted and doomed to punishment the criminals.

Now out of these facts arise some very important considerations, chief of which is this, that by this case at Bombay the first direct blow has been struck by the law itself against fanaticism. It is a heavy and most important blow—surely fatal though slow in its effects. The purity of the stern decision which this case affords, namely, that *the law will permit the exercise of no power given to a man by a superstition, to the injury, disgrace, or even annoyance of his fellow subject*, levels a blow at caste which wealth or creed cannot long withstand. Let but the proceedings of this case be published throughout the land, and the principle of religious liberty and free conscience is established for ever; for, to say the plain truth, the only hold of superstition on men's minds, and the sole support of idolatry here as elsewhere, has rested on pretended powers which this decision renders impossible of pretence any longer. Every man may now rest secure from every let, hindrance, or harm, arising from authority or power not *legal and material*. The exercise of authority not given by enactment is penal. And from the sweeping force of this declaration, that the use of superstition as the means of coercion is illegal and penal, there is no man, not even if a whole race believe him to be a god, excepted.

Let all reformers rejoice, then, and let the members of the Brumho Sumáj of Lucknow learn, and use the strength of the weapon thus put into their hands by law. May we be pardoned for suggesting that, if it be in the power of this body to confer or offer an honour, the strongest friends of their cause who have yet declared themselves, are the prosecutor in this case, and Sir Joseph Arnould, the judge.—*Oudh Gazette, January* 1, 1862.

## XIX.—*The Samáchár Hindustani.*

THE MAHÁRÁJ LIBEL CASE.—All things have an end. The sun himself, as Thomas Campbell says, must die, and even the great Maháráj case could not occupy the Bombay Supreme Court for ever. After dragging its slow length along for an unusual duration, it has come to a stand with the decision of the Bench, and we can now safely moralize upon it.

In Western India there is a large sect of Hindus called Vallabhácháryans, from Vallabh, their founder. The Baniá and Bháttiá castes compose the laity of the sect, and the Mahárájás the clergy. Both in doctrines and in practices, Vallabhácháryans appear to us to be worse than the very dregs of the modern Vaishnavas. Had the facts not been proved in a court of justice, the practices of the Vallabhácháryans would have been incredible to our readers. The Vallabháchárya laity allow their priesthood to take, and the latter are not slow to take, liberties with the former's females, which we had thought hardly possible. But we will not anticipate. Mr. Karsandás Mulji, the editor of a Gujaráti paper in Bombay, the *Satya Prakásh*, or the "Light of Truth," and the defendant in the present action, as a Vallabhácháryan of the Baniá caste, could not but be aware of practices which were too notorious. The progress of intelligence had opened his eyes as those of other young Vallabhácháryans to their enormity. But he and his friends did not content themselves with merely seeing and perceiving—they tried to remove the evil. They promoted the education of girls that these might learn the sin of their parents' ways. They tried to introduce the re-marriage of widows, that these may not have an irresistible temptation to buy—it is literally bought as the reader will see by and bye—at the hands of the Mahárájás satisfaction of their animal desires. They exhorted the Mahárájás personally to mend their conduct. The plaintiff, Jadunáthji Maháráj, came to Bombay in 1860, and thought fit to ingratiate himself with the reformatory party by the most liberal assurances. He even went the length of founding a girls' school, and appeared to be earnest in the cause of widow-marriage. Some time after his ardour cooled, and his next appearance in public must have surprised the young reformers. He set on foot a periodical called the "Propagator of our own Religion," for the purpose of, we believe, neutralizing the effect of the attacks upon Vallabhácháryanism so often made by the reformers in the papers. In this periodical he openly invited criticism. The reformers were not backward in responding to the call. Meanwhile the defendant was horrified to discover that the immoral practices of the Mahárájás were sanctioned by the sacred authorities of the Vallabhácháryans. At the same time he was informed on good authority that the plaintiff was as immoral as his class. On the 21st October in 1860 the defendant published an article in the *Satya Prakásh*, in which he tried to prove that the Vallabhácháryans are a new sect heretical in respect of the ancient Hindu religion, and whose sacred books inculcate the grossest immorality, and roundly charged the Mahárájás as a body, and the plaintiff as one of them, with immoral practices in the name of religion. At this the plaintiff brought the action for libel. In regard to the second plea of the defendant, justification, both the judges agreed in their verdict in his favour. We, along, we are happy to say, with the entire press of Bombay, regret that on the technical plea of "not guilty," the Chief Justice prevailed against his Puisne in recording a verdict for the plaintiff for Rs. 5 damages. We regret because, as was to have been expected, the plaintiff's party, as we learn from the *Bombay Times*, tried to take advantage of it by announcing that he had gained the victory, explaining the nominal nature of the damages by suggesting that the judges took pity upon the defendant's poverty, and that the award was made in reference to his condition. But fortunately the bazaar was too shrewd to swallow such a transparent falsehood, and all classes of the natives have understood the decision properly. Those of the plaintiff's friends who had prepared sweetmeats to distribute as soon as the decision in his favour, upon which they counted as certain, should be given, were too crest-fallen to assume the airs of a fictitious triumph.—*Samáchár Hindustani, Lucknow, May* 17, 1862.

## XX.—*The Ceylon Times.*

We recently received from Bombay a copy of the proceedings in the libel case tried in the Supreme Court of that city, in which Jadunáthji Brizrattanji, Maháráj or high priest of the sects of Bháttias, Banians, Bráhmins, was the plaintiff, and the proprietor and publisher of a Gujaráti newspaper at Bombay called the *Satya Prakásh* were the defendants. The libel complained of was to the effect that the Mahárájes of these sects inculcated doctrines opposed to the Shástras of the Hindus, and that this Jadunáthji in particular was, under the cloak of religion, guilty of the grossest immoralities with the females of his sect.

In the plea of justification as filed by the defendants, it is declared that the leaders of the said sect assert that they are the incarnations of the gods Brahma and Krishna, and are themselves gods, and are and ought to be worshipped, implicitly obeyed, and served as gods by the members of the said sect, with all the minds, bodies, and properties of such sectaries, and that the neglect of any such to perform the said worship, implicit obedience and service, is a sin of the gravest character, and that it is the duty of the female members in particular of the sect to love the said leaders with unhallowed love, and to perform worship in implicit obedience and service with their bodies whensoever called upon or required by any of the said leaders so to do; albeit such female members are, or may be, unmarried maidens, or wives of other men, and in no wise married or betrothed in marriage to the said leaders. The plea goes on to allege that adultery and fornication are by the religious books of the sect encouraged and commended, and that the surest way of procuring eternal happiness is by acquiescence in such practices. Horribly disgusting as these statements may sound in our ears, they are mild enough compared with the awful disclosures made in open court and reported in the volume before us.

We have no desire to do more than record our utter detestation of such practices as those which, under the pretence of religion of any kind, appear to have prevailed in and about Bombay. With such a code of religious morality, the natives of India must remain debased to the level of the brutes. Until they be utterly purged of these iniquities they must not talk about equal rights and social advancement. We are, however, glad to find that there is a small band of reformers at work amongst them ; and we tender our cordial acknowledgments to the Editor who, having braved the hostility of his countrymen, has boldly proclaimed the truth at all hazards.—*Ceylon Times, June 24,* 1862.

## XXI.—*People's Friend.*

The libel case brought forward in the Supreme Court of Bombay by Maháráj Brizrattanji, one of the gurus of the Vallabháchárya sect, against the editor of the *Satya Prákash* newspaper, has at last been decided in favour of the defendant with costs. The case pended in the above Court for several months and excited great interest among the native community. Its particulars are these :— The defendant, who seems to be a member of the *Soodhar Lele* or reforming party of the natives, and edits the *Satya Prákash,* a Gujaráti newspaper, disclosed in one of his articles the indecent and immoral practices of the Vallabhácháryan gurus, and accused the plaintiff (one of those gurus) of adulterous conduct towards his female disciples. The plaintiff instituted this law suit against him, and the defendant pleaded that what he had stated in the article was correct. Many rich and influential bankers and merchants gave their evidence in favour of one side or the other, and the Judges came to the conclusion that the abuses brought to light were such as deserved a public denouncement. On the technical plea of not guilty they awarded Rs. 5 as damages to the plaintiff, but acquitted the defendant of the higher charge of defamation and libel, and awarded to him costs of the defence. The plaintiff is said to be intending to appeal to the Privy Council. We trust that on reading this case, the Vám-márgis, who notoriously surpass the Vallabhácháryan priests in their immoralities, will feel ashamed of themselves, and mind their religion's charter, and that many more Hindu reformers will be encouraged to denounce publicly the defects which they may observe in the manners, customs, and rites of their countrymen.—*People's Friend, Etawah, May* 23, 1862.

ENTS OF THE BOMBAY VERNACULAR PRESS ON
E IMMORAL PRACTICES OF THE MAHÁRÁJAS.

### I.— *The Bombay Sámáchar.*

cial general meeting of the respectable and sensible persons of the
caste was assembled, and, after consultation, it was resolved that the
· which their Mahárájas exercise over them, is, on many occasions,
and pernicious ; and, in consequence of this, their money is wasted, and
offered to their understanding, and a blot is cast on the respectablity of
uly.   Therefore these persons came to the resolution that as much as
possible the Hindus should not ask the opinion of the Mahárájas on any
ind that females, after they have arrived at the age of puberty, should
)ermitted to pay *darshna* (divine homage) to the Mahárájas in their
. . . . .  It is not necessary for us to say that if the authority of
hárájas be not undermined at present, they will have the more to repent
, when their money is wasted and a stain cast on the reputation of their
—*21st December*, 1855.

### II.— *The Jám-e Jamshed.*

; manner sensible and right thinking Hindus have seen their error, though
have made fit and proper arrangements with respect to it.   They have
meeting of their own caste men, and have arrived at this resolution :—
o case unconnected with matters of religion they should ask the opinion
religious preceptors, as they on many occasions exercise over them
authority, and cause them to commit acts which reflect shame on the
n of their families; and that after a certain hour of the day they should
it their females to pay *darshana* (divine honours) to their religious pre-
ι their temples. . . . . . . .   Thus very often they gave to their
preceptors, with great willingness, permission to destroy the reputation
families, and thought it an act of holiness, sufficient to carry their
;o the seventh generation in heaven.   But all this folly has spontaneously
made public. . . . . . .   The meaning of our words is simply
t they should be backward in respecting the notoriously immoral, the
;troying, and the unrighteous as well as improper commands of their
s of religion.—*25th December*, 1855.

12

### III.—*The Samáchár Darpan.*

Much discussion is now raging regarding the improper conduct of the Mahárájas of the Hindus, and many complaints have been made to us in respect to it; also several communications have reached us, wherein more is written than the improper conduct of the Mahárájas. If the Mahárájas, not dreading God, commit evil acts, they ought to be punished.

The more the people advance in civilization the more tyrannical their acts will appear; and the Hindus will not now believe, as they formerly did, the tyrannical acts of the Mahárájas as the commands of God. At present their knowledge has held a torch before them : by its light they emerge from darkness into day. Therefore they will not now approve the acts of the Mahárájas, and will not see their families dishonoured.—*29th November,* 1855.

### IV.—*The Bombay Chábúk.*

The Gosáinji Mahárájas of the Vaishnavas of this place, instead of giving religious instructions, carry on debaucherous practices on their followers. This appears nothing, looking on them with the eyes of a savage man; but thinking justly it appears a wicked practice. These Mahárájas appear totally divine to the Hindus, but their acts seem extremely base, and their heart full of sin, and their conduct out of the way of social arrangements, and their practices opposed to religion. Their followers expose the vices of their religious guides with respect to all this. . . . . . . . Oh S'iva! S'iva! that aged matrons like their (Mahárájas) mothers, young women like their sisters, and maidens like their daughters, who come to touch the feet of these true religious guides in their temples, who come to pay *darshana* (divine homage) to these godly Mahárájas, who repair to pay *darshana*, believing them to be God—that they should be made victims of carnal intercourse by the Mahárájas, instead of giving them religious instructions. Fie! Fie! upon this incarnation, oh! damned (burnt) your Vaishnava religion.—*21st June,* 1859.

### V.—*The Rást Goftár.*

"You Mahárájas! cease to fine, to excommunicate and to interfere in the private domestic affairs of your followers. You will sometimes be involved in trouble instead of gaining any benefit in the shape of money; and you and your creed shall fall into dust by this (interference). Hindu Mahárájas! many young men of your class are immersed in debauchery; withhold your hand from that, otherwise you will have to taste its fruits sooner or later. Hindu Mahárájas! keep yourselves aloof from all tyranny, immorality; give religious instructions and moral admonition to your followers, and endeavour to act accord-

those religious instructions, that thereby you may gain glory in this world, good place in another world. Otherwise, if you continue to conduct your- is you do at present, nothing but repentance and sorrow, shall you have at Be assured of this.—*6th June*, 1858.

## VI.—*The Satya Prakásh.*

then why do not the Vaishnavas select a single and honest Maháráj, and out the other Mahárájas from their holy office? Why wanted foppish, tyrannical, and adulterous Mahárájas in the holy office of religious pre- t! Oh Vaishnavas; how long will you suffer oppression? How long will · dragged under the restraint and awe of tyrannical Mahárájas? Oh! reflect, and devise means whereby your own reputation and that of the of Vallabháchárya may be preserved.—*20th March*, 1859.

## VII.—*The A'pektyár.*

temple of the Hindu Mahárájas is proved a brothel; their private dwel- le home of a corrupt and disrespectable family; their eyes wanton licen- ss; their senses the seat of wicked appetites (desires); every pore of their unrighteousness, uncleanliness, dirtiness; and, in short, they have been incarnations of devils, and possessed of the qualities of Satan, instead of arnation of God.—*22nd June*, 1859.

## VIII.—*The Samshir Báhdur.*

religious preceptors ought so to conduct themselves as to do good to their rs, and ought not to possess a desire of riches and women. Instead of that, sent Mahárájas become guilty of great sins by committing debauchery with males of their followers. Again, the Mahárájas ought to treat alike their nd poor followers; instead of which they cause the poor people to be ed with cords, and allow rich persons to make *darshana* by admitting them und.—*10th September*, 1858.

## IX.—*The Dost-e Hinda.*

cause of all this is that the Mahárájas are defective. They are themselves al, themselves avaricious, themselves partial, themselves ignorant, and per- ly sunk in pleasures; whereby many of their sensible Vaishnava followers ently disgusted, and, owing to the cowardice of the headmen of the Hindu are obliged to remain in slavery.—*21st April*, 1861.

### X.—*The Sudharma Bodhak.*

Oh God! how much iniquity happens on this earth! Several religious guides (who are known by the name of Mahárájas), under the name of religion, and under the pretence of religion, plunder the estates and properties of simple people, (and) by committing adultery with their sisters, daughters, and wives, pollute their modesty. Oh God! is there no one on this earth to punish these religious preceptors! How much guilt, how much immorality, that the properties of men should be plundered in the broad light of day! Not only property is plundered, but the chastity of people's wives is robbed, and adultery committed with them in a manner as to make it known to all. Oh! other criminals are punished in this world, but how do these religious impostors escape punishment! Oh God! how this iniquity can last in Thy reign!"—*20th January,* 1861.

### XI.—*The Pahrejagár.*

When the king (Maháráj) contemplates on his riches, what words can describe his joy! A gentle fragrant cool breeze blows; wreaths of flowers are scattered around; melodious sounds of the cymbals of the Gopis (females) fall on the ears; rich clothes lie on the body; and the Gopis and Gope (Maháráj) sport with each other. How can the poor have a chance of redress in such a temple! If the king were to acquire large stores of wealth, even then the poor shall never receive benefit at his hands.—*18th December,* 1855.

### XII.—*The Pársí Reformer.*

In this manner these Mahárájas, claiming to be your spiritual guides, enjoy your young daughters (and) sisters, destroy your domestic comfort, and stain your character. Therefore (you) Vaishnavas! should keep anxiety about it, and, as the "reformed party" of your caste, have used their prudence to shun these refuges, it behoves you to be on your guard. It is a credit to you to keep off your females from these debaucherous (Mahárájas), and to observe the dictates of religion with prudence.—*29th May,* 1861.

### XIII.—*The Khojá Dosta.*

Most of the simple and ignorant female devotees are entrapped into this religious snare, and, giving money to the Mahárájas, practise adultery with them. But these immoral creatures, the Mahárájas, are not content with this, and they many a time use violence on the tender body of the maidens (of their devotees), the instances of which are not uncommon. Such are these Mahárájas—the pretended preceptors of religion—and their acts.—*25th August,* 1861.

## XIV.—*The Vruta Sár.*

Should the temple of the Mahárájas be a place of religious topics and admonitions, or that of dancing of prostitutes? Does it become the Maháráj to encourage a prostitute?. . . . . . . . We recommend the Vaishnavas to ponder upon these questions. It is necessary for them to devote their attention to these questions. They should (also) pay attention to the present state of the Mahárájas. The Mahárájas act according to their own fancy, (and) it is necessary to give a check to this at once. If the Gujaráti (people) pay proper attention to the conduct of the Mahárájas, their *gurus* themselves will act in consonance with their duties. If, however, any Maháraja do not behave properly, he must be expelled (from his holy office).—*25th August,* 1859.

## XV.—*The Dhuma Ketu.*

An Anecdote.—Some old gentlemen, assembling in one place, were discussing as to who is happy in Bombay; when one of them decided that in Mumbássur (*i.e.,* the town of Bombay) there are two happy beings: one, the Maháráj of the Baniás, and the other, the (stallion) buffaloe of Banáppá the milkman.—*14th September,* 1855.

## XVI.—*The Prabhákar.*

On this account, the Bháttiá Maháráj has created a disturbance about the *Chappan Bhoga,* and what will the meeting of the Bráhmans do (to him) when his mind is absorbed into the jingling of the foot-ornaments of the Gopis (female devotees) attending his temple. He thought that if the income of the Bráhmans, which was all in the hands of his Bháttiá devotees, be stopped, they (the Bráhmans) themselves would be compelled to side with him.—*16th September,* 1855.

## XVII.—*The Parbhodaya.*

Not only are their bodies and wealth dedicated to the service of these Mahárájas, but their daughters, sisters, and wives, with their persons, are dedicated to these debaucherous religious preceptors. We feel much pain and shame at seeing this. That there are such blind religious guides (the calves of kine) amongst mankind is a disgrace. The authority of the Mahárájas is exercised over their followers without any restraint.—*August,* 1859.

## XVIII.—*The Dnyánodaya.*

The Gujaráti people are very pious: so much so, that some (of them) touch the feet of their *gurus* (spiritual guides), some touch their body with their hands, and when the Mahárájas—their *gurus*—wash their body, they (the devotees) drink the dirty water dropping from their *dhotara* and body with such feelings as if this water were from a holy place. . . . . . . . The females of the Gujaráti (people) show piety towards their *gurus* even much more; it is an injunction of the S'astras to select a *guru*, and to consign to him these three objects—*tan, man,* and *dhan* (body, mind, and wealth). That is to say (the females) make over their body (in a literal sense)   In fact, the *guru* of the Gujaráti (people) is their God. —*1st March,* 1845.

## XIX.—*The Bámdád.*

We had often heard of the wicked conduct of these religious guides—the Mahárájas; but several of the narratives were such that we could not believe them. That they who pretend to be religious preceptors should entertain evil thoughts and do wicked things was to us incredible; but now we are compelled to believe.—*October,* 1858.

## XX.—*The Guru and Woman.*

At this time a few Mahárájas may be going in the right path. The majority of them follow the wrong path. The youthful fops are given to ostentation. The present children of Vallabha disgrace the name of their ancestors. . . . . . The lálají (showy) Mahárájas, when the *darshana* time has commenced, and people crowded, sit in their bed chamber inside the temple, and by the gesture of the eyes, or through some persons kept for the purpose, invite the female designed (for evil purpose), and commit evil act with her.   In Surat, once upon a time, a Maháráj, exerting his wild strength upon a girl who had not attained the age of puberty, had almost caused her death.   Similar horrible events have happened at (Katch) Mándavi, with which the Rájá and his subjects (Bháttiás) of that country are not unacquainted.   In many places such a thing has happened. What kind of oppression is this! what kind of debauchery this! what kind of religious guides these!   I blush to write more of such things.   Many of the Mahárájas are almost blinded by these immoral practices with females.—1858.

## XXI.—*The Debaucherous Gurus.*

The Mahárájas, for these evil purposes, through certain females and males, order sooner or later the female whom they have singled out from those who have come to pay *darshana* (divine homage).   Sumptuously dressed females, who are wantons, are invited by the Mahárájas merely with a beck of their eyes.   An invitation from the Maháráj is an invitation from Krishṇa, and thinking she has met God, she hastens with delight and precipitation to touch the person of the Mahárájas. . . . . . . . . For these purposes, they (the Mahárájas) do not use females of their own age; but upon tender youthful girls they exert their beastly strength.—1859.

## XXII.—*The Whippings (Chábaká).*

I have seen the deceit of the Mahárájas. Now, lady! none of you should go into the Mahárájas' temple. Inviting a girl of tender age, they give the sacred sweetmeats, and, representing the story of the Kúhn Gopis, make a wanton assault. If they see wealth they invite with affection, otherwise they heed not; robbing the wealth and bloom of youthful beauty! See the honesty of religious instructors !—1860.

## XXIII.—*The Authority of Gurus.*

The Mahárájas should behead the Vaishnavas, or cause them to be beheaded, plunder their property, defile their females; and should not their followers lay a complaint of their wrongs before government. Ha, ha! they should not drag them to court, but shamelessly submit to these impious *gurus*, for doing that which is opposed to the laws of social union, opposed to the law of God. These Mahárájas, like savage bulls, thrust their heads into the domestic concerns of their devotees, cause dissensions by misrepresentation as to their family, caste, and friendship, and accomplish their evil designs.—1859.

## XXIV.—*The Ancient Religion of the Hindus, etc.*

The conduct of the Gosáinjis (Mahárájas) of the present day is so notorious that it is not necessary to say much about it. Besides, their acts are so disgraceful that (our) pen does not move to describe them in this work. Being possessed of affluence, they are from their childhood brought up in indulgence, and are allowed to do as they fancy, and receive no education whatever. Most of the present Gosáinjis, therefore, are ignorant fools; they do not possess as much knowledge as is required for the office of a *guru*. What admonition can one impart to others who does not possess any knowledge. . . . . . The Gosáinjis pass their time in eating daintiest viands, in wearing fancy clothes and jewels, in driving carriages, in committing adultery with strange women, and in repose.—1861.

www.ingramcontent.com/pod-product-compliance
Lightning Source LLC
Chambersburg PA
CBHW030906270326
41929CB00008B/599